25,00

THE HISTORY OF OPERA
A series planned to cover the history of opera in approximately
26 volumes to appear between 1980 and 1990. Each volume is
written by a specialist and is intended to give not only the
musical and operatic history of the period covered, but to fit
events and the artists who created them into the framework of
the social and intellectual history of their time.

Other titles published or in preparation

The Birth of Opera by Jane Glover

The High Baroque by Lesley Orrey

The History of Opera in Russia by Dora Ramadinova

Also by T.J. Walsh

Opera in Dublin 1705—1797
The Social Scene

Monte Carlo Opera 1879—1909

THE HISTORY OF OPERA

SECOND EMPIRE OPERA

The Théâtre Lyrique, Paris
1851—1870

by

T. J. Walsh

JOHN CALDER · LONDON
RIVERRUN PRESS · NEW YORK

First published in 1981 by John Calder (Publishers) Ltd,
18 Brewer Street, London W1R 4AS and Riverrun Press Inc,
175 Fifth Avenue, New York 10010

© 1981 T.J. Walsh

British Library Cataloguing Data
Walsh, T.J.
    Second Empire opera. – (History of opera)
    1. Théâtre Lyrique *(Company)* – History
    I. Title   II. Series
    782.1'06'04436   ML 1727

ISBN 0–7145–3659–8

Typeset in 11 on 12 point Plantin by Margaret Spooner
Printed by Offset Lithography at Whitstable Litho Ltd.
Bound by G. & S. Kitcat Ltd.

CONTENTS

For Victoria
with much love

Illustrations

Preface

This book was conceived at Listowel Writers' Week in County Kerry in Ireland. There was even a touch of comedy reminiscent of a Charles Lever novel in the circumstance, for two Dr. Walshes were being confused, one with the other, while the publisher's identity for a time was concealed under the misprinted name of 'Colder'. I should like to think that I have managed to convey some of the light-hearted atmosphere which attended that occasion into the book itself, for, on the surface at least, the Second Empire was above all, light-hearted.

Not all was Offenbach however and in this book I have tried to describe a facet of the Paris opera scene, which, whatever its subsequent shortcomings assuredly began with serious artistic intentions. Over one hundred years later its success may seem sadly limited. Among all the creations of this quondam opera house how many are now remembered by the general opera-goer? — just a few, Gounod's *Faust* and *Roméo et Juliette*, Bizet's *Les Pêcheurs de Perles* and, irony of ironies, Berlioz' maltreated *Les Troyens à Carthage*. Yet when compared with productions of the same period at the Opéra and Opéra-Comique this is quite a good showing. True, the Opéra can boast of Verdi's *Les Vêpres Siciliennes* and *Don Carlos* besides Meyerbeer's *L'Africaine*, but in the repertoire of the Opéra-Comique one has to exhume such little known works as Massé's *Les Noces de Jeanette*, Meyerbeer's *Le Pardon de Ploërmel*, Maillart's *Les Dragons de Villars* and Bazin's *Maître Pathelin*.

Where the Théâtre Lyrique scored highest however was not in its creations but in its revivals; five operas by Mozart, five by Weber, two by Gluck, four by Verdi, and possibly the most significant revival of all, *Rienzi*, the second of Wagner's operas ever to be performed in Paris. As we know, not all of these productions were presented as the composers had intended or would have wished. But performed they were in whatever manner, and perhaps the real import of the theatre's function is best understood when one remembers that they were all performed in the vernacular. So little and so seldom was opera in German then performed in Paris that it was almost unknown there, but the Théâtre Italien held an annual season made up of a programme of Italian favourites. At the Théâtre Lyrique the audience could also hear Verdi, Mozart and Bellini, and there follow the story as well.

Naturally each of the three 'French' opera houses in Paris had its own social and intellectual *ambiance*. The Opéra was the theatre of the aristocracy and the *nouveau riche*, the Opéra-Comique that of the *bourgeoisie*. The Théâtre Lyrique stood as the opera house of the working man and woman and the hard-up artist. For its time it had created an artistic domain not dissimilar to Sadler's Wells Opera in London eighty years later.

With the ending of a book comes the pleasure of thanking libraries and their staffs as well as friends who have helped in the making of it. The libraries on this occasion are the Bibliothèque de l'Arsenal and Bibliothèque Nationale, Paris, as well as the British Library and University of London Library. In the last, the Music Librarian, Dr. M.A. Baird was particularly kind and hospitable to me. As always, I include with gratitude Miss Kathleen O'Rourke, County Librarian and the Misses Kathleen Lucking and Anna Drury through whose help and attention the Wexford County Library has become for me, the London Library. Then there is Helen Gregory, old friend and co-worker who has seen this book through all its trying years, not always in agreement with my findings perhaps, but never-failing in her support.

T.J.W.

Introduction

Once again 'it was the best of times, it was the worst of times,' for it was the year 1851 in Paris, the dawn of the Second Empire. The epoch was being celebrated musically by the opening of a new theatre for French opera, an intrepid enterprise, all the more hazardous because so many similar ventures had already failed.

As early as 1820 there had been opera comique at the Théâtre du Gymnase; then, from 1824 to 1829, such works as Rossini's *Il Barbiere di Siviglia* and *Otello* and Mozart's *Le Nozze di Figaro* and *Don Giovanni* had been given in French at the Odéon. Next, at the Théâtre des Nouveautés, from 1827 until 1831, opera comique and more French versions of Rossini and Mozart were performed, while at the Théâtre de la Renaissance, briefly, between 1838 and 1840, productions fluctuated between opera comique and the first French performance of *Lucia di Lammermoor*.[1] None of these theatres were devoted exclusively to opera; in fact, it formed a very small part of their general repertory. Moreover, all such performances were given under special licence, for Napoleon I by a decree of 29 July 1807 had suppressed twenty-six of the thirty-five theatres then existing in Paris[2] and had reduced the number where French music might be performed to two—the Opéra and the Opéra Comique.

When opera failed at the Renaissance in mid 1840, the administration did not seem inclined to re-establish it elsewhere. However, on 14 May 1842, a number of composers and dramatists, including Hector Berlioz, Adolphe Adam and Ambroise Thomas petitioned the Minister of the Interior, M. Duchâtel, to create a third French opera house.[3] A special Commission was set up and by August it seemed that the request would be granted, since plans for the new theatre were announced, but then on 28 October the application was rejected.[4] In September 1844 another attempt was made, when a petition, signed this time exclusively by laureates of the Prix de

Rome, sought to have a new lyric theatre established where young and unperformed composers and librettists might, like poor expectant souls, at least find a purgatory which in time would admit them to the paradise of the Opéra and Opéra Comique. Again, it was rejected.[5]

Then, where groups had failed, one man, entirely on his own, succeeded. He was the composer Adolphe Adam, best known today for his music to the ballet *Giselle* and among opera enthusiasts for a few agreeable scores which include *Le Postillon de Lonjumeau*. By coincidence his first immature operas had been among those performed at the Nouveautés, following which he became established at the Opéra Comique. About 1845 Crosnier, who was director of the Opéra-Comique, resigned and the theatre was taken over by Basset. Basset promptly fell out with Adam and told him that as long as he was director of the Opéra Comique, Adam's works would never be performed there.

In despair of finding a new stage, Adam turned to Crosnier who had meanwhile become lessee of the Théâtre de la Porte-Saint-Martin, and suggested that they establish a theatre to present the old opera comique repertory which was then being neglected by the Opéra Comique itself. Seemingly Adam had got the idea from a production of Grétry's *Richard Cœur-de-Lion* which, re-orchestrated by him, had been very successful at the Opéra Comique a few years earlier. His plans came to nothing, however, for Crosnier discovered it was more rewarding to rent his theatre to others and so Adam had again to look elsewhere. But first he sought a licence to allow him to withdraw his operas from the Opéra Comique and to present them, with new works by other composers, himself. This he obtained with Crosnier's help and, with his licence secure, Adam found his new theatre.[6]

It was the Cirque Olympique in the boulevard du Temple. This was indeed an indoor circus, the culmination of a travelling 'spectacle équestre' introduced into France by Philip Astley during the first years of Louis XVI's reign. Early in 1847 the theatre became available and Adam, in partnership with Achille Mirecour, a sometime artist of the Odéon, took it over at a cost of 1,400,000 francs[7] under an arrangement whereby 250,000 francs were to be paid at once, with the remainder in annuities over the following ten years.[8] As Adam tells it, his tribulations before he could gain possession of the theatre read like the book of Job. Had he but known it, his real troubles would only begin once he was installed.

First, the building had to be refurbished or rather rebuilt, for the architect Charpentier seems to have retained little but the four walls. This renovation would cost a further 200,000 francs. The old circus ring now became the parterre of the auditorium, fitted out with fauteuils and surmounted by three semi-circular floors of boxes and galleries in the customary theatre style. The acoustics were poor, but since the stage projected as an apron much further into the auditorium than was usual,* this at least helped the singers. Decoratively, the stage boxes were supported by the usual caryatids, while the inevitable allegorical groups representing Music, Poetry and Dance, interspersed with floral garlands, ornamented the ceiling.[9]

It was ready by the autumn and, having named it Opéra National, Adam opened this 'third lyric theatre' on 15 November 1847 with a musical prologue, *Les Premiers Pas, ou les Deux Génies* and a new opera by Aimé Maillart called *Gastibelza*. The prologue, 'a brilliant mosaic'[10] by Adam, Auber, Halévy and Carafa, was topical. It referred to the boulevard 'du Crime' (by which name the boulevard du Temple was then popularly known, due to the lurid melodramas produced in its theatres) and encouraged the Parisian dilettanti to visit the new Opéra National there. There was also much play made of the newly inaugurated railway between Paris and Tours—the marvel of the day.[11]

Financially the project was in trouble from the start and it seemed unlikely that it would last out the year. Artistically its chances cannot have been much higher, for a report of one production relates that it 'obtained but a mediocre success owing to the detestable style in which it was executed,' and adds, 'The singers were frightful, the chorus almost as bad as those at the Italiens, and worse than those at the Opéra Comique; the orchestra weak and coarse.'[12] In the event, history would take a hand to give it a much shorter life span than anyone could have

*

Circus theatres of the period frequently included large scenic stages in addition to the traditional ring.

contemplated, for on 23 February 1848 revolution would break out, on the following day Louis-Philippe would abdicate and the resulting political upheaval would give the Paris public other things to think about besides opera.

A last-ditch stand was made before the venture finally expired. Having been closed for several days, the theatres were allowed to re-open provided that the first receipts were given for the benefit of the wounded. A 'pièce de circonstance' called *Les Barricades de 1848* was mounted on 6 March—to compete with all the other theatres which were presenting the same type of patriotic fare. But a disillusioned public had no interest in barricades in the theatre, there had been a surfeit of them in the streets and so, on 28 March 1848,[13] just over four months after it had opened its doors, the Opéra National closed them again and Adolphe Adam retired from his position of opera director, a ruined man.*

By coincidence, exactly five days earlier, on 23 March, a 'tree of liberty' had been planted in front of another theatre just a stone's throw down the boulevard du Temple. The same evening the façade of this second theatre was brightly illuminated and since it had the unusual and convenient feature of an outside balcony, the theatre's conductor, Alphonse Varney, surrounded by the members of his orchestra, gave a concert, followed by a ball for the public who danced in the street below.[14]

Varney must have been very popular just then, for he had lately composed the music for some verses known as the Chant des Girondins or 'Mourir pour la Patrie'—the Marseillaise of the 1848 revolution. The verses had been written by Alexandre Dumas père** for inclusion in his (and Auguste Maquet's) play *Le Chevalier de Maison-Rouge*, and it was outside Dumas' theatre—the Théâtre Historique—that the public was now dancing to Varney's music. By coincidence it would also be in the Théâtre Historique that the presently extinct Opéra National would find a new home.

*

For details of the programme of operas performed during Adam's four-month season and members of his company, see Appendix E.

**

The refrain is borrowed from Rouget de Lisle.

Dumas's theatre had been newly opened just over a year before, and the story of its establishment has all the romantic insouciance of one of his own novels. He was friendly with the sons of King Louis-Philippe, and the Duc de Montpensier, who was present at the first performance of *Les Trois Mousquetaires* at the Théâtre Ambigu Comique, offered to use his influence to procure him a licence for his own theatre. Duchâtel objected on the grounds that there were too many theatres in Paris already, so the Duc approached his father instead. The result was that Dumas had his licence by 14 March 1846. This granted him the right to present dramas and comedies in prose and in verse and, during two months of each year, lyric works with chorus. The new theatre was to be situated on the corner of the boulevard du Temple and the faubourg of the same name (close to the present place de la République) near six other well known theatres. A company was formed to administer the project.[15]

Apart from the inevitable financial difficulties involved in building a new theatre, the present structure presented an unusual problem due to the limitations of the site. Its unconventional outline required the new theatre to be wedged between and behind two other buildings and gave it a frontage on the boulevard only eight metres wide. The architect was Dedreux and he ornamented his narrow façade, three times as high as its width, with ionic columns, caryatids and figures from Corneille and Shakespeare, and also devised the singular outside balcony already mentioned. The front of the theatre joined the auditorium by a long narrow vestibule, and here again the design was unusual, for the auditorium was 20 metres wide by only 16 deep.* This unusual design at least had the advantage of giving the audience in the boxes and various galleries a more direct view of the stage than was possible in the then more orthodox 'horse-shoe' theatres. The increased width of the stage also helped in the presentation of spectacle.[16]

The theatre was intended to accommodate two widely differing types of audience. What was desired therefore was a

*

This form of theatre, employed by Palladio at Vicenza, had been suggested again in Paris during the 18th century. See *Projet d'une salle de spectacle pour un théâtre de comédie* by Charles Nicolas Cochin. Paris 1765 (Reported by Lasalle).

a) Façade

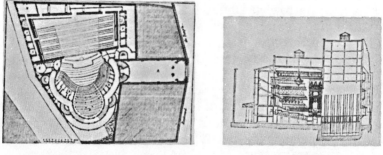

b) Floorplan   c) Section

Architectural details and decorations of the Théâtre Montpensier
(Historique)

building so arranged that the élite of Parisian 'society might find in it every provision for their comfort without in any way trenching upon that of the ordinary public of the theatres of the boulevard.' The problem was satisfactorily if snobbishly resolved by making 'provision for the inferior audience mentioned . . . by two large amphitheatres . . . extending behind the second and third tiers of boxes.'[17]

Originally it had been intended to name it after its patron the Duc de Montpensier but, whereas Louis-Philippe may have helped to acquire the licence, with characteristic bourgeois caution he had no intention of permitting his son's name to be blazoned on the façade of a boulevard theatre, and so the Théâtre Montpensier became the Théâtre Historique.

Under the direction of Hippolyte Hostein (Dumas remained titular head), it opened its doors for the first time on 20 February 1847 with Dumas's *La Reine Margot*. It had been an event awaited with much anticipation and gallery 'first-nighters' began gathering over 24 hours beforehand—and in winter too, although there must have been some braziers about.

There was also sustenance, for at about ten o'clock soup-sellers began to circulate among the queues, to be followed at midnight by bakers with bread, hot from the ovens. Meanwhile, neighbouring shop-keepers had sold bundles of straw to those who wished to lie down. The scene was lit by hundreds of lanterns carried by the crowd who, from time to time, would break into the chorus of a song, and so the night passed in music, conversation and what may be comprehensively described as amusement. At dawn, the commissariat returned, selling hot coffee and little cakes, while some people stopped the water-carriers as they passed on their way into the city and, having bought water, washed themselves in public. Later in the day, sausage-sellers came, leaving a trail of garlic behind. There was even a ballad singer promoting a ballad which he had just composed for the occasion. Shortly before performance time, celebrities, including the Duc de Montpensier, arrived. Among opera composers present were Auber, Adam, Halévy, Clapisson and Carafa. At seven o'clock the curtain rose; it did not finally fall until three o'clock the next morning.[18]

The theatre naturally was occupied mostly by Dumas's dramas, but the clause which allowed the performance of lyric works for a short period each year was availed of at least once, when on 10 August 1848 a 'drame lyrique' called *Atala* by Dumas fils, taken from Chateaubriand, and with music by Alphonse Varney, was performed. It was a story about Indians (but no cowboys!) the warring Natchez and Seminoles, and was much concerned with their conversion to Christianity. It may have been an oratorio, for it was sung or recited by ladies in white dresses and men in black robes. Among the singers who took part was the bass Junca, late of the Opéra National.[19]

The Théâtre Historique survived the 1848 revolution, but from 1849 onwards it was in financial difficulties, with frequent changes of directors and strikes by unpaid actors and stage-hands, until it finally closed on 20 December 1850.[20] It would remain so for almost a year.

Following the revolution, living had become precarious for artists. Writing in July 1848, Berlioz recounts: 'I am sadly affected by the deplorable state in which I find music and musicians in Paris after my long absence [in London]. All the theatres closed, all the artists ruined, all the professors idle, all the pupils absent . . . Some of the first violins at the Opéra on a salary of 900 francs [£36] per annum! . . . Without pupils, what must become of these wretched musicians?'[21]

Nevertheless, although the Théâtre Historique had closed late in 1850, early in 1851 there were rumours that it was to be re-opened by a most unexpected body, the dormant Opéra National.

This decision to change the theatre into an opera house brought forth many candidates for the post of director—among them Adolphe Adam's bête noire, Basset[22]—but the appointment went to Edmond Seveste.[23] Seveste came of a theatrical family. His father, Pierre, had joined the ballet school of the Opéra as a child and had had a successful career there until the revolution of 1789. He then became a member of the Théâtre du Vaudeville and later assumed the management of the theatre at Saint Cloud. Edmond and his brother Jules joined their father in 1822, Edmond would subsequently become director of the Comedie Française for a very brief span, but the family interests lay mainly in the suburban theatres of Paris, (such as the Théâtre de Belleville in the rue de Belleville, opened by the brothers in 1828) where they enjoyed the privilege of presenting

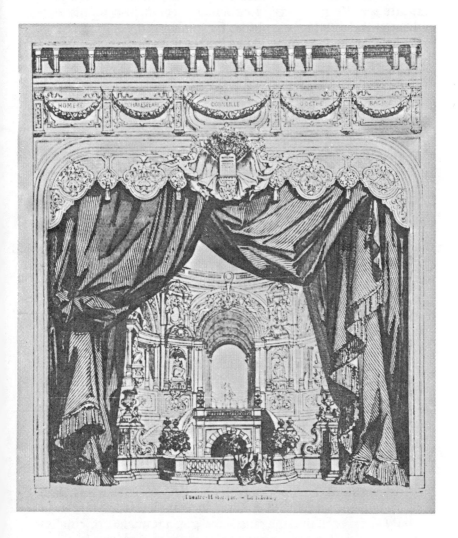

Théâtre Historique. Proscenium and front curtains.

new plays as well as borrowing from the repertory of the city theatres.[24] Varney was re-nominated conductor to his old theatre, and a comic bass named Grignon was brought from the Opéra Comique as stage manager.[25]

By June, new opera scores were reported to be arriving for the director's attention by the cart-load. However, about mid-July, disagreement between Seveste and the original owners of the theatre concerning essential repairs precipitated a crisis, and for the second time in the history of the Opéra National there were reports of its being housed in the Théâtre de la Porte-Saint-Martin. The difficulty was quickly resolved and during the last week of July, Seveste signed a contract leasing the Théâtre Historique. This done, he set off to audition singers throughout France and northern Spain 'in the hope of making some marvellous discovery.'[26]

Meanwhile, refurbishing of the theatre began. It seated 2,000 and was said to have excellent acoustics for opera. When it was built it had been decorated in the fashionable theatre colours of red and gilt and had been lit by two large chandeliers. The decorators employed had been the sculptor Klagmann and artists Dieterle, Despléchin and Séchan. (This time the ceiling decoration represented Apollo, god of the arts, driving his chariot across an illuminated sky.) Yet another artist, Joseph Guichard, had decorated the external cupola.

Now there was fresh paint (white and gold), new furnishing for the fauteuils (fuchsia coloured), a new drop curtain (painted by Auguste Rubé), and four new candelabra attached to the pillars of the stage boxes. The foyer too was newly papered in deep red imitation damask, but was furnished only with a grand piano supporting an enormous bust of Weber. It was said that on first nights, critics used to assemble to discuss their views in the corridor behind the first tier boxes, while Massenet, who in his youth had been a tympanist in the Théâtre Lyrique orchestra, would later recall that the musicians' green room had originally been a stable for the horses taking part in Dumas's historic dramas.

Little alteration was needed therefore to turn the playhouse into an opera house. Indeed, nothing significant was changed except that busts of Lully and Gluck now took the place of the busts of Corneille and Molière which had surmounted the stage

(Théâtre-Historique. — Details de l'hémicycle. Quatrième panneau de la frise, peinture de M. Guichard.)

(Théâtre-Historique. — Details de l'hémicycle. Cinquième et dernier panneau de la frise, peinture de M. Guichard.)

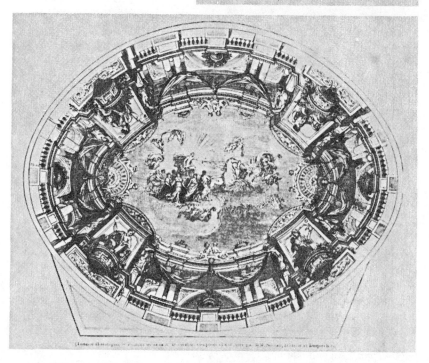

Architectural details and decorations of the Théâtre Historique.

boxes, and names of opera composers were substituted for names of dramatists throughout the theatre. There was one other innovation—the mounting of a large clock guarded by the names of Cherubini, Dalayrac, Grétry and Mozart above the stage.[27] A common enough decoration in Italian theatres, it caused adverse comment in Paris, even evoking a thought from Murger's *La Vie de Bohème*—he likes not the clock because it ticks away his life.[28]

The Duc de Montpensier's salon elegantly furnished in silk, now became the director's office. In an excess of sentiment, Dumas used to keep the Duc's box illuminated on first nights as if expecting his arrival after the Orleanists had been swept from power. Prices of admission seem to have remained as for the Théâtre Historique and ranged from six francs for the front boxes down to 75 centimes for the second amphitheatre.

Throughout August, while work progressed at the Théâtre Historique, rehearsals were taking place at the Théâtre Ventadour—courtesy of Benjamin Lumley, the English impresario who was then directing a season of Italian opera there. The operas being prepared were Xavier Boisselot's *Mosquita la Sorcière* and Félicien David's *La Perle du Brésil*[29] and, with MM. Tariot and Croharé added to the company as chorus master and accompanist, and Fosse as assistant stage manager*, the curtain rose on a reborn Opéra National on 27 September 1851.

---

*

Singers for the season are recorded as: Mmes Rouvroy, Duez, Guichard, Léon Petipa, Vadé, Guyard, Mendez-Loustauneau, Dupont, Lambert, Clemence, Octavie; *Ténors*, Michel, Philippe, Biéval, Dulaurens, Menjaud; *Ténors Comiques*, Leroy, Soyer, Gastineau; *Barytons*, Meillet, Ribes, Grignon (fils), Mutel, Willems; *Basses Nobles*, Bouché, Junca, Prouvier; *Basses Comiques*, Grignon, Dumonthier; *Orchestra*, 60 players; *Chorus and Ballet*, 60.[30]

Chapter 1

The brothers Seveste as directors 1851—1854

1851–1852

The opera chosen by Edmond Seveste for the occasion was *Mosquita la Sorcière*, music by Xavier Boisselot, libretto by Scribe and Vaëz. (It may be noted here that French opera librettists of the time, like certain animal species, constantly travelled in pairs.) Following the opening, E. Viel rhetorically asked in *Le Ménestrel*, 'Why a third opera house?' and then supplied answers that were predictable and well known.

The Opéra was inaccessible to debutant composers and so could be dismissed at once. The Opéra Comique by its regulations was obliged to perform a one-act work by any prize-winner of the Conservatoire who might submit it, but the delay before actual production made the realisation of this idea almost a fantasy. And how many prize-winners could ever hope to see a three-act work performed there? Besides, not every composer could hope to become a Conservatoire prize-winner, and for them what offered?[1]

The story of *Mosquita la Sorcière* had been set in Mexico, a romantic country sufficiently remote at the time for yet another fanciful plot by Scribe. Berlioz, in the *Journal des Débats*, obviously not impressed by Boisselot's music, took refuge in declaring that it was very difficult to appraise it with justice and accuracy after only one hearing. He had no doubts about the chorus, however. They were numerous enough and the men had been well chosen—a sonorous mass—the tenors especially were excellent, but the women's voices were thin, squally and out of tune.[2] Although Berlioz would emphasise the point later, it can be said here that the principal singers engaged for the Opéra National were of promise rather than renown. (Occasionally some renowned singers appearing towards the end of their careers there could be thought to have shown promise.) Two of some note engaged for the first season were Auguste Meillet (who with his future wife Mlle Meyer would have a highly successful career at the Opéra National) and the bass Junca, who would have the dubious distinction of creating Mefistofele when Boito's now famous opera would be whistled off the Scala stage in 1868.

The orchestra under Varney was praised. The musicians were described as young and energetic. Many had been recruited from among prize-winners at the Conservatoire and the *Moniteur Universel* was confident that they would match the orchestra similarly formed for the Odéon when opera was performed at that theatre during the 1820s.[3]

Withal, Boisselot's opera enjoyed a fair success which, incidentally, demonstrated Edmond Seveste's primary difficulty as theatre director—the necessity of reconciling the theatre's declared policy of presenting works by unknown composers and authors with the need of attracting audiences. For the Opéra National's audience, like every audience in its approach to the arts, knew well what it liked, which was what it knew well; in this instance, popular works by well-established composers. Consequently Seveste was obliged to give revivals of successful operas in order to find the money to present new operas—frequently to an apathetic public.

He approached his problem with the command of a forthright business man, by presenting on the second evening of his season, 28 September, two surefire winners, Rossini's *Le Barbier de Séville* and Paër's *Le Maître de Chapelle*. That his approach, at least from a box-office viewpoint, was right is well proven by the number of performances which each of these three operas would have during the theatre's 20 years' history: *Mosquita la Sorcière* had 25, *Le Barbier de Séville* 126 and *Le Maître de Chapelle* 182.

Briefly, the arrangement then existing in Paris opera houses allowed the Opéra and Opéra Comique to perform works only by French composers or by non-French composers if they were composed to French texts. Italian opera remained the prerogative of the Théâtre Italien and could not be performed in translation at the two state-aided theatres although, for whatever reason, there were occasional exceptions, notably *Lucie de Lammermoor* in 1846 and *Le Trouvère* in 1857, both at the Opéra. But the Opéra National was exempt from this regulation as in fact the earlier non-subsidised French opera seasons had been; so Seveste was able to pick the most successful pieces from the Italian repertory and present them in the vernacular. Moreover, this policy of having important works performed in translation having proved successful, it remained a very important influence on repertory throughout the theatre's history.

Le Barbier de Séville was performed in the Castil-Blaze version with spoken dialogue as performed at the Odéon in 1824 ('after Beaumarchais and the Italian drama, words adapted to Rossini's music').[4]

Until late in October, *Mosquita la Sorcière* was the only new opera to enter the repertory. Seveste was indeed playing a cautious hand when he introduced instead two further old favourites—Niccolò Isouard's *Les Rendez-vous bourgeois* and François Adrien Boieldieu's *Ma Tante Aurore*. The latter opera is rarely spoken of today except to mention the romance 'Deux jeunes gens s'aimaient d'amour', remembered because three notes only, C, D and E are used in it over a passage of 36 bars.* The title page of the libretto used at the time of its creation records: 'hissed in three acts on 23 nivôse [13 January 1803], applauded in two, the 25th of the same month...'.[5] A two-act opera it still remains.

Such deviation from the theatre's declared plans naturally drew critical fire which Jules Lovy in *Le Ménestrel* tried to deflect. 'Epigram and his brother Persiflage begin to attack the new theatre,' he reports. 'Our young composers must be content with their lot, declares one musical rag, with reference to *Ma Tante Aurore* and *Les Rendez-vous bourgeois*. The petty spite of this paper had already appeared with *Le Maître de Chapelle* and *Le Barbier de Séville*. Happily epigrams do not demolish a theatre, neither however do they help it to prosper, so at last

---

*

Albert de Lasalle, *Mémorial du Théâtre Lyrique*, p. 19, reports an earlier example by Jean Jacques Rousseau in an air 'Que le jour me dure', but for 16 bars only.

here is a little brand new one-act piece which should stop these venomous tongues.'[6]

The little one-act piece was a bit of French Irishry called *Murdock le Bandit* by Eugène Gautier to a libretto by Adolphe de Leuven. Murdock was a sort of rapparee Fra Diavolo and some of the action was said to have been reminiscent of Auber's opera. The music, too, was declared to be reminiscent of unspecified composers, and included a predictable duet, 'Irlande chérie, ô mon doux pays' based on an Irish melody.[7] Berlioz, who also referred to the introduction of some Irish themes, commented more favourably and described the opera as 'the work of a musician, complete and clever.'[8]

Nevertheless there was some ironic questioning from the critic of *L'Illustration*. Referring to first-night enthusiasm (created no doubt by Gautier's and de Leuven's friends and an efficient claque), 'What are we to conclude?' he asks. 'We have witnessed similar ovations at the first performances of *Le Val d'Andorre* and *Le Prophète* . . . M. Eugène Gautier is taking the first steps in his career [but] masters as eminent as Halévy and Meyerbeer are at the apogée of theirs'.[9] He advises his readers to hear *Ma Tante Aurore* instead and proceeds to praise Boieldieu, then long and safely dead, finally signing himself 'Georges Bousquet'. And who was Georges Bousquet? He was an opera composer and a contemporary of Eugène Gautier! Life consequently was not easy for Edmond Seveste; admonished when he did not put on the works of young composers, admonished by the same critics even when he did, what was he to do? In this instance he reached a wise compromise. He presented an opera by Bousquet in the following year.

Seveste was nevertheless doing reasonably well, for the box-office was taking an average of 2,000 francs a performance. 'Courage, then, M. Seveste,' urged J. L. Heugel, director of the ever loyal *Le Ménestrel*. 'Call upon the new composers, the young artists, the movement is towards the as yet undiscovered. Follow it freely without becoming involved in exaggeration and you will succeed.'[10] He did, by presenting an important work a month later, but first there were small-scale revivals of Dalayrac's *Maison à vendre* and *Ambroise, ou Voilà ma Journée*.

The new opera was Félicien David's *La Perle du Brésil* and would be the Opéra National's first important success. In 14 years it would be performed there 144 times. In his review of the first performance Berlioz observes, 'There are two musicians in Félicien David, the melodious dreamer, singing the charms of solitude and starry nights . . . with true accent, elegant style, vibrant harmony, pure and picturesque orchestration. Then there is the musician whom I will call lazy, who seems to be satisfied with forms of almost infantile simplicity, of choruses in unison accompanied by an orchestra in unison, of primitive rhythms, slack harmony, immature melody and occasionally much noise but little motif.'[11]

This schizoid attitude may have developed from David's involvement in Saint-Simonism and from his years spent in the East. His eastern impressions certainly influenced his 'ode-symphonie' 'Le Désert', highly effective programme music which was his first and remained his most popular success.

La Perle du Brésil seems to have been given a very poor production. Once again Berlioz describes it as 'sometimes good, often bad and in all, of little advantage to the composer. At every moment the ear is pained by instruments or voices which commit unpardonable faults. Here a discordant harp, there a damned piccolo that plays out of tune [the Conservatoire 'lauréats' must have been having an 'off' night] . . . On stage all the small roles are sung in one manner only . . . terrible, and the ladies of the chorus of whom I have already spoken have voices of cruel perfidy'.[12] But its success was great and it consolidated the credit, both financial and artistic, of the new opera house. Today all that is even vaguely remembered of it is the air, 'Charmant oiseau', a Galli-Curci favourite.

The Musical World had earlier reported: 'the Opéra National is not doing very well. Perhaps, however, when the new opera of Félicien David comes out, things may change for the better.'[13]

They had every appearance of so doing, but then the history of France was altered again when, in the early morning of 2 December, Louis Napoleon staged his coup d'état against the Assembly.* Once again barricades went up in Paris, to be torn

---

*

One anecdote concerning the event relates how the Comte de Morny (Louis Napoleon's half-brother) on the evening of 1 December went to the Elysée from the Opéra Comique. He had been present until the main interval of the first performance of a now completely forgotten opera, *Le Château de la*

La Perle du Brésil (David) 1851 Act 3 Setting by Chéret.

down within a few days, but meanwhile the general unrest had closed the theatres.

The plight of the performers is described in a letter from Augustus Harris, senior: 'I found all the shops closed, and very few people in the street, except in front of the seven theatres; before each, except the Opera National,* there was a knot of persons, which I recognized as the companies of each theatre. They had very long faces, and seemed anxiously waiting the result of the day, to know if they played at night, having been obliged (in consequence of the military occupying the Boulevards) to close the previous evening...'[14].

The closure of the Opéra National (in the boulevard du Temple) seems to have lasted less than a week. Just before the disruption, Albert Grisar's *Les Travestissements* had been revived there. An unimportant little work for two singers, it failed to repeat the slight success it had won when first staged at the Opéra Comique in 1839.

Before the year ended, there was also an announcement of what would become the longest ongoing non-event ever to take place at the Opéra National, news of a forthcoming production of Balfe's *The Bohemian Girl*, here called *La Bohémienne*.[15] That it was not just journalistic gossip is confirmed by its repetition in the following January [16] and since Balfe was in Paris at the time, he may have been trying to negotiate a performance. He would eventually get it, almost to the day, 18 years later. Instead, the new year of 1852 saw a production of an opera comique by Adrien Boieldieu (son of a more famous father) called *La Butte des Moulins*. The libretto by Gabriel and de Forges was partly based on the attempt to assassinate Napoleon I which occurred on Christmas Eve, 1800. (A cart loaded with explosives had been planted in the rue Saint Nicaise to intercept him as he drove to the Opéra for the first performance in Paris of Haydn's *The Creation*). It was an unlikely subject for an opera comique which, according to

Barbe-Bleue, by de Saint-Georges and Armand Marie Ghislain Limnander de Nieuwenhove.

*

Probably the Opéra (in the rue Le Peletier)—at this period called Théâtre de l'Opéra National and so, today, sometimes creating confusion.

The theatres of the boulevard du Temple (1760–1862) showing the Théâtre Lyrique, late Théâtre Historique on the left.

Berlioz, had been hurriedly written to augment the repertory of the Opéra National. The music was 'thickly interlarded with Imperial reminiscences',[17] which was opportune at the time. Yet the opera did not succeed and as Berlioz observed, Seveste's position was difficult; 'we believe he should be much more discriminating in his choice of new operas.'[18] The 'extravagant enthusiasm the friends of this theatre display on every first representation'[19] was also noted.

Another opera comique of even less importance followed, *Le Mariage en l'Air*, a one-act piece by Eugène Déjazet. After the performance Grignon, the stage manager, came before the curtain to announce that the librettists wished to remain anonymous[20] (perhaps they had been reading Berlioz!). In fact they were Jules Henri Vernoy de Saint-Georges and Jean Henri Dupin, the first surpassed in fame only by Scribe, the second a sometime collaborator with Scribe himself. They seem to have been wise in trying to hide their identity for it was said: 'never has a play made so painful an impression, never have we been so bored'.[21] Déjazet's music was treated with more respect— probably a polite reception accorded to a beginner, for subsequently he never succeeded as a composer.

Next there was the revival of yet another opera comique, but one that was more entertaining as well as having some historical interest. This was François Devienne's *Le Pensionnat de jeunes Demoiselles*, which had had its first performance in 1792 under the title of *Les Visitandines* (Nuns of the Order of the Visitation). A scabrous plot in a convent setting conformed to the French anti-religious sympathies of the late 18th century. After the Restoration it was banned from the Opéra Comique, and later under Charles X it was allowed to be staged only in its new form and under its new title. When it was revived in 1872 at the Folies-Bergère and in 1900 at the Opéra Comique, religious sensibilities had turned full circle and once again, in setting and in title, it became *Les Visitandines*.

With the present revival Seveste was rebuked for not performing the original version which, he was told, the Imperial (that is, Napoleonic) censorship had authorised up to 1814. Besides, religious habits were now commonly seen on the stage, for example in *La Favorite* and *Le Domino Noir*.[22]

Devienne was a virtuoso flautist and the musical style of his opera is described as light, easy, natural, full of gaiety and frequently subtle.[23] Gustave Héquet of the *Revue et Gazette Musicale*, reviewing this revival, notes close similarities between certain passages and a duet from *Il Matrimonio Segreto*, an air by Zingarelli and the introduction to Gluck's *Iphigénie en Tauride*. The latter, however, he explains, was a deliberate parody.[24] What was no parody and certainly similar was the air 'Enfant chéri des Dames', for its first ten notes are identical with the beginning of Papageno's air 'Ein Mädchen oder Weibchen' in *Die Zauberflöte*.[25] Whether this was coincidence or plagiarism, either intentional or from some forgotten performance of the air which had lingered in his subconscious mind, remains a matter for academic debate. It certainly did nothing to help performances at the Opéra National, for there were only 16.

Les Fiançailles des Roses by Villeblanche followed, with no greater success. Edmond Seveste's brother Jules had had a hand in the libretto. The programme included a second opera which even now is vaguely remembered for it was Adolphe Adam's *La Poupée de Nuremberg*. Adam relates that he was ill when Edmond Seveste brought him the libretto. He composed it in eight days without leaving his bed and, getting up on the eighth day to play it over on the piano, found that he had recovered. The work had cured the illness.[26] It was a great success. 'Since *Les Rendez-vous bourgeois* we have seen nothing so cheerful in any opera house'[27] declared one report. 'This is a little [one] act destined to remain in the repertory.'[28] proclaimed another, while Berlioz wrote, 'This farce contains a whole emporium of waltzes, galops, pot-pourris . . . worthy of the Nuremberg fair'.[29]

After *La Perle du Brésil* it was the only genuine success that the Opéra National had yet had. Hence it was all the more ironic that Edmond Seveste, who appears to have been ailing for some time, should die on 28 February while it was in performance. At his obsequies a Mass composed by Adolphe Adam was sung by members of the company conducted by Varney.

Later Adam, in a letter published in *Le Ménestrel*, appealed to the Minister of the Interior to help Seveste's widow and children and to appoint Jules Seveste to the post of temporary director— 'so recognising the rights of the family of the theatre's founder.'[30] Jules was provisionally appointed until 1 May from among 20

Interior of the Théâtre Historique.

candidates, one of whom was the celebrated tenor Gilbert Duprez.[31]

Duprez' name did not appear on the list by chance. He was then aged 45 and had begun to compose operas. What is said to have been his best work, *L'Abîme de la Maladetta*, had been performed in Brussels during the previous November and had been announced for the Opéra National in January.[32] The libretto was by his brother Edouard (Gustave Louis Oppelt is also said to have lent a hand), and in the production he had one very good card to play, for the prima donna would be his daughter, the excellent soprano, Caroline Duprez. She was born in Florence in 1832 while her father was appearing in that city and had made her debut at the Théâtre Italien, Paris in 1850. Engagements in London and Brussels followed and now in 1852 she had arrived at the Opéra National. Later she would create Catherine in Meyerbeer's *L'Étoile du Nord* at the Opéra Comique.[33]

She had of course created the soprano role in *L'Abîme de la Maladetta* in Brussels and would appear for the first time at the Opéra National on 11 March in the same opera, now called *Joanita*. The cast was a strong one and included Balanqué (later the first Méphistophélès in Gounod's *Faust*) and a 'ténor de force', Poultier who, having been declared too old and no musician by Cherubini when he sought admission to the Conservatoire,[34] nevertheless had had an important career at the Opéra.

The Duprez assemblage did not please everyone. 'We do not like family operas any more than we like family dinners and reunions,' snapped Cornélius Holff, who described the ending of the overture as if all the horns, basses, violins and wind instruments in creation were giving forth their 'ut de poitrine'— the high C from the chest of which Duprez was so proud. He dismisses the performance by declaring—'That evening the claque really earned its money.'[35] But Paul Scudo of the *Revue des Deux Mondes* reported that the finale recalled the first-act finale of Rossini's *Otello*.[36] Duprez, 'discarding false modesty', was brought on stage at the end by Caroline to receive a shower of bouquets.[37] It is probable that he was being applauded more as a past singer than as a present composer, for by the end of the month the press was referring to 'longueurs' in the music and to

The boulevard du Temple showing the Théâtre Lyrique, late Théâtre Historique, with what would appear to be an orchestra playing on its outside balcony.

empty seats, especially in the cheaper parts of the house, said to be due to the lack of spoken dialogue.[38]

On 12 April, while *Joanita* was in performance, the Opéra National took the name of Théâtre Lyrique,[39] a name it would continue to hold thereafter. Nationalism throughout France was making an uneasy exit. On the previous 20 December a plebiscite had converted the Second Republic into a Second Consulate. A majority of seven million votes indicated that a Second Empire could be confidently expected. Sure enough, in due course, the Théâtre Lyrique became the Théâtre Lyrique Impérial.

But finding another opera to replace *Joanita* with its dwindling audiences was more pressing than finding a new name for the theatre. Rossini and Castil-Blaze once more came to the rescue, this time with *La Pie voleuse*, better known as *La Gazza Ladra*. The press again spoke out about foreign importations. 'There is considerable loss of time, work, money,' reproved Holff, 'but I recognise the desire of M. Seveste to satisfy the public. They say that the new director is besieging our poets and composers. In return can he discover some youthful and vital work that will give his theatre a more brilliant future than its past?'[40] Loss of time, work and money there appears to have been, for *La Pie voleuse* ran for only seven performances. But it filled a gap, permitting the season to run its course until the theatre closed on 30 April with a last performance of *Joanita*.

Earlier, on 18 April, it had been announced that the wishes of the press had been heard and that Jules Seveste had obtained the privilege of the Théâtre Lyrique. It was also announced that he was seeking a subvention of 50,000 francs for the year.[41] The matter had in fact been raised in February, long before Seveste's appointment had been contemplated.[42] The usual vacillation followed. On the one hand it was asserted that the theatre could not last out the season without the help of the state.[43] On the other, it was regretfully announced that a subsidy could not be granted for the coming year as the budget had been already voted.[44]

As will be seen, the jocular comment concerning Jules Seveste which the *Revue et Gazette Musicale* made in an article summing up the season's activities had an element of tragic prescience about it. Seveste, it recounted, had succeeded his

View of the new Théâtre Lyrique

deceased brother as director of the theatre—'without hesitation, without a quiver. Heroism must be a virtue of the family.'[45]

1852–1853

Meanwhile Jules Seveste industriously set about organising his next season. There had been rumours of a new opera by Ambroise Thomas to re-open the theatre but these were promptly denied; the work went instead to the Opéra Comique. J.L. Heugel in *Le Ménestrel* approved the decision and once again commended the cause of young authors and composers to the 'third lyric theatre'.[1] Equally unreliable was news of a certain Count de V..., a very grand, very powerful 'seigneur' but, principally, a very rich capitalist. Inspired, it was said, by the example of some English milords who had recently taken over Her Majesty's Theatre in London, he was reported as emerging in princely fashion to ensure the future of the Théâtre Lyrique.[2]

Alphonse Varney, the conductor, resigned his post to spend his time composing and conducting in Ghent. He was replaced by his deputy M. Placet, whose position in turn was filled by the violinist, Louis Michel Adolphe Deloffre, lately returned from London.

For some reason Seveste had introduced a clause into the contracts of the choristers and orchestral players insisting that they become members of the Association des Artistes Musiciens. Most of them joined though at this remote period the advantage to Seveste is difficult to comprehend. One would have thought that a 'unionised' chorus and orchestra would have been the last thing he would have encouraged.[3] Perhaps it pleased him to introduce so many new members paying an annual subscription of six francs a year to the Association. Alternatively, he may have decided that it was easier to deal with his chorus and orchestra as one homogeneous group rather than as irate individuals.

The opera chosen to open the season was Adam's *Si j'étais Roi*, the libretto reputedly taken from a tale of *The Thousand and One Nights*, although the scene had been changed from Arabia to Goa. So confident was Seveste of its success that a dual cast of principals was engaged to allow the opera to be performed on successive evenings. It would account for half of the performances at the Théâtre Lyrique between 4 September and the end of the year.

That remarkable partnership in French literature, the Goncourt brothers, have left a colourful description of the production which, they noted, was staged sumptuously and with understanding. 'A word about the costumes,' they continue. 'M. Ballue has designed like a Humayun of Delhi or Bombay. His talent lies in the creation of oriental costume. He piles on precious stones, deep red garnets. He arrays silk on velvets, gold on gauze with the lavishness of a nabob. This time M. Ballue has spared nothing. He has remembered a traveller's tale that about a million gems are worn away each year in India merely through being handled. He has brought out his entire jewel case. He has given to the different characters the flared appearance which one finds on Indian soapstone miniatures. He has shod his principal artists superbly and draped about their shoulders fabrics of gold and silver interwoven with scarlet. He has appliquéd roses in profusion on the tunics, and if he has not costumed his dancers in yards of rose and blue muslin bordered with silver, it is because the corps de ballet protested'.[4] Although the Goncourts were writing rhapsodically, it is evident from this description that not all Théâtre Lyrique productions can have been shabby.

Amidst this Indian-Arabian Nights' splendour it was only just that Adolphe Adam should also find an Aladdin's cave for, having lost his fortune in the first Opéra National, he would now partly recoup it in the theatre which ensued.

A month later Eugène Gautier presented another one-act opera comique, *Flore et Zéphire*, to follow *Murdock le Bandit* of the previous season. The story was adapted from two old vaudevilles, *La Danse interrompue* and *Les Vieux Péchés*, and his librettists were de Leuven assisted on this occasion by Deslys. The press was critical of all three, Héquet stating, 'Unhappily, here the dialogue is not always as lively as the situations, and the music is even worse. The buffo style requires vivacity.'[5] In spite of the critics this trifling work had 126 performances over the next four years.

Just as remarkable was the fact that it was followed 12 days later by another Gautier—de Leuven (this time joined by

Michel Carré) opera comique called *Choisy-le-Roi*. This was a period pastiche about Mme de Pompadour, set in Louis Quinze's favourite hunting lodge. One critic noted that this piece was less noisy and less heavily orchestrated than *Flore et Zéphire* and that its style was more accomplished.[6] Once again the audience would disagree, for the opera would have only 22 performances in one season.

Towards the end of the month there was another opera comique, this time with a Scottish pastoral setting, called *La Ferme de Kilmoor*. It was an effort of Alphonse Varney (late conductor) and was being compared with Halévy's then popular *L'Éclair* as an opera without chorus. The critic Cornélius Holff obviously hated Varney, whom he refers to constantly as 'l'illustrissimo maestro Varney'. 'The opera is heavy,' he declared, 'the details are utterly silly . . . As for the music, if you could call it music, it is even more painful than the libretto. The overture consists of nothing but a cor anglais solo producing the most woeful effect.'[7] But Holff's was not the only bad review. 'It is a very inferior work about which the most benevolent critic cannot find a good word for anyone,' declared Gustave Héquet.[8] In spite of Varney's aspirations, it became evident when he retired as conductor of the Théâtre Lyrique that composition obviously was not his forte.

During October, news was also circulating about the engagement of the famous and now aging tenor, Jean Baptiste Marie Chollet. Earlier in his career he had created the tenor roles in *Fra Diavolo, Zampa*, and *Le Postillon de Lonjumeau*. He was a member of the French opera company that sang at the St. James's Theatre, London in 1850, when it was said of him that 'he was well received on account of his easy, gentlemanly and vivacious acting and his command both of humour and pathos, which atoned for loss of voice.'[9] The same source reported that his engagement at the Théâtre Lyrique was unsuccessful, which is enlightening in view of the eulogies he would receive in the French press.

It was natural that he should appear in some of his old and well-tried successes, and so he began his season as Chapelou in *Le Postillon de Lonjumeau*. He was then 54 although, since he would live to be 93, he presumably could be considered to be still in his prime. At least one review made it appear so when

Gustave Héquet announced, 'Chollet has lost nothing of his talent from the old days. He still has his figure, his comic gestures, his delivery (clear and energetic) . . . You can imagine how he was received in the role in which he always triumphed. It was like a family gathering, a return of the prodigal son . . .'[10] Berlioz, too, describes how he was 'acclaimed, applauded, recalled'. He was also showered with bouquets, a practice which Berlioz abhorred. 'This form of ovation is nowadays discredited,' he declares. 'The Opéra Comique no longer employs it, and most actors have renounced it.'[11]

Less than a week following the production of *Le Postillon de Lonjumeau*, there was a revival of a much less important opera by a much less important composer: Narcisse Girard's *Les Deux Voleurs*. By coincidence de Leuven and Brunswick were librettists of both works. It was popular and had been first performed at the Opéra Comique in 1841.

Something a little more substantial followed, *Guillery le Trompette*, a two-act opera comique by the Sicilian composer, Salvatore Sarmiento. Although a reputed pupil of Donizetti, he seems to have borrowed his style from Rossini, even to a crescendo in the overture. 'If he is lacking in originality, at least he is a melodist and he writes well for the voice, as do most of the Italians,'[12] wrote Gustave Héquet. Berlioz was also non-committal except for some ironic words concerning bouquets thrown to Mlle Rouvroy. 'For the past year, bouquets have replaced catcalls,' he tartly comments, 'and one could not give greater affront to an artist than to throw even one rose!'[13]

The last opera for the year, performed just before Christmas, was *Tabarin*, by Georges Bousquet (our critic of Eugène Gautier from the previous season and also a Prix de Rome winner in 1838 with Gounod). Indeed in May 1840 Fanny Mendelssohn was said to have preferred Bousquet's music to Gounod's,[14] apparently on very limited hearing of either. The libretto, by Alboize and Andrel had a historical basis. It concerned Tabarin, a strolling jester, and Mondor, a mountebank, who in the time of Louis XIII used to perform at fairs on the Pont Neuf in Paris. 'Since *Si j'étais Roi*, no new work has been so well received at the Théâtre Lyrique or produced so much effect,' proclaimed Gustave Héquet.[15] Jules Lovy in *Le Ménestrel* agreed, but had reservations about the performance which, he

Tabarin (Bousquet) 1852 Act 2

stated flatly, was 'incompetent'. 'Above all,' he ironically reported, 'we will keep quiet about the execution of a certain chorus, which almost made the audience collapse. Never was there such obstinate persistence in singing out of tune. Perhaps it was for a bet?'[16]

The year for the Théâtre Lyrique had nonetheless been successful, culminating in December with a visit to the 60th performance of *Si j'étais Roi* of Princess Mathilde, daughter of King Jerome Bonaparte and a cousin of Louis Napoleon, now Emperor Napoleon III. The theatre was as crowded as for the first performance of the opera, and her Highness was so pleased that she promised Jules Seveste she would come again to hear Chollet in *Le Postillon de Lonjumeau*.[17]

Princess Mathilde's patronage was something worth having, for she exercised a unique influence on cultural life in Paris during the period of the Second Empire. She had been engaged briefly to Louis Napoleon but in 1840 had married Anatole Demidoff, an extremely wealthy Russian. Later she became the mistress of Alfred-Emilien O'Hara, Count de Nieuwerkerke. Even before the advent of the Second Empire she had established a salon at her house in the rue de Courcelles and at her country estate, Saint Gratien, near Enghien. Her entertaining included not only conventional dinners and receptions but also glittering fancy dress balls and theatrical soirées. She painted in water-colours, from what we can learn, not badly. Works by her once hung in the Luxembourg Museum and at Lille. It seems that she did not enjoy music. But it was her ability to successfully gather together musicians, painters, singers, poets, critics, ministers of state and Academicians at the rue de Courcelles which was her paramount contribution to art and to the Paris of her time.

Early in January 1853 Berlioz wrote with enthusiasm of the work Jules Seveste was doing at the Théâtre Lyrique. He pointed out that Seveste had opened his doors to all young composers not alone French, but of all nationalities; but one must not expect to hear first-class singers there—no Sontag, Jenny Lind, Mario or Tamberlik—one must count on adequate performances only. He advised Seveste not to try to compete with his grands confrères (of the Opéra and Opéra Comique); instead he should attend to the quality of what was being produced on his own stage. Berlioz commends the justice of the

Théâtre Lyrique's claim for a subvention of 100,000 francs; he admits that it is a lot of money but believes that it could be worse spent.[18]

The first opera to be performed in the new year was another Adam revival for Chollet, *Le Roi d'Yvetot*, originally produced with Chollet as Josselin, at the Opéra Comique in 1842. This was always one of Adam's less successful works and proved to be so again here.

A vignette of the Théâtre Lyrique audience comes from a performance which took place on Sunday, 6 February. This commenced at a quarter to six to allow time for two works. One was *Si j'étais Roi* and, in an attempt to shorten playing time, the overture was cut. But the audience would have none of it; they insisted on the overture being played, with the result that the curtain did not finally come down until after midnight.[19]

Towards the end of January, a new form of entertainment was introduced. It was described both as an 'opera-ballet' and as a 'mimodrame'.[20] Although not entirely successful, the experiment would be repeated during the following year. The title of the first opera-ballet to be performed was *Le Lutin de la Vallée* and the impetus for its staging came from a singular artist named Arthur Saint-Léon. His true name was Charles Victor Arthur Michel, and he was born in Paris on 17 September 1821 but brought up in Stuttgart, where his father was master of the theatre ballet and court ceremonies. He studied dancing with his father and Albert, and the violin with Paganini and Mayseder. In time he would perform as dancer and violinist before most of the crowned heads of Europe, and be decorated by many of them. He would also become an important choreographer and very indifferent composer.

In 1845 he married the renowned ballerina Fanny Cerrito. It has been said that the parish priest of the fashionable church of St Roch refused to perform the ceremony on the hardly canonical grounds that he did not marry theatrical people! Perhaps a more likely reason can be deduced from a notice which appeared in the *Illustrated London News* of 11 January 1845. This announced the forthcoming marriage, adding, 'The Pope has granted a bull for the union, Saint-Léon having been converted from Judaism.' But Saint-Léon was not a Jew, he had been baptised as an infant in the Reformed Church in Paris.

However, to a conservative prelate of St Roch there would be nothing to choose between Judaism and Lutheranism, no matter what Pope Gregory XVI might have granted, and so the marriage was solemnised in a church in the more liberal suburb of Batignolles. Within five years they had separated. He was the choreographer and, with Nuitter, the adapter of the story of the ballet *Coppélia* for which Delibes composed the music and which was first performed in May 1870. Three months later, he would be dead, and at his burial service in the Lutheran church in the rue Chauchat, Delibes would play an excerpt from *Néméa*, another Saint-Léon ballet, as the coffin was borne down the aisle.[21]

Le Lutin de la Vallée was yet another work composed by Eugène Gautier for the Théâtre Lyrique. Adolphe Adam and Saint-Léon were also said to have interpolated some of their compositions into the score. Saint-Léon had resigned his engagement at the Opéra, where he had recently been dancing, bringing with him Mme Guy-Stéphan. Ten years earlier, when the latter first appeared in London, she was described as 'a stoutish young lady, with a pretty face, who moves with great flexibility, and dances with an easy careless grace that is very pleasing, without representing any sentiment by her movements ...'[22]

The most popular item of the evening was a violin solo composed and played by Saint-Léon, entitled 'Une matinée à la Campagne', in which he reproduced all the noises of the farmyard![23]

The opera-ballet's success, although ephemeral, was good while it lasted, and receipts of over 4,000 francs a performance were announced.[24] Of the first performance we learn that there were flowers and recalls in plenty as well as 'a typically Italian ovation in the form of a dove'[25]—presumably lowered on to the stage.

The Emperor's marriage with Countess Eugénie de Montijo, having been formally announced on 22 January 1853, took place a week later. There were the usual festivities and celebrations. There were also the usual intrigues, including one report that the Odéon, having been promised the title of Théâtre de l'Impératrice in honour of the new Empress, was now having its distinction disputed by the Théâtre Lyrique.[26] Neither theatre acquired the honour, but there was some compensation for the Théâtre Lyrique when, on 28 February, their Majesties attended a performance there.

'From the beginning of the evening,' we read, 'the boulevard du Temple was illuminated with the initials N.L. announcing the advent of the Emperor and Empress to the Théâtre Lyrique'.

At nine o'clock, with customary ceremonial, Seveste received them at the foot of the staircase leading to the auditorium, while the choir of Les Enfants de Paris struck up the 'Hymne à la Gloire', more commonly known as 'Partant pour la Syrie'.[27] This air, which would become to the Second Empire what La Marseillaise had been to the First Republic, was written and composed by Queen Hortense, the Emperor's mother. At least so the story goes, but a member of the Queen's household, an eminent flautist named Louis François Philippe Drouet, was so ungallant as to tattle that he was obliged to give musical form to tunes which the Queen hummed. Still, there have been few Emperors who had even the treble line of their national anthem composed by their own mother.

Indeed, Queen Hortense's compositions were due for a revival, for an album of her songs would be published in May in editions costing 40, 100 and 150 francs, the latter approved by the Emperor in a special portfolio bound in silk moiré.[28] Sales must have been slow, for within a month the price had dropped to 120 francs.[29]

The entertainment arranged for the evening consisted of *Flore et Zéphire*, *La Poupée de Nuremberg* and *Le Lutin de la Vallée*. It was a brilliant occasion 'which brought a new impetus to M. Seveste's theatre'.[30] It also brought a reward to Mme Guy-Stéphan in the form of a bracelet ornamented with diamonds as a mark of the Empress's approval.[31] This was presented by Count Baciocchi, the Emperor's first chamberlain, who had lately been appointed superintendent of the imperial theatres.[32]

Napoleon III was in fact a helpful force to music and to the theatres during his reign. As early as April he would receive in private audience Eugène Scribe, President of the Association of Authors and Dramatic Composers, accompanied by some fellow members. They were seeking an extension of the period of their rights in favour of their heirs beyond the then legal 20 years after death.[33]

Not that he could be accused of being musical. It is said that he 'could so little remember a musical theme that you might have played the same thing twice over to him, and given it two different names, and he never would have known it.'[34] At the Compiègne house parties, a piano organ was used to accompany the guests for dancing. The tunes were ground out by the male members of the party—usually the older; the younger men would be dancing. It merely needed the mechanical turning of the handle to play, but a certain ear for time was also required. We read that 'the worst offender, the most hopeless performer was undoubtedly the Emperor himself'.[35] He was reputed to sleep through opera performances,[36] although it should be added that by this time he was a sick man, but all in all where music was concerned, he seems to have liked only polkas, waltzes, mazurkas and to have enjoyed the military 'tralalas' at the changing of the guard; 'for him the jingling johnny had charm and the big drum was full of excitement'.[37]

Neither was the Empress musical, although she is said to have sung arias from Bellini's *Norma*. It is also said that her mother once declared that she had a voice like a crow![38] Her musical preference, like the Emperor's, was for popular waltzes.

A four-act opera comique (described also as an opéra féerie), *Les Amours du Diable*, by de Saint-Georges and Albert Grisar, was the next work to be presented. It was successful and in time would travel to both North and South America. The same story had been originally used some 20 years earlier for a ballet, *Le Diable Amoureux*, with libretto again by de Saint-Georges. Berlioz even found some similarities between it and Meyerbeer's *Robert-le-Diable* and, although not over-enthusiastic about the opera ('If I have nothing more to say about the score of *Les Amours du Diable* it is because I find some embarrassment in speaking about it'), at least counselled, 'Well then, let all who know neither *Robert the Devil* nor *The Devil in Love* rush to the Théâtre Lyrique to see *The Loves of the Devil*.'[39]

Berlioz too found a noticeable advance in the standard of musical performance. 'The orchestra has improved,' he reports, 'it is almost in tune.' He also comments favourably on Deloffre, who seems to have been the leader on this occasion, as he does on the singers, with the continued exception of the ladies' chorus. 'When it comes to the spoken dialogue, however,' he writes, 'one cannot find criticism sufficiently severe. It is the animal kingdom to perfection. They do not speak, they bawl, and with what accents, what inflexions of voice . . .'[40]

The next opera was a new work by Adam for Chollet, *Le Roi des Halles*. Once more his librettists were de Leuven and Brunswick, and this time their story was set in the mid 17th century during the time of the Fronde. Berlioz perhaps found this production more satisfactory, though he appears to have written about it with tongue in cheek.[41] In spite of a lavish production by Seveste which in part was said to rival that of the Opéra, [42] the work in fact proved unsuccessful. Adam was inclined to blame Chollet for the failure, citing the latter's resentment at the audiences' warm reception of the young singer Laurent as the reason.[43] It was as unfair a charge as it was regrettable, for Jean in *Le Roi des Halles* would be Chollet's last creation. Like *La Poupée de Nuremberg*, it was a hurriedly written opera; unlike it, it did not succeed. The reviews were universally cool, and time has proved them to have been right.

A one-act opera comique, *Colin-Maillard* by Aristide Hignard, which was then performed, may have been originally intended for the theatre of his native city, Nantes. The only fact of interest to survive from it is that one of its two librettists was Jules Verne (also born in Nantes about the same time as Hignard), today universally known for *Around the world in 80 days, 20,000 leagues under the sea*, and so much more. He was also for a time secretary of the Théâtre Lyrique and was reputed to have had a hand in many of the operas produced there.[44] The work itself was dismissed as a harmless vaudeville for which Hignard had composed an equally artless score—he certainly could not be accused of revolutionary tendencies.[45]

L'Organiste dans l'embarras, which followed, seems to have been just as insubstantial. Its composer, J.B.T. Weckerlin, was primarily a musicologist interested in reviving old songs. Alboize's libretto is said to have been derived from E.T.A. Hoffmann[46] whose fantastic tales were then serving French librettists so constantly and so well, long before Offenbach would enshrine some of them in the title of his most famous opera.

The 1852–53 season ended on 31 May. Three days earlier, an 'epilogue' entitled *Le Présent et l'Avenir* was given as the final production. This was a 'pot-pourri' of items from the repertory (everything from a duet in *Le Barbier de Séville* to a duet in *L'Organiste dans l'embarras*) strung together on a thin story line about a composer who, having waited 35 years to have his opera performed, was at last offered the stage of the Théâtre Lyrique. A precedent for this style of closure was reported to have been introduced at the Comédie Française by Beaumarchais at the end of the 1775–76 season, when all the artists in the company took part in a performance. Previous to this, the Comédie Française used to end its season with a single final address traditionally spoken by a leading actor.[47]

The Théâtre Lyrique took advantage of both styles of ending, for after the performance the 'composer' appealed for a government subvention for the theatre and the curtain finally descended following a witty anecdote charmingly told by Mlle Guichard.[48]

1853–1854

The theatre re-opened for the 1853–54 season on 3 September. Throughout the summer there had been much activity. New singers were engaged*, new operas were announced for production including, to commence the season, a prologue composed by six young musicians all making their debuts in this one work.[1] New chorus members were also auditioned, allowing the chorus to be considered 'much better than last year.'[2]

An important appointment was the promotion of Adolphe Deloffre, the principal violinist and assistant conductor of the previous season, to the post of principal conductor. As a young violinist he had set out for London from Paris with the renowned orchestral conductor Jullien. Later he became principal violinist at Her Majesty's Theatre under Balfe. He used to return to Paris each year to give concerts and finally he settled there permanently in 1851. He was to remain at the Théâtre Lyrique until 1868 when he changed to the Opéra Comique. There his greatest distinction would be to conduct the first

*

Artists announced were: Mmes Cabel, Chevalier, Colson, Girard, Meillet; MM. Cabel, Grignon, Junca, Laurent, Legrand, Meillet, Menjaud, Ribes, Sujol, Tallon.

performance of Bizet's *Carmen* in 1875, but he died not long after, on 8 January 1876.

From the early part of the 19th century, French opera orchestras (as in Great Britain and Ireland) were conducted by the principal violinist who occasionally, and mainly in ensembles, would beat time with his bow. (The accompagnateur or maestro al piano was relegated to a secondary position of accompanist or vocal coach. In France a pianist or organist would then have been in charge of a choir.) By 1850 the conductor-violinist had all but dispensed with his instrument and had begun to beat time exclusively, still using his bow as a baton. His violin would still remain close by, perhaps on a shelf beneath his desk. Meanwhile his position amidst the orchestra players had been determined. He might stand at the extreme end of the orchestra pit, facing the players with the stage on his left—as at the Opéra Comique and Théâtre Italien, or be seated in the centre behind the prompter's box (the position today)—as at the Opéra and Théâtre Lyrique.

Throughout the first half of the century, almost all the regular opera conductors in Paris were violinists. By 1850 their importance corresponded with their ability to control the players under them. Moreover, it was then widely believed that a conductor must be either a composer, an instrumentalist or a singer in order to successfully direct the playing or singing of others. As the 19th century progressed, this divided involvement became unworkable, due to the increased complexity of operatic music. At the same time we learn that the personality or individuality of a conductor was hardly recognised by the mid 19th century. Virtuosity in singers or instrumentalists might be recognised and appreciated, but never in conductors. Neither was he a box-office draw and his name did not usually appear on theatre bills, which might have included the scene-painter, costumier and régisseur.[3]

Judged by present day standards, Deloffre was a poor conductor. Fétis describes his method of giving the beat as flabby and indecisive, failing to clearly indicate the time. However he confirms that he was a painstaking artist. Berlioz also takes him to task and relates that while he conducted with his bow, he also beat time with his foot, stamping so noisily on the floor as even to drown out the sound of the bass drum.[4] His added comment that the tap of the bow on the prompter's box was traditional although stamping the foot was not, indicates that Deloffre was standing or seated in the centre of the orchestra.

French orchestras included a small group of soloists (virtuoses d'élite) who, from the end of the 18th century, were exempt from ordinary orchestral playing. They performed solo pieces only. Deloffre had at least one such virtuoso among his players. He was Jean Rémusat, a gifted flautist from Bordeaux who, like Deloffre, had given much of his career to Her Majesty's Theatre, London. Throughout his life he used the old style of flute, rejecting the notable improvements introduced to the instrument by Boehm. Towards the end he visited Shanghai, where he founded a music school and where he died in 1880.

Prior to the opening of the season, there was the Emperor's fête day on 15 August. This was the birth date not of Napoleon III, but of his illustrious uncle Napoleon I. Such diversions kept the Napoleon Bonaparte myth alive. On this day, free performances were offered to the public in all the theatres.* At the Théâtre Français, Rachel drew enormous crowds to see her perform in *Phèdre*, and the Théâtre Lyrique was equally crowded for a programme which consisted of *Le Maître de Chapelle*, *Ma Tante Aurore* and *Flore et Zéphire*. These performances took place at one o'clock in the afternoon and the day, having begun with a *Te Deum* sung in all the churches,

---

The first free performance for the Parisians was given at the Théâtre Italien in 1682 in honour of the birth of the Duc de Bourgogne. The façade of the theatre was illuminated with over 1000 lights and 60 maroons were set off. Another took place in 1744 to celebrate the recovery of Louis XV from serious illness and was again given by the Italian players. Many casks of wine were placed on the balconies of the theatre to slake the thirst of the populace. There were free performances at the Opéra and Théâtre Français to commemorate the birth of a daughter to Louis XVI and Marie Antoinette in December 1778 and the birth of the first Dauphin in October 1781. On the former occasion *Castor et Pollux* by Rameau and a ballet *La Chercheuse d'Esprit* were performed at the Opéra, and the evening ended with a tumultuous reception of the chorus 'Chantons, célébrons, notre reine' from *Iphigénie en Aulide*.
(Information derived from John Lough, *Paris Theatre Audiences in the 17th and 18th Centuries* London 1972, and Emile Blavet, *La Situation*, reported M. 18 August 1867)

would end with a concert in the Tuileries Gardens attended by their Majesties.[5]

Seveste eventually commenced his season on 3 September but not, as originally announced, with a work by many authors now entitled *La Princesse de Trébisonde*. This was his intention but at the last moment he judged it imprudent to detain his audience until two in the morning, so the season's prologue was held over until the following evening.[6] Consequently he began with a four-act opera called *La Moissonneuse* by Adolphe Vogel. Although the title of *The Harvester* does little to indicate it, the libretto was loosely based on an episode concerning Cagliostro, here called by his true name, Balsamo. The work did not succeed (musically it was highly derivative) and the only feature to really attract attention was the setting for act two, painted by Enrico Robecchi to represent the then well known painting of *Les Moissonneurs* by Léopold Robert. Emile Lerouge, the choreographer, was also praised for a tarantella danced with an agility and daring reminiscent of the dancing at the Closerie des Lilas.[7]

When *La Princesse de Trébisonde* was performed the next evening, it was found to be nothing more than another pastiche in the same style as the epilogue with which the previous season had ended. The librettists, according to the *Revue et Gazette Musicale*, remained anonymous, but Jules Lovy in *Le Ménestrel* identified them as Alboize and de Leuven. Nor did all the six composers turn out to be either young or making their debuts, for they were Nicolas Louis, Morin, Weckerlin, Gautier, Rossini and Rameau.[8]

Later in September there followed a first opera comique, *Bonsoir Voisin*, by Ferdinand Poise, a successful pupil of Adam, which would continue to be performed for several years. The idea for the plot was said to have come from a cartoon by the unique artist-journalist, Gavarni.[9] Berlioz declared it to be an imitation of Massé's *Les Noces de Jeannette*, produced at the Opéra Comique during the previous February (and successfully revived there as late as 1960) and asked what was to be gained by the Théâtre Lyrique presenting facsimiles of its subsidized rival.[10] M. and Mme Meillet, the sole artists in the cast, were most successful.

But the greatest success of the season, and for seasons to come, would be a new opera by Adolphe Adam, *Le Bijou perdu*.

Fortuitously, a new star had been discovered to enhance its success. She was a soprano named Marie Cabel, who had been born Marie Josèphe Dreullette in Liège, the daughter of a sometime French cavalry officer. While still a child, a great future had been predicted for her by Pauline Viardot Garcia, yet from 1847 until 1849 she would perform at the Opéra Comique almost unnoticed. She then changed to the Théâtre de la Monnaie in Brussels, where she was at last acclaimed. Next she returned to France to sing at Lyon at a reputed 3,000 francs a month, when Jules Seveste discovered her. She had earlier married her teacher, taking his name, but the marriage proved unhappy and so they were divorced. (Louis Cabel, who was also performing in the company, was her brother-in-law.) Her husband's tuition cannot have been entirely successful for she was said to have many faults of vocalisation, but her voice remained sweet and flexible. Charles Dickens, who heard her in Auber's *Manon Lescaut* at the Opéra Comique, wrote that she was 'the most delightful little prima donna ever seen or heard.'[11]

Georges Bousquet declared that for him the outstanding items in *Le Bijou perdu* were Cabel's singing of the air 'Ah! qu'il fait donc beau cueillir des fraises,' which became the 'hit number' of the opera, and Rémusat's playing of a concerto in the overture.[12] Berlioz was not enthusiastic. Never an admirer of Adam's music, he was by the third act writing in exasperation, 'My God, how long an opera seems to take!'[13] His exasperation may have been fuelled by the fact that both Liszt and Wagner had lately arrived in Paris[14] and it was reported that Liszt would superintend the production of one of Wagner's operas at the Théâtre Lyrique and conduct the opening performance.[15]

Not that his views affected the box-office, where the first 15 performances brought in receipts of over 60,000 francs. Marie Cabel had truly brought the carriage trade to the boulevard du Temple, and shining equipages with prancing animals formed ranks where previously stood the occasional fiacre with its drooping-headed horse.[16] The *Illustrated London News* had placed the Théâtre Lyrique seventh among the Paris theatres in order of social prestige, but now boxes had to be engaged four or five days in advance. In December the Emperor and Empress would attend, thereby placing the ultimate seal of success on the opera.[17]

In order to grant Marie Cabel some little respite from her success, a century-old opera comique, *Le Diable à quatre*, was now revived. The genesis of this work begins with the old ballad opera, *The Devil to Pay, or the Wives Metamorphos'd*, first performed in 1731. The libretto was by the Irish playwright Charles Coffey, and in 1756 a French translation by Claude Pierre Patu had been published. During the same year Philidor arranged the music for a version of J.M. Sedaine which was performed at the Opéra Comique. Then in 1809 A.F. Creuzé de Lesser adapted Sedaine's libretto for which Jean Pierre Solié composed a new score, and it was this version (rescored by Adam) that was performed at the Théâtre Lyrique. Its revival made little impact, however, and it had only 23 performances during that one season.

Another opera-ballet, *Le Danseur du Roi*, doubling as a vehicle for Saint-Léon, followed. Predictably he was the dancer (and violinist) to the King—Louis XIII. On this occasion he brought as his partner Nathalie Fitzjames from the Opéra. At some time in her career Mme Fitzjames had been both singer and dancer, but dancing was unquestionably her principal vocation. Some confusion exists concerning who composed the score of *Le Danseur du Roi*. Both Soubies and Lasalle credit Eugène Gautier with it, but Gustave Héquet records, 'All the music . . . dance tunes, chorus, song and symphony are by Saint-Léon' and comments, 'his orchestration is not very varied'.[18] Whoever it was, and Gautier seems the more likely candidate, less than a month after it was produced, and following a run of only 11 performances, Saint-Léon had fled the scene and the opera was suspended.[19]

Its place was taken by a one-act opera comique, *Georgette, ou Le Moulin de Fontenoy*, with music by Gevaert. The locale of Vaëz's libretto had a very nominal association with the epic battle of Fontenoy, but Seveste was complimented for presenting a style of 'opera-bouffe' which had already succeeded so well with *La Poupée de Nuremberg*.[20]

The year ended (literally) with a performance on 31 December of a Donizetti opera called *Elisabeth, ou La Fille du Proscrit*. At least that is how Grignon described the work when, as stage manager and dressed in a black suit and white tie, he came before the curtain to announce it prior to the first performance.

Its true identity however was more involved. Originally it had been produced at the Teatro Nuovo, Naples in 1827 under the title *Otto Mesi in Due Ore, ossia Gli Esiliati in Siberia*, and it enjoyed varying success in other Italian theatres, including La Scala, until 1835. It was subsequently performed throughout the Continent.

There was determined opposition by E. Viel of *Le Ménestrel* to its revival both on stylistic grounds as an indifferent work of a good composer as well as the perennial protest against 'interminable exhumations'. Such exhumations were no less damaging to the interests of living authors than they were to the memory of the illustrious dead. The Théâtre Lyrique, because of its privileged position, was all the more culpable in yielding to such temptation—it was hoped—for the first and last time.[21]

Elisabeth seemingly had been intended for performance at the Opéra Comique during the early 1840s but was withdrawn when Eugénie Garcia was not re-engaged there.[22] The Italian libretto of the opera had been based on a French mélodrame by Guilbert de Pixérécourt* and was now retranslated by de Leuven and Brunswick. Unfortunately the music had also been 'translated' by one of Donizetti's innumerable pupils, Uranio Fontana, who added music of his own to the overture and to the first and second acts, including new airs for the tenor. He also introduced an entirely new third act, whether his own composition or arranged from early Donizetti works it is difficult to decide.[23]

Nevertheless Berlioz found the score, while not very original, to abound in agreeable pieces and declared the performance to be one of the best he had heard in that theatre. At the same time he pointed out that the singers had contracted shocking habits of prosody which offended both the ear and the meaning of the words. The majority, both French and Italian, now emphasised the penultimate note in a phrase: Plus de *bo*-nheur! Mon *a*-mour! Son toit *pro*-tecteur! in order to spin out interminably the sound of the 'o' or the 'a'. He concluded by describing the decor and production of *Elisabeth* as first class.[24] While not very successful (only 35 performances were given), the opera enjoyed

---

*

Who in turn took his story from a well known novel *Elisabeth ou les Exilés de Sibérie* by Mme Cottin (Sophie Risteau) 1770–1807.

a more successful run than it had ever had while Donizetti was alive.

No new opera entered the repertory in 1854 until early in February and then it was merely a one-act opera-ballet, *Les Étoiles*, composed by Auguste Pilati. This slender piece, described as a 'ballet, sung, spoken and danced'[25] (it was outside the terms of the Théâtre Lyrique's licence to present ballet in any other form), anticipated *Schéhérazade* in setting if not in story, for the action took place in the harem of the Shah of Persia. The critics were mainly impressed by the principal male dancer, Alfred Chapuy from the Opéra; Berlioz speaks of him as outstanding. Presumably he had been engaged to fill Saint-Léon's place. There was praise, too, for the choreography of M. Barrez, also from the Opéra.

It may be explained here that *Les Étoiles* formed only part of the evening's programme. When shorter operas were produced, a successful work from the repertoire, *Le Bijou perdu*, for example, was always added to ensure a satisfying length of entertainment. It was a rare occasion when one opera only was performed, and evenings when six acts from two or three operas were given were not uncommon.[26] On the evening that *Les Étoiles* was produced, the performance started late and had not ended by midnight. Jules Lovy of *Le Ménestrel* was critical of the situation and advocated the return of the clock over the proscenium—seemingly earlier removed—as a corrective to the administration's casualness.[27]

Later in February there was a more noteworthy offering from Adrien Boieldieu called *La Fille invisible*, but even with Mme Meillet leading the cast it had no greater success than his effort of two years previously. *The Musical World* thought the music to be 'much the same style as his former works—neither better nor worse.'[28] Berlioz, on the other hand, acknowledged notable progress, but reproached him for his abuse of the bass drum and trombones in his scoring.[29] The setting of the opera was across the Rhine and endorsed Wagner's assertion, written from Paris in 1841, that French librettists sought their stories abroad, principally in Germany. Ironically he observed, ' "What extraordinary places," they think, "Silesia, Thuringia and the lands around them must be!" '[30] Yet with the works of writers such as E.T.A. Hoffmann and Jean Paul for models, who will say that they were not justified. Of this production Jules Lovy wrote that it was time that the French stage made an end of German corporals speaking Alsatian gibberish while dressed in Austrian and Russian uniforms.[31]

La Promise, with a libretto by the established partnership of de Leuven and Brunswick, set in Provence during the time of the First Empire, and with music by Clapisson, was next produced. Clapisson was a violinist and a well known composer, a pretentious man who held himself in much greater esteem than posterity has ratified. He would at least gain the morbid distinction of having Rossini's 'Pietà Signore' (then attributed to Stradella) played at his requiem mass by his confrère the renowned violinist Sarasate.[32] Even during his lifetime he was not universally acclaimed and B. Jouvin, writing in *Le Figaro*, stated that 'far from having a style [he] does not even possess a manner, a musical signature, by which his works may be recognised . . . a tap of clear water which no one has taken the trouble to turn off is more productive than M. Clapisson; talent without originality denotes the working musician but not the artist.'[33] Yet he had gained a reputation and because of it *The Musical World* would sagely if equivocally predict of *La Promise*, 'Although not a work of the first class, it will probably have a run, owing to the manner in which the principal part is sustained by Mlle Marie Cabel . . .'[34] It did, at least for that year, when it was played 57 times.

The only opera by Ambroise Thomas, the composer of *Mignon*, ever to be performed at the Théâtre Lyrique, was now presented. It was a revival from the Opéra Comique of an early one-act work, *Le Panier fleuri*, but it passed almost unnoticed.

A two-act opera comique which followed, *Une Rencontre dans le Danube*, had music by Paul Henrion, a composer of romances and popular songs, of whom it was remarked that he had lost his footing in the theatre. The story concerned two men who meet when one rescues the other from drowning in the Danube. Again the romantic beyond-the-Rhine influence is apparent, for it was noted that the Danube had nothing to do with the story—the Sarthe or any French river would have done as well.[35] Whatever the river, the opera sank without a trace.

A revival of an early opera by Adolphe Adam, *La Reine d'un Jour*, with a libretto by the eminent pair, Scribe and de Saint-

Georges, was scarcely more successful.

An opera which would survive until the beginning of the 20th century was Ernest Reyer's *Maître Wolfram*, with libretto by F.J. Méry. Reyer was unquestionably the most progressive composer to have an opera performed at the Théâtre Lyrique at this time. Like many of his literary friends, indeed like so many French artists of the period, he was influenced by the Orient, but his music in time would be influenced by Wagner, and 30 years later he would compose an opera, *Sigurd*, based on the Nibelungen legend, which in story corresponds roughly to *Götterdämmerung*. It was his most important work and even now is occasionally performed. Although *Maître Wolfram* did not achieve many performances it was favourably received, but its success 'was mainly attributable to the singing and acting of Mme Meillet.'[36]

It would seem that at this time even final rehearsals were frequently perfunctory, for in April the Minister of the Interior circularised all theatre directors that the general rehearsal, which the Inspector of Theatres attended, must take place with costumes and decor.[37] His reason may have been one of censorship against the subsequent introduction of indecorous costumes or scenery into the production.

In May Marie Cabel, on leave and singing at Bordeaux and Nantes, was announced to return to take part in a benefit performance of *La Promise* for the stage manager (Grignon?) on 1 June.[38] This she may have done, but the evening's programme also included a revival of Grétry's opera comique, *Le Tableau parlant*. First performed at the Comédie Italienne in 1769, its success until the end of the 18th century was widespread, but from then onwards performances dwindled, and at the Théâtre Lyrique it was played only three times.

The theatre having closed for the summer, many of the company left for London where they would give a two months' season at the Saint James's Theatre, commencing with Cabel in *Le Bijou perdu*. The *Illustrated London News* described the opera as 'exceedingly immoral—a thing of no importance in Paris, but not yet disregarded, we trust, in London.'[39]

This was not an official visit of the Théâtre Lyrique. Lafont was in charge and Jules Seveste made it clear that he was in no way associated with it but instead was remaining at home to prepare for the autumn re-opening.[40] He had sound reasons for so doing, for on 21 May it had been announced that the Minister of the Interior had confirmed him in the Théâtre Lyrique licence first awarded to his brother Edmond, for ten years.[41] Moreover, there was even talk of a formal promise regarding the long-sought subvention.

Then, with a stroke of drama which occurs so frequently in opera and an element of irony which can happen only in real life, on 30 June Jules Seveste died suddenly at Meudon, near Paris. The jest concerning his bravery, made at the time he accepted the position had become tragically true. Following a service at the church of Saint Nicolas des Champs, where the orchestra of his theatre paid him final homage (the singers were in London) he was buried in Montmartre cemetery. Many theatrical and artistic personalities attended his funeral and graveside orations were delivered by de Saint-Georges and Baron Taylor.[42]

The frequency with which Isidore Justin Séverin Taylor (created Baron by Charles X) delivered orations at funerals testifies both to his importance and his humanity. The events of his life were so diverse that one can become acquainted with him only by consulting many different sources: the archaeologist for the Luxor obelisk which stands in the place de la Concorde and which Taylor helped to bring from Egypt; to theatre history to know that he staged Victor Hugo's *Hernani* when Director of the Théâtre Français; to military history to learn of his part in the Spanish expedition of 1823; to the antiquarian to know of his restoration of theatrical monuments; to the lithographer for his studies on the origins of that art. He made many voyages abroad, was a connoisseur of Spanish painting, held the position of Inspector General of Fine Arts; and as a sociologist did much work in the foundation of philanthropic societies. This last labour he began in 1840 with the formation of the Association des artistes dramatiques, to be followed by the Association des artistes musiciens, and it was as founder of these associations that he spoke the last words at so many gravesides. When his own turn came to be buried at the great age of 90, speeches were delivered by no less than seven colleagues, all artistic nonentities. The many reference books that grant him Irish ancestry through his father may be right, for there were Taylors settled in Ireland from the end of the 13th century. Those who describe his mother as also being of Irish descent are on much less secure ground. Her name, Walvein, could be a continental corruption of Walwyn, but Walwyns are to be found not in Ireland but in Hereford, England.

So with the parting words of Baron Taylor winging them to heaven (for he had eulogised at Edmond's funeral as well), the era of the Seveste brothers ended at the Théâtre Lyrique. Both appear to have been more than competent administrators. They had to be, for theirs was very much a 'boulevard' theatre without subvention and with the highest priced seats costing no more than five or six francs. Besides, we can be sure that Cabel's carriage trade customers were by no means regular.

As for artistic standards, in spite of the Goncourt brothers' colourful prose and praise, these must have been impaired by financial exigencies. The routine level of singing, with a few notable exceptions, has already been mentioned. No doubt a budget would occasionally be found to decently mount a work that might be expected to have a run, but as can be seen in the period already covered, such successes came only about twice a year. Between, there must have been much mediocrity. Yet, within the theatre's policy, there was much that was good, and Soubies confirms this when he writes: 'After all, thanks to the proven ability of the direction, the theatre had remained alive. In less than three years the brothers Seveste had played or, to be more exact, had mounted, since the theatre was their creation, 46 works of which 29 were new, a very great proportion of the latter being by debutants. In sum they had undertaken a double obligation—seemingly contradictory—both to serve art and please the public, thus ensuring a decided chance of success for young composers'.[43]

Chapter 2

Perrin and Pellegrin 1854–1856

1854–1855

When through sudden death a political seat becomes vacant there is never any lack of candidates to fill it. So it was with Jules Seveste, for show business is a form of politics. Among many who sought the nomination, the best remembered today are Léon Escudier, Verdi's French publisher and sometime director of the Théâtre Italien, Emilien Pacini, the librettist and French translator of *Il Trovatore*, and Jacques Offenbach. M. Vedel, who had been the provisional administrator, was also mentioned but the post eventually went to Emile Perrin. This created some surprise for at the time Perrin was director of the Opéra Comique and his temerity at undertaking a second lyric theatre must have suggested symptoms of an unbalanced mind. He certainly gave indications of operatic madness for, having first had an inauspicious career as a history painter (he was a pupil of Gros and Delaroche and exhibited at the Salon), he would later hold appointments as director of the Opéra, the Opéra Comique (on two separate occasions) and the Théâtre Lyrique, finally ending for good dramatic measure with the Comédie Française. He was born in Rouen on 19 January 1814 and would die in Paris on 8 October 1885.

His first appointment to the Opéra Comique came through the then Minister of the Interior, Ledru-Rollin, following the 1848 revolution. Between 1857 and 1861 he would temporarily quit operatic management and return once more to painting, seemingly with success.

Wagner, while in Paris in 1860 remembered him as 'a well-to-do bel ésprit and painter . . . [who] had heard *Lohengrin* and *Tannhäuser* performed in Germany, and expressed himself in such a way as led me to suppose that he would make it a point of honour to bring these operas to France should he at any time be in a position to do so . . .'[1]

He seems to have been a good administrator, while the composer Edouard Lalo describes him as 'a stern man of dictatorial manner'. In 1877 he spoke kindly at the unveiling of Bizet's monument at Père Lachaise cemetery, though he had spoken vehemently against *Carmen* when it was first produced two years earlier.

But whereas the Théâtre Lyrique now had a director, it had at the same time lost its star artist, for Marie Cabel had been under contract to Jules Seveste, not to the theatre and so was now both free and eager to make a new engagement with the highest and most prestigious bidder. There was some talk of the Opéra but Perrin eventually succeeded in wooing her for a period of five years at an annual salary of 40,000 francs and three months annual leave. It was agreed that she would continue to sing at the Théâtre Lyrique for one year and then transfer to the Opéra Comique.[2]

This ambiguous arrangement caused anxiety as to how the Théâtre Lyrique would now be run vis-à-vis its more powerful rival, which led to the following reassuring announcement. 'Each of the two establishments will have a separate company and special repertory. The Théâtre Lyrique will not be the vassal of its elder brother; on the contrary, every effort will be made to keep up a noble spirit of emulation between the two, which cannot fail to be profitable to the art.'[3]

Certain onerous conditions were also imposed on the new director. He was obliged to keep his theatre open for ten months of the year, from 1 September until 30 June, and during this time to present at least three acts by previously unperformed composers. Not more than six acts by composers who had already had four works performed at the Opéra Comique could be staged. (The number of acts rather than the number of productions is always stipulated, presumably to prevent Perrin and other directors from evading the conditions of their privilege by presenting, say, only two one-act pieces by the unknown composers and, on the other hand, transferring more than two three-act works from the Opéra Comique.)

Works from the Opéra Comique which had remained unperformed there for two years could however be transferred and in special circumstances the Minister could assign any work from the repertory of the Opéra Comique to the Théâtre Lyrique, though not conversely.

Perrin's privilege was to run for three years, at the end of which the Minister could withdraw it without indemnification if the experiment had not proved successful, but Perrin could not give up one theatre without renouncing the other.[4]

In practice, this latter clause would never be enforced. Equally casual was a proviso which guaranteed Prix de Rome winners the right to have an opera of at least two acts performed at the Théâtre Lyrique in the year following their return to Paris.

Then in September a misunderstanding arose between Perrin and Baron Taylor's Societé des Auteurs et Compositeurs Dramatiques, and Perrin tendered his resignation from the Théâtre Lyrique to the Minister of State, Achille Fould, who on 1 July had taken over the direction of Paris's non-subventioned theatres from the Minister of the Interior. The committee of the Societé was demanding 15 per cent of the receipts of performances plus a number of free tickets plus agreement that two operas at least would be played each evening—'as the Théâtre Lyrique is to be dedicated to young authors.' Furthermore it required—'All translations and reproductions of foreign composers to be ABSOLUTELY prohibited as the theatre is intended exclusively for national composers, ABSOLUTE separation of the repertoire of the two theatres'—and an assurance that works which had been accepted by Jules Seveste would be put into production.[5]

In due course concessions were made by the Societé; Perrin withdrew his resignation, and by mid-September it was announced that 'the greatest harmony now prevails between all the parties concerned.'[6]

Harmony was also prevailing in the theatre itself, and on Saturday 30 September it re-opened for the season. There had been some concern whether this would be possible: a week before, we read, 'at this moment the theatre is full of workmen who have even taken possession of the stage, so that the actors* are obliged to rehearse in the foyer.'[7]

Improvements to the theatre, as we know, had been started by Jules Seveste, resulting in a splendid sight for the audience at the re-opening. The first amphitheatre had been elegantly fitted out with private boxes to which small salons were attached. The already existing side boxes had been brought forward and lowered by removing a row of stalls so that the entire auditorium and stage was now fully visible from them. An added row of fauteuils in front of the boxes also offered excellent seats, while the second gallery had been converted into stalls.[8]

Improvements were also being made in other departments— in costumes, decor, orchestra and chorus, even among the principals. The change may have begun earlier with the engagement of Marie Cabel. Certainly the Théâtre Lyrique could no longer be considered a simple boulevard theatre, of which a visiting critic in 1851 had written that he had wanted to come to Paris but had got only as far as the boulevard du Temple. Due no doubt to Perrin's standing, the tone of the theatre, both artistic and social, was being raised. Cabel's carriage patrons were not only returning, their visits were becoming more rewarding.

The opera performed at the re-opening was *La Promise*, with Marie Cabel a surefire revival, but the season really began on 7 October when *Le Billet de Marguerite*, with text by de Leuven and Brunswick and music by Gevaert, was first produced. Once again the scene was Germany, to be exact, Bamberg, but neither the libretto which was considered overly involved nor the music which was thought frivolous found favour with the audience.

*

Perrin's company for the season is listed as follows: *Chanteuses*: Mmes Marie Cabel, Deligne-Lauters, Colson, Meillet, Amélie Bourgeois, Vadé, Chevalier, Garnier, Girard; *Ténors*: MM Rousseau de Lagrave, Sapin, Achard, Sujol; *Ténors comiques*: MM Allais, Colson, Legrand, Leroy; *Barytons*: MM Meillet, Crambade, Cabel, Ribes; *Basse chantante*: M. Marchot; *Basses*: MM Junca, Adam, Grignon. Deloffre was the principal conductor, the orchestra numbered 63, the chorus 55. It was probably about this time that M. Arsène joined the company as general stage manager, a post he would still retain in 1866. The baritone Pierre Laurent had died shortly before, aged 33, 'in consequence of having taken a bath too soon after dinner.' (MW 2 Sept. 1854)

Gevaert's *Georgette* had been quite successful when performed during the previous year but that, it was pointed out, had been a short opera. *Marguerite* commenced at eight o'clock and even by midnight one could not be sure when it would end.[9] And, once again, Berlioz had harsh things to say about the scoring for trombones.[10]

Praise was lavished instead on a young mezzo-soprano from the Brussels Conservatoire, Pauline Deligne-Lauters, who would later have an outstanding career at the Opéra as Mme Gueymard-Lauters, and on a young tenor named Léon Achard from the Paris Conservatoire. (He was the son of a distinguished actor.) Achard would later create Wilhelm Meister in *Mignon* at the Opéra Comique and, having sung for a time in Milan and Venice, would return to Paris to appear at the Opéra. On his debut in *Marguerite*, Gustave Héquet thought his voice too delicate for the theatre.[11] Nevertheless the passable success which the opera achieved was due entirely to these two young artists.

Less than a month later another and (as far as the Théâtre Lyrique was concerned) final opera bouffe came from Eugène Gautier. The subject was eastern, as the title *Schahabaham II* indicates, and the 'music throughout lively, spontaneous and natural, the melody abundant, the inspiration fresh'[12] yet it failed to outlast the following year. It was followed by *Le Roman de la Rose*, composed by Prosper Pascal, which fared even worse.

The prolific Adolphe Adam then returned to the theatre which for long had been his first love. It happened that he had not one but two operas on hand, *Le Dernier Bal** for the Opéra Comique, *Le Muletier de Tolède*, with a libretto by d'Ennery and Clairville, for the Théâtre Lyrique. With Perrin directing both theatres it was thought that two works by the same composer presented concurrently would lead to jealousies, so a choice had to be made. Since he had composed *Le Muletier de Tolède* for Marie Cabel, Adam did not hesitate, this was his choice. It achieved merely a relative success, and that success was due entirely to Cabel, for *Le Muletier* is generally considered to be one of Adam's weakest operas. Yet Berlioz would observe, 'In short, I repeat, the score of *Le Muletier de Tolède* is one of the

*

Subsequently never performed.

most successful of M. Adam.'[13] This drew the following acerbic comment from his colleague Paul Scudo in the *Revue des Deux Mondes*. 'M. Berlioz who detests M. Adam's music has extravagantly praised *Le Muletier de Tolède* so that M. Adam who detests M. Berlioz' music would in turn extol *L'Enfance du Christ*.'[14]*

The performance was summed up as follows. 'The orchestra is good and well conducted by M. Deloffre. The choruses are well drilled, the scenery pretty, the mise en scène superb. There is also a good corps de ballet who dance nicely. In short, nothing is wanting for the opera save originality in the libretto and melody in the music—two very trifling omissions!'[15]** Nothing was wanting at all for Cabel who is described as 'neatly bound as to the feet in the very jauntiest little morocco boots... She is the fauvette of the boulevards, the very sweetest of warblers; and her acting is quite equal to her singing.'[16]

Perrin wished to have a curtain-raiser to precede *Le Muletier de Tolède* so Adam composed a one-act sketch, *A Clichy*, for an all-male cast of three. The tenor Leroy who was one of them is described as 'he with the nose'.[17] Although far less pretentious than *Le Muletier*, this operette would survive for three seasons with a total of 89 performances.

As in 1854, the New Year of 1855 was again ushered in with a new production, this year a one-act opera by Clapisson called *Dans les Vignes*. It had only 18 performances and was forgotten after one season.

So 1854 had passed. Historically in France it could be said to be the end of the beginning. The Second Empire was now firmly established and the coming year would see the inauguration of

*
L'Enfance du Christ* was first performed on 10 December 1854. Berlioz has described the *Revue des Deux Mondes* (and Scudo, with whom he was then waging musical warfare) as a journal 'whose music criticism is in the hands of a monomaniac.' (*The Memoirs of Berlioz*. Trans. and Ed. David Cairns. London 1970. 583.)
**
In the opera world of the time little was ever entirely lost: d'Ennery and Clairville's libretto was taken over by Augustus Harris and Edmund Falconer (Edmund O'Rourke). Set to music by M.W. Balfe, it became *The Rose of Castile*, which was produced at the Lyceum Theatre, London on 29 October 1857 where it ran for over a hundred performances. It was later revived many times in several countries.

the first Exposition Universelle with all its attendant glories. Not that 1854 had not had its problems. Even as the new year began, the horror and suffering of the Crimean war was at its most depressing. Sebastopol was still holding out. A docile French press was too effectively controlled for the truth of the situation to be published. In Paris vexatious news was limited to such announcements as a report that the first bal masqué of the season at the Opéra was 'less brilliant than usual on account of the predominance of plain black coats and the comparative rarity of costumes.'[18]

Indeed, scarcely a ripple could be discerned throughout the social and artistic life of the city. The re-opening of the Opéra for the 1854–55 season was characteristic. The director, Nestor Roqueplan, had opportunely decided upon a solemn inauguration with a cantata written by L. Belmontet, to music composed by the late Queen Hortense. 'The greatest efforts are being made,' we read, 'to attain the highest degree of perfection possible, both in the musical and choreographic departments; rehearsals are held every day, and M. Roqueplan is doing his best to justify the high honour to which he has been raised.'[19] That was the real Second Empire Paris and Sebastopol was a long way away. Besides, if people would only subdue 'their ignorant impatience', all was progressing slowly but surely and Sebastopol would eventually fall. It did, but not until the following September, an occasion which presented an opportunity for further cantatas.

In relation to the Théâtre Lyrique, Berlioz had lately written: 'It is on the road to prosperity; it has many serious-minded singers with real voices, the chorus is well assembled and sufficiently numerous, there are several virtuosi of merit among the instrumentalists of the orchestra, its audience has become more civilised. We begin to see a musical future there.'[20]

But that was in October 1854, and before Perrin had presented what can only be described as six failures in a row. By January 1855 a success in one or other form was essential if he was to survive. He may have foreseen the danger as early as the previous November, for it was then that he had announced a revival of *Robin des Bois*, a renowned French travesty of Weber's *Der Freischütz*. This version, adapted and translated by Castil-Blaze and Sauvage, had been presented at the Odéon in

December 1824. About three years later the same version had
been performed at the Opéra Comique and although other
versions had since been produced in Paris (in German at the
Théâtre Italien in 1829, in French at the Opéra in 1841) it was
the Castil-Blaze version which was once again being staged.

It demonstrated the stagnation of opera as an art form at the
Théâtre Lyrique, for when *Der Freischütz* had been composed
in 1821, romanticism in Paris was very much avant garde.
Géricault's 'Raft of the Medusa' had been shown—and
denounced—and both *Hernani* and the performance of Beethoven's symphonies still lay in the future there. We read that
'Tragedy [then] walked in stately guise, in hoop and farthingale;
and the barbarous Shakespeare was shaven, trimmed down,
begloved, and berouged, until he was shorn of those horrid
excrescences which made his name a bye-word in the country of
Racine and Corneille.' Amidst this ambience, Castil-Blaze had
travelled to Florence and Frankfurt* where he 'had purchased
80 to 90 pounds' weight of the various modern compositions
then most in vogue . . . [and] finding himself possessed of a
masterpiece in savage shape, he immediately determined to fit it
with breeches, bagwig and sword, and make it worthy of the
then French lyrical stage and of himself.'[21]

A distraught Weber tried to remonstrate with him at the
injustice being done, to which Castil-Blaze coolly replied that it
was his alterations which had ensured the opera's success, and
that Weber showed ingratitude to reproach him for popularising
his music in France.

The result was that the Parisians crowded the Odéon, while
in the provinces audiences also filled the theatres to hear *Robin
des Bois* and to give a firm endorsement to the superiority of the
adapter over the composer. Moreover, to add financial insult to
artistic injury, it was Castil-Blaze (and presumably Sauvage)
who collected the performing fees. That such a situation should
exist in 1824 is perhaps understandable, that it should remain 30
years later confirms that nothing survives so tenaciously as bad
taste.

*

The Musical World has got its cities confused. In a letter published in J.D. of 21
January 1826 Castil-Blaze states that he bought his forty kilogrammes of
scores in Mainz.

Castil-Blaze's alterations were both textual and musical. The setting was changed from Bohemia to either Scotland or Yorkshire, Robin Hood's realm. Both places are mentioned. The score gives Yorkshire during the reign of Charles I, but Sir Walter Scott's novels may equally have influenced the new terrain. Whether Scotland or England, the Wolf's Glen scene became the crossroads of Saint Dunstan. Worse was his meddling with Weber's scoring and his introduction of the duet, 'Hin nimm die Seele mein!' from *Euryanthe*, although in justice to Perrin the latter seems to have been excluded from his production.

At the Théâtre Lyrique, the opera's earlier Odéon success was repeated. It was performed intermittently almost every season until 1886, when a version newly translated by Trianon and E. Gautier helped to restore Weber's original score and coincidentally helped to prove that Parisians could now take *Der Freischütz* 'neat'. It also led to a Weber revival. Since elsewhere romanticism was being supplanted by realism, not surprisingly perhaps the Théâtre Lyrique was now discovering romanticism. Within five years, four more of his operas would be produced there.

Concerning the standard of performance, Berlioz, writing in the *Journal des Débats*, found the production and settings good, and reported that the men's chorus acquitted itself well but that the wind instruments perpetrated faults 'the gravity of which was indicated by the murmurings of the audience.'[22] Paul Scudo, for once agreeing with Berlioz, confirms that the orchestra 'was at its wits' end' and adds that the singers with one exception left much to be desired.[23]

The exception was Pauline Deligne-Lauters. She had been coached for the role by Gilbert Duprez, of whom it was said, 'Never could singer be under a more unfit master for an opera like *Der Freischütz*. M. Duprez seems to have considered the masterpiece from the Castil-Blaze point of view; and as the "maestro" had taken liberties with the great composer's text, the "professore" thought he might, with equal good grace, embellish and vary the melodies. He set himself to work and spared not roulades, shakes and ricercate, whereof Weber had no idea, and which, had he heard them, would have driven him mad . . .'[24] Mme. Deligne-Lauters, having read a number of suchlike

unfavourable reviews of her style, decided to change it, so that
the same critic could report of a subsequent performance with
satisfaction—'I have heard her again, and was delighted to find
she has discarded M. Duprez and returned to Weber.'[25]
Nevertheless, all were agreed that in spite of the work's
imperfections, its success was assured and that the public would
'flock for many a day to hear those delicious melodies which M.
Castil-Blaze has kindly not excised from the opera.'[26]

Weber was now followed by Poise, and one-act Poise at that,
Les Charmeurs, which must have been something of an anti-
climax. The libretto by de Leuven was adapted from Favart's
Les Ensorcelés, ou Jeannot et Jeannette. '*Les Charmeurs* is a
composition of M. Poise,' observed Scudo, 'that is to say it was
done first by M. Auber and afterwards revised by M. Adam'.[27]

This in turn was followed by a two-act opera comique, *Lisette*,
set in the period of Louis XV, by Sauvage. The composer was
Eugène Ortolan, but while Poise would achieve quite a satisfactory success with his small work, Ortolan scarcely got a
hearing. His music was said to show originality overshadowed
by inexperience, and there was 'too much noise throughout.'[28]

The next production, presented on 14 May, was much more
impressive. It was a three-act opera, *Jaguarita l'Indienne*, with
libretto by de Saint-Georges and de Leuven and music by
Fromental Halévy. One reviewer announced that the plot had
been derived from a story by James Fenimore Cooper, but
obviously he had got his Indians—or his Americas—mixed, for
Jaguarita was a native of Dutch Guiana. (A more likely source
may have been a story by Eugène Sue.) There was certainly
cause for confusion, since one reads of a trapper and of redskins
brandishing tomahawks and scalping knives. As Jaguarita,
Cabel caught the merest breath of criticism, offered as 'a word
from a friend':—'She is chief of a Red Indian community', she
was told, 'and she alone among them appears as a pale-face. She
is queen of the savages, and her costume is too suggestive of a
Parisian modiste. Some red ochre would be well applied...'[29]
Monjauze, a new tenor who sang the role of Maurice, had
originally been an actor who had played comedy at the French
Theatre in Saint Petersburg and drama at the Odéon. As a
singer, he was said to have a metallic voice, but was complimented
for not 'rushing at the ut de poitrine which has ruined so many

singers.'[30] Concerning the production, we read, 'The mise en scène is gorgeous, superb, and almost unequalled for splendour. Nothing like it has been seen for many a day in Paris, and such a collection of Indian dresses, weapons, curiosities, and nic-nacs, could probably not be found in many museums in Europe.' The orchestra too 'was excellent, the choruses well drilled ... the ballet graceful and pretty, and the success of the whole unquestionable.'[31] Halévy's name and music combined with Cabel ensured the opera a satisfactory run. Following the action of Adam with *Le Muletier de Tolède*, Halévy now wrote a curtain raiser for *Jaguarita*, named *L'Inconsolable*. Prudence or downright embarrassment at the result must have prompted him to present it under the pseudonym of Alberti. There is a further link between *Jaguarita l'Indienne* and *Le Muletier de Tolède*. The latter, it will be remembered, became a successful opera by the Irish composer, Balfe. *Jaguarita* was now adapted, once more by Harris (and by T.J. Williams), and in 1863 became *The Desert Flower*, the last opera to be composed by the Irish composer, William Vincent Wallace.

Aristide Hignard's *Les Compagnons de la Marjolaine* was the final creation of this season. Evidently his earlier opera, *Colin-Maillard*, had created sufficient small-scale interest when it was performed to encourage the Théâtre Lyrique to present this second work. The season then came to an end with a revival from the Opéra Comique of Auber's *La Sirène*, the only work of this composer ever to be performed at the Théâtre Lyrique. It was another 'brigand' piece so favoured by the composer and librettist of *Fra Diavolo*. For whatever reason, this revival did not succeed, but it did introduce three new singers to the company: Mlle Pannetrat, who came from Algeria via Toulouse and the Paris Conservatoire (she had a good voice but was never a rival to Marie Cabel); M. Dulaurens, a tenor who possessed 'a pleasant voice and an unpleasant appearance'[32]; and M. Prilleux, 'an admirable comedian'.[33] The theatre finally closed on 30 June, and did not re-open until 1 September.

In the circumstances this was surprising, for the Exposition Universelle had been opened with much pomp by the Emperor on 15 May. (The event had been celebrated with the production of *Jaguarita* at the Théâtre Lyrique.) But visitors from abroad were slow in arriving, and reports such as that 'the operas and theatres show a sad falling off in their receipts'[34] may indicate the reason for the theatre's closure. Moreover, the weather was most unseasonable. Spring had set in with unusual severity, and as late as 31 March we read, 'the famous horse-chestnut of the Tuileries is covered with snow in place of leaves.'[35] But by the end of April spring had come at last, and we learn that 'Paris is putting on its best face, and never since the world began was there such whitewashing, cleaning, scrubbing, painting and furbishing ... The lodging-house keepers are demanding prices quite fabulous even for attics and fourth-floors back'.[36] At the same time M. Winterhalter was 'busily engaged in finishing for the exhibition a picture of the Empress surrounded by her Ladies of Honour, drawn size of life'.[37]

It was not until August and the arrival of Queen Victoria— when historians recalled that not since the time of Henry VI, over four hundred years before, had an English monarch set foot in Paris—that both weather and occasion combined to create an unqualified success. The Queen, accompanied by the Emperor, attended a performance of Auber's *Haydée* at the Opéra Comique, when the chorus was specially augmented by the chorus from the Théâtre Lyrique and at last it could be announced, 'the operas and theatres are making more money than at any previous period on record, and are compelled to turn away thousands every night'.[38]

The exhibition helped to divert 'public attention [from] the colossal war, which the two great representatives of civilisation are now waging against the champion of brute force, ungovernable passions, and abject slavery.'[39] Since the time of the Directoire, exhibitions had always been considered an effective remedy to allay national disquiet. This was the 12th such exhibition.

Although closed for the summer, the Théâtre Lyrique was nevertheless not entirely idle. First there was a performance of a 'drame lyrique' called *Paraguassù* on 2 August, composed by J. Villeneuve and Joseph O'Kelly. This was oddly described as a 'Brazilian chronicle' and seems to have been an imitation of Félicien David's *Le Désert*. Singers who took part were Mme Deligne-Lauters and MM Dulaurens, Junca and Ribes, while the actor Jouanni spoke at intervals to explain what it was all about. *La Sirène* and *Les Charmeurs* were then performed to a full free house on the Emperor's fête day. It could well have been his last fête day at that, for within a month, while driving from Saint Cloud to the Théâtre Italien, he was shot at in the rue Marsollier. His assailant, a shoemaker named Bellemarre, had what is now known as a police record, although it was also admitted, 'There seems little doubt, however, that he is deranged.'[40]

1855–1856

So September came round. When the previous season had ended, the artists, as was customary, had scattered to other theatres for the summer. Marie Cabel had gone to Baden-Baden, but Rousseau de Lagrave, Crambade and Colson (the latter taking his wife who was then at the Opéra Comique) had crossed the Atlantic to perform at the French Theatre in New Orleans. One member who would not be rejoining the company was the maître de ballet, M. Lerouge, for he had died in June at the early age of 44.

The theatre re-opened on 1 September with Marie Cabel in a revival of *Jaguarita l'Indienne*. Then on Sunday 9 September Sebastopol surrendered at last. On the following evening all the theatres were brilliantly illuminated, while 101 guns thundered from the Invalides. On Tuesday 11 September, free performances were given as for the Emperor's fête day. The Théâtre Lyrique chose *Jaguarita*, and both there and at the Opéra Comique a cantata, *Victoire*, was performed, the words by Michel Carré, the music by Adolphe Adam. This was sung at the Théâtre Lyrique by Dulaurens, Achard, Meillet and Marchand.

The first creation of the season, performed on 14 September, was a one-act opera comique, *Une Nuit à Seville*, by Frédéric Barbier, with libretto by Nuitter and Beaumont. It had a scarcely passable 26 performances, although this did not prevent all three authors having another one-act work performed there in November. This was *Rose et Narcisse*, which received only 11 performances and so effectively finished M. Barbier's career at the Théâtre Lyrique, although his librettists remained to become much involved in the translation of foreign works for the theatre. Among the singers, Mlle Garnier, who sang Rose, later joined Offenbach's Bouffes-Parisiens, where she enjoyed a 'succès de beauté' as Venus in *Orphée aux Enfers*.

In order to make a full evening's entertainment with *Une Nuit à Seville*, there was a revival of Hérold's three-act opera comique *Marie*, first performed in 1826. It was considered to be one of his most attractive works, yet failed to win approval. This seems to have been due not to any weakness in the opera but to the extreme feebleness of the production. It was obviously under-rehearsed and, according to A. de Rovray (Fiorentino) in *Le Moniteur Universel*, the singers had taken as their motto 'each for himself and God for us all.' The prompter was panic-stricken, the conductor thrashed about like a devil in a holy water font. Calamity followed calamity. Achard lost his voice completely. Mlle Pannetrat launched into her great vocalises with confidence, but left them not always as she would have wished but as she was able. Prilleux, so entertaining in *La Sirène*, was here woeful. Only Grignon was irreproachable in the role of the Baron.[1]

At the same time M. Delaforest of *La Gazette de France* offered some observations concerning the difference between *Marie* and *Jaguarita*, and the artistic revolution which had occurred within a generation. The libretto and score of the former, he thought, yielded charm and sweetness, the whole ensemble intended to please an urbane society with its agreeable and elevated style. As for the subject and composition of the latter, there were extravagances, hence there was noise without any feeling for truth, character, attractiveness or social content.[2] M. Delaforest should have lived to see *Jesus Christ Superstar*, or whatever worse the future may hold.

Whether such an unsatisfactory outcome was the cause or the consequence of his decision, Perrin now resigned as director of the Théâtre Lyrique. He is said to have been disappointed with the results he was achieving there, and *Marie* may have been the last straw. The Opéra Comique was also suffering. His resignation was not entirely unexpected, since it had been reported during the previous April, with Halanzier, then director of the Strasbourg theatre and later director of the Opéra, announced as his successor.[3] When he did resign, however, his place was taken by someone entirely different.

He was M. Pellegrin, who had been director of the Grand Theatre, Toulon from February 1845,[4] and from 21 November 1847 until 31 May 1852 director of both the Grand and Gymnase Theatres, Marseille.[5] Here his greatest achievements appear to have been a successful production of *Le Prophète* with Meyerbeer present in 1850, and the engagement of Mme Charton-Demeur for his 1851–52 season. Later he became organiser of theatrical performances at the military academy of Châlons-sur-Marne recently established by Louis Napoleon.[6] This may explain his appointment to the Théâtre Lyrique which was ratified on 29 September 1855[7] for there is little else to explain it. His time there was very short. It was said that he had lasted only as long as the roses last, the space of a day. Indeed one report indicates that he had left even before the end of the year.[8]

Meanwhile, having appointed M. Lemaître, an old colleague from the provinces* as treasurer of his new theatre, Pellegrin was finding plenty to occupy him there. Most troublesome, Perrin was insisting that under the terms of Marie Cabel's contract, he could command her services either at the Opéra Comique or the Théâtre Lyrique, and naturally now wished to have her perform exclusively at the former, where he remained as director. Not surprisingly, Pellegrin objected.[9] One thing was certain, and he knew it; without Cabel heading his roster of artists, failure was inevitable.

He inaugurated his engagement with a three-act work by Gevaert, *Les Lavandières de Santarem*—an inauspicious opening for him. Gevaert seemingly had not lived up to the promise of his two earlier Théâtre Lyrique operas, for it was reported that 'though not actually still-born', *Les Lavandières de Santarem* was 'almost as dead as Julius Caesar.'[10] Berlioz did not agree, and recorded, 'It seems to me Gevaert's best score.'[11] His librettists, d'Ennery and Grangé, were also said to have used him badly, and one reviewer was incensed at what he considered

*

Le Ménestrel (21 October 1855) describes him as Pellegrin's 'former treasurer at the time he directed the theatres of Toulouse'. *Le Mousquetaire* (2 July 1854) also mentions 'M. Pellegrin (of Toulouse)', so either he was a native of that city or he may have held an appointment in the theatre there after leaving Marseille.

to be an unsavoury scenario. 'A mad king [of Portugal], a pimping courtier, a young lady who sets fire to the palace so that she may preserve her chastity, washerwomen who become duchesses, a colonel of 15 just weaned from his nurse whose husband is a sort of whipper-in, a soldier who threatens his sovereign in his very palace...' 'Such dirty linen,' the writer thought, 'should be washed at home!' (What passed for dirty linen gives amusing insight into the political and moral mores of Second Empire Paris.) He then adds, 'Nothing is damned now-a-days in Paris. A new piece, if bad, is allowed to discover its own alacrity in sinking, and the manager soon knows from the state of his box-office when it should be withdrawn.'[12] *Les Lavandières de Santarem* survived for a little over two months and then disappeared with the coming of the new year.

With Barbier's *Rose et Narcisse* interposed between, Pellegrin's next production was 'a pretty little trifle'[13] by de Lajarte and Boisseaux named *Le Secret de l'Oncle Vincent*. Then followed a revival of a three-act opera by the Neapolitan composer Carafa called *Le Solitaire* which had been first performed at the Opéra Comique in 1822. The subject was based on a renowned novel of the period, *Le Solitaire* by Vicomte d'Arlincourt, when the brown cloak of the mysterious hermit (Le Solitaire) created a fashion which coloured parasols and umbrellas, the gowns, hats, pelisses and laced boots of the ladies, cloaks and frock coats of the men; even carriages were painted brown. Besides, there was the famous rondo 'C'est le solitaire' that travelled the world and was relentlessly drummed out by all the barrel organs and vaudeville orchestras.[14] But all that had been 30 years before; the time of Le Solitaire had passed. Not that the present revival had helped to reinstate it, for A. de Rovray in *Le Moniteur Universel* again announced that the performance was of 'a feebleness that drives one to despair,'[15] while Saint-Étienne in *L'Union* ominously observed, 'This exhumation was not successful.'[16]

It was about this time that the Minister of State set up a commission to examine the auditoria of the Paris theatres and to suppress all uncomfortable and uninhabitable seats—an unpopular move with the Society of Dramatic Authors, whose thoughts were centred more on the box office than the stage.[17] They need not have worried. 120 years later, the Opéra still sells seats 'sans visibilité'. During September theatre directors had also been instructed to ensure that their employees offered the greatest consideration and courtesy to the public.

On 8 December there was a benefit performance for Meillet which consisted of Adam's *Le Toréador* performed by artists from the Opéra Comique, *Le Bijou perdu* with Marie Cabel, and a scene from Offenbach's lately produced *Les Deux Aveugles*. Meillet, we learn, was warmly received.[18]

The year ended for Pellegrin with a production no more successful than his earlier ones. Again it was a one-act piece, *L'Habit de Noce*. It was composed by Paul Cuzent, who had the added distinction of being a celebrated bareback horse rider. Alas, the reviews confirm that his best work was done in the circus ring.

The end of the year also saw the departure of Marie Cabel to the Opéra Comique, of Mme Deligne-Lauters to a concert tour in Brittany, and of the tenor Dulaurens to Ghent. The bass Junca was performing in New Orleans.

But there were also new arrivals of promise and of merit: Mlle Pouilley, who had already appeared once or twice at the Opéra, the bass Hermann-Léon from the Opéra Comique, and above all Mme Miolan-Carvalho, whose debut had been announced the previous October. A flurry of new compositions also arrived, most of which would never see the stage. They included one called *Les Chevrons de Jeanne* with libretto by Clairville and music by M. Bellini 'nephew of the great composer'.[19]

The new year of 1856 was ushered in by the Emperor having all the musicians of the Garde Nationale (over 200 of them!) serenade him under the great balcony of the Tuileries with Queen Hortense's air, and by the appointment of Charles Gounod and the critic Pier Angelo Fiorentino (alias A. de Rovray) as members of the Légion d'honneur.

The presentation of a 'petit opéra de salon' during musical soirées had earlier become the vogue. At a splendid reception given by the Comte de Morny, *A deux pas du bonheur* by Felix Godefroid and Mme Roger de Beauvoir was performed to an audience of 500, headed by Princess Mathilde. On the following evening, the Minister of State and Mme Fould presented, as part of their evening's entertainment, *La Volière* by Gustave Nadaud. The enormous gathering included not alone Princess Mathilde but her brother Prince Napoleon (Plon-Plon) and her cousins the Prince and Princess Murat as well.[20]

At the Théâtre Lyrique Pellegrin produced a one-act opera by Adam called *Falstaff*, with a revival of *Le Sourd*. *Le Sourd* would have many years of success at the Théâtre Lyrique, but *Falstaff*, specially composed for Hermann-Léon would not survive. Whatever the merits of the music, which was described as 'light and facile but without inspiration,' it was frankly stated of the libretto: 'Not a vestige of the Shakespearean quaintness and drollery is to be detected. The role was well padded and acted indifferent ill by M. Hermann-Léon, who appeared to me to entertain no idea of the original.'[21]

So, without a single success to his credit, Pellegrin would leave the Théâtre Lyrique after this production—if he had not already left it. His tenure there, whether due to lack of flair or of finance, could hardly have been less propitious. Artistic standards seem to have been very low, and Alberic Second, writing in *L'Artiste*, describes a performance of *Le Barbier de Séville* as 'at every point unworthy of the Parisian stage . . . sung in pitiable fashion by a tin-plate company amidst impossible scenery and decrepit stage properties.'[22]

By early February the press was noting that disagreement concerning the forthcoming opera, *La Fanchonnette*, had arisen between its librettists and composer (Clapisson) and the Théâtre Lyrique.[23] Soubies throws some light on the situation by explaining that although Pellegrin had Miolan-Carvalho under contract, he had at the same time to file a petition for bankruptcy[24]—ironically, had he known it, just as he was on the point of having his first great success. The artists then tried to form a société or commonwealth, but to no effect. Instead, Clapisson approached Mme Miolan-Carvalho's husband to invite him to take over the direction of the theatre. He consented and so, on 20 February, Pellegrin's resignation having been officially accepted, the Minister appointed Léon Carvalho to his post.[25] Whether through luck or judgement, he could not have chosen a better man.

Chapter 3

Léon Carvalho 1856–1860

1856–1857

For success in the theatre, a certain flamboyance is essential. Léon Carvalho, born Carvaille in Port Louis, Mauritius in 1825, was above all flamboyant. He began his career in Paris singing lesser baritone roles at the Opéra Comique, and it may have been the frustrated ambitions of a singer manqué which later made him persist in trying to alter operas by new composers which he presented at the Théâtre Lyrique. The culmination of this mania was an attempt to introduce wild animals onto the stage to accompany a dream sequence in Saint-Saëns' *Le Timbre d'Argent*. Nevertheless, in his time he was the most perceptive impresario in Paris, daring and imaginative. Although he personally preferred the light frivolous music of Auber, Hérold, Clapisson and the like, he nevertheless revived the operas of Mozart, Weber, Beethoven and Gluck and launched those of Gounod, Bizet and Berlioz. Moreover, not only did he encourage young composers, he was polite to them. His colleague at the Opéra, Nestor Roqueplan, described him as 'this indomitable and inventive director, who has done more for the spreading of great music than all the other lyric theatres in Paris put together.'[1]

Carvalho lived and entertained extravagantly. For a man who did not 'sincerely want to be rich', this was a form of self-indulgence which could lead only to chronic debt, eventually forcing him into a succession of bankruptcies. The greatest blow of all befell him towards the end of his career in 1887 while he was director of the Opéra Comique. The theatre burned down during a performance, with the death of 131 people, and he was fined and imprisoned for negligent management. Following a successful appeal, he was reinstated in his former position in 1891.

In 1859, while director of the Théâtre Lyrique, he would enter into negotiations with Richard Wagner, although the outcome led to nothing positive. In letters written from Paris by Wagner to Liszt and to the Wesendoncks he describes Carvalho as '(a really pleasant, decent man)' and records, 'I have seen his theatre and liked it tolerably well ... If they are prepared to work extra hard there, I could allow them my *Rienzi*—provided that I could insist on an opera [production] without dialogue, just once ... The Director is prepared—and would like—to present the opera [Tannhäuser]. However, how long his theatre will be allowed to stand—(because of cracks it is to be demolished) he himself does not know—possibly it will be demolished in March. A large new theatre is to be built for him.'[2] Regretfully this pleasant relationship would not last and in a letter written ten years later to a friend in Paris, Wagner declares: 'I want nothing more, absolutely nothing but to be rid of the wretch Carvalho, to be free.'[3]

Much of Carvalho's success at the Théâtre Lyrique was due to his wife, the soprano Marie Miolan-Carvalho, whom Reynaldo Hahn describes as 'his terrible wife. Oh! yes, terrible.' He explains that 'this great singer combined a talent which was certainly not exaggerated, a talent which indeed was miraculous, with ineffable bad taste, an immense arrogance concealed under bourgeois charm and an implacable will, to which her husband lent the support of his effective directorial powers. Surrounded by admirers and stupid idolators, she demanded of composers the most extraordinary caprices of virtuosity, and took monstrous liberties with classical music, when she sang it, which was seldom ... With Adolphe Adam, with Clapisson and with Victor Massé she had a ball, to put it vulgarly. She could allow herself full rein without fear of overdoing it or of overloading their music with the craziest arabesques, the most scintillating sequins, the most elaborate ornaments ... Is it necessary for me to refer yet again, amongst the musical mutilations attributed to her, to the ending which she substituted for that of Mozart in Cherubino's air?'[4]

She had been born in Marseille on 31 December 1827 and had her first singing lessons from her father, an oboe player. Later she studied with Duprez at the Paris Conservatoire. Her first successes were in *Le Pré aux Clercs*, *Giralda* and *Les Noces de Jeannette* at the Opéra Comique. She married Léon Carvalho, then a fellow artist of that theatre, in 1853. In time she would become internationally famous.

Léon Carvalho accordingly commenced his career at the Théâtre Lyrique with the dual advantage of having a wife who was a star attraction (and who, it might be emphasised, had been originally engaged by Pellegrin) and with Clapisson's *La Fanchonnette*, also contracted originally by Pellegrin, which would turn out to be a smash hit. First, however, he had difficulty in taking possession of his theatre, since Emile Perrin, the tenant, and M. Pellegrin both maintained that part of the 'matériel', costumes and scenery belonged to them.[5] He resolved the problem by bringing an action before the President of the Civil Tribunal.

To be sure, there were a few carping comments about *La Fanchonnette*. 'Clapisson,' wrote Scudo, 'has not yet been able to overcome either Adam's popularity, or the opinion of unfavourable reviewers' and there was his oblique observation that the production was 'sufficiently well finished for a boulevard theatre.'[6] But on the whole, Héquet considered it 'a success, a great success,'[7] so much so that Soubies compared it (with its story of a street singer who writes her own satirical songs and becomes involved in a number of quasi-historical intrigues) to Lecocq's famous *La Fille de Madame Angot* of 16 years later.[8] Its success moreover was immediate, and the first 30 performances grossed 135,941.90 francs at the box office.[9]

Carvalho's next two productions failed to maintain this success. The first, *Mam'zelle Geneviève*, was Adolphe Adam's last work for the Théâtre Lyrique, the theatre for which he had composed so much and had worked so hard, and his second last work for any stage. He would die six weeks later in the early morning of 3 May, worn out by his efforts in trying to recoup the enormous sum of 150,000 francs, lost when he had first tried to establish the Théâtre Lyrique in 1847. Between then and 1856 he had toiled without a break and could now leave a store of 13 operas and two ballets to show for his seven years' work. Of these operas, eight remain recorded in Loewenberg, an extra-ordinary number of comparative successes for a composer forced to work against time. *Mam'zelle Geneviève* is not listed among them.

It seems to have been a weak composition although once again Berlioz describes the music as 'sweet, melodious, easy, well composed and always good on the stage . . .'[10] However, an opinion that the opera lacked freshness and vivacity of colour[11] seems to have been closer to the mark.

A one-act opera comique, *Le Chapeau du Roi*, set in the time of Louis XI, followed. It was the first work to be presented there of an as yet inexperienced composer named Henri Caspers, and Héquet announced that it would not 'cause any revolution in musical art.'[12] Nevertheless Caspers would have other operas performed at the Théâtre Lyrique.

Adolphe Adam was buried in Montmartre cemetery with the usual solemnity on 5 May. Halévy spoke the last address; Baron Taylor was one of the pallbearers. As a mark of respect, both the Théâtre Lyrique and the Bouffes-Parisiens (where his last operette *Les Pantins de Violette* was playing), remained closed that evening. At the Opéra, there was a performance of his ballet *Le Corsaire* the receipts of which, by the Emperor's direction, were given to his widow. They were said to amount to 10,000 francs. The Minister of State later granted her a pension of 1,200 francs a year, which amount Carvalho equalled. It was to come from the theatre's treasury. One wonders how payment was maintained throughout Carvalho's many vicissitudes, for 'Mme veuve Adam' did not die until 1880.

Following his friendly reviews, it was appropriate that Berlioz should be elected to Adam's seat at the Institut, gaining 19 votes to Gounod's six and David's four.

On 23 May Carvalho showed remarkable judgement in presenting Grétry's famous *Richard Cœur-de-Lion*. The orchestration arranged by Adam when the work was revived at the Opéra Comique in 1841 was now used again. The success of the production was enormous.

The tenor Michot, who had arrived at the Théâtre Lyrique from a café-concert situated in the rue de la Lune[13] but with an aristocratically named A. Guillot de Sainbris for his teacher,[14] made a highly promising debut as Richard. Meillet as Blondel in his famous air 'O Richard, ô mon Roi!' seems to have created the same effect as had occurred when on 1 October 1789 Louis XVI and Marie Antoinette made an unexpected appearance at a banquet given by the Bodyguard of the Assembly then meeting at Versailles.

At the Théâtre Lyrique, we read of 'excitement, tears, enthusiasm, applause without end and obstinate cries of 'bis' which the conductor was forced to obey',[15] which corresponded to what had occurred (intermingled with cries of 'Vive le roi') in the theatre at Versailles 70 years earlier.

It has been said of *Richard Cœur-de-Lion* that it was composed 'when the operatic revolution in French music, brought about by the harmony of Rameau, the melody of Italy and the German orchestral amplitude of Gluck, was an accomplished fact, and when the troubadour experience, with its pseudo-revival of the Middle Ages was just catching sight of romanticism, still a long way off.'[16] Noteworthy then that it should now establish itself on the Paris stage (it was concurrently being performed at the Opéra Comique) when romanticism was already becoming passé. But establish itself it did, and at the Théâtre Lyrique it was performed each year without a break until 1868, achieving the extraordinary total of 302 performances.

The ill-fated Prince Imperial had been born on 16 March, and to mark the occasion free performances were given in all the theatres the following evening. At the Théâtre Lyrique these included a cantata, the words by Carvalho, the music by the always available Clapisson.[17]

Three months later there were similar celebrations when the official christening took place at Notre Dame. On this occasion *Si j'étais Roi* and *Bonsoir voisin* were performed, and there was another cantata, this time written by M. Rollet with music by Charles Réty, the solos of which were sung by M. and Mme Meillet and Michot.[18] There were celebrations too for de Saint Georges who was promoted officer of the Légion d'honneur and for Victor Massé and Arthur de Beauplan who were appointed 'chevalier'.

It was in a blaze of imperial glory therefore that the theatre closed for the annual 'relâche' on 30 June. There was much glory too from the brilliant successes of *Richard Cœur-de-Lion* and *La Fanchonnette*. Miolan-Carvalho was reported to have sung La Fanchonnette four times each week since it was produced, and at the close of the season 'was singing better than she had ever sung.'[19]

Even prior to the theatre's closing, rehearsals were under way for an opera by Maillart to be produced during the forthcoming season. There was also talk of an opera by Massé.[20] In time both would be enormously successful. Consequently it must have been with a feeling of optimism that during the vacation Carvalho set about improving the standard of his chorus and orchestra. It was announced that Saint Léon would be in charge of choreography.[21]

Earlier in the year, just after Carvalho had taken over, Berlioz had written: 'The Théâtre Lyrique is now on the way to success. The impetus which it got from its new director is vigorous and well directed. Musically the performances are improving and details of production seem more polished. The vogue for *La Fanchonnette* by filling the coffers should enable the director to make important reforms for which he needs money. On the completion of these reforms the future of the theatre depends. For long it was assumed that one could succeed in the boulevard du Temple with methods which ignored the more refined tastes of the public from the boulevard des Italiens. That was a serious mistake. The audience recognised the defects of performance . . . and in the end they ceased [to attend] . . . Out of 50 scores which have been already presented in this theatre, at least 30 did not deserve to see the light of day. There must be limits to indulgence, especially where a director is concerned. To inflict such dreadful works on decent people indicates not alone a lack of ability but also a lack of good manners. There are some transgressions which cannot be excused.'[22]

Once again the artists scattered during the vacation. Hermann-Léon, who had taken a benefit early in June, set off on a 'tournée departementale' which brought him to Orléans. M. and Mme Meillet were fêted in Nevers as one might expect since it was Meillet's home town. Others returned to Paris, M. and Mme Colson from New Orleans. While they did not rejoin the Théâtre Lyrique, they brought back with them a young French mezzo-soprano, Juliette Borghèse, who became very successful there. In July Caroline Duprez married Amédée Vandenheuvel, an accompanist attached to the Opéra, and at about the same time *Le Ménestrel* was publishing a selection of patriotic choruses composed by Queen Hortense for the use of French and Belgian choral societies.

All this was of minor consequence however when compared with news that the renowned Dr Véron, late distinguished director of the Opéra (only one of his surfeit of professions) and now a member of the Corps Législatif, had risen in the Chamber of Deputies to propose that the Théâtre Lyrique be granted a subvention of 100,000 francs a year. He pointed out at some length that the theatre as presently constituted, even having the support of a very talented woman singer, nevertheless existed precariously. This was a matter of concern to theatres throughout France, not just Paris, for whereas the Opéra Comique presented elaborate works requiring luxurious costumes and decor as well as highly competent artists, their cost would be the ruin of provincial theatres if they were to be transferred to them. Provincial theatres—to which it was difficult to attract audiences in any case—were consequently dependent on the Théâtre Lyrique for their repertoire. With adequate support, the Théâtre Lyrique could produce a number of suitable two-act operas each season which would enable both the theatre to survive and the state to avoid considerable losses in the provinces. In voting for such a subvention, the members would be protecting two great industries, and Véron hoped that if the amount could not be included in the present budget, it would be included in the next one.[23]

Reading the report, one finds that Véron puts his case well. It is a nice political touch to find him emphasising that he is attempting to save not alone a Paris theatre but numerous provincial theatres as well. But irrespective of country or period, the outcome of such applications is immutable. We read that 'unfortunately the eloquence of M. Véron has been checked by circumstances and the subvention was not passed, but at least the cause is a good one and let us hope that next year it may have greater success'.[24] Inevitably it did not. Inevitably too the subvention would come sometime. It nearly always does, if the theatre can survive that long.

The summer passed and the Théâtre Lyrique re-opened unofficially on 31 August 1856, a day earlier than advertised, to allow a benefit performance (items from *Si j'étais Roi* and

Richard Cœur-de-Lion) for M. Arsène, the general stage manager. The official opening took place on 2 September—having been postponed from the previous day because *Zampa* was being revived at the Opéra Comique that evening—with Miolan-Carvalho in *La Fanchonnette.*

For the remainder of the year Léon Carvalho would present only two creations, but so great was their success that nothing more was needed, for they were Maillart's *Les Dragons de Villars* and Massé's *La Reine Topaze.* (A revival of *Masaniello* was transiently discussed, but whether it was Carafa's opera or Auber's *La Muette de Portici* which was intended is not made clear.)[25]

Les Dragons de Villars, which still holds the stage in the French provinces, had its first performance on 19 September. (Maillart is said to have created an effect by sending orchestral parts which were urgently required to the Théâtre Lyrique by a mounted dragoon, an exotic 'chasseur d'Afrique'.[26])

The story of the opera was said to have been borrowed from a novel by Georges Sand, *La Petite Fadette,* the period of which the librettists Lockroy and Cormon had transferred to the reign of Louis XIV.[27] Paul Scudo considered the best item in the work to be the tenor-soprano duet, 'On ne m'avait jamais dit cela' and declared, 'M. Maillart will certainly come to take a distinguished place among the dramatic musicians of our country.'[28]

It will be recalled that it was with Maillart's first opera *Gastibelza* that the Opéra National had opened in 1847. Maillart subsequently had two works produced at the Opéra Comique, but with so little success that Emile Perrin rejected *Les Dragons* for that theatre as being 'too dramatic'. One of the Seveste brothers and Pellegrin are also said to have rejected it for the Théâtre Lyrique. Of them all, Carvalho was the only one to realise its potential.[29]

During October, Victor Massé's *La Reine Topaze* went into rehearsal. Léon Achard, who was to have sung the principal tenor role, resigned following a dispute with the administration.[30] His place was taken by Monjauze. The production continued to be postponed due to the overwhelming success of *La Fanchonnette* and *Les Dragons de Villars* and eventually did not reach the stage until 27 December 1856.

Queen Topaze (Miolan-Carvalho) was yet another of the

many gipsies, with Azucena in *Il Trovatore* and Catherine in *Les Diamants de la Couronne*, who pervaded 19th century opera. She is unique however in that her realm is—of all places— Venice, where it seems her power outranks the Council of Ten. When *La Reine Topaze* was produced, Massé was a well- established composer who even today is still vaguely remembered. But the real success of the opera seems to have sprung not at all from his music but from an air universally known as 'The Carnival of Venice', at best only arranged by him. This he had adroitly introduced for Queen Topaze into a festive scene in the opera designed to represent Paolo Veronese's famous 'Marriage at Cana' at the Louvre.[31] The air itself was said to be an 18th century Neapolitan folk song called 'La ricciolella'. It gained its title by being introduced into a ballet named *Le Carnaval de Venise*, composed for the Opéra in 1816 by Rodolphe Kreutzer and Luis de Persuis.[32] A number of composers wrote variations to it, the best remembered among them being Jules Benedict, but it appears that Miolan-Carvalho had chosen variations composed by Paganini,[33] presumably to demonstrate that what he could do with his violin she could do better with her voice. By all accounts she did just that and the resultant exhibition of musical bad taste seems to have been astounding. She sang three variations and of the third, Scudo records, 'the singer answered with infinite art, notes sung from the chest with notes from her upper register. It was with this see-saw oscillation that she ended her vocal entertainment amidst frantic applause.'[34] 'Such an authoritative display' declared another review, 'has not been heard since the days of Catalani or Persiani.'[35]

Virtuosity was what the public wanted and so they flocked to *La Reine Topaze* while *Les Dragons*, although successful, fell behind. But without the virtuoso Miolan-Carvalho to sustain interest, the lack of merit in the music became only too apparent, a lack which even at the height of its success prompted Scudo to write: 'It is not a chef d'œuvre and contains nothing which was not already more or less known beforehand.'[36] For this reason *Les Dragons* can still be occasionally heard, but *La Reine Topaze* has long since vanished from the repertory.

Nevertheless, because of *La Reine Topaze*, 1856 ended* for

*

Inevitably during the year some singers had left the company and some had

Carvalho with what was aptly described as 'a resounding success'. At the same time, *La Fanchonnette* had passed its 100th performance, while *Les Dragons* was close to 50. By the end of 1857 *La Reine Topaze* would have achieved 115.

In spite of thronged houses, however, it must not be assumed that opera at the Théâtre Lyrique—or indeed in any Paris theatre—at this time was artistically on a very elevated level. If the following report from the *Indépendance Belge* is to be believed, it was in fact very much the contrary. It records: 'The Burmese Ambassadors now at Paris [to conclude a treaty between both countries] seem rather astonished at the customs of the most witty people on the face of the earth. If they write their travelling impressions, in the style of the *Lettres Persanes*, it is not unlikely they will hold us up to the derision of trans-Gangesian India. Seven of them visited the Opéra on Monday, in two boxes on the second tier, and witnessed a performance of *Le Prophète*. The rattling in the throats of the male singers, the screaming of the lady vocalists, and the tempest raised by the orchestra, made a profound impression on their sensible hearts and they manifested an inclination to throw themselves at the feet of the Emperor, for the purpose of obtaining the grace of M. Roger. M. Feuillet de Conches, who was with them during this ordeal, explained that what they took for a kind of torture was simply a fashion and that, for the last five-and-twenty years, people have not amused themselves differently at Paris.'[37]

But whatever opera might lack artistically, things could not have been better socially for the Théâtre Lyrique at the commencement of the New Year of 1857. Prince Napoleon had attended the initial performance of *La Reine Topaze* and had rewarded Mme Miolan-Carvalho with a diamond pin.[38] Then their Imperial Majesties attended. There had been a couple of disappointments concerning this important visit, the first on 19 January due to the infant Prince Imperial suffering a slight

joined. Among those who left (including Achard) were M. Prilleux for the Opéra Comique and Mlle Garnier for the Bouffes-Parisiens. Among those who joined and who have not been mentioned already were—Mme Numa-Blanc, a soprano; Mlle de Corcelles, a dugazon; MM Froment, Scott and Cœuilte, tenors; MM Lesage and Grillon, baritones; MM Balanqué and Serène, basses; and M. Jollois. Balanqué had in fact sung at the Théâtre Lyrique in 1852 in Duprez' opera, *Joanita*.

ailment. The following Wednesday evening was then considered inappropriate since it was 21 January—the melancholy anniversary of the execution of Louis XVI. Eventually, they were present on 26 January.[39] There was also the extraordinary story of the renowned and retired tenor (for he was now over 50) Gilbert Duprez. It was reported that he was about to return to the Théâtre Lyrique to sing the baritone role of Rigoletto. *Le Ménestrel* dismissed the idea, commenting that all it required was for Duprez to sing some passages from the role in his small private theatre (which he had already done) for 'that smoke to produce a fire—almost a conflagration.'[40] It was agreed 'that some such project has been on foot; but besides the secondary difficulties of carrying it out, the greatest obstacle is said to have arisen on the part of the ministry, who could not allow it to be supposed that the repertory of the Théâtre-Italien had become public property.'[41] So nothing further was heard of the matter.

A more practical proposition was Carvalho's decision to produce Weber's *Oberon*. Perhaps he had decided that more than three winners in a row of creations was too much to expect, or perhaps he had merely decided to continue the policy of his predecessors of combining new works with translations of proven foreign ones, undoubtedly the only policy if he was to keep his theatre filled.

Oberon had already been performed in Paris at the Théâtre Italien in 1830 by a German company, but this was an entirely new version translated by Nuitter, Beaumont and de Chazot. It was reported that the music had been transcribed from a score in the Conservatoire by Deloffre 'who religiously conserved the text. Two morceaux only have changed position because of the libretto and the French authors have followed the English poem almost to the letter. Two non-singing characters only have been introduced, the captain of the Calif's guards, and Aboulifar, the chief eunuch.'[42] These two roles were introduced as comic relief. The other alterations mentioned were the transference of Rezia's cavatina 'Mourn thou, poor heart' from Act 3 to Act 1, and the ending of the opera with the slaves' chorus 'Hark! what notes are swelling?' instead of the chorus 'Hail to the Knight' which properly concluded it but which now was inserted at the beginning of Act 3.[43]

The mediaeval French poem, *Huon de Bordeaux, Pair de France et Duc de Guyenne* is one source of *Oberon.* Christoph Martin Wieland, German poet and man of letters, partly inspired by Shakespeare (he had translated 22 of the plays into prose) and having developed an interest in the orient, combined these three sources for his romantic epic of this name which was published in 1780. This was translated into English by W. Sotheby, and James Robinson Planché, dramatic author and Rouge Croix Pursuivant of Arms, is said to have founded his libretto on this translation.

In the course of composition, Weber had written to Planché from Dresden: 'The cut of an English opera is certainly very different from a German one. The English is more a drama with songs; but in the first act of *Oberon* there is nothing that I could wish to see changed, except the finale . . . I thank you obligingly for your goodness of having translated the verses in French; but it was not so necessary because I am, though yet a weak, a diligent student of the English language.' Later, having received Acts 2 and 3 which seem to have pleased him, he wrote: '. . . I must repeat, that the cut of the whole is very foreign to all my ideas and maxims. The intermixing of so many principal actors who do not sing—the omission of the music in the most important moments—all these things deprive our "Oberon" of the title of an opera . . .'[44]

When it was produced at the Théâtre Lyrique, the work was described as an 'opéra fantastique'. The French librettists would appear to have returned to Wieland's original poem for their translation. One review states, 'The name of the English librettist is unknown to us and is of little consequence,'[45] and Berlioz records that a direct translation of the libretto had not been made but that a combination of Planché's libretto and Wieland's poem had been used.[46]

Regrettably audience reaction seems to have been most stimulated by the newly introduced buffoonery for Aboulifar, and at least one critic described the libretto as 'a little cold in the first and second acts, becoming more amusing in the third thanks to greater action and to the performance of Girardot as the chief eunuch.'[47] Musically, Berlioz records that Weber's score had been respected except for the changes mentioned above; moreover he praises highly the chorus coached by M.

Bousquet and the orchestra conducted by Deloffre.

Carvalho, in that oft-repeated theatrical phrase, had spared no expense and had increased the string section by ten, even adding to his expenditure by taking out the front row of stall seats to make room for them. 12 extra female choristers were engaged for the chorus of spirits, and we read that the apotheosis of Titania and Oberon was 'most poetic'.[48] Another review describes the production as having 'created the liveliest emotion among the musical dilettanti of Paris.' It reports that 'the papers lay great stress on the spectacle, the dresses and appointments,' and then adds obliquely, 'from which it may be naturally inferred that the execution of the music was not remarkable . . .'[49]

To this criticism, however, Parisians showed complete indifference, and within a month after it was produced, *Oberon* 'was bringing in money in the same proportion' as *La Reine Topaze* which had netted 202,986.20 francs after only 40 performances.[50] Indeed, so great was the success of these two operas that it was a full three months before the next creation was mounted at the Théâtre Lyrique.

This was *Les Nuits d'Espagne*, the first opera of Théophile Semet, then a modest timpanist at the Opéra who in later life would become a sometime teacher of Emmanuel Chabrier. Little can be said for it except that it anticipated Bizet in having not alone one toreador but a supporting chorus of toreadors and a feminine lead called Carmen. Berlioz judged that the applause it had received at its first performance presaged a reasonable success. Its run of 46 performances proved him to be correct.

The season ended with two unimportant one-act works, *Le Duel de Commandeur* by de Lajarte, and *Les Commères*, by an Italian composer, Montuoro.

The unlikely reason given for the production of 'these two poor scores, tossed about for so long'[51] was that the season was coming to a close; one of them was said to have been in rehearsal since the previous October. But with *La Reine Topaze* and *Oberon* each playing to houses of 5000 francs nightly up to May (although it had been reproachfully noted that the production of *Oberon*, instead of improving, was becoming slacker all the time[52]), who would want to change programmes? Besides, the 'two poor scores' turned out to be complete flops.

The theatre closed for the usual summer recess with *La*

Fanchonnette on 30 June and, apart from the fête day performance on 15 August, when *La Reine Topaze* was performed, it remained closed until 1 September.

1857–1858

When Carvalho followed up the success of *Oberon* by beginning his new season with *Euryanthe,* he was pushing his luck. Inevitably Castil-Blaze had been there before him, having included two pieces from the work in a pastiche called *La Forêt de Sénart* at the Odéon in 1826. Five years later a more responsible production, still translated by Castil-Blaze was given at the Opéra.

At the Théâtre Lyrique the work was 'Castil-Blazed' yet again, this time by de Saint-Georges and de Leuven, from whom better might have been expected. The new libretto was partly remodelled on a romance, *Histoire de Gerard de Nevers et de La Belle Euriant, sa mie* by a Count de Tressan.[1] Names of characters were altered and recitatives suppressed, with spoken dialogue introduced instead. 'The original libretto,' Durocher relates, 'was considered a little bold, a little risqué for the French theatre',[2] so the distinguished librettists took the matter in hand and 'livened the plot and altogether made it a more agreeable drama than the German original . . . the serious parts being relieved by a couple of cowardly serving men who furnish the farce of the opera,'[3] after the fashion of the comic pair introduced into *Oberon.* An intriguing incident about the translation is that de Chazot, lately a colleague of de Saint Georges and de Leuven in preparing *Oberon,* took legal action against de Leuven because of numerous similarities between the translation used in performance and one which de Chazot had earlier submitted to the Théâtre Lyrique.[4]

There was the usual transition of music from one act to another: an air and duet from Act 2 to Act 1. The 'Invitation to the Waltz', scored by Berlioz, was introduced into Act 2 for a ballet, and Act 3, although now very much cut, included the Gipsy March from *Preciosa.* These modifications were said to passably resemble what picture restorers achieve when they produce a new painting from an old one.[5]

As with *Oberon*, the orchestra was augmented. Rehearsals were conducted by Charles Gounod because Deloffre was ill. He recovered in time to preside at the first performance on 1 September, [6] although it was scarcely a success. 'The piece,' we read, 'is well got up both as regards the scenery and the dresses.' But the singers are dismissed as 'mediocrity on all sides', and although the orchestra 'did its best . . . that was not superlative. The audience was cold and apathetic.'[7]

A singer who received considerable praise in some reviews was Juliette Borghèse, but before the month was out she had married a master mariner and left the company. Her place was taken by Mathilda Cambardi who had previously sung at the Théâtre Italien and in Germany.[8]

Early in October, a one-act opera comique, *Maître Griffard*, introduced a young composer, just 21, who had an important career ahead of him, for he was Léo Delibes. Today still remembered for his opera *Lakmé* and his ballet *Coppélia*, he had come from the Folies Nouvelles where in 1855 his very first production had been a sketch, *Deux sous de Charbon*, and from the Bouffes Parisiens. He had become an accompanist at the Théâtre Lyrique in 1853 and indeed may still have held the position when *Maître Griffard* was produced. Remarkably, Berlioz, usually so generous, was uncommonly critical, even sardonic, commenting that Delibes was known in musical circles through a polka that was having a ready sale.[9] Generally, however, the work was well received, one tenor air in particular, 'Je suis Blaise', winning special praise.

What was not well received at all was an over-rated work which followed—Clapisson's *Margot*. Yet it had all the elements for success—Clapisson, de Saint-Georges, de Leuven and Miolan-Carvalho—the identical mixture that had made *La Fanchonnette* so successful. Instead, from Léon Durocher we read, '*Margot* is a mistake by two men of spirit and talent'—which disposed of the librettists. The composer fared no better. The music was summed up as 'predictable'—'an interminable album of romances'. Vulgar seems a better description, for the overture, following a pastoral introduction, proceeded to give forth farmyard noises. (It was a pastoral opera with a story somewhat reminiscent of *La Sonnambula* combined with other well known opera plots.) Even the vocalises composed for

Margot (Clapisson) 1857 Act 2.

Miolan-Carvalho, so important to the opera's success was thought by Durocher to be more suitable for the violin or piano.[10] Nevertheless, Berlioz gave the opera unstinted praise, describing it as 'written with exceptional care. The melodic style is easy, lively, brisk, piquant; the harmonies and modulations succeed one another in the most agreeable and natural fashion...'[11] One sometimes gets the uneasy feeling that Berlioz frequently wrote his music criticism with a considerable leavening of irony.

The cause of the abrupt departure of Mme Meillet for the Opéra Comique is made clear by an announcement that the secondary role of Artemise, now being sung by Caroline Vadé, had been originally offered to her. She had summarily rejected it. Such an insult was not to be borne.[12]

Meanwhile the 'Carnival of Venice' business, not to mention the practice of vocalise, was getting seriously out of hand. At the Opéra Comique, an opera of that name (by Ambroise Thomas, no less) was performed before their Imperial Majesties, in which Marie Cabel won new triumphs. 'The execution of an air without words, imitating a "concerto (!) for the violin", as we are informed, was a prodigy of vocalisation.'[13] With *La Fanchonnette* now nearly two years old, and nothing better than a mediocre *Margot* to compete with it, Miolan-Carvalho cannot have been pleased with that sort of opposition.

The last opera of the year was *La Demoiselle d'Honneur*, a second work by the little-known Semet to be performed within 12 months, and later reported to have cost 25,000 francs to produce.[14] It was a cloak and sword venture, and a duel which was staged seems to have been one of its most applauded episodes. Berlioz indulgently declared it to be as good as, if not better than, Semet's earlier *Les Nuits d'Espagne*;[15] but not so Paul Scudo in the *Revue des Deux Mondes*, who criticised the use of pedal notes in the harmony and of the piccolo which 'never ceased to prattle above the orchestra.'[16] For the public, however, the opera's significance was its introduction to the Théâtre Lyrique (from the Opéra and Opéra Comique*) of the popular tenor Marius Audran, father of the operetta composer,

*

Where he created a host of roles including (of Irish interest) Le Comte de Salisbury in Balfe's forgotten *Le Puits d'Amour*.

Edmond Audran. He failed to make any impression however and quickly left the company again in February 1858.[17]

The year 1858 began with a work by the composer whose operas would bring the Théâtre Lyrique its greatest fame and who in turn would make his name there, for he was Charles François Gounod. The opera was Le Médecin malgré lui, his third. Two others had previously been produced at the Opéra. Although still performed today, this opera comique never won universal acceptance, but was nevertheless the first opera by Gounod to gain international recognition. The text was taken from Molière almost unchanged, with only slight alterations by Barbier and Carré. In his play Molière, then a sick man, satirised the medical profession.

Ridiculous as it may seem, the libretto—almost 200 years old at the time of Gounod's production—ran into censorship problems. These were not on moral or religious grounds as would later occur with Faust, but because of objections by the Comédie Française that opera was trespassing on the dramatic field. It was here that Princess Mathilde came to Gounod's aid (he had lately joined her salon) and jealous rivalry was won over. Gounod expressed his thanks by dedicating his score to her.

The opera was first performed on 15 January, the anniversary of Molière's birthday, and when it had ended, the curtain rose again to reveal a scene on Olympus with the playwright's crowned bust in the background. The entire company filled both sides of the stage, and Miolan-Carvalho (who had not taken part in the opera), dressed as a Greek muse and bearing a golden palm, came forward to sing a hymn in Molière's praise in which the chorus joined. The music was said to have come from Gounod's first opera, Sapho.[18]

It may be noted that this was not the first time that Le Médecin malgré lui had been set to music. In 1792 it had been performed at the Théâtre Feydeau with a score composed by Désaugiers père which, appropriate to the period, included the revolutionary air, 'Ça ira'.[19]

Gounod in his style of composition reverted to the 17th and 18th centuries. Jules Lovy in Le Ménestrel described it as 'a delightful pastiche of Lully, Monsigny, Grétry', combined with the melodious nuances of modern music. He also discovered Italian influences, and even something of Mozart and Cimarosa.[20]

Berlioz also commented on how closely Gounod had copied Lully, but in more practical vein wondered if the opera would make money. He ended by surmising that the musical style of the work was rather delicate and subtle for the Théâtre Lyrique audience, and demonstrated his knowledge of Shakespeare (acquired from Harriet Smithson) by declaring in Hamlet's words that it would be 'caviare to the general'.[21] His judgement was here correct for while its artistic success was great, the work did not really draw at the box office.

But on this first night finance could be ignored, for the opera, conducted by Deloffre, was genuinely well received, and afterwards Gounod was called for enthusiastically. Meillet in his role of Sganarelle the woodcutter is said to have descended to one of the parterre loges and to have lifted Gounod in his arms as one lifts a faggot on to the stage to the joyous acclamations of the entire theatre.[22] One sad event only marred the occasion. On the following day Gounod's mother to whom he was deeply attached, died. She had been too ill to ever realise that he had at last achieved success.

This production was followed by a highly unusual concert held on 30 January, a farewell benefit for Caroline Duprez-Vandenheuvel, who was setting off for a season at Marseille. A number of artists took part with her in scenes from *Les Noces de Figaro*, *La Fille du Régiment* and Rossini's *Otello*, but the main interest converged on Gilbert Duprez, her father, who, assisted by his Swedish pupil, Euphrosyne Leman was appearing in Act 2 of *Rigoletto*. At last he had achieved his wish to sing (part at least) of this great baritone role and coincidentally to challenge—unsuccessfully, one suspects—Ronconi, who was then performing it at the Théâtre Italien. The right to perform Verdi's work in translation at the Théâtre Lyrique seems to have been decided by the Civil Tribunal only that very day.[23] Duprez also sang, as a tenor, in the final scene from *Otello* with his daughter as Desdemona and Leman as Emilia.

A packed audience thoroughly enjoyed their evening until curtain fall. Then, as Jules Lovy expostulates, 'Would to God that the same spirit of order and fidelity had reigned in the cloakroom of the theatre! But, alas, many a spectator having rediscovered Duprez' voice [he had retired 12 years before] would have been happy also to have found his overcoat on leaving. On that evening mesdames the usherettes seem to have lost their heads. Thanks to them and to the bizarre organisation of their cloackrooms—we say bizarre so as to remain parliamentary—the evening was enriched by a supplementary performance not on the programme. Total: five hours of music in the theatre plus two hours of uproar in the foyer.'[24]

During mid-February, influenza, which had been raging since January, caused both cast changes and postponements. There was a revival of *La Perle du Brésil* which pleased Berlioz not at all. So little did he like it that he enumerated its imperfections to make known his opinion of the Théâtre Lyrique. 'Musical performances are not improving in this theatre,' he wrote. 'Nearly all [Carvalho's] singers, men and women, are afflicted with goat bleat, if one is to give it its correct name. Goat bleat at the Théâtre Lyrique has become so insistent that if a singer tries to produce a sustained note, one thinks it is a trill, and if a singer trills, one thinks he is trying to produce a sustained note. The female chorus is very bad at present, the men less so. The orchestra does not play together. This is a very serious defect and I advise M. Deloffre to attend to it. An orchestra must play together. If you have bad instrumentalists, get others. If their instruments are defective, get better ones. An orchestra must play together.'[25] (He repeats this admonition five times at the end of his review.)

Historically, if one is to accept facts as they have been contemporaneously and authoritatively recorded, what is one to make of the foregoing? Was the overall standard at the Théâtre Lyrique reasonably good, was it mediocre, or was it simply rank bad?

Although *Euryanthe* had been less than successful, Carvalho tried his hand once more at Weber. This time he chose *Preciosa*. It too had been performed at the Odéon in 1826 under the title of *Les Bohémiens,* arranged not by Castil-Blaze on this occasion, but by his *Robin des Bois* confrère, Thomas Sauvage. Berlioz recalls having attended more than ten performances.[26] The new Théâtre Lyrique version by Nuitter and Beaumont included two items from Weber's earlier opera *Silvana.* The original German melodrama for which Weber wrote his music had been in four acts, but these Carvalho had reduced to one. The knockabout 'Laurel and Hardy' couple which had been introduced into all Weber's operas for comic relief at the Théâtre Lyrique were in this production taken by Gabriel and Serène. Once again they amused the audience by their eccentricities.[27] As a one-act piece, *Preciosa* had been preceded by another opera comique, *Don Almanzor*, by Renaud de Vilbac, a composer whose now forgotten reputation seems to have rested on the composition and transcription of ephemeral pieces for the piano and organ. 'It is not one of those things which repels the public,' wrote Berlioz, 'it is rather one of those which leaves them indifferent.'[28]

In April there was news of Berlioz working on an episode from the *Aeneid*,[29] but of more interest to the audience was an announcement that Delphine Ugalde would join the company to appear in *Les Noces de Figaro* and to create the role of Marguerite in Gounod's new opera, *Faust*.[30] Delphine Beaucé (she subsequently performed under her first husband's name) was born in Paris of a musical family and first came to notice at the Opéra Comique where, among other roles, she created and was renowned as Galathée in Massé's opera of that name. Her career was very successful there but a laryngeal condition caused her to transfer to the Théâtre des Variétés, where she played with less success in *Les Trois Sultanes ou Soliman Second* by Lockroy and Favart. She next re-joined the Opéra Comique and then the Théâtre Lyrique. Her stage career ended as directrice of the Bouffes Parisiens.

A concert in the style recently given by Duprez was now presented on 26 April, the principal artist taking part being the celebrated tenor Enrico Tamberlik from the Théâtre Italien. He sang, in French for the first time, the trio from *Guillaume Tell* with Meillet and Battaille and, in Italian, the duet from *Otello* with the baritone, Corsi, introducing his famous 'ut dièse' or high C sharp from the chest. Receipts of 15,000 francs were anticipated[31] and it seems likely that this amount was reached, for from the morning a queue had formed in the boulevard du Temple—so much so that the police had to maintain order. Never was the house more crowded. Even Duprez was reported to have announced as he entered, 'Here are receipts a semitone higher than mine,' but whether the reference was to Tamberlik's range or receipts is not made clear. Miolan-Carvalho and Ugalde were among the other artists, both vocal and instrumental, who took part. The former sang the 'Carnival of Venice', the latter her air from *Galathée*.[32]

At last the evening—8 May—which 'tout Paris' had expectantly awaited, arrived, bringing *Les Noces de Figaro* to the Théâtre Lyrique. Mozart, like Weber, had been much performed in Paris during earlier years and the first of five performances of *Le Nozze di Figaro* translated into French by F. Notaris, was given at the Opéra on 20 March 1793. The recitatives were replaced by spoken dialogue taken directly from Beaumarchais, but the arrangement proved unsatisfactory. The singers at the Opéra were unused to speaking their lines, neither could they act. The dialogue, moreover, extended the length of the performance beyond the audience's patience.[33] Castil-Blaze (but naturally!) arranged a version which was performed throughout the French provinces, ultimately reaching the Odéon in 1826. There was even a pastiche performed, made up of excerpts from Mozart's *Figaro* and Rossini's *Il Barbiere di Siviglia*.

In view of the objections earlier expressed at the use of Beaumarchais's text, it is interesting to find that a number of reviewers noted their disappointment that this had not been done—'as was formerly done in *Le Barbier de Séville* and, quite recently, in *Le Médecin malgré lui*'[34]—when the recitatives were suppressed. Once again it appears that the Comédie-Française actors had protested, and so 'the dispute was settled by an ingenious compromise: let Beaumarchais's prose be translated into verse, and the Théâtre Français will ignore it.'[35] So Barbier and Carré were called in again to lightly adapt Beaumarchais as they had recently arranged Molière. Berlioz makes the same point about the dialogue, but praises the theatre for at least not altering Mozart's orchestration 'by adding trombones, ophicleide, big drum and cymbals, as is practised in London where they rescore even Beethoven.'[36]

Nevertheless the production appears to have been highly individual. Deloffre conducted extracts from Mozart's symphonies during two intervals[37] and Léon Durocher reported: 'Mad. Carvalho [Chérubin] sings her first act air and that of the second act, "mon cœur soupire" [Voi che sapete] with unsurpassing delicacy and charm except that she ends the first with a B flat not to be found in the score, and which, introduced as it is and not supported by the orchestra seems rather harsh. Perhaps she takes "mon cœur soupire" too quickly ... The duet commonly known as the "letter duet" is not in her part but in Suzanne's. Mad. Carvalho considered it to be lawful spoil and took it for herself, just as the lion claims the best part of the deer ... To effect this transfer from one role to the other, it was necessary to change the character of the piece and turn a piece of banter, full of grace and lightness, into a plaintive elegy ... The combination of these three artists [Miolan-Carvalho, Caroline Duprez and Ugalde], di primo cartello, as they say in Italy, will no doubt prove an irresistible attraction for the public, and double that which the great name of Mozart and the incontestable merit of his work must exercise ... The voice of M. Balanqué was dull in the part of Almaviva which he played rather coldly. He will probably acquit himself better as he becomes more acquainted with it. Let me also hope that the orchestra will acquire more accent, colour, brilliance and energy when its conductor, to whose intelligence I have often done justice, has learned more of Mozart's intentions. Surely it is to be regretted that there was no one in the theatre to give the real tempo of so many pieces, the effect of which is diminished sometimes by being taken too slowly, but more frequently by a too petulant vivacity?'[38]

The above review sums up the Théâtre Lyrique's *Les Noces de Figaro*. Individual or general, artistic or vulgar, it enjoyed a great success and was a staple of the repertory for many years.

With this success on his hands Carvalho next presented, of all things, a revival of Maillart's *Gastibelza*, the opera with which Adolphe Adam had opened his Opéra National in 1847. But its vogue had passed and it would barely limp into the following year, with only 15 performances in all.

One other one-act opera comique, *L'Agneau de Chloé*, would be the last new production of the season. It was composed by Jean Baptiste Montaubry, an orchestral conductor at the Théâtre du Vaudeville and brother of a then well known French tenor. It possessed the unique distinction of having, instead of the omnipresent operatic 'drinking song', an 'eating song' sung by Mlle Girard in honour of the mutton cutlet![39] Chloé's lamb 'played his role with an intelligence and calm that delighted the audience and provoked two or three salvoes of applause on his own account'![40] Once again Berlioz indulgently praised the music[41] but the work did not survive the season.

Regulations for the prompt commencement of theatre performances were being enforced by the Prefect of Police about this time.[42] It may have been a regulation more frequently honoured in the breach, and late starting times seem to have been common. A rumour was also published that M. Vandenheuvel, Caroline Duprez' husband, was about to take over the direction of the Théâtre Lyrique and that Gilbert Duprez was financing the venture. This was quickly scotched by Duprez[43] but one is left wondering if he might not have had some idea of supplanting Carvalho, news of which had reached the press before his plans were ready.

So the Théâtre Lyrique ended another season on 30 June, following performances of *Les Noces de Figaro* on three successive evenings, whereupon the company disbanded. Shortly afterwards some at least of the singers were to be found performing in Montmartre and Saint Germain for, as Berlioz observed, 'Without singing, how can they survive?'[44]

1858–1859

During the summer recess there was the usual gossip concerning new artists, new productions and the numerous novelties with which theatre directors ever strive to convince their patrons that the next season will be the best of all seasons. It would open on 1 September with *Les Noces de Figaro* which two months later could be reported to be producing 'the most splendid receipts.' The announcement continues: 'The management is carefully preparing Mozart's *Don Juan*, ... *La Fée Carabosse* by M. Massé and *Faust* by M. Gounod ... Mozart's *Don Juan* promises to prove very attractive, as there is a report that M. Carvalho has determined on playing the part of Leporello ... A new tenor of the name of Guardi is to make his debut in M. Gounod's *Faust*. M. Carvalho is taking the greatest care of this gentleman. If it were possible he would shut him up in a case till the day of his first performance. It is impossible to describe the precautions with which M. Guardi is surrounded. Whenever he visits the theatre or the green room, it is always in the most mysterious manner. Whenever he sings, no one is allowed to stop and hear him, and the other artists are turned out. It is well known that M. Carvalho is not wrong to take care of this suckling Tamberlik who possesses a very fine voice, and if his acting is only on a par with his singing, M. Carvalho will not have had his trouble for nothing.'[1] In the event he did have his trouble for nothing. Nevertheless Guardi will appear prominently in the *Faust* story when we reach it.

The first new production was *La Harpe d'Or*, described as an opéra-légende and composed by the eminent harpist Felix Godefroid. The most solemn moment of this naive piece occurred when by a miracle a statue of Saint Cecilia came to life on a crowded stage 'and with her stone fingers' executed 'a brilliant fantaisie on her golden harp'[2]—the composer at the same time helping her out by performing the fantaisie in the wings. A tenor lately arrived, named Michot, who was replacing Monjauze, turned out to be the hero of the performance in both senses. His voice is described as warm and vibrant, but he attracted most attention by attempting to compete with Tamberlik's renowned C sharp from the chest. He achieved a B natural in a trio 'which was encored with enthusiasm' (whether it was the note, the phrase containing it or the entire trio that was encored is not made clear) and it was remarked 'that when the new diapason* arrives the tenor Michot will find that he has a C from the chest for Arnold in *Guillaume Tell*.'[3] There was also praise for a new mezzo-soprano, Mlle Wilhème. 'She does not bleat!!!!!' declared Berlioz. He also drolly pointed out that in the interests of dramatic truth Godefroid should play his harp like an olden day saint—'that is to say, very badly.'[4] Obviously Godefroid was a better harpist than composer, for his opera had only nine performances.

Some weeks later, an opera comique, *Broskovano*, by Louis Pierre Deffès, did better. 'What a fine thing bandits are for MM the librettists,' commented Saint-Yves in *Revue et Gazette Musicale*. 'Broskovano is a bandit and, as if that were not enough, he is also a vampire!'[5] The setting of the work is

*

A Commission had lately recommended that the pitch in France should be lowered from an A of 896 to 870 vibrations.

Walachia, which may help to explain this singular character. Berlioz thought the music 'tasteful' but reproved the composer for plagiarising 'the little dance air in A major from *Oberon* [For thee hath beauty].' 'Patience, you go too quickly', he advised him. 'It is not yet 50 years since *Oberon* was written.'[6]

It may seem strange that these two unimportant works were the only new productions to be staged before Christmas in that season. It must be remembered however that one other opera at least, *Les Noces de Figaro*, was sustaining its very successful run. Moreover, 19th century technology had begun to help the theatre in a most unexpected fashion. We read that 'the railroads bring, every day, to Paris eight or ten thousand travellers; who, when their business is transacted, have no other means of employing their evenings than by going to the theatre.'[7]

In such a situation it needed only the vision and determination of M. Voisin, Receiver-General of the department of Maine et Loire and president of the Philharmonic Society of Angers (a nice blending of art and public service) to organise a train to transport 500 fellow Angevins to Paris (almost 200 miles away) for a performance of *Les Noces de Figaro*.[8] (One wonders was this the first opera train ever, three quarters of a century before Glyndebourne?) It was hoped that such enterprise would encourage other French cities to send their musical amateurs.

On 23 November the 'convoy of pleasure' set off in 25 carriages drawn by two engines. On their arrival at the boulevard du Temple, they found the façade of the theatre illuminated in the form of a lyre surrounded by laurels and decorated with groups of flags and the arms of Angers, an enormous key. A curious crowd stationed itself at the approaches to the theatre, for the day's playbills had announced a special programme requested by the Angevins. An audience of Parisians also assembled, both to enjoy the enthusiasm of a new-found public as well as to make up its mind about them. Condescendingly they trained their lorgnettes but failed to see anyone who did not appear to be a fellow Parisian, 'for Angers is an ancient city with a distinguished population made up of nobility and bourgeoisie, between which two branches of society love of the arts lies.'[9] To make the visitors feel thoroughly at home, Carvalho also had an interval curtain painted to represent a panoramic view of

Les Noces de Figaro (Mozart) 1858 Act 2.

Angers.[10] The Angevins returned the compliment by bringing bouquets all the way from their native city. These were graciously accepted by the three leading lady singers.

The last performance (for the time being) of *Les Noces de Figaro* would take place early in the new year—due to an engagement elsewhere of Duprez-Vandenheuvel. Then it would be the Limousins, headed by the Maire of Limoges, who would make the journey on 10 January. Again, it was successful—M. Chaumont, music publisher of the locality, had alone collected 400 subscriptions—and again the visitors were warm in their applause.[11]

The financial importance of *Les Noces de Figaro* to the Théâtre Lyrique can now be understood. Where receipts were concerned, it would be one of Carvalho's major successes. Indeed, financially 1858 would be his best year ever in that theatre, although the box-office had shown an increase each year since he had assumed management.

Administratively, too, it seems to have been an undisturbed year for him. True, some slight contretemps had arisen between him and the Commission of Dramatic Authors which was claiming rights on works such as those of Mozart which were in the public domain,[12] but the matter was satisfactorily resolved. Besides, he could point out that through the Commission he had paid a sum for authors' rights on *Les Noces de Figaro* to Mozart's son, living in reduced circumstances in Milan, and 4,000 francs to Weber's son for *Euryanthe.*[13] If the story of the Mozart donation is true, the money arrived just in time, for Karl Thomas, Mozart's elder son, would die in Milan on 31 October 1858.

Throughout the winter months, two new works of anticipated importance were in rehearsal. They were Massé's *La Fée Carabosse* and Gounod's *Faust*. The original casting was for Miolan-Carvalho to take the lead in *La Fée Carabosse* with Ugalde singing Marguerite in *Faust* but, having heard *Faust* in rehearsal, Mme Carvalho with the prescience of a true prima donna opted for this opera and so the roles were reversed.[14] *Faust* was also to be the first work performed but its vicissitudes in rehearsal, as will be recounted, led to a postponement, and so *La Fée Carabosse* was given first instead. It was intended that both operas would be played on alternate evenings, but the failure of *La Fée Carabosse* would make this arrangement impossible.

Because of all the difficulties involved, *La Fée Carabosse* was not staged until 28 February 1859. It was in three acts and a prologue (the prologue was considered a praiseworthy innovation) and it was described both as an opera comique and as a féerie. The plot concerns a fairy queen who through jealousy transforms a young and attractive member of her realm named Mélodine into a wrinkled white-haired hag with a hump on her back; so she must remain until she can find a fiancé who will embrace her, and another gallant who will consent to shoulder the burden (literally, it would seem) of her hump. While awaiting the outcome (happy, of course) Mélodine changes her name to the more appropriate Carabosse.

As an experienced composer, Massé must have been distressed to find his music labelled 'painless',[15] although Ugalde as Mélodine was given an attractive 'Song of the lark' which was described as a companion to the 'Song of the bee' which he had composed in *La Reine Topaze.*[16] An inconsistency in stage design was also noted for while the settings were superb and the costumes splendid, the former were from the 17th century while the dresses belonged to the 15th. All in all it was not a production which seemed set fair for success and even the attendance of Prince Jerome at a performance on 24 March[17] did little to revive its sagging fortunes, for the receipts for the evening reached only Fr 2651. 25c.[18]

The Faust story in legend and in literature began in the early 16th century. Where Gounod is concerned, it commenced with a play, *Faust et Marguerite*, by Michel Carré, produced at the Théâtre du Gymnase, Paris, on 19 August 1850. Then, in 1855, Gounod met Jules Barbier. Barbier was much taken by him and explained that he would like to dramatise *Faust* as an opera libretto, to which Gounod is said to have replied, 'I have been thinking of that for 20 years.' Barbier next called on his friend Carré, who did not express much enthusiasm—his play had not had much success—nevertheless he agreed to collaborate.

On completion the work was first submitted to Alphonse Royer, the director of the Opéra, who rejected it on the grounds that it lacked opportunities for spectacle. The three authors then took their score to Carvalho who was more receptive. It was now 1858 and no sooner had the work been accepted for the Théâtre Lyrique than the first obstacle arose. Another *Faust*—a 'drame fantastique' by d'Ennery with music by Amédée Artus—was presented at the Théâtre de la Porte-Saint-Martin on 25 September and Carvalho, wary of competition, decided to shelve the opera for the time being. But d'Ennery's play, which had cost a considerable sum to stage, although successful, was not sensationally so. Consequently the director and authors began to think again.

At the time *La Fée Carabosse* was already in rehearsal with Miolan-Carvalho as Mélodine but, as has been noted, she quickly assumed the role of Marguerite instead. Since a note in Carvalho's hand, 'To be played at the Théâtre Lyrique, 17 November 1858'[19]* occurs in the original manuscript libretto of *Faust*, this may have been his original projected date of production. Rehearsals had commenced in October[20] but from the beginning they proved difficult. First of all there was the necessity of cutting what was obviously an overlong score to a manageable length. Then Carvalho's insistence on altering other people's operas (too frequently recorded to need comment here) delayed production further. We can trace these alterations from Barbier and Carré's manuscript libretto and although certainly they were not all for the worse, they are nevertheless considerable. Finally there was Mme Carvalho who, having got her hands on the role of Marguerite, was making certain that no one would upstage her in it. Hence at least one air for Siebel, 'Versez vos chagrins dans mon âme,' occurring in Act 4, was excised on her authority.[21]

At the same time it must be understood that *Faust*, even as first performed at the Théâtre Lyrique, differs not inconsiderably from *Faust* as we know it today. Perhaps the most striking change occurs in the present use of recitative instead of the original spoken dialogue. It is not clear when this alteration first took place. One report suggests that it was at Strasbourg,[22] the first French city outside Paris to stage *Faust*. Conversely a press announcement in September 1859 reports that when *Faust* would be revived at the Théâtre Lyrique during the following

*

An earlier operatic setting of *Faust* by Louise Angélique Bertin was produced in Paris at the Théâtre Italien in 1831.

month, it would be 'with recitatives instead of dialogue'.[23] However when the revival did take place there is no mention of new recitatives, only 'a new symphony which Gounod has introduced into the score at the beginning of Act 5 during the diabolical fêtes of the Walpurgisnacht.'[24]* Lastly, an announcement giving a precise date records that the change occurred at the Grand Théâtre de Bordeaux, with Gounod present, on 2 April 1860.[25]** The significance of the alteration is that it turned a work which bore the suspicion of being opera comique (indeed the manuscript libretto indicates that Barbier and Carré wrote certain passages, particularly in Act 2, with this intention) into a truly grand opera. As such Carvalho might have hesitated to stage it; his audience was not a grand opera audience. We know how even Weber's operas had to have farcical scenes written into them. Once the opera had succeeded, however, Gounod or perhaps Choudens, his publisher, took over and a note appears in the vocal score from the second edition onwards stating that the work must be performed by the theatres' grand opera troupes, and recitatives employed.

Three examples may be quoted to illustrate differences occurring in the early editions of the score. In Act 2, Valentin's fine recitative, 'O sainte médaille' first appears in the second edition. (As is known, the Invocation 'Even bravest heart' was specially composed for Charles Santley only in 1864.) In Act 3, the garden quartet which now commences with 'Seigneur Dieu, que vois-je!' originally began with spoken dialogue supported by a mélodrame down to Faust's 'Prenez mon bras un moment,'

*

This may have been a 'witches' chorus' which was cut just before the first performance, later restored and then withdrawn for good. It was not the ballet music as we now know it, which was composed for the first production of *Faust* at the Opéra in 1869. Lasalle (*Mémorial du Théâtre Lyrique*) states incorrectly that the ballet music was composed for the first performance of the opera at the Théâtre de la Monnaie, Brussels in 1861. He may have been confusing it with a ballet of *Faust*, the music by Panizza, in the repertory of the Monnaie from November 1858.

**

The writer has been unable to find contemporary evidence of this. *Le Ménestrel,* 15 April 1860, reports that Barbot has been called to Bordeaux to sing the role of Faust. The same source, 22 April 1860, describes Gounod attending a performance of his opera in Rouen. In neither instance are specific dates given.

while in Act 4 the same style of 'melodramatic' dialogue precedes Méphistophélès' Serenade.

Other alterations introduced into subsequent performances include deleting the small part of a beggar who sings some lines in the Kermesse scene.[26]* (The rondo, 'Le Veau d'Or' began life as 'Couplets du Scarabée'[27] or 'Song of the beetle', presumably as close as Barbier and Carré considered it necessary to get to Goethe's 'Song of the Flea'. Gounod, it appears, was dissatisfied and, having rewritten the air 12 times, the well known 'Veau d'Or' was the result that reached the stage.)[28]

When the opera is given complete, Act 4 consists of three scenes—a room in Marguerite's house,** the church, and the public square where Valentin duels with Faust and is killed, and since the 1869 production at the Opéra, this is the usual order in which the scenes are performed. But at the Théâtre Lyrique the act ended with the church scene which Carvalho believed would make the better effect.[29] It certainly made the better effect for his wife, since the act then finished with her big set piece instead of Valentin's, but to be fair this is the order in which Goethe had set the scenes of his drama and presumably Barbier and Carré had simply followed it. Indeed Carvalho appears to have had more interest in the theatrical effect of a transformation scene from square to church, achieved by the sudden disappearance of the outside wall of the church from the square.

He was very proud of this scene (his designers for the opera were Cambon and Thierry) and later when he revived *Faust* at the new Théâtre Lyrique in the place du Châtelet, which had a much smaller stage, he found that it would no longer fit. He recalls, 'It was necessary to give up installing the scenery for the public square, a remarkable job of painting and machinery which transformed itself without effort into the cathedral, getting bigger and bigger to the eye, and deploying its vaulted

---

*

In his production of the opera during the 1960s, Jean Louis Barrault introduced a mute role of a beggar into this scene and into Act 4.

**

In this scene, almost invariably cut, Marguerite sings at her spinning wheel. Possibly it is the deletion of the scene which has created a tradition of having her sing 'Il était un roi de Thulé' seated at a spinning wheel in Act 3, as there are no directions for it in the early scores.

roof to grow higher and wider...'[30] The Ministry of Fine Arts' concern that the same church scene would cause a diplomatic incident with the Vatican—matters were rather delicate just then with the impending entry of France into a war for the unification of Italy—and Carvalho's successful appeal to the Papal nuncio, Monseigneur de Ségur, that it should be retained have been recounted elsewhere. Less well known is the censor's deletion of Méphistophélès' line to Faust in Act 2, while encouraging him in his pursuit of Marguerite: 'Is it that you have been sprinkled with holy water?'[31]

Possibly the most amazing story of the genesis of *Faust* is that the chorus, 'Gloire immortelle de nos aïeux', the famous 'Soldiers' Chorus', does not appear in the manuscript libretto and was a complete afterthought, taken from Gounod's uncompleted opera, *Ivan le Terrible*. Another borrowing, this time a Dies irae from a Requiem Mass performed in Vienna in 1842, became Marguerite's final air in Act 5, 'Anges purs! anges radieux!'[32]

The foregoing gives a brief sketch of how *Faust* went into the furnace of production and of how it was moulded during its early performances. Delays and difficulties have already been mentioned, but the most unfortunate delay of all arose over the tenor Guardi who was to sing Faust, and of whom it will be remembered Carvalho was taking the greatest care. Guardi was not an Italian as his name might suggest but a Frenchman whose real name was Hector Gruyer. He was a pupil of Georges Bizet's father, who was a singing teacher. It has been said of Georges Bizet that Gounod was 'the strongest musical influence'[33] in his life; consequently should a problem arise over Guardi and *Faust*, the repercussions in the Gounod-Bizet circle would not be professional alone but personal and social as well. It would be incorrect to say that a problem did arise over *Faust* since quite obviously the problem existed already, only no one seemed to have recognised it—except perhaps Carvalho—since for what other reason was he surrounding his young recruit with so much secrecy?

A review of Guardi which appears some six months later relates: 'I do not know where [he] is from, nor who is his teacher, but he seems to be only a pupil whose strident badly placed voice is already affected with that unbearable vibrato which denotes more than fatigue, I mean a real impairment of the larynx. It is doubtful that M. Guardi has the potential for a long career, especially in the first rank...'[34] In other words Guardi was singing with a faulty technique and Bizet père was his teacher. How much influence was brought to bear on Carvalho through the Gounod-Bizet connection to accept him we do not know—probably none at all. Good tenors were no easier to find then than they are today and, as is now well known, *Faust* requires a good tenor.

Meanwhile rehearsals were proceeding and on 20 February the opera was advertised to have its first performance on 23 February, with *La Fée Carabosse* to be performed some days later.[35]

The following week, however, the situation was reversed; *La Fée Carabosse* was now announced to be performed first [36] which, as we know, it was on 28 February. What had occurred was that Guardi had lost his voice at the dress rehearsal, probably the first occasion on which he was obliged to sing his role 'flat out'. The result does not need to be imagined, it is recorded in Georges Bizet's correspondence written to his mother from Rome where he was then a student.[37] Inevitably it caused a temporary coolness in his friendship with Gounod when Guardi was replaced.

Guardi's successor was Joseph Théodore Desiré Barbot, who was reputed to have been a colleague of Carvalho's at the Conservatoire.[38] He was also said to have very little voice, of poor timbre.[39] He was one of those singers who for no particular reason seem to make some sort of career where better artists have failed although, like other male singers, his career seems to have been helped by his wife, Caroline Barbot, who did have some success at the Opéra and in other continental theatres.

Barbot learned his new role in 15 days[40] and, with some extra time for stage rehearsal, *Faust* was eventually produced on 19 March. Even on that day an announcement advised the public that the performance would commence at seven precisely but that it was undecided what intervals would be required, especially at the first performance, because of the very complicated decor of the last scenes.[41] So, after all its months of rehearsal, *Faust* was reaching the stage by no means a finished production. Deloffre would conduct and the orchestra, as for

Faust (Gounod) March 1859 Act 5 Scene 2 Setting by Cambon and Thierry

most important productions, would be augmented.

It has been more or less universally accepted that *Faust* opened to an unenthusiastic press and that it did not become an immediate box-office success, but on scrutiny there is little to support either of these opinions. Taking the box-office first: apart from an incomprehensible sum of Fr 425.75* taken on the first night, the receipts for 30 performances throughout the rest of the season up to early June never dropped below Fr 3,000 a night, and on ten occasions exceeded Fr 5,000. Four out of five later performances did fall below these amounts,[42] but by then it was summer, an exceptionally warm summer and besides, France was at war. Neither were the reviews entirely critical. Certainly Léon Escudier in *La France Musicale* reproached Gounod for 'bringing to the theatre what he should have left at a concert'[43] but Berlioz in his customary fashion wrote generously, although in a letter to his friend Humbert Ferrand he privately professed, 'I will tell you that Gounod's *Faust* contains some of the loveliest things and some of the most mediocre.'[44] Léon Durocher (Gustave Héquet) singled out the music of Act 3, 'where one recognises almost everywhere the hand of a master.'[45] D'Ortigue described the Soldiers' Chorus as being in the style of Verdi and making a thrilling effect, and concluded that 'the opera of *Faust* is the work of a master.'[46] Paul Scudo too praised the Soldiers' Chorus and found the church scene admirable, although he thought Méphistophélès' Serenade an insignificant piece which proved that the devil had brought no luck to Gounod. He ended his review: 'M. Gounod is perhaps destined to occupy in contemporary art the role of a Cherubini . . . that will be a fine field of action to fill, and one which will allow the composer of *Faust* no cause for complaint.'[47] All critics were eulogistic about the sets, especially those for the church scene.

As can be seen, therefore, in no manner was criticism completely hostile. Indeed, in retrospect, much that was written shows acute perception. Only one reviewer went so far out on a limb as to say 'It is not at all likely that M. Gounod's new opera

---

Was it that the house had been almost entirely 'papered' for a first performance, or was it that Théâtre Lyrique audiences were reluctant to attend new productions until they had had some news of them, or, just possibly, was it simply a misprint in Soubies & de Curzon?

will ... [take the place of] the *Faust* of Spohr. Why so hackneyed and unmalleable a subject for dramatic purposes should have been selected it is difficult to say ... I cannot argue a prosperous career for the new opera'![48]* At the Théâtre Lyrique *Faust* would in fact achieve 306 performances, the greatest number of any work ever performed there. Its later success throughout the world is beyond reckoning.

What may have militated against the early performances of *Faust* was not the music but the singers. Barbot received favourable notices on the whole although Scudo refers to 'his unpleasant tenor voice and Toulousain accent'[49] but Miolan-Carvalho seems to have been a disappointment at first and there is mention of her voice tiring. Perhaps the real problem was that both critics and audience, accustomed to hearing her toss off the 'Carnival of Venice' variations, could not immediately appreciate her singing of more refined music.

One reviewer suggests this when he writes: [Miolan-Carvalho is] 'as sparing of ornament in this part as in others she is prodigiously lavish, producing her effects by the force of simplicity and naif-grace and, when the situation demands it, the breadth and energy of her expression.'[50] Her appearance in the role was compared to Ary Scheffer's many paintings of Marguerite, and on these she may have modelled her performance.

With only one break of a week, caused by Miolan-Carvalho's illness, *Faust* continued to be performed regularly until 15 June. Then Miolan-Carvalho was obliged to leave for an engagement at Covent Garden.

On the following 10 September the opera was revived and once again Guardi was given his chance, but after four performances he had to withdraw. Bizet, who rarely corresponded with his father, now wrote, 'I needn't tell you that even

---

*

A critic whose good opinion Gounod sought was Richard Wagner, as the following letter sent 'towards the end of 1859' to Charles Réty, then secretary of the Théâtre Lyrique, indicates: 'My dear friend, I am most anxious that M. R. Wagner hears my score of *Faust*. His approval as well as his criticism are of the kind one seeks and I should be very grieved if the performances were to end without him knowing my work. I would entreat you therefore to reserve a good box for him for Tuesday's performance.' (J. G. Prod'homme et A. Dandelot. *Gounod 1818–1893*. Paris 1911. 2 v. II 24).

from far away I feel as deeply as you do your sorrow over Hector's failure. I am horribly depressed today. The disappointment is all the more cruel because we hoped for so much.' To Guardi he also sent a sympathetic letter. 'If you had succeeded, mon cher ami, I would perhaps have delayed writing to you, but as fate is against you, I hasten to tell you how much I sympathise with you . . . I am furious and at the same time heart-broken over the behaviour of a man in whom I had faith [Gounod] . . . '[51]

Faust then had to be retired until Michot could be released from other roles to take over the part, and so the next performance did not take place until 15 November. By the end of the year it had been performed 57 times. Since it is sometimes said that this is a relatively small number for what became so successful an opera, it should be pointed out that this again seems to have been due to lack of a suitable cast rather than lack of interest by the audience. While it may be conceded that *Faust* never enjoyed the tremendous success of, say, *La Fanchonnette* or *La Reine Topaze* when they were first produced, these were ephemeral successes. *Faust's* success has lasted till today.

Following *Faust*, there were only two new productions before the season ended, both on the evening of 11 May. Each in its way was a minor classic, for they were Weber's *Abou Hassan* and Mozart's *L'Enlèvement au Sérail*.

Abou Hassan was, strangely enough, having its first production in Paris, where its success would be limited. It had been translated by Nuitter and Beaumont who, it will be recalled, had adapted earlier Weber productions for the Théâtre Lyrique.

The plot of the opera, taken from *A Thousand and One Nights*, had been used earlier by Marmontel and Piccinni as *Le Dormeur éveillé*, produced at Fontainebleau in 1783. At the Théâtre Lyrique the music which gave most pleasure was Hassan's air, 'O Fatime! ô toi que j'aime!', sung by Meillet.

L'Enlèvement au Sérail, its companion piece, combined stylistically with it to make a suitable middle eastern double bill. It was of course a far stronger work and, unlike *Abou Hassan*, had been previously played in Paris, both in German and in French, translated by Moline. The present production had been translated and 'arranged' by Prosper Pascal, the erstwhile composer of *Le Roman de la Rose*, who here gave Mozart a helping hand by orchestrating and introducing the 'Rondo alla

Turca' as an interval piece before the second act.

Berlioz wrote forthrightly of the production as follows: '*L'Enlèvement au Sérail,* to quote almost all my colleagues, has been performed at the Théâtre Lyrique with the most scrupulous fidelity. So one has only to turn into two acts a work composed in three, transpose the running order of some of the pieces, transfer a great air from Mme Meillet's role and give it to Mme Ugalde, and introduce between the two acts the famous Turkish March so familiar to pianists who play Mozart. Splendid! That is what is meant by scrupulous fidelity.'[52] (Paul Scudo records the insertion of an air from *La Clemenza di Tito,* the suppression of the Constanze-Belmonte duet, 'Ha, du solltest' and the changing of the denouement.[53]) Berlioz continues, 'Mme Ugalde performs with address and a happy audacity the ungrateful vocalisation with which Blondine's role bristles. The proportion of high notes must surely tire her, and since they have shown so much respect for Mozart's score as I have already mentioned, they could perhaps have pushed fidelity to the point of lowering certain airs by a semitone, thereby bringing them back to the old diapason for which they were composed.'[54] It is, in fact, confirmed that both Ugalde and Meillet sang a modified version of the score, for Léon Durocher states: 'They do not attempt to sing textually all that Mozart has written. The thing is impossible.'[55]

The work introduced a distinguished bass as Osmin. He was Charles Amable Battaille* who was born at Nantes. The son of a physician, he acceded to his father's wishes and first qualified as a doctor but soon gave up practice in his native city and set out for Paris to become a singer. He was a pupil of Manuel Garcia at the Conservatoire and from 1848 had a highly successful career at the Opéra Comique for ten years. He then contracted a laryngeal condition which ended his singing for a time. As Osmin he was making a come-back to the stage, but he was either beyond it or else the role was much too low for him, for although 'he played well and sang with talent it was to be regretted that his voice did not possess more force and timbre.

*

Not to be confused with the bass Eugène Bataille who created Lothario in *Mignon* at the Opéra Comique in 1866.

There were a number of low passages which could hardly be heard and which did not make their effect.'[56]

Mlle Nelly, evidently a pianist as well as a comedy actress, for she played the piano part of the Gounod-Bach 'Méditation', had been the beneficiary of a concert given at the Théâtre Lyrique on 15 April. She was supported (though in the circumstances supported is hardly an appropriate term) by Tamberlik, who repeated his *Guillaume Tell* trio with Meillet and Battaille, as well as by the sopranos Mmes Frezzolini, Carvalho and Ugalde, the dancer Amalia Ferraris, the actor Bressant and the actress Mme Arnould-Plessy who performed a short evanescent play.[57] If fees to her 'supporters' were not too high, Mlle Nelly should have made a profit, for the gross receipts of her benefit came to Fr 13,407.50.[58]

Miolan-Carvalho took her benefit on 24 May. Stalls cost 30 francs, boxes 150 and 200 francs, but all were taken up. Not only did the Théâtre Lyrique orchestra take part, but the orchestra of the Opéra was at hand as well. Félicien David was one of the conductors. Duprez was present to sing Act 4 of *Otello* with Pauline Viardot and a scene from *La Juive* with Miolan-Carvalho. Miolan-Carvalho then joined Ugalde to sing the waltz from *Faust*, generously arranged for the occasion by Gounod. Next, each sang her incontestable 'Carnival of Venice' and *Galathée* airs. Both were encored. The tenor Gueymard and Caroline Barbot from the Opéra sang the great Act 4 duet from *Les Huguenots*, and Amalia Ferraris, also from the Opéra, danced. The Gounod-Bach 'Méditation' was again heard, this time with Vieuxtemps playing the violin solo. The evening ended or more correctly the morning ended, for once more it was 2 a.m., with Niccolò Isouard's *Les Rendez-vous bourgeois*. A distinguished audience had included Prince Jerome and the singers Roger and Borghi-Mamo[59] and the concert's receipts came to exactly Fr 18,703.50.[60] A newspaper report a week later stating that they had reached Fr 24,000[61] suggests that all such reports, including reports of figures earlier quoted, must be accepted with caution and perhaps disbelief.

Word was again circulating about Carvalho's retirement, with Emile Perrin now announced to replace him, but once more the news was denied.[62] Later news which was affirmed was that both the Opéra and the Théâtre Italien were trying to engage

Miolan-Carvalho and—of even greater concern to M. Carvalho—
(since presumably he could contend with his wife's affairs) that
the Opéra was seriously trying to engage his principal tenor
Michot.[63] In this the Opéra was not being just gratuitously
predatory. Alphonse Royer, the Opéra's director, also needed a
principal tenor, for his renowned Roger had lately lost his right
arm in a shooting accident. Carvalho naturally fought to retain
his singer, protesting to the Minister of State that it would be
impossible for him to open his theatre for the forthcoming
season if he were to be deprived of the tenor who sang all the
principal roles there.[64] So a compromise was reached. Michot
would remain at the Théâtre Lyrique until the end of the year (it
seems that he had earlier signed such a contract) after which he
would join the Opéra. In turn he would be replaced by
Delaunay-Ricquier from the Opéra Comique.[65]

Since France and Sardinia were now at war with Austria, the
season wound down rather than progressed to a normal close.
Besides, as earlier mentioned, it was an oppressively warm
summer, and in July it would be dolefully announced that, 'our
theatres at the moment are going through a terrible period.'[66]
But it was ideal weather for celebrating victories and, following
the battle of Magenta on 4 June, the Paris theatres were
illuminated for three nights.[67] Then, after Solferino, the Théâtre
Lyrique had a cantata, *La Voie Sacrée*, with words by Raymond
Deslandes and music by Aimé Maillart, sung in celebration.[68]
This was followed two evenings later, on 27 June, with another
'song of victory', this time by Jules Cohen and Mme Louise
Colet, called *L'Armée d'Italie*.[69] Most of the celebrating must
have remained on the boulevards however for, although but-
tressed by performances of *Richard Cœur-de-Lion* and *Le
Médecin malgré lui*, the receipts for the evening came to a paltry
Fr 157.50.[70] Mercifully the theatre would close for the season
three nights later.

During this summer a number of the principal artists
combined with others from the Opéra Comique to bring some
entertaining French opera to Madrid. Ugalde was the star of the
company, Deloffre the conductor.[71] At home a victorious army
returned from Piedmont and Lombardy on 14 August to find
the windows and balconies decorated and the boulevards
crowded to welcome them. Official banquets were held, both on

14 and 15 August, most appropriate to the Emperor's fête day. Verdi attended in a political capacity but left for Busseto immediately afterwards.[72] The proceedings ended with a solemn Te Deum sung at Notre Dame.

Carvalho was meanwhile planning his own campaign, and productions of Gluck's *Orphée* and Gounod's new opera *Philémon et Baucis* were announced for the coming season. He must have found it difficult to remain tranquil when he read the news that the municipality of Marseille had voted a subvention of 160,000 francs for their opera house. As *Le Ménestrel* observed, 'A provincial subvention that would well satisfy our Théâtre Lyrique of Paris.'[73]

1859–1860

The new season opened with a three-act opera comique of little distinction, *Les Petits Violons du Roi* by Deffès, probably staged because of the passable success of his *Broskovano* a year before. The now aging Scribe had a hand in the libretto, which recalled the adventures of the musician Lully while he was employed as cook's helper in the kitchen of Mlle de Montpensier, before becoming director of the orchestra, 'Les Petits Violons', established for him by Louis XIV. Historically it was not especially accurate and dramatically it was described as 'badly cooked'.[1] Deffès' music was said to make some recompense, but not enough to outweigh the weakness of the libretto. The most intriguing fact about the music was that Deffès used an arrangement of 'God save the King', seemingly both in the overture and in the finale of the opera.[2] The production of the opera was thought to be an error on Carvalho's part[3] and its comparatively few performances would confirm this. Indeed its only real success was gained by Mlle Girard who played Lully 'en travesti'.

A one-act work which followed, *Mam'zelle Pénélope* by de Lajarte, an updated version of the Penelope story in which Catherine, the latter day Penelope spends her time knitting a pair of stockings, had even less distinction or success. 'Entre nous,' declared Jules Lovy in *Le Ménestrel*, a very small event.'[4]

At this time a decision was reached to build a new Théâtre

Lyrique. The opening of one of Baron Haussmann's new boulevards required the demolition of the theatres in the boulevard du Temple, and the Paris municipality had decided that two of them should be built elsewhere. These were the Cirque Impérial and the Théâtre Lyrique. The place du Châtelet had been chosen as a suitable site.[5] Situated on the right bank of the Seine, it was a hub traversed by Haussmann's great streets from north to south and from east to west. The municipality had decided to undertake the construction of the two theatres and meanwhile had purchased the present Théâtre Lyrique building for 1,400,000 francs with the intention of demolishing it when the new theatre was ready.[6]

So far the 1859–60 season had presented nothing of importance. Wagner had arrived in Paris during September and was said to be in negotiation with Carvalho[7] [about Tannhäuser] but, as we know, nothing came of it. New singers who had joined the company with Delaunay-Ricquier were Lucien Bourgeois, another tenor, Vanaud, a bass, and the sopranos Moreau, Marimon, Durand and Marie Sax. Much more would be heard of the last artist.

But another singer was about to join the company of whom much had already been heard. Moreover she would join in a production which would enhance even her reputation. She was the famous mezzo soprano Pauline Viardot, younger daughter of Manuel Garcia and sister of Maria Malibran. Born into an artistically accomplished family, she had grown up accordingly, and from childhood had developed an aptitude for languages and for painting. At the age of eight she could play the accompaniments for singing lessons given by her father, and in time became a singer herself, having studied with her parents. She made her first appearance in Brussels in 1837. 12 years later she would create Fidès in Meyerbeer's *Le Prophète* at the Opéra. She married the writer and impresario Louis Viardot in 1841.

It has been said that it was when Carvalho heard Pauline Viardot sing at his wife's benefit concert on the previous 24 May that he first got the idea of staging Gluck's *Orphée*[8]—against all the odds for a commercial success because Viardot had not appeared in opera in Paris for over eight years, not since she had created the name role in Gounod's *Sapho*, an unsuccessful production, and although she was only 39 years old, her voice had for some years shown unmistakable signs of wear. More ominously still, it had 'long been the fashion to talk and think of Gluck as "heavy" and to believe that his works would not bear representing as a whole.'[9]

Carvalho nevertheless went ahead and engaged Berlioz to revise the French version of the score which Gluck had adapted in 1774 for the counter-tenor Legros, and to restore it to the original version sung by the castrato Guadagni in order to suit Viardot's more florid mezzo soprano voice. He also increased the string section of the orchestra and augmented the chorus by 20.[10] The auxiliary choristers were specially released from the Théâtre Italien by the director Calzado. Carvalho had also placed Berlioz in charge of rehearsals, especially rehearsals for Viardot. The settings were as elaborate as they had been for *Faust* and once again were by the same designer-scenepainters, Cambon and Thierry. The choreography for the ballet was by Lucien Petipa. Deloffre conducted.

Staged in this fashion, *Orphée*, to everyone's surprise, became an immediate popular success. Both serious opera-goers and those who visited the theatre for relaxation were equally impressed. Gluck's classical masterpiece had been accepted by the Second Empire. The reviews were stippled with superlatives.

Henry F. Chorley, the London music critic, wrote: 'As personated by Mme Viardot it left nothing to desire. Her want of regularity of feature and of prettiness helped, instead of impairing, the sadness and solemnity of the mourner's countenance; the supple and statuesque grace of her figure gave interest and meaning to every step and every attitude. Yet, after the first scene (which recalled Poussin's well-known picture of "I too in Arcadia") there was not a single effect that might be called a pose or a prepared gesture . . . Further, the peculiar quality of Mme Viardot's voice, its unevenness, its occasional harshness and feebleness, consistent with tones of the gentlest sweetness—was turned by her to account with rare felicity, as giving the variety of light and shade to every word of soliloquy, to every appeal of dialogue. A more perfect and honeyed voice might have recalled the woman too often to fit with the idea of the youth . . . Her bravura at the end of the first act . . . showed the artist to be supreme in another light—in that grandeur of execution belonging to the old school, rapidly becoming a lost

Orphée (Gluck) November 1859 Act 2 Setting by Cambon and Thierry

art. The torrents of roulades, the chains of notes, unmeaning in themselves, were flung out with such exactness, limitless volubility and majesty as to convert what is essentially a commonplace piece of parade into one of those displays of passionate enthusiasm to which nothing less florid could give scope.'[11] There was scarcely a critic who did not echo his words.

Meyerbeer attended the third performance,[12] Prince Jerome the sixth, after which he presented Viardot with 'a magnificent bracelet in antique style, ornamented with two cameos.'[13]

But Pauline Viardot was not the only first class artist taking part. There was also Marie Sax, who had been born and christened in Belgium, Marie Constance Sasse. On the death of her father, a military band-master, she was admitted as a pupil to the Conservatoire of her native Ghent. She appeared first in Brussels and then came to Paris, singing in a number of cafés-concerts, ending at the Café Géant close to the Théâtre Lyrique. There she was heard by Ugalde who gave her some singing lessons and introduced her to Carvalho. She made her debut at the Théâtre Lyrique on 27 September 1859 as the Countess in Les Noces de Figaro. The following review can be taken as representative of her performance.

'Mlle Sax possesses a magnificent voice, but both as a vocalist and as an actress, she is in the state of raw material—material however of undeniable quality and extraordinary aptitude, and which will undoubtedly reward the discoverer ... It is fortunate that Mlle Sax's talents were discovered at an early stage as her voice is still fresh, and she has not been long enough in the exercise of her calling to form any vicious habits.'[14]

Her success was so great that after one season she would be engaged for the Opéra to create Elisabeth in the notorious production of Tannhäuser, a second Elisabeth in Don Carlos and Selika in L'Africaine. Her early assumed name created one extraordinary circumstance. M. Adolphe Sax, that renowned manufacturer of brass instruments, still remembered today for his saxhorn and saxophone who, when not inventing new instruments, seems to have spent his time taking actions against competitors for infringing his patents, brought a case against Marie Sax in 1866 for using his name![15]

Immediately following Orphée's success, there was talk of productions of Armide, Fidelio and Verdi's Macbeth (with the

Italian baritone Varesi), all for Viardot.[16] Of these, *Fidelio* alone reached the stage. *Orphée* would remain in the Théâtre Lyrique repertory for five years. In it Viardot would make her farewell to the opera stage. The new year of 1860 brought a one-act opera comique, *Ma Tante dort*, by Hector Crémieux and Henri Caspers. 'A great deal is expected of this work,' reported *The Musical World*, and so it turned out—'A gay and sparkling little composition.'[17] Berlioz too thought it much more amusing than 'most one-act pieces.'[18] It proved sufficiently amusing for Ugalde, who had enjoyed a great success in it to have it staged at the Opéra Comique when she returned to that theatre in the following autumn.

This was followed by a three-act opera of which a great deal was also expected, for it was Gounod's *Philémon et Baucis*, but it failed to live up to expectations. With Gounod, much the same personnel was involved as in *Faust*—Barbier and Carré as librettists, Cambon and Thierry as designers, Miolan-Carvalho and Balanqué (and Marie Sax) among the singers, yet this time the result never sparkled; it merely fizzled out after 13 indifferent performances.

Originally the work was in two acts and was intended for the Baden-Baden theatre. The plot, taken from La Fontaine, about the descent of the gods Jupiter and Vulcan to earth to assess man's goodness and the restoring of youth to the aged Philémon and Baucis because they were kind, is too thin a tale to be expanded to a three-act opera. The second act was an interpolated orgy scene showing how the other half of Philémon and Baucis' world lived. Elaborately designed after the then celebrated painting 'Romans of the Decadence' by Thomas Couture,[19] it failed to rouse the audience in any fashion. Indeed, the only excitement of the evening seems to have come from a bouquet thrown to Mme Carvalho which caught fire from the footlights but was retrieved by a fireman without causing any damage.[20] Berlioz was about the only critic who had a favourable word for the opera, too favourable, in fact, for he thought it 'one of the most pleasing that [Gounod] had written.'[21] Paul Scudo expressed the opinion that, reduced to two acts, it could become an elegant little chef d'œuvre.[22] Sagely enough this is what was done when Emile Perrin as an ad interim director revived it at

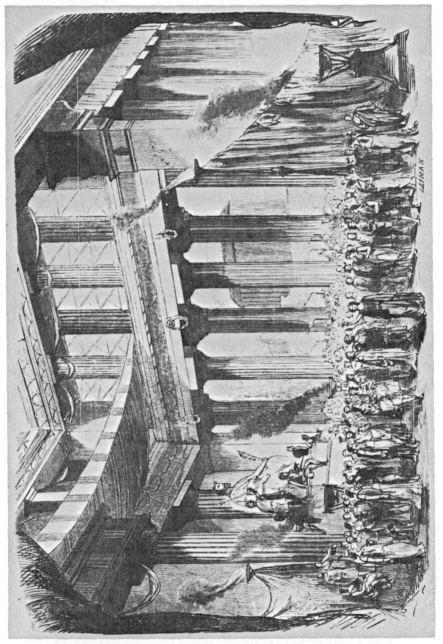

Philémon et Baucis (Gounod) February 1860 Act 2 Setting by Cambon and Thierry

the Opéra Comique in 1876.* There *Philémon et Baucis* remained in the repertory up to 1940, having received 240 performances.

Snippets of opera news continued to appear throughout the season. In March we read: 'Notwithstanding the late gales, the rain and the cold, the theatres have been as full as ever—fuller indeed...'[23] Composers and librettists had collected 59,976 francs in authors' rights from the Théâtre Lyrique during 1859.[24] Both Wallace's *Maritana*[25] and 'a great score on the *Don Juan* of Lord Byron by Massé[26] were promised for the following season but remained unperformed. It was announced that Berlioz' *Les Troyens* would open the new Théâtre Lyrique, which was to be renamed Théâtre Municipal de la Ville de Paris.**[27]

Work had commenced on the new building towards the end of April. M. Bellu 'to whom Paris owes the building of several theatres' had gained the contract to rebuild both the Cirque Impérial and Théâtre Lyrique under the direction of G. Davioud, the city architect. The agreement had lately been signed between Bellu and the Prefect of the Seine, Baron Haussmann. The contract price was 4,300,000 francs, and Bellu had undertaken to have the work finished within 18 months from the day on which he was given possession of the ground, not only the exterior 'but in a state perfectly fit to enter.'[28] Davioud was doing serious work on the acoustics. He also had a surprise in store, a luminous ceiling to take the place of the traditional inconvenient chandelier. The heating and ventilation systems would be the very latest.[29]

Miolan-Carvalho's widowed mother died during March,[30] which permitted the suspension of performances of *Philémon et Baucis.* Instead, the audience could look forward to Pauline Viardot's benefit performance, which would be held on 20 April. The programme ranged from Octave Feuillet's play *Le Cheveu*

---

*

Diaghilev revived the opera without success at Monte Carlo in 1924. Because he detested spoken dialogue, he had Georges Auric compose recitatives, as he had earlier asked Erik Satie to compose recitatives for *Le Médecin malgré lui.*

**

Today, almost identically named, Théâtre de la Ville.

Blanc performed by Rose Cheri and Dupuis, and a pas seul from *La Sylphide* danced by Emma Livry, to excerpts from *Armide* and *Macbeth,* including the sleep-walking scene sung by Viardot, joined by Sax in *Armide* and Francesco Graziani in *Macbeth.*[31] In view of the late hour at which these concerts were ending, there may be some significance in an announcement published just before that all Paris theatres were obliged to close by midnight 'under penalty of a fine.'[32]

The final production before the season ended was *Gil Blas,* another libretto by Barbier and Carré, the music by Semet. The plot consisted of five scenes from Alain René Le Sage's novel, *Gil Blas de Santillane,* and it was described as 'a comic opera in five acts, a thing almost unheard of, Mozart being nearly the only one who had ever brought out one so long.'[33] It seems to have been at least two acts too long, for, as Joseph d'Ortigue summed up in the *Journal des Débats:* 'Semet is a knowledgeable musician, he has the knack, the finesse, he understands the stage, but there is twice too much music in his opera and nothing is more difficult to sustain than a light style.'[34] The show in fact was carried by Mme Ugalde as Gil Blas (travesti parts appear to have been fashionable just then) and, we read, she 'fills the role of the hero to the great delight of the public, for whatever charm may now and then be found wanting in her voice she supplies by her animated acting... nothing is equal to the song she sings before the door of the inn where the villagers are feasting, accompanying herself with a mandoline. He is expressing the hunger he feels, and when they will not listen to him he changes his tone to diabolical menaces. The air was rapturously encored.'[35] Not only was it encored, but it became a mainstay of barrel organs for the next two or three years.[36] What more popular acclaim could Semet wish for?

On 1 April 1860, long threatening, as the saying goes, the moment came at last when Léon Carvalho resigned as director of the Théâtre Lyrique. The failure of *Philémon et Baucis* had probably provoked the final crisis. He was replaced by Charles Réty who some years earlier had joined him as secretary-general. Réty in turn was now replaced by the dramatist Philippe Gille.[37] The Théâtre Lyrique artists honoured Carvalho with a banquet and afterwards presented him with a splendid 'souvenir'. A letter of address was also read—'Sir and dear

Gil Blas (Semet) March 1860 Act 1

comrade. We will never forget your indefatigable efforts to make the Théâtre Lyrique a refuge for serious artists and illustrious authors . . .' etc![38]

He then left with Mme Carvalho for London where she was opening the Covent Garden season in *Dinorah* on 10 April. His resignation was certainly a financial gain, for Miolan-Carvalho was in effect subsidising the Théâtre Lyrique whereas, singing in other opera houses, she commanded high fees.

Léon Carvalho was unquestionably in financial straits at the time, as the following press announcement makes clear. 'All is not roses in the profession of director of the Théâtre Lyrique,' it reports, 'and we have been much surprised to learn that M. Carvalho whom we supposed to be well in credit has instead an overdraft of 250,000 francs. It is true that he has assets estimated at 400,000 francs, but the first 100,000 francs paid over to him by M. Réty's "backer" was in the form of eighty-five 1,000 franc promissory notes. The balance of 15,000 francs was in gold. M. Réty's "backer" is making certain that his first payment will not also be his last, especially if Mme Miolan [Carvalho], as we are given to understand, is unlikely to remain a member of the new director's company.'[39]

There is no doubt that Carvalho's extravagant productions caused his downfall, but where is an unfortunate impresario to draw the line? If he cuts back financially, it shows artistically. The critics comment and the audience stay away. Alternatively, if he overspends in order to attract an audience, he is patronisingly censured when the inevitable crash occurs. It is an exercise in the law of diminishing returns, and the impresario rarely wins.

So it was with Carvalho who, following his resignation, was described as 'nothing more than a simple national guard.' The article continues, 'M. Charles Réty has secured possession of the Théâtre Lyrique. M. Carvalho's post as director has not made him rich. [Artistically] he has had a great success but he indulges himself in his productions. When M. Carvalho is preparing a new opera he calls on all the artist painters, designers and decorators, assembles gunsmiths, silk and velvet merchants, bead embroiderers, the lot. Eagerly he orders the richest fabrics and these he unrolls in his office so as to admire them. The costumier is given carte blanche. [Carvalho] resolves to do better than all his colleagues and, what is more, he does.

Thus, the cost of the soldiers in *Faust* was insane . . . The decor of the garden scene was truly a chef d' œuvre. The costumes for the opera were remade five times [and] for the Walpurgisnacht scene M. Carvalho called upon the imagination of M. G [ustave] Doré . . . *Faust* was a magnificent production, but M. Carvalho had spent 150,000 francs on it, that is to say 120,000 francs too much.'[40]

With Miolan-Carvalho gone from the company, Réty was left somewhat low in vocal quality. Fortunately he would have Ugalde until the end of the season and Viardot both in *Orphée* and in a production of *Fidelio* which Carvalho had been rehearsing. This would give him time to organise his 1860-61 programme. He was also benefiting greatly from the fact that shortly before Carvalho's resignation the privilege of the theatre, due to expire in 1861, had been extended to February 1867.[41] This would mean both a guaranteed seven-year term of office—if he wished to retain it—and also a lease of the splendid new Théâtre Lyrique when it was completed. So Réty for the present had little cause for complaint.

So too, it seemed, had the city of Paris, or at least that select part of it which centred on the Tuileries. Regrettably the weather even in mid-April had remained 'atrocious—snow, hail, wind and rain.' 'But,' we are assured, 'bad weather here never hinders gaiety; and as the time to leave Paris approaches, the fever grows fast and furious. Suppers, quite in the English style, are the fashion now. The other night a ball was given at the Marquis d'Aligre's, and dancing was prolonged all night: two suppers took place, and the guests departed at eight o'clock in the morning. That beats England. The grand ball, that has been as much talked of as a state affair, has come off, and nothing now remains but the brilliant recollection. The Empress did not wear her much-talked-of costume of Diana, but was in a domino. The great affair of the evening was the quadrille of the "Elements", composed of 16 of the greatest ladies of the court and court society, with a beautiful Polish lady as the goddess of the earth. But what fairy pen can describe the scarlet and gold and diamonds of fire; the ethereal blue of air (in which element Mme de Morny appeared), the pale translucent green and silver of water—the fruits and flowers of earth, whose fair represent-atives, more wonderful than Atlas, bore the globe on their heads.

They performed a fancy quadrille with, of course, the grace and charm only great ladies can ... Imagine, however, all that is fairy-like, all that taste could devise or money procure, in the decorations of the room, the wondrous costumes of all nations and ages, animated butterflies, Spanish flies, etc., and you will have a faint view of the fancy ball.'[42]

A French artist named Henri Baron imagined such a scene. Seven years later he would paint it and give it the title, 'Fête officielle du Palais des Tuileries'.

Chapter 4

Charles Réty takes over 1860–1862

1860 continued

Charles Réty was born about 1826 and had at first studied to become a composer, but early in his career had changed from composition to criticism. He was a member of the theatrical press when he first joined the Théâtre Lyrique as secretary-general in March 1856.[1] For a quarter of a century until his death in 1895, he was to be music critic of *Le Figaro*, signing his articles with the pseudonym Charles Darcours.[2] His period as director of the Théâtre Lyrique would be neither very long nor very distinguished.

He entered into his engagement there with the advantage of having another classic already in rehearsal under Carvalho, Beethoven's *Fidelio*, and with Viardot again playing the leading role. This opera had had earlier performances in Paris, both in German and Italian, but two French versions which had been prepared, one for the Odéon in 1826, were never staged, perhaps for political reasons. The present version had been translated by Barbier and Carré, who had 'enriched the dialogue in some details and given other names to the principal characters.'[3] They had in fact given the opera an entirely new setting, transferring the action to the plottings of the Sforza family in Milan at the end of the 15th century. So, in turn, Leonore became Isabella of Aragon; Florestan became Gian Galeazzo Sforza, her husband; Pizarro became Ludovico Sforza, his uncle; and Don Fernando became Charles VIII of France.

Berlioz states that this was Carvalho's idea in order to have the finale end in 'costumes less sombre than those of the original opera.'[4] This change may have improved the decorative appearance of the artists, but as Léon Durocher astutely remarked, 'One will go to the Théâtre Lyrique to hear Beethoven's music but not to see metres of silk and velvet.'[5] Apart from this alteration of place and period, Beethoven's score appears to have been left relatively untouched. The opera was produced in three acts, and there was some interchanging of music from its normal position. The short duet, 'Jetzt, Alter' sung by Pizarro and Rocco was omitted, and a duet for Leonore and Marcelline from the 1805 version of the work included instead. Regretfully it must be said that, great as Viardot's success had been in *Orphée*, equally great was her failure in *Fidelio*. As reviews of her *Orphée* have revealed, her voice was by no means an unblemished instrument, but quite apart from this, she seems to have been utterly incapable of sustaining Leonore. 'The role is generally too high for her voice, and it imposes painful efforts . . . this new creation will add nothing to her glory.'[6] She had 'to contend with a role which was much too high for her . . . [but] to what heights of virtuosity did she raise the magnificent air in act two, ending it with an appoggiatura of unparalleled audacity on the final high B.'[7] These are two examples of the general opinion of her performance. The spoken dialogue too seems to have given her trouble and her inability to overcome the difficulty caused embarrassment to her audience.[8]

The remainder of the cast was no better. Guardi, making another appearance following his two failures in *Faust*, is recorded by Durocher as having 'a ringing and sympathetic voice' but, he adds, 'he will be more consistently agreeable when he has learned to overcome the quavering which too often mars it.'[9] Durocher also thought that Serène and Amélie Faivre were inadequate.[10] Battaille alone was satisfactory in the role of Rocco, 'which he played with spirit and sang with good volume.'[11]

The best that could be claimed for the production was that it had been received respectfully but coldly. (By a fascinating coincidence, when the opera was originally performed in Vienna, the then indifferent Theater an der Wien audience consisted almost entirely of French officers in the army of Napoleon I, who had lately occupied the city.) Berlioz summarises the situation when he asks rhetorically, 'Can [this] performance

Fidelio (Beethoven) May 1860 Act 3.

of *Fidelio* be praised unreservedly? Undoubtedly, no, but it is better than one has the right to expect from a theatre so little encouraged and with such modest resources. Aided entirely by the public, it has done more in the past two years for the true interests of art than all our other opera houses together . . . The young director M. Réty is motivated by the best intentions, he is a musician, he knows the theatre, with the smallest support, sustained by the most miserable subvention, brave as well as prudent as he is, he will do wonders.'[12]

Nevertheless a weakness existed in the new director which *The Musical World* was quick to detect. 'Unluckily, however,' it reports, 'with M. Carvalho has departed the prestige of the establishment, which bids fair to sink once more into the position of mediocrity from which that gentleman with indomitable spirit and eminent ability delivered it. Had *Fidelio* been brought out at the Théâtre Lyrique while he was manager, success—nay, triumph—would have been a matter of certainty; but he having seceded, that sudden rage for the classical repertory which seized the Parisians some time since, and with which they themselves were even more astonished than their neighbours, has abated.'[13]

Réty's real problem probably lay in the fact that 'the public had been spoilt under the previous direction and had become accustomed to high standards of performance combined with costly staging. It had now become absolutely necessary to reduce the costs of the enterprise.'[14] In other words, lacking a subvention, the public was now getting no more than it was paying for.

Early in June it was announced that the *Fidelio* performances had ended, due to the compulsory departure of both Viardot and Battaille,[15] but unquestionably it was the audience and not the artists who had left.

The dismal scene was partially brightened by Mme Ugalde's benefit concert which took place on 14 May and which was a benefit to end all! It included Adelaide Ristori in a scene from Schiller's *Maria Stuarda*, Boieldieu's opera *Les Voitures versées*, Viardot and Sax in the last act of *Orphée*, Ugalde herself in scenes from *Le Toréador* and *Gil Blas* and, as a final principal feature, the Gounod-Bach 'Ave Maria' sung by Ugalde, accom-

panied on the piano by Massé, on the violin by the young
Sarasate, and on the organ by Gounod.[16]
Having failed with his revival of a classic, Réty now sought to
complete his first partial season by introducing a few superficial
works, mostly in one act. It is significant that the first of these,
Les Valets de Gascogne, had Philippe Gille, the theatre's new
secretary-general, for librettist and his brother-in-law, Alfred
Dufresne, as composer. Of the two, Dufresne's music was
said 'to have received the better welcome.'[17]
This was followed a few days later by a revival of Hérold's
early opera *Les Rosières,* first performed at the Opéra Comique
in 1817 and now rehearsed and staged in 15 days to fill the gap
left by the unsuccessful *Fidelio.*[18] *Les Rosières* was in Hérold's
early style, showing the influence of his teacher Méhul and
differing considerably from his later operas such as *Zampa.* Its
revival was well received, and it and *Les Valets de Gascogne* each
had about 30 performances.
This however did not allay apprehension for the theatre's
future, for we read, 'With these two works and *Orphée* for which
the vogue still continues, the Théâtre Lyrique will gently pass
the month of June and console itself for the succès d'estime of
Fidelio. It is certain that a non-subventioned theatre cannot live
on a succès d'estime.'[19] It was during mid-June that—'At the
command of the authorities all the theatres in Paris broke
out . . . into lyrical ecstasies of patriotic enthusiasm at the
annexation of Savoy and Nice.'[20] The Théâtre Lyrique did its
part on 14 June with a cantata, *France, Nice and Savoie,* sung by
Guardi, Raynal and chorus.[21]
One other work was staged before the season ended, an 'opéra
de salon' which was furtively slipped on to the playbill on
Sunday evening, 17 June. Sunday was so unusual a day for a first
performance that it created a sense of mystery and intrigue
exceeding any interest in the work itself— *Maître Palma*—a
fantasy of renaissance Venice. The composer was an unknown
Mlle Rivay (Gille was one of the librettists) and the opera was
performed three times only, although it was reported by Jules
Lovy as being 'musically worthy of a better fate than that which
it received.'[22]
Consequently it was like a ship that had been buffeted by
winds while sailing in shallow waters that Réty eventually

piloted to reach the safety and seclusion of the end of his first season on 30 June. The theatre closed with performances of *Les Valets de Gascogne* and *Orphée*, but opened again unofficially on 4 July with a benefit concert for M. Quinchez, a stage manager and singer. The same programme was repeated, with an added interlude in which Mme Ugalde, Mlle Faivre and MM Balanqué and Ribes took part.[23]

Réty then spent his summer, as Carvalho had previously done, engaging new singers and commissioning new operas, although the published announcements suggest that in both pursuits he lacked his colleague's flair. Even before the theatre was closed in June, he was auditioning choristers.[24] If the fees they received were comparable to those paid by the Opéra, they certainly were not lavish, for the yearly salary of most Opéra choristers was then a miserable 800 francs.[25] There were also places vacant in the company for two virtuoses d'élite—a violin and violoncello soloist.[26]

New solo singers whom he engaged were Mlles Blanche Baretti, Roziès, Durand, Orwil or Oprawil (the name is spelled both ways; she was a German and protegée of Viardot)—sopranos; Ida Gilliess, mezzo-soprano (a Scottish girl, she would sing with the Royal English Opera in their 1865–66 season at Covent Garden); Mme Zevaco; MM Verdelet, Laveissière, Peschard, tenors; M. Petit, baritone.

It was advertised that Miolan-Carvalho was returning to sing in *Faust* and *Philémon et Baucis*,[27] but this expectation did not materialise. Viardot however did remain with the company, and at her former fee of 3000 francs a month. She was announced to appear in *Orphée* and in another Gluck opera, 'either *Alceste* or *Iphigénie*.'[28]* Among a number of new operas commissioned was a five-act opera comique for which the music of each act would be composed by a different young composer![29]

About this time they were having difficulties at the Opéra with the 'normal diapason' which had recently been introduced there. We learn that it was 'especially obnoxious to the bass singers. The "pif-paf", for instance, is, with the new pitch, in

*

en Aulide or *en Tauride?* The announcement does not say. Neither opera was performed during this season.

some parts beyond the range of any but the most exceptional voices. The character of the music is also considerably modified by the change, and in some instances, as for example, the air of the "Couvre Feu", loses not a little of its original colour'.[30]* At the new Théâtre Lyrique, the diapason for the moment was confined to the sound of workmen's tools. Progress was reported from time to time. By July the building had reached ground level;[31] by August it was approaching the level of the first floor, and it could be seen that the ground floor was arcaded in the same style as the Odéon.[32] Then, three weeks later M. Bellu announced a delay in construction. The new Théâtre Lyrique would not now be ready until 25 September 1861.[33]

A more immediate problem for Réty was a particularly aggressive claque which had taken control of performances to the annoyance of most of the audience. Claques were endemic in Paris theatres as they were and as they still remain in theatres throughout the Continent, although in most Paris theatres they at least exercised a decent restraint. But at the Théâtre Lyrique, we read, 'the claque is three times, six times, perhaps ten times more numerous than elsewhere, because there it is recruited from unemployed choristers, obliging amateur choral singers and that formidable cohort of vocal enthusiasts who are only too happy to pay by overindulgent applause to satisfy their own domineering taste. We would hope that the new direction will suppress this abuse . . . [for] if this state of affairs continues, the real public, the independent public will be obliged to [go elsewhere].'[34]

With this question to be considered, undoubtedly only one of many, Réty approached his first full season at the Théâtre Lyrique.

---

*

In Paris, in less than a century, the diapason had risen as follows:

1784	*Richard Cœur-de-Lion*	A equalled 820 cycles per second
1807	*La Vestale*	A equalled 848 cycles per second
1829	*Guillaume Tell*	A equalled 860 cycles per second
1831	*Robert le Diable*	A equalled 865 cycles per second
1859	*Faust*	A equalled 896 cycles per second

1860–1861

It began on 1 September with two new operas, a two-act work, *Crispin rival de son maître*, with music by Adolphe Sellenick, described as a 'brave soldier' (from the recent Italian campaign) and 'military bandmaster',[1] preceded by a curtain-raiser, *L'Auberge des Ardennes*, by Hignard. Hignard's collaborators were Carré and Jules Verne. He was said to have deserved 'a more substantial libretto', nor was he helped by 'two unsuccessful debutants'[2], Durand and Verdelet.

The libretto of *Crispin rival de son maître* was based on Le Sage's comedy, but Sellenick's music seems to have added little to the play. One reads of 'inexperience' and 'tentative gropings'. The cast was mediocre and Amélie Faivre in the leading female role was admonished that 'to scream is not to sing.'[3]

A dispute had arisen between Réty and the composer Ernest Reyer. Reyer had written an opera to a three-act libretto by Barbier and Carré which had been accepted by Léon Carvalho to open the present season. On assuming management, Réty had sought permission to have its production postponed until December, to which the three authors had agreed. However, on the pretext of having to make new arrangements, Réty then tried to have the production further postponed *sine die*, to which the authors naturally objected. They threatened legal action, but the Society of Authors stepped in, with the result that the matter was amicably arranged, and it was announced that the work would shortly appear on the stage.[4] It speaks badly for Réty's judgement that he should have hesitated to stage it, for the opera was *La Statue*, the second most successful creation he would present during his time at the Théâtre Lyrique.

A benefit performance in aid of the Association des Artistes Musiciens was presented on 6 October. The programme consisted of a play from the Gymnase, *La Partie de Piquet*, a military band interlude and *Les Rosières*—somewhat poor fare for so worthy a cause.

Then came a revival of a well known opera comique, *Le Val d'Andorre*, by de Saint-Georges and Halévy. Réty had been lucky to obtain this work from the Opéra Comique. Agreement had been reached with Nestor Roqueplan, who had then resigned from the theatre, and although the present director, Beaumont, wished to rescind it, he felt honour bound to respect an arrangement reached by his predecessor.[5] It would turn out to be the first genuine success among very few that Réty would enjoy. There were several reasons for this. Firstly, the opera had won considerable success when first produced in 1848. Secondly, Battaille, the original performer in the important role of Jacques Sincère, was now a member of the Théâtre Lyrique, and furthermore Réty had made a determined if not entirely successful effort to improve the standard of his casting. On paper it seemed admirable, for with Battaille there was also M. and Mme Meillet and Monjauze, all of whom had been induced to return to the Théâtre Lyrique.

The mise en scène was described as 'splendid', the costumes 'rich', and chorus and orchestra under Deloffre were unreservedly praised.[6] In passing it may be noted that by now the new 'normal diapason' had been introduced at the theatre.

Where the principal artists were concerned, time however had brought change. Mme Meillet's singing was no longer entirely in favour, while her approach to the role was considered provincial. (She had just returned from an engagement in Marseille.) Above all she was sharply criticised for wearing a blonde wig. Monjauze seems to have been received more kindly although he had retained his 'white and barking' voice and had put on weight, 'which was a compliment to Belgian cuisine.' M. Meillet acquitted himself well. 'Martin of old* could not have done better.'[7] Battaille, 'not long since the king of this feast, gloriously retained his crown.' The revival consequently won 'a fresh baptism of success in its new adopted land ... and the child of Saint-Georges and Halévy was joyfully acclaimed by all the echos of the boulevard du Temple.'[8]

Viardot had returned to Paris, and so some performances of *Orphée* were given, commencing on 5 November. Mlle Orwil sang Eurydice. So successful was the revival, which alternated with the equally successful *Le Val d'Andorre*, that a new opera

---

*

Jean-Blaise Martin (1768–1837). A famous baritone with a very high range whose name is now used to describe the high French baritone voice.

of Maillart's was temporarily deferred. It was also announced that the Théâtre Lyrique had received word that some unknown person was holding 50,000 francs to enable *Les Troyens* to be staged worthily when it opened the new theatre.[9]

In November Achille Fould resigned as Minister of State, and since the Ministry of the Emperor's Household had been abolished, Count Walewski, the new Minister of State, was now given control of all the Imperial Theatres—but these did not include the Théâtre Lyrique.[10] He was assisted by Count Baciocchi, the Emperor's Master of Ceremonies, who was appointed superintendent on 8 December 1860.[11]

When Maillart's opera comique, *Les Pêcheurs de Catane*, eventually did reach the stage on 17 December, it turned out to be a complete disappointment. A number of critics had discovered a similarity between the plot and a story by Lamartine called *Graziella*, but Léon Durocher indignantly refuted the suggestion. 'It is not so, thank God!' he righteously declared, 'The virginal dress of Graziella has not been rumpled by the rough hand of modern opera comique.'[12] More damaging, Maillart's score was considered repetitious of his earlier works. One feature only was unequivocally admired—the decors, especially the second act setting which represented the Ionian Sea bordered by high Sicilian cliffs shimmering in moonlight while fishermen arrived in their barques with flaming torches. Even Berlioz mentions this scene and relates that during it 'one hears a charming muted violin solo played by M. Lenoir, the first violin soloist.'[13] Mlle Baretti, making her debut, had taken over the role of Nella originally intended for Miolan-Carvalho, who was then singing at the opera house in Nantes.

The production at least permitted Paul Scudo to mount a full-scale attack on opera in general as then produced in Paris. He writes: 'Every time one attends the first performance of a lyric work, one is surprised and asks oneself, how is it possible that such an absurd fable as that being unfolded can have been accepted, first by the composer, then by the director, and then by the 30 or 40 people who take part in the production. One leaves the theatre weighed down by boredom and perplexed by all the absurdities and twaddle that the Paris public must endure. Then, eight days later, you see another play with music which makes your head swim, and you are plunged deeper into the domain of stupidity and effrontery. I do not think that anyone could imagine anything more inane, more monotonous and more hackneyed than the libretto of *Les Pêcheurs de Catane*... After a succession of scenes, some more trivial than others, Nella, who learns that Fernand intends to marry his cousin Carmen, becomes mad and slowly expires before the eyes of a public fatigued from all the clichés which have been around the theatres for the past 30 years. It is *Lucia*, it is *Muette* [*de Portici*]. It is all that one can expect— the inevitable drinking chorus, the ballad, the mysterious apparitions, the ballerinas and the 'tableaux vivants', derived from old engravings depicting the merriment of people from southern countries in the last century...'[14] From our knowledge it cannot be gainsaid that Scudo was basically right but, as we also know, Réty was scarcely the man to alter the situation.

The year ended bleakly. Performances were being poorly attended, and the young baritone Cibot, aged only 26, who had sung Wagner in the first performances of *Faust*, died after only three days' illness.[15] The only stimulating news was that rehearsals for *Les Ruines de Balbeck* [*La Statue*] had commenced in the foyer of the theatre and that the decors for the opera would be by Cambon, Thierry, Nolau and Rubé, based on photographs brought back from Baalbek itself by the French writer Maxime Du Camp.[16]

Neither did the new year bring anything of significance into the repertory, at least not during the first two months. A one-act work, *La Madone*, by Louis Lacombe, which had been promised for years, at last reached the stage. The libretto by Carmouche was said to be 'absurd even beyond the wide limits of toleration allowed to operatic writers.' It was a very slight story of a young girl who is sitting as an artist's model for a portrait of the Madonna and who has a jealous lover. But the affair is quite innocent, and all ends happily. 'M. Lacombe's music is a fit match for this ridiculously empty nonsense...' reported *The Musical World*; he 'has evidently no other vocation than that he has previously proved to the world, the perpetration of unendurable symphonies and crabbed digital performances on the pianoforte. Let him adhere to it.'[17] He did however introduce one novelty into his composition; spoken dialogue was accentuated by an instrumental continuo as later used so effectively by Massenet in *Manon.*[18]

A second one-act opera comique which followed soon after received more performances but no greater critical acclaim. It was *Astaroth* by Boisseaux and Debillemont, and had previously been performed at Dijon, the birth place of both librettist and composer. 'Abominably stupid' is how *The Musical World* describes the libretto, 'all about a drunkard who has a bad dream, in which the foul fiend appears to him, and he is so frightened that he gets up not only sober, but a model of temperance and teetotalism. The composer who has had to find fitting strains for this would not be much advantaged by the mention of his name.'[19]

A great deal had been expected from a three-act work composed by Clapisson, with which it was hoped to repeat the success of *La Fanchonnette.* Almost up to production time it was intended to call it *La Nuit de Mardi Gras,* but ultimately it came out as *Madame Grégoire.* It was said to have been the last libretto in which Eugène Scribe had taken a hand, and although it concerned the romantic adventures of Mme Pompadour, a subject familiar to the audience, the complexities of the plot made it extremely difficult to follow. The critics at best were ambivalent—Clapisson's established position no doubt protected him—though Berlioz would declare it 'an important work' and 'one of the best to come from the composer's pen.'[20] The public was more forthright; it allowed *Madame Grégoire* just 17 performances.

This continued lack of success must have been disheartening for Réty, and indeed shortly after the production of this opera, we read of the 'Théâtre Lyrique which we should like to see escape the crisis which threatens its fragile existence.'[21] Actually, at the time word was again circulating that the theatre was to receive a subvention of 200,000 francs, [22] but it never came during Réty's management.

Matters improved slightly with the next production, another curtain raiser called *Les Deux Cadis,* composed by Théodore Ymbert. The libretto, again partly written by Philippe Gille was, as the title indicates, about two rascally cadis, magistrates by day and highwaymen by night. Berlioz found the music to be better written than was customary with minor works at the Théâtre Lyrique.[23]

The next opera to be performed would be Reyer's *La Statue*, Réty's only production of any lasting importance during his two years at the Théâtre Lyrique. It was acclaimed by both critics and audience alike. 'The mise en scène,' Lovy assures us, 'has splendour which attests to the importance which the Théâtre Lyrique direction gives to this work. The settings of the ruins of Baalbek and of the underground palace are amazing.'[24] Reyer was unreservedly praised for his music. 'It cannot be denied,' writes Durocher, 'that this remarkable young composer who hates what is commonplace, possesses elegance, harmonic invention and a great capacity for combining instruments. His scoring is done with extreme care, full of varied, unexpected and piquant effects. He is of the school of "musiciens coloristes" and one will find few who have a richer palette. His master is Weber. One recognises this immediately, and since one must tell all, at times one discerns the master a little too much. In short, he is one of today's musicians in whom one can place the greatest confidence.'[25]

That both Reyer and his librettists, the redoubtable Barbier and Carré, were also satisfied, is indicated by a report that on the evening of the first performance, Deloffre found on his desk a conductor's baton on which the following inscription was engraved: 'Théâtre Lyrique—the authors of *La Statue* to M. Deloffre.' Then, to endorse the opera's success, Choudens acquired the publication rights of the score 'on very favourable terms for the young and brilliant composer.'[26]

This one swallow failed to make Réty's summer, however. Moreover he was suffering the minor setbacks which are a way of life in all opera houses. In January, Simon Libert, his chorus master and assistant conductor, had died.[27] In March, Viardot had raised her fee from 3000 to 4000 francs a month, provoking the comment from *Le Figaro*, 'little enough for the tragedienne, but a great deal for the singer.'[28]

Le Figaro also announced that Réty was about to enter into agreement with Richard Wagner (lately in Paris for the production of *Tannhäuser* at the Opéra) for performances at the Théâtre Lyrique of *Lohengrin, Rienzi*, and *'Iseult'*. One cannot be sure if the news is to be taken seriously, for the writer continues, 'I do

La Statue (Reyer) 1861 Act 2

not know if it is a good idea, but at least it is original... *Le Figaro* is offering a prize of 500 francs for the invention of a whistle rayé [29] [to be used at the performances].'

Two other one-act works performed in May were the only new productions for the remainder of the season. The first was *Au travers du Mur* by de Saint-Georges and Poniatowski. Anyone who remembers the Victorian ballad, 'The Yeoman's Wedding Song', will know Prince Joseph Poniatowski—Italian by origin, birth and upbringing, (though the family had been long established in Poland) French by antecedents (his uncle was created a marshal by Napoleon I) and by his position as senator of the Second Empire. Poniatowski was both socially prominent and wealthy, yet he composed too fluently, even though he lacked individuality, to be dismissed as a rich amateur. He was also a singer. Berlioz states, 'He had moreover been gifted with one of the most entrancing tenor voices that I have ever heard.' [30] His brother Charles and Charles' wife Elisa were also singers, and when his early opera *Giovanni da Procida* was performed privately in Lucca in 1838, all three took part. [31] (Elisa and Charles are also recorded as having sung Lucrezia and Don Alfonso in Donizetti's *Lucrezia Borgia* at Livorno in 1832.) Poniatowski also maintained a private theatre in Florence where, in April 1839, a company of amateurs performed Méhul's *Une Folie*, Boieldieu's *La Fête du Village voisin* and Halévy's *L'Eclair*. [32]

His best known if scarcely remembered operas are *Don Desiderio* (Pisa, 1840), *Pierre de Medicis* (Opéra, 1860) and *Gelmina*—written for Patti—(Covent Garden, 1872). Poniatowski, as a prince, was of course aware of the antagonism towards him as a composer, and in a letter to Verdi, who was friendly with him, he complains of 'deep-rooted prejudice that, because I am a prince, it follows that I must be a blockhead.' [33] Not that this prejudice was entirely unwarranted. It is related how he once took two of his operas to play over to Rossini so that the maestro might advise him which should be staged first. Having played through the first score he was about to start on the second when Rossini who had dozed off, suddenly woke up and touched him gently to stop him. 'It is not necessary, mon cher,' he advised, 'stage the other.' [34]

Au travers du Mur was greeted with the same ambivalence.

Critical opinion fluctuated between the complimentary 'Very lively and amusing... easy, natural and without pretension'[35] of Paul Scudo, to a damning 'The subject seems to have been selected to prove the truth of the saying, "The weakest goes to the wall" for a very weak and commonplace vapid and villainous affair it is.'[36] 'Some people say I should admire such twaddle if I had not been previously informed it was by a prince, but they are mistaken. I should require no such previous information; for I should know only a prince could write such twaddle—and get it played.'[37]

The opera had been presented as part of a benefit for Battaille (he played the leading role) who was leaving the Théâtre Lyrique to return to the Opéra Comique. The rest of the programme consisted of Act 3 of *Armide* with Viardot and Orwil (as La Haine), and Act 3 of *La Sonnambula* with Vandenheuvel-Duprez as Amina. In *Armide* the chorus was either too small or insufficiently rehearsed, but J.L. Heugel comments, 'If the Théâtre Lyrique encouraged by this attempt, brings back *Armide* to the stage as it has done with *Orphée*, nothing will be left undone to assist Mme Viardot, who remains sublime in Gluck.'[38] The three principal singers shared the honours of the evening, 'which would have been more profitable if seat prices had not been increased so much.'[39]

The last new work before the season ended was included in another benefit performance, this time for Viardot. It was *Le Buisson vert* by Léon Gastinel. Lasalle states that the librettist's name Fonteille was a pseudonym of Michel Carré.[40] The title, which was the name of an inn, had little bearing on the plot, which was set in Stockholm during the time of Gustavus III and the poet and song composer, Carl Michael Bellman. The story had no historical basis, but Jules Lovy described the music as having been 'written with talent and conscience, the two dominant qualities of the composer.'[41] The programme also contained fragments from Acts, 2, 3 and 4 of *Alceste* with Viardot—'which created such enthusiasm at the last Conservatoire concert'[42]—Act 3 of *Otello* with Viardot and Duprez, Act 1 of *Maria Stuarda* with Ristori—and ended with *Les Rendez-vous bourgeois* with Battaille as César.

The theatre closed for the season on 31 May with a performance of *La Statue*.

1861—1862

The same theatre in the boulevard du Temple would still be in use when the 1861—62 season commenced on 1 September. As early as the previous May, it had been announced that the new Théâtre Lyrique would be ready to be occupied in October, but because the neighbouring Salle du Cirque would not be ready until January 1862, it had been decided to inaugurate both places together.[1] This January date was confirmed when the new season began in September. Meanwhile, in July, Charles Réty had reached agreement with the municipality and had accepted the terms of his new lease. Again it was forecast that the theatre would be transferred to the place du Châtelet by the coming January.[2] Not surprisingly there were the usual rumours of architectural blunders having been made in the building. We learn that the stage had been designed two metres too narrow to allow for the moving of scenery.[3] When the previous season ended, Réty had found himself not only without Bataille but threatened with the loss of another important bass singer, Balanqué who, for a time at least, though he later relented, had declined to renew his contract. During the summer recess, however, he had engaged some new artists: M. and Mme Labat 'from the provinces', three tenors; Surmont, a 'trial'*; Mathieu, husband of Mlle Caye; and Bonnet, from the theatre in Batavia, as well as Jules Lefort, a well known concert and salon baritone. A second baritone, Jules Petit, had joined the company at the end of the previous season, but the greatest prize, in fact the only prize—or so it seemed at the time—was the re-engagement of Marie Cabel, who was to re-enter the theatre in one of her greatest successes there— *Le Bijou perdu*.[4] The orchestra too had been enlarged, choristers would number 60, and there would be 18 dancers which would make 'a very respectable corps de ballet.'[5]

The new season opened on the customary 1 September with a revival of *Les Dragons de Villars*. This was followed on the next

---

* or tenor comique after Antoine Trial, 1736—95.

evening by *La Statue*, after which came *Le Bijou perdu*, bringing back Marie Cabel to the Théâtre Lyrique in a role she had created there eight years before. It was reported that 'the house was crowded and the reception of the brilliant songstress was of the most enthusiastic description.'[6] Ironically this was not sustained. When she had earlier left the Théâtre Lyrique, her place had been taken by Miolan-Carvalho who seems to have refined public taste in singing. In 1861 Cabel 'still retained a voice of surprising agility',[7] but by then her automaton coloratura style had been supplanted in public taste by the less elaborate, more emotional manner of singing required for operas such as *Faust*.

This new attitude to vocal technique was emphasised following a revival of Halévy's *Jaguarita*, also with Cabel, in November when, it was declared, 'This opera is in fact one of the worst specimens of that odious tour de force school for which the Théâtre Lyrique became the arena from its commencement under Adolphe Adam and to which, after an interval of pseudo Gluckism, it now returns after the manner of the sow and the dog in the powerful figure of the Scriptures. Such perverted productions as these, in which the voice is treated as an instrument of brass or wood, intended to obey merely mechanical impulses rather than the grand and noble organ of human emotion, have ruined all the best singers whom France has recently produced, and by all who have any regard for pure art, ought to be energetically reprobated.'[8]

The first creation of the season took place on 22 October and was an opera-ballet by Boisseaux and de Lajarte. It had been rehearsed under the title of *Le Voyage dans la Lune* (the second act took place on that, then still unvisited planet) but when produced it was called, with little reason, *Le Neveu de Gulliver*—perhaps because like his distinguished uncle (Jonathan Swift's Gulliver), John Gulliver in this opera was a great traveller. There was nothing original about the setting on the moon, but the libretto reveals an early interest in 'women's liberation', for the moon was inhabited entirely by ladies who indulged in the minor vices of 'smoking and drinking absinth.'[9] As a composition it was said to be agreeable opera-ballet music, the sort that Napoleon I liked because it did not hinder him from thinking of his affairs while he listened to it.[10] The main interest in fact centred on Hortense Clavelle, a young dancer borrowed from the Opéra, in the role of Soudha-Jari, and her feminine corps de ballet, and Berlioz records, 'In the last analysis the success was for Lefort [the baritone singing John Gulliver] and the elevations of Mlle Clavelle.'[11]

Almost certainly it was financial difficulties at the theatre which now forced Réty to reduce his new productions to just four one-act curtain raisers for the rest of the year. The first of these, *Le Café du Roi* (the king was Louis XV) was a revival which had been performed earlier at Ems. The author was Henri Meilhac (it was his first opera-comique libretto), the composer Deffès, who 'had tried for the second time [*Les Petits Violons du Roi* was the first] some of the old tunes of Lully and Rameau.'[12]

This was followed by *La Nuit aux Gondoles*, a fantasy with a story impossible to relate. 'How to explain what one does not understand?' asks Durocher.[13] 'A complete flop, resounding and without remedy,'[14] reports Lasalle.

The next, *La Tyrolienne*, was described by Scudo as 'a one-act opera which will not make the fortune of the Théâtre Lyrique.'[15] The libretto, by de Saint-Georges and d'Artois, was taken from an old vaudeville. The composer was a little-known Belgian named Leblicq whose music was described, also by Scudo, as 'a tissue of commonplaces current in the streets of Paris for thirty years.'[16] Berlioz was kinder, commenting that 'his style is clear . . . he does not abuse the orchestra too much, nor does he torture the singers. One can only censure his melodies for lacking originality.'[17]

The last of these four operas was *La Tète Enchantée* by Dubreuil and Paliard. The composer Paliard came from Lyon where he kept a wallpaper shop,[18] and his opera was said to have been first performed there many years previously under the title of *L'Alchimiste*. Musically, Jules Lovy reported that there was nothing outstanding in the score, although it did liven up a little towards the end.[19] Dramatically, we read: 'The subject is composed of incredibly stale material being of the same class as the *Poupée de Nuremberg*, in which some old fool with a daughter or ward believes in magic and is duped by a trick of the lovers.'[20]

During October, evidently in an attempt to attract an

audience, Réty engaged the sisters Julia. They were two children aged five and eight years, who played violin fantasias during the evening.[21]

Having continually affirmed that the new Théâtre Lyrique would open in January (even as late as 20 October it was reported, 'It seems certain that the new auditorium of the Théâtre Lyrique will be inaugurated on 1 January 1862—the most explicit orders have been given to have the work finished by this date'[22]), now, late in December, it was announced that it would not open until the following autumn. Moreover readers were warned against paying attention to rumours which had begun to appear in the press. It had been lately reported that dressing rooms for the artists, and storage for scenery, had been forgotten in the construction. This was now vigorously denied. The truth was that 30 dressing rooms for both male and female singers had already been constructed, approached by a private staircase. As for the scenery store—there was never a question of having one. The new Théâtre Lyrique would stow scenery in current use in the scene dock—like all the other theatres in Paris.[23]

In spite of his many difficulties, Réty continued to engage new singers, including a young German soprano, Georgine Schubert.[24] But his policy of presenting one-act works by unknown composers was obviously not succeeding either artistically or financially and so, in an attempt to retrieve his losses, he had recourse to the plan originally adopted by Carvalho: revive a classic. The classic Réty decided upon was Méhul's *Joseph.*

While it had excited the enthusiasm of musicians and singers, French audiences had always remained indifferent to *Joseph.* This revival in January 1862 proved no different, although its lack of success was due not so much to Méhul's music or to Duval's oratorio-like libretto as to the incompetence of the tenor chosen to sing Joseph. He was M. Giovanni, a pseudonym which concealed M. Burzin or Bazin, until recently an outside broker on the Paris Bourse. A year earlier, when over 30, he had relinquished his profession to become a salon singer.[25] But such engagements in drawing-room surroundings hardly offered the preparation needed to undertake a difficult role in opera, a conclusion confirmed only too well by events. Berlioz reports:

'*Joseph* was in fact not performed that evening. The debutant, Giovanni, they say, suffered from stage fright. He was terrified! Ah, what terror. That can well be believed. When someone is not used to the stage, nor to singing, nor to words, nor to the orchestra, nor to the public, and goes on for the first time before an audience of 1200 in a theatre to try to act and sing and speak, that can indeed be upsetting. He almost lost gestures, words and voice all at the same time. He seemed to have difficulty in his movements. His coat weighed him down... The public was cold, but not severe. They seemed to say to him, "This evening does not count, we will come again".'[26] Giovanni appears to have had a baryton-Martin voice rather than a true tenor and was accused of having transposed down the air, 'Vainement Pharaon', a charge which he vigorously denied.[27] The only artists completely successful in the production were Amélie Faivre as Benjamin and Jules Petit as Jacob, 'who roused the entire auditorium'.[28] Even Méhul's music was no longer universally accepted, one reviewer complaining that 'the style unsupported by the genius of Gluck or Lully appeared terribly antiquated.'[29]

Miolan-Carvalho had returned to Paris for a fortnight in February. A benefit performance for her was announced, which would include the garden scene from *Faust*, an act from *Les Noces de Figaro* and an interlude given by all the great artists who were her comrades at the Théâtre Lyrique.[30] It is not certain that this ever took place.

Two months after he had produced *Joseph*, Réty enjoyed the greatest success of his management, with a three-act opera by Albert Grisar, called *La Chatte Merveilleuse*. The role of the cat had been composed for Marie Cabel. It was a fairy subject, the plot borrowed by Dumanoir and d'Ennery from Perrault's *Le Chat Botté* (*Puss in Boots*) and a vaudeville, *La Chatte metamorphosée en Femme*, by Scribe. Musically Grisar was said to be on his own ground. 'Not for him the strong situations, grand sentiments, violent passions; instead ask him for comic verve, gaiety, charm and you can have all you wish. The first act was a little weak, but the last two were charming.'[31] Production and scenery were elaborate, particularly in Act 2 where different landscapes were projected, dissolving one into the other, after the fashion of a magic lantern. 'This moving panorama,' declared Jules Lovy, 'is worth a dozen fine decors.'[32] Cabel won the applause of the evening, receiving recalls and bouquets. Monjauze as Urbain was also praised, but Leroy as the king is reputed to have sung as if he had another cat in his throat. Despite its early triumph, the opera would disappear from the repertoire in little more than a year, never to be revived.

Following this success, from now on it was all downhill for Réty. La Chatte was followed by yet another curtain-raiser, L'Oncle Traub. The music was by Eugène Delavault and the opera was dismissed as 'a little one-act piece of the most trifling description.'[33]

Two weeks later, something of slightly more consequence was brought forward. This was a two-act work, La Fille d'Égypte, with a libretto by Jules Barbier and music by Jules Beer, who had the artistic advantage of being a nephew of the renowned Giacomo Meyerbeer. Beer was described as a 'rich Prussian' and it was observed that he had 'proved by his score that the author of Les Huguenots was one uncle from whom musically he had inherited nothing.'[34] The libretto had nothing whatever to do with Egypt (it was about a gipsy and gipsies originally came from Egypt, hence the title). More specifically, it was a manifest copy of Prosper Merimée's Carmen, still set in Spain, but with the heroine rechristened Zemphira. Barbier—without Carré—was considered by Léon Durocher an unsatisfactory arrangement not to be encouraged.[35] The publication of the vocal score—a rich man's privilege—dedicated to Rossini, was announced in July[36] although the work had had only an unlucky 13 performances.

Two days after this production, 'a very modest but agreeable curtain-raiser' called La Fleur du Val Suzon was staged. The music was by Georges Douay, the libretto by Turpin de Sansay. Its setting was during the time of the Fronde and in it M. Guyot, a bass lately recruited from the Bouffes Parisiens 'made a no less agreeable debut.'[37]

Early in May, M. Arsène had what seems to have been his annual benefit when Le Val d'Andorre was performed.[38] The Théâtre Lyrique was then due to close in the boulevard du Temple on the last day of the month and to re-open in the place du Châtelet on 1 September, but, before closing, two new works remained to be performed.

They were *Le Pays de Cocagne*, for which Pauline Thys had composed 'melodies, tender and gracious, melodies, animated and piquant'[39] and *Sous les Charmilles*(these arbours ornamented the palace gardens of an unspecified king of Spain) with music by Lucien Dautresme, who was said by Jules Lovy to be 'more contrapuntist than melodist, less inspired than informed.'[40]

Although relocation at the new theatre was now imminent, the old Théâtre Lyrique would not be demolished for some time. Achille Lafont (Eyraud), who had been granted the licence for the new Théâtre du Prince Impérial, would temporarily assist in presenting drama there.[41]*

Late in July a pre-dress rehearsal of Berlioz' *Béatrice et Bénédict* had taken place at the 'old' theatre prior to the opera's production at Baden-Baden. We read that members of the orchestra and musicians among a specially invited audience broke into spontaneous applause several times, 'the better augury for the success of the work.'[42] It was the last performance of any opera ever given in that theatre.

Before the season ended, there had been what was described as a pilgrimage to the boulevard du Temple, presumably to bid the old theatre a nostalgic farewell.[43] But time as always was relentless, and not only were old theatres falling and new ones rising, but modern inventions were being employed to accommodate theatre-goers. At the new Hôtel de la Paix, for example, a room was being set up containing plans of the auditoria of all the Paris theatres, where visitors could choose their seats and then reserve them at once by the electric telegraph.[44]

On 30 June the Minister of State, Count Walewski, accompanied by Camille Doucet, Director General of the state theatres, and Charles Garnier, the architect of the new Paris

---

*

This undertaking was inspired by Edouard Brisebarre, a dramatist who had obtained a licence for a new Paris theatre from the Minister of State. The theatre re-opened as the Théâtre Historique with *Le More de Venise* (translated from Shakespeare by Alfred de Vigny), on 29 October 1862. Alexandre Dumas objected to the theatre being called Historique and so, by order of the Minister, for its second production on 14 November it was called Théâtre du Boulevard du Temple. Brisebarre and Lafont's partnership survived until 21 October 1863. The theatre was demolished immediately afterwards. (*Le Théâtre Historique* 121–124)

Opéra, visited both of the new theatres at the place du Châtelet and offered congratulations to the architect, Gabriel Davioud. The new Théâtre Lyrique was to be handed over by the municipality to Réty on 15 July, and it was regretted that it could not be put into use right away.[45] The opening date was now given as 15 September with Marie Cabel in *La Chatte merveilleuse* as the inaugural opera.[46] But Cabel was demanding a fee of 7000 francs a month with the proviso that she would not have to perform more than 13 times within that period, conditions which Réty was believed to have refused.[47]

Then on 28 July a reception was held at the two new theatres. This was attended by Prince Napoleon, Count Walewski, Baron Haussmann, Prefect of the Seine and the Municipal Council, and an immense crowd of the public, invited or not. The Théâtre Lyrique was lavishly decorated with flowers for the occasion. In order to test the acoustics, Pasdeloup and his orchestra performed excerpts which included the *Oberon* overture and, with the help of the Paris Orphéonistes, choruses from *Preciosa* and *Jaguarita*. A young baritone from the Conservatoire, M. Caron, sang the air from Verdi's *Le Trouvère*, and it was regretted that a woman's voice had not also been employed, to complete the test. J. L. Heugel was certainly doubtful of the result, and he concludes his article by invoking 'God, that science might have conquered the acoustic hazards in the year of grace 1862.'[48] Whatever the outcome, Davioud was appointed Chevalier de la Légion d'honneur on the Emperor's fête day.[49]

It was now announced that, following the opening production of *La Chatte merveilleuse*, there would be a new opera by Semet called *L'Ondine* and, after that, Balfe's *La Bohémienne*. The cast was given for the latter: Cabel, Mlle Moirico, Monjauze and Bonnesseur;[50] and Balfe was expected to arrive in Paris in September,[51] probably in connection with the performance. Nevertheless it was well known that Réty was in serious financial difficulties. There is evidence of this on 14 September when the opening of the theatre was postponed once again until 1 October[52]—and there would be even a further postponement. His problem was that the theatre's receipts had fallen by 124,000 francs at the end of 1860, and by a further 90,000 francs at the end of 1861.[53] Receipts during the previous year consequently had been a depressing 470,000 francs, little more than half the amount Carvalho had taken in during his best year of 1858. Faced with these figures, Réty was left with only one decision, however much he might struggle to avoid it. As Soubies has recorded, 'it was not written that he should enter into the promised land, he would never pass over Mount Nebo.'[54] And so on Saturday 4 October at 5 o'clock in the afternoon, he accepted the inevitable and tendered his resignation.[55] His debts amounted to 773,000 francs.[56] Carvalho, Charles Desolme of *L'Europe Artiste* and Pasdeloup were each mentioned as his possible successor.[57] Carvalho was appointed to the post on 8 October; his licence was to run for seven years.[58]

Chapter 5

Carvalho at the place du Châtelet
1862—1868

1862–1863

The Grand Châtelet was a fortress which stood on the right bank of the Seine guarding the Pont au Change at the entrance to the Cité. In 1802 it was demolished as serving no further purpose and a rabbit warren of small houses which surrounded it was razed at the same time. The cleared ground which resulted became the place du Châtelet. As has been noted, Haussmann's Paris required the demolition of theatres in the boulevard du Temple. The decision to rebuild the two principal ones, the Cirque Impérial and the Théâtre Lyrique (recently retitled Théâtre Lyrique Impérial) on this vacant ground located them on what was a main cross roads of the new Paris, besides bringing them closer to its centre and to its more fashionable districts. Today, still retaining much of their original form, the buildings remain facing one another, although they have undergone changes of name. The Cirque Impérial quickly became the Théâtre du Châtelet, the Lyrique was later called the Théâtre Sarah Bernhardt.

The architect, Gabriel Davioud is perhaps better remembered today as a designer of Paris parks and fountains than as a designer of Paris theatres.[1] His assistant was M. Senèque. *The Builder* described the two buildings as 'a combined eyesore' and stated that 'the effect of the whole from any distant point of view, is in simple truth, a vile blot on the picture.'[2] An account of the Théâtre Lyrique alone relates that 'this square mass with its campanile of a ventilator which crowned the building resembled an enormous travel trunk surmounted by a hat box.'[3] It had been built on a site of 1850 square metres. Fronting the Seine, the ground floor consisted of a range of small shops which the thrifty municipality had planned to provide rents, but with their signboards they affronted the aesthetic sensibilities of the Paris press. The main entrance to the theatre faced the place du Châtelet and consisted of an arcade of five openings which gave access to a vestibule 25 metres wide by six deep. From here one entered the orchestra stalls* ('where the ladies are admitted as at the Italiens'[4]), or ascended a double staircase of carved stone which led to the upper parts of the auditorium. Two coloured enamelled medallions by the Italian ceramist, Giuseppe Devers, representing Poetry and Music decorated the façade. The Emperor's entrance was in the avenue Victoria, whence he could ascend by a staircase to his box. Ventilation also came from the north side of the building originating in an airshaft in the square Saint-Jacques and passing underneath the avenue Victoria to the theatre basement where the air could be warmed in winter. Coursing through flues it entered the auditorium by openings covered by trellis work which surrounded the stage and by apertures beneath the front of the boxes and galleries, finally escaping through the ventilator in the roof. There would be a report that the occupants of the orchestra stalls were being troubled with draughts, but on the whole the ventilation was thought to be very satisfactory.

Inside the theatre one arrived at the principal tier of boxes on reaching the top of the grand staircase. On the same level was the grand foyer, of similar proportions as the vestibule directly beneath it. It was ornamented with sombre arabesque motifs, and with busts of celebrated musicians. Five large arcaded windows with balconies overlooked the place du Châtelet and at either end there was a small square salon with a fireplace, furnished with sofas. These two rooms were set aside for conversation during the intervals. On the storey above was a foyer for smokers, but this seems to have been a loggia. 'Cigars legalised in a Paris theatre!'[5] declared a scandalised *Musical World.*

---

*

A pit, situated behind the stalls and presumably not very extensive, is mentioned in some reports.

The auditorium measured 20 by 20 metres in extent and was 19 metres high. It was variously said to hold both 1750 and 1500 spectators. One source gives both figures, although at an interval of some years[6] but the lower number is probably the correct one. The stage was 11.5 metres wide but was quite inadequate in depth. Sightlines were reported to be good— satisfactory for the period might be a more accurate way of expressing it—except that the footlights inevitably concealed the artists' feet. The really bad seats were in the fashionable stage boxes where patrons could see the artists only in profile, could hear only those parts of the opera which happened on their side of the stage and had to endure the heat of the footlights. The two principal tiers of boxes had ante-rooms attached. Stall seats were said to be most uncomfortable, 'To allow a person to pass, you must get up,' we read 'and your seat follows you.'[7] The ornamentation was of neo-classic design, interlaced along the front of the five tiers of boxes and galleries. The cove of the ceiling was lavishly decorated with allegorical figures. The names of Auber, Halévy, Meyerbeer and Adam ornamented the proscenium arch while around the wall just under the ceiling one read the names of Hérold, Méhul, Gluck, Mozart, Weber, Boieldieu and Rossini. The decoration was mainly in white and gold with the boxes lined in red. Two examples only of bad taste are recorded. The stage boxes were considered garish because of gilt over ornamentation (they were also thought to be 'of a marvellous magnificence'[8]), and the stage curtain was said to be too sombre—'The colour is cold and dull,'[9] we read. Nevertheless, everything in the new Théâtre Lyrique proclaimed the luxurious state in which everyone wished to live in those days, especially the nouveaux enrichis of a 'haussmannised Paris'.[10]

The most striking and best advertised feature of the new theatre was the lighting. The customary huge chandelier had been abolished and in its place a system called 'exclusive lighting' had been installed. This consisted of a huge horse shoe-shaped ceiling of ground glass elaborately ornamented with arabesques of varied colours. Above this a cupola housed several hundred jets of gas (one report gives 1200) backed by a huge reflector which projected an even vari-coloured, softened and equalised light down on to the audience. There were disadvantages, mechanical, financial and social. 'Exclusive lighting' had first been used in the chamber of the Corps Legislatif where the temperature above the ceiling was said to have reached 90° centigrade with consequent risk of fire. (The roof trusses of the Théâtre Lyrique, and of the Cirque Impérial where this form of lighting had also been installed were made entirely of iron). The amount of gas used with the new system was said to be three times greater and therefore three times more expensive. The ladies in the audience complained 'that their toilettes were submitted to too bright a scrutiny.'[11] There were advantages as well. Theatrically, the most important was that when the performance began the light in the auditorium could now be dimmed 'to exactly the point calculated to give just the proper amount of due prominence to the lighting of the stage, without, at the same time, leaving too little light in the house, upon which the full power of light is again thrown between the acts'[12]* The advantage to the occupants of the upper galleries was twofold. With the disappearance of the ineluctable chandelier, glare was eliminated, as was the oppressive heat, especially in summer, now that the gas jets were placed above the ceiling, in which position besides lighting the auditorium better they also helped to improve the ventilation. Nevertheless, for whatever reason, 'exclusive lighting' failed to become popular in Paris theatres. By 1877 the only luminous ceiling still remaining was in the Théâtre du Châtelet.[13]

Today it is difficult to comprehend the heat and smells of the upper strata of a large theatre one hundred or more years ago. 'Who would voluntarily enter a *salle* heated by hundreds of gas-lights, without air, and infected by noisome smells of all kinds . . . ?' asks a reviewer at the old Théâtre Lyrique.[14] Such discomfort tended to produce remedies often no better than the affliction. The Russian composer, Glinka, would write of his visit to Paris in 1852 'I rarely went to the theatre because the Parisians use perfume so unsparingly that the air becomes unbearable.'[15] An English visitor wondered how people could

---

*

Of corollary interest is the information that up to this time house lights were left undimmed during Théâtre Lyrique performances. Indeed even the partial reduction of light mentioned brought some complaints of 'crépuscule.'

'live' in the upper galleries, 'or enjoy anything in the stifling heat as that of all the older theatres.' He incidentally relates that in Paris theatres you could vacate your seat in a box or orchestral stall during an interval and return certain of finding it unoccupied just by leaving your handkerchief or a bill of the performance attached to it.* 'When you enter the theatre you are directed to your seat by a logeuse or box-keeper.' he explains. 'There is no thrusting to get in; the police would prevent that; and indeed no one helps to make confusion as do the various classes of ill and well dressed "roughs" at English places of amusement, going in and coming out.'[16]

Administrative changes had also taken place in the new Théâtre Lyrique for Count Walewski had decreed that in all the new theatres, the supplementary fee for booking a seat in advance of the evening of performance should be abolished. Arrangements were also to be made so that patrons could collect their tickets on arrival at the theatre without having to queue** as heretofore. It was announced that these arrangements were for cheaper seats only, regulations for dearer seats, whatever they may have been would remain as they were.[17]

This was then the Théâtre Lyrique that Léon Carvalho opened on 30 October 1862. His return came as a surprise for at the same time he was a candidate for the Opéra Comique,[18] then about to be vacated by Emile Perrin who would become director of the Opéra. The Opéra Comique post would go to Adolphe de Leuven. To celebrate the opening of the new theatre the monumental fountain in the place du Châtelet was illuminated

---

*

It was not until July 1866 that a change in the style of theatre tickets was introduced. It was then decided to print them in the form of return railway tickets, 'one half to be handed to the contrôleur as you enter, and the other kept as authority for taking your seat. Each half has the date, number of place and number of row printed upon it. All the places will be numbered, and the officious intervention of box-openers etc., and the necessity of leaving a glove or a newspaper on your fauteuil in order to secure your place, will be dispensed with'. (0. 14 July 1866)

**

'Black market' queues were in operation at Paris theatres as early as 1839. *Briefwechsel zwischen Eduard und Therese Devrient,* ed. Hans Devrient, Stuttgart 1909.

over the chestnut trees that surrounded it, a triple girdle of light encircled the theatre itself, while its near neighbour, the recently opened Théâtre du Châtelet, was also lit up in welcome.[19]

It was a miscellaneous programme that Carvalho presented commencing with a 'Hymne à la Musique' specially composed (?) by Gounod to words by Barbier and Carré in which the entire company took part. The soloists were Miolan-Carvalho, Faure-Lefebvre, Viardot and Cabel. This was followed by a religious march by Adolphe Adam—a compliment to the original founder of the enterprise—after which the curtain rose on the first part of a concert, with the artists in day dress (habit de ville). This consisted of airs from La Juive (Battaille), La Reine Topaze (Miolan-Carvalho) and the Gounod-Bach, 'Ave Maria', sung by Duprez-Vandenheuvel, Cabel, Faure-Lefebvre, Miolan-Carvalho, Girard and Moreau, accompanied by four violinists, one of whom was Sarasate, three harpists, which included Godefroid, two pianos played by Ketterer and Vandenheuvel, two organs played by Delibes and Miolan, and, if we are to believe Le Ménestrel the entire orchestra conducted by Deloffre![20] 'This simple and touching melody' we read 'was superiorly performed and encored by acclamation from all the house.' In the circumstances one is relieved to learn that the Oberon overture which opened the second part of the programme was also encored. The artists now appeared in stage costume and gave scenes from La Chatte Merveilleuse, Joseph, Les Dragons de Villars, L'Enlèvement au Sérail, Orphée and Les Noces de Figaro. Miolan-Carvalho following her 'Chanson de l'Abeille' in the first part, had been recalled and showered with bouquets from the stage boxes, and in spite of the advanced hour at which the concert ended the house remained well filled throughout. The Mozart pieces gave the liveliest pleasure.[21]

Successful as the inaugural concert had been, Carvalho was not without difficulties. Cabel was still insisting on a fee of 6,000 francs or more a month. Since she was eventually engaged, presumably she got it. She was negotiating from a strong position for the opera which had been announced to open the season, Semet's L'Ondine was not ready, and prior to Carvalho's unexpected assignment his wife had accepted engagements for both Lyon and Marseille. It was now being pleaded that these engagements were only provisional 'in expectation of the situation which has now come to pass' and the telegraph lines were said to be humming in efforts to extricate her from them.[22] Carvalho's only solution therefore was to have recourse to Cabel and *La Chatte Merveilleuse.*

He was also impeded because of alterations which were found to be necessary both to the auditorium[23] and to the stage,[24] the latter probably to enable the scenery from the old and larger stage to be fitted on the new one. He had purchased the old theatre's scenery and costumes from Réty at their original cost of 200,000 francs.[25]

The augmentation of the orchestra and chorus which was announced[26] seems to have been a matter of form rather than a matter of fact. This was about the tenth time over the years that we read of an increase in numbers. So, at what did they now stand? Apart from the orchestra, chorus and minor artists, Carvalho was not required to retain other artists previously engaged by Réty,[27] although in many instances he was obviously only too pleased to do so.* Bonnesseur, who had been engaged for a principal role in *L'Ondine* had some disagreement with him[28] and accepted an engagement at the Opéra instead. Raynal had gone to sing in Toulouse but would rejoin the company in December. [29]

In mid-November there was 'talk' of producing Handel's *Rinaldo* 'in a French dress'[30] and *The Bohemian Girl* was trotted out yet again, this time with Miolan-Carvalho announced for Arline.[31] With more point it was stated, 'During the weeks that followed [the inaugural concert] and until the end of the year, playbills of the Théâtre Lyrique resembled those regimental flags on which are inscribed the names of all the victories.'[32] The victory with which Carvalho commenced his campaign proper on 31 October was *La Chatte Merveilleuse* with Marie Cabel. This was quickly followed by performances by *Les Dragons de*

*

His company was announced as: Mmes Viardot, Cabel, Miolan-Carvalho, Faure-Lefebvre, Girard, Moreau, Gonetti, Wilhème, Dubois, Vadé, C. Vadé, Duclos. MM. Battaille, Monjauze, Sainte-Foy, E. Cabel, Balanqué, Bouvard, Bussy, Petit, Ribes, Legrand, Bonnet, Wartel, Gabriel, Girardot, Leroy, Martin. Conductor: Deloffre. Chorus Master, Bousquet. M. 2 Nov 1862. Maitre de Ballet, M. Théodore. U. 10 Oct 1863.

Villars, Orphée, L'Enlèvement au Sérail, Le Medecin malgré lui and *Robin des Bois.* Financially it was successful. Receipts for the month of November totalled Fr. 119,557.50,[33] an average of just over 4000 francs for each evening.

But the real success of the repertory, *Faust* could not be revived until 18 December* due to Miolan-Carvalho's commitments in Lyon. The performance was described as the 'definitive reopening of the Théâtre Lyrique.'[34] There were some modifications in the production. The alterations in the church scene have been noted earlier, but we also learn that 'the Walpurgis was simplified and purged of a number of horrors' and it was here that the spinning wheel scene was suppressed for the first time. The opera's success was greater than ever.

Countess Walewska who was present in a stage box threw her bouquet to Miolan-Carvalho—'It was almost official homage'[35]— and receipts for the performance came to 6,800 francs.[36]

During December there had been a change of personnel in the theatre. Jules Lovy, who as it happened would not have long to live, became secretary-general replacing Guy-Stéphan who was promoted to administrator.[37] A strong lobby was once again exerting pressure for a subvention,[38] while audiences were 'more and more in agreement on the good disposition and excellent sonority of the theatre.'[39] So, with a good theatre, a good company of artists and stout advocates to back him, all seemed set fair for Léon Carvalho on his new voyage with the Théâtre Lyrique.

His first new production, the postponed *L'Ondine* would at last be performed on 7 January 1863. It was generally agreed that it did not fulfil Semet's earlier promise shown in *Nuits d'Espagne* and *Gil Blas.* The libretto, by Lockroy and Mestépès was based on La Motte Fouqué's fairy tale, employed in a number of libretti, notably Lortzing's *Undine.* Paul Bernard of *Le Ménestrel* while noting that *L'Ondine* was the work of a talented and experienced musician, devoted a great part of his review to urging Carvalho to present Balfe's *La Bohémienne*[40] then being performed widely throughout the Continent. In

---

*

short 'the work was coldly received by the public'[41] and ran for only seven performances. Carvalho, consequently, quickly had to find a replacement. His choice fell on Mozart's *Così fan tutte*, or rather, a radically altered version of this opera. It was Mozart's score all right, or most of it, but the libretto by Barbier and Carré (who else?) was now an adaptation of Shakespeare's *Love's Labour's Lost* and the whole gallimaufry was retitled *Peines d'amour perdues!* Such desecration would not be tolerated today, but in the late eighteenth and nineteenth centuries, especially in Germany, it was almost routine procedure that the work could not be presented without someone attempting to improve on Da Ponte. Nor was such meddling confined to rewriting the libretto. Otto Jahn reports the score of a Coronation Mass, allegedly by Mozart, which, apart from the Credo consisted of entire pieces and fragments from *Così fan tutte*.[42] It was all part of the nineteenth century, not to mention the early twentieth century attitude, to what was considered to be Da Ponte's impossible libretto.

While Barbier and Carré pursued their discreditable task there was much artistic socialising at the Théâtre Lyrique. On 5 January the theatre was en fête for a visit to *Faust* by Napoleon and Eugénie, who remained until the end of the performance.[43] In fact all fashionable Paris was crowding there. There was the added compulsion of an early visit since Miolan-Carvalho was under contract shortly to leave for Marseille.[44] Carvalho endeavoured to mitigate his wife's absence from Paris by reaching agreement with his fellow director Halanzier whereby for part of the Marseille season her place would be taken by Marie Cabel.[45] There is some evidence that a similar arrangement had been effected with Lyon.[46] Coupled with Balfe, a second Irish composer William Vincent Wallace was having an opera, *Love's Triumph* (lately produced at Covent Garden) put forward for the Théâtre Lyrique.[47] The hundredth performance of *Faust* would be celebrated there on 24 March,[48] and about the same time it would be necessary to postpone *Peines d'amour perdues* due to Cabel being ill and for 'lack of a tenor such as Naudin [who had recently sung Ferrando at the Théâtre Italien] to sing "Un'aura amorosa".'[49]

Peines d'amour perdues was at the same time coming under

heavy critical fire. Most critics were furious, and epithets such as sacrilege, profanation, abomination and desolation were freely published. 'There will not be enough "cat calls" in France to punish those who would be guilty of such an outrage against the greatest musician who has ever existed,' declared Paul Scudo.[50] Against this the critics were reminded of Carvalho's conscientiousness towards the works of Mozart, Weber and Gluck already presented by him and were assured that Mozart's music would remain intact—his 'work will not be disparaged by exchanging the glass beads of Da Ponte for a diamond of Shakespeare.'[51]

This particular diamond of Shakespeare had not been chosen by Barbier and Carré merely by sticking a pin in an index of Shakespeare's plays. Certain similarities exist, although mainly reversed, with the original libretto. In *Love's Labour's Lost* four men renounce the companionship of women for a period of three years. Four women arrive and overcome their resistance, one by one. In one scene the men enter disguised as Russians. The resemblances here are obvious.

Carvalho was probably attracted to the opera, (remembering his earlier successes with Mozart) because it had been opportunely revived at the Théâtre Italien during the previous November after a lapse of over 40 years. This revival which had provoked universal praise for the score and universal condemnation for the libretto may have decided him to have an entirely new libretto fashioned. He did not lack precedence for this because the first Paris performance of *Così fan tutte* in French had taken place at the Opéra in 1813 in a pasticcio version adapted to a new libretto, *Le Laboureur chinois* by several hands, dramatic and musical. Musically, the Barbier and Carré version was in the hands of Prosper Pascal 'who [had] given all his attention to the transformation of the work, and by M. Léo Delibes.'[52] The presentation seems to have been satisfactory enough. Production, we read was 'splendid. Scenery and costumes of incomparable richness. Nothing could equal the décor of the garden.'[53] The cast* too was more than competent, with the exception of one

*

The new version allotted the music as follows: Faure-Lefebvre, *Princess/Fiordiligi*, Cabel, *Rosaline/Dorabella*, (but she seems to have annexed Fiordiligi's aria 'Per pietà'). Girard, *Papillon/Despina*, Duprez, *Prince/Ferrando*, Petit, *Biron/Guglielmo*, Wartel, *Don Armando/Don Alfonso*. Deloffre conducted.

débutant, Léon Duprez (the great Gilbert's son, who had been chosen to compete with Naudin in singing 'Un'aura amorosa') and of whom it was said, he 'proved his father's son in everything but voice.'[54]

It is only when one reads of the revised work itself that one begins to understand the extent of the interference which took place and the extent of the failure. 'Never did literary moles work deeper in the dark than Messieurs Barbier and Carré,' recounts *The Musical World.* 'Not a vestige of the poetry and romance of the original melodrama remains. The book Da Ponte compiled for Mozart—one of the silliest ever written for music—is a marvel of grace and gaiety compared to the concoction of the two popular French scribes.'[55]

But it is Paul Scudo in the *Revue des Deux Mondes* who most devastatingly dissects this hybrid specimen. The following is a précis of his review:—The Théâtre Lyrique has the courage of its convictions and has given the first performance of a work in four acts under the piquant title of *Peines d'amour.* It is a forced marriage, one might say a monstrous coupling of a strange play by Shakespeare with the exquisite music of Mozart's opera, *Così fan tutte.* The scene is now transported to a princely court of the sixteenth century. The overture was preserved intact. At the rise of the curtain, the Prince of Navarre, Biron and other courtiers agree to renounce for three years all social pleasures including love. [In order to devote themselves to study and meditation.] They sing the first trio in the score, pass over the second, and later distribute the other pieces according to the needs of the action, the demands made by the newly introduced characters, and the division of the work into four acts. The quintette, 'Di scrivermi ogni giorno' is unrecognisable, not alone because the comic part which Don Alfonso sings hardly exists, but because it is the men who now weep and no longer the women. All the rest is in keeping. The charming trio for the three men 'E voi ridete' is ruined because the syllabic rhythm is no longer present. In compensation they have retained after a fashion the admirable trio 'Soave sia il vento'. The first act finale in which sword play takes place [instead of the 'poison' scene] is much more improbable and less gay than in *Così fan tutte.* It is indeed absurd to see a prince fighting a pretended rival before a princess and her ladies in the hope of touching their hearts. Such clowning is much less amusing than Da Ponte's arrangement which inspired in Mozart one of the finest pages of dramatic music that exists. Mozart's recitatives were suppressed and replaced by interminable dialogue which interrupted the musical flow and lowered the general temperature. Nor must we forget the rash hand that dared to introduce into the new arrangement symphonic fragments borrowed from other works of Mozart. An absurd story, a hundred times more tedious, more improbable than Da Ponte's anecdote, a mutilated score from which eight pieces have been omitted from the original and in which the others are unrecognisable.[56] Scudo could have added that instead of Despina's entry as a notary at the dénouement of the last act, Papillon enters as a fortune teller to utter some prophecy.[57]

'The concoction,' to again quote *The Musical World*, 'was a failure.'[58] *Le Ménestrel* might come to its defence by proclaiming, 'criticism has had its reservations, that is its right, but the public keeps its own counsel. In time it will appreciate the sweet music of Mozart, the excellent interpretation and sumptuous production.'[59] It was a plea for a lost cause. The opera would have a mere 18 performances. Marie Cabel sang Rosaline for the last time on 8 May and then set off for Marseille to enable Miolan-Carvalho to return to Paris.[60]. There the latter would give six further performances of *Faust* before leaving for London, where at Covent Garden she would sing 11 more.

Carvalho was now leaning heavily on successes from previous years to form his programme and so the only new operas to be presented before the season ended were two ephemeral one-act pieces. The first, *Les Fiancés de Rosa* (originally titled *Le Mariage à l'Épée*) was by a lady composer, Clémence Valgrand. In real life she was Marie Félicie Clémence, Vicomtesse de Grandval, and presumably it was her exalted station which had caused *Le Ménestrel* to announce, 'Grandval directs the rehearsals in person like the musician she is.'[61] Yet, her social position should not make us prejudge her ability as a composer for Léon Durocher would write—'One can easily see from the first bars of the overture that Mme Clémence Valgrand is well above the class of ordinary amateurs . . . She writes well for the voice and her instrumentation is very correct. She has given Miss Jenny an air in which the principal theme is extremely elegant.'[62] He alas has to admit that in general, and in spite of the passages he has mentioned, the score was weak, and that the second opera, given on the same evening, was received more favourably by the public. This was *Le Jardinier et son Seigneur* composed by Léo Delibes to the old La Fontaine fable of the sycophantic gardener and his attempts to ingratiate himself with his equally overbearing seigneur. Philidor had composed a significant opéra comique to the same story a hundred years before. The libretto for the Delibes work by Barrière was said to be 'lively, gay, humorous and very well played.' The music had the same qualities. As a pupil of the late Adolphe Adam it was said in praise of Delibes and his opera, 'If one had given *Le Jardinier et son Seigneur* to the public as a posthumous work of Adam, no one would have thought of protesting.'[63] With performances of *Faust* on 30 May and *Oberon* on 31 May the season ended (a month early, it would seem) until the usual 1 September.

Earlier in the year Delibes, who had been accompanist at the Théâtre Lyrique since 1853, became second chorus master at the Opéra. He was replaced by Hector Salomon who had for his assistant Edouard Mangin, later to become conductor at the Théâtre Lyrique.[64] He would help to found a new musical conservatoire in Lyon in 1872. In June, Jules Lovy died.[65] M. Bousquet, the chorus master held auditions for male and female choristers[66] and, as was customary, many of the principal Théâtre Lyrique singers found engagements at Baden-Baden during the summer break.[67] In fact, rehearsals for Henry Charles Litolff's opera, *Nahel,* which would be produced at Baden-Baden in August, were even then taking place in the closed theatre.[68] Marie Cabel rejected Carvalho's approaches for another season (competition with Mme Carvalho must have been trying) and opted for Lyon instead.[69]

But far more significant affairs had been taking place in the Chamber of the Corps Legislatif. In April a Baron de Ravinel had proposed that the subvention to the imperial theatres be reduced by 300,000 francs because of an urgent need of money for other purposes. (So, the reduction of subsidies to the arts in times of economic stress is neither as new nor as confined to some parts of Europe in the late 20th century as people sometimes believe.) Fortunately M. Busson was there to rise to the defence of opera. He cogently made the point that the subvention paid annually to the Théâtre Italien was now about to cease (with the forthcoming liberty of the theatres). Was it not time that this money should now be given to encourage the Théâtre Lyrique, which had proved its worth by its perseverence, its artistic standards and the talents which it had produced?[70] It was believed that the proposal would surely have the support of the Minister of State, Count Walewski—but, just then, the Minister was resigning his post. (Amidst the vexed Papal-Italian question, Walewski, Napoleon III's cousin, had taken the clerical side.) He obliged just before his retirement—a neat political gesture. Carvalho was at last decreed an annual subvention of 100,000 francs and Le Ménestrel would affectionately declare, 'The theatres and the arts will not forget with what lively solicitude and courtesy the Count Walewski presided over their destinies for three years.'[71] The bouquet thrown by Countess Walewska to Miolan-Carvalho during the performance of Faust had been symbolic.

1863—1864

When the Ministry of State passed from Count Walewski to M. Billault it was shorn of some of its trappings. The imperial theatres and the Conservatoire of Music now entered the domain of the Minister of the Imperial Household and Fine Arts, Maréchal Jean Baptiste Vaillant,[1] who had Camille Doucet for his director general.[2]

One of Doucet's first official acts was to establish a competition for the staging of operas by untried composers. A three act libretto chosen as having the most merit would be submitted to the young musicians, and the work resulting judged to be the best would be performed at the Théâtre Lyrique. In an attempt to keep everyone at least satisfied, if not completely happy, it was agreed that the competitors themselves should elect three of the five members who would form the jury, the other two to be Léon Carvalho and an appointee from Doucet's administration.[3] The conditions of Carvalho's subvention in fact demanded that a three act work by a Prix de Rome lauréat who had not previously had a work staged in Paris be performed at the Théâtre Lyrique each year,[4] and it was believed that Doucet's attempt to supply a competent libretto would give the inexperienced composer a better chance of success.

On 20 August Mme Miolan-Carvalho returned to Paris from the Carvalho summer residence in Dieppe to commence rehearsals for *Les Noces de Figaro*.[5] The season began with the 146th performance of this opera on Thursday 3 September.* Miolan-Carvalho retained her role of Chérubin, but the rest of the principals were new, the Countess was now sung by Brunetti, Susanne by Ugalde, Figaro by Lutz and the Count by Petit. The first new production of the season on 11 September was a revival of Grétry's *L'Épreuve villageoise*, presumably the version rescored by Auber for the Opéra Comique in 1853. It was reasonably successful, but of much greater significance were three operas then in rehearsal, which, although when first produced (all within a span of little over three months) would break no records, yet would nevertheless be works by which, with *Faust* and one or two others, the Théâtre Lyrique was to be most remembered.

The first of these was Georges Bizet's *Les Pêcheurs de Perles* commissioned by Carvalho in the previous April—even before his subvention had been confirmed. It had started out with the title of *Léïla*, and the locale of Mexico. Both were subsequently altered, the setting being changed to Ceylon. The libretto, as is now well known, was weak, and it is equally well known that Eugène Cormon, one of the librettists, later admitted that if he and his colleague Michel Carré had realised the quality of Bizet's talent they would not have encumbered him with so feeble a plot. Such belated acknowledgement of poor judgement must have brought Bizet much consolation as it does to all artists who have to suffer for the stupidity of their collaborators.

---

*

Artists engaged by Carvalho for the 1863–64 season included: Mmes Miolan-Carvalho, Ugalde, Charton-Demeur, Faure-Lefebvre, Brunetti, de Maësen, Ebrard, (Rosine) Bloch, Mézeray, Dubois, Estagel, Vié, Wilhème, Reboux, Doria, Duclos, Albrecht, Bayon, Martin.

MM. Monjauze, Morini, Petit, Ismaël, Lutz, Cabel, de Quercy, Pilo, Péront, Girardot, Gabriel, Wartel, Legrand, Caillot, Trillet, Masson, Guyot, Teste.

Conductor: Deloffre. Principal solo violin: Albert Vizentini.
RGM 9 Aug and 30 Aug. 1863. Accompanist: Leopold Ketten M. 18 Oct. 1863

Numerous changes were made in the opera during rehearsals—as might be expected with Carvalho about. Later there would be alterations of the original score, particularly in relation to the ending. These changes have all been annotated, notably by Winton Dean. Suffice it to say here that the first production of the opera ended with the theme of 'Au fond du temple saint' sung by the lovers in the distance as they sail away to safety.

The opera was advertised as having 'Not one line of prose . . . it will be sung as in the theatre of the rue Le Peletier'[6] (the Opéra). The role of Leïla may have been intended originally for Julia Ebrard,[7] a débutante from the Conservatoire, but in performance it was taken by Léontine de Maësen.* Because of the latter's illness the first performance had to be postponed from 14 until 30 September.

As is known the work was damned almost universally by the Paris critics. There was resentment not against the music alone but also against the man. Because he appeared before the curtain at the end of the performance, Gustave Bertrand of *Le Ménestrel* wrote, 'Before ending we will make a small comment addressed not to his talent, but to his tact and modesty. There was general astonishment to see him come on stage to bow to the audience at the end of the performance. This may be customary in Italy, but we are in France and M. Bizet is French. We dislike such exhibitions except when they result from the most extraordinary success, and even then we would prefer the composer to remain behind until dragged on in spite of himself—or, at least seeming to be.'[8]

The same critic was also hostile to the music. He relates, 'It is a grand opera in four [sic] acts, a heavy burden for a debutant, and it appears that M. Bizet has faltered under the load, for the last scene was far below the standard of the first. The duet "Au fond du temple saint" contains the best music of the opera, so knowing the worth of this godsend the composer repeats the motive eight or ten times in the score. [At Bizet's funeral service in 1875 the duet adapted as a 'Pie Jesu' by Guiraud was included in the musical programme]. "Je crois entendre encore" was also

---

* Who had a younger sister, Camille de Maësen who would later sing at the Opéra.

much applauded, but the remainder, and above all the ensembles are strained in style and ponderous in effect. He is influenced by Gounod and Félicien David [which was true] and also by the new Italian school' (which meant Verdi). Bertrand's summing up: 'There is too much shrieking in this score of *Les Pêcheurs de Perles.*' [9]

The rest of the press took the same line. Benoît Jouvin in *Le Figaro* complained that there were neither fishermen in the libretto, nor pearls in the music. [10] Léon Durocher in the *Revue et Gazette Musicale* emphasised Bizet's alleged borrowings from Wagner. 'We have not been present at such an entertainment since M. Wagner's concerts, since the overture of *The Flying Dutchman* and the famous *Lohengrin* choruses. Except for the few passages that we mentioned earlier and which are exceptional, the instrumental and vocal tempest roared and bellowed from one end to the other of this terrible opera.' [11] A critic with the rather incredible name of Dishly Peters writing for *The Musical World,* who claimed he had seen the opera 'with M. Berlioz who was polite enough to give me a place in his box,' grandiloquently announced, 'The piece is rubbish, and only a " *Prix de Rome*" could have produced music so full of sound and fury and so signifying nothing... The house was choked with the friends and partisans of the young Bizet, who recalled him in a tempest at the end.' [12]

Hector Berlioz was alone in reviewing the work sympathetically. Writing his last notice for the *Journal des Débats* he concluded, 'The score of *Les Pêcheurs de Perles* does M. Bizet the greatest honour and he will have to be accepted as a composer in spite of his exceptional talent as a pianist.' [13] It found favour only among the more enlightened members of the audience and had a sparse 18 performances, the last of them on 23 November. Bizet himself considered it a failure.

That this should be Berlioz' last review for the *Journal des Débats* was made possible by the fact that the next opera to be presented by Carvalho was *Les Troyens à Carthage,* part two of Berlioz' massive five act opera, *Les Troyens.* A special prologue was composed to replace the first part which comprised *La Prise de Troie.*

On 5 February 1863 Berlioz had sent a letter to J.W. Davison of *The Times* telling him of his future plans. They included the production of *Les Troyens* of which he writes: 'If within a week's time the Minister does not begin rehearsals of it at the Opéra, I will yield to Carvalho's persuasions and try our luck at the Théâtre Lyrique for December. For three years they have been shilly-shallying with me at the Opéra; and I do want to hear and see that big musical concern before I die. We will not, as I need not tell you, be able to accomplish such an enterprise with the actual resources of the theatre, but endeavours will be made to get together a really grand lyrical company; and Carvalho declares he can do it.'[14]

As affairs turned out Carvalho hardly succeeded. In the circumstances it is difficult to understand how Berlioz could have expected him to do so, for in rehearsal it was found that the work included numerous small roles, which although secondary could not be given to mere coryphées.[15] Uncertain news that artists were being sought from outside the company suggests that it was not Carvalho but Berlioz who was trying to recruit them; there was even an unknown Mlle Morio singing at Marseille, to whom he wrote—'Mademoiselle. I will be very happy if you are engaged at the Théâtre Lyrique and if they mount my opera of *Les Troyens* I offer you the role of Cassandre which to me appears to suit your voice and your talent.'[16] Mlle Morio does not seem to have been engaged nor, with the elimination of *La Prise de Troie* did her promised role survive, but Berlioz' letter confirms that in late April the production of the complete *Les Troyens*, in some form, was still envisaged.

A singer whom Berlioz did introduce to the production was Anne Arsène Charton-Demeur who during the previous year had created Beatrice in his *Béatrice et Bénédict* at Baden-Baden. She had sung first in the French provinces and then in Brussels. In 1849 she had a short spell at the Opéra Comique and then set out on a career in Italian opera, singing in Madrid, St. Petersburg, Paris (Théâtre Italien), New York and in South America. She returned from an engagement in Havana in April to sing Dido.[17] Her voice was mezzo-soprano, strong, extensive and well practised. She sang with impetus and passion, sometimes overstepping the line of sincerity.[18]

Although Berlioz, as he states in his letter to Davison, and later in his *Memoirs*, recognised that the enterprise was beyond

Les Troyens (Berlioz) 1863 Act 5

Carvalho, yet within his financial and technical means Carvalho did try to present the opera in a responsible fashion. He assembled the best cast at his disposal and, we learn, arranged for as many instruments of every kind as Berlioz wished. From behind stage the instruments of Sax would respond to the strings in the orchestra. (Berlioz relates that he paid for some of these extra players himself.) As for the production, Carvalho had already spent 70,000 francs on it. Of Berlioz it was said that he drives the rehearsals with that frenzy and utter confidence that he brings to all aspects of his art, and which he so amply demonstrated four years before when rehearsing *Orphée*.[19] Ever volatile in his moods during this period, he seems to have alternated between the apex of optimism and the depths of despair. We read that 'In the intervals of rehearsals [he] would come to the house of our friend d'Ortigue to rest. He would arrive in floods of tears, weeping in admiration of himself. "Oh! how good it is!" he would say sobbing, "how good it is! The musicians of the orchestra embraced me, Carvalho is wild with joy and enthusiasm".'[20] As late as 29 October the optimism would remain and he would write briefly to Davison—'Come, it is settled, Wednesday, November 4. [date of first performance] At the rehearsal this morning the success was terrific.'[21]

It was all in vain. Berlioz in his *Memoirs* has described all that went wrong, although he was then writing with hindsight and in the depression of disappointment, but even a sympathetic reviewer like Gasperini had to record: 'The dress rehearsal was on Monday, at which time the first performance was promised for Wednesday. I only half believed the good news. Order had not been established in newly built Carthage nor in the camp of the Trojans. The dancers dressed in bizarre costumes, their faces ambiguously made up still seemed to be uncertain whether they were supposed to be citizens of Sidon or from the banks of the Niger. I searched for Salammbô but could not see her. On the other hand some shapeless cloaks were ranged beside the triumphal costume of Monjauze [Aeneas] without disgrace. The scenery, which mistakenly recalled a commonplace village on the outskirts of Paris was stacked in disorder beside Phoenician structures. In brief I could not imagine how one could create order out of this chaos within forty-eight hours. We were all proved wrong... The first performance took place. I would not say that all went well, that the orchestra, the singers, the stage hands had done their tasks with exemplary precision, but it is clear that these occasional imperfections will vanish by the second performance . . . the orchestra was magnificently conducted by Deloffre.'[22]

A list can be made of two teams of critics, one which voted 'for', the other 'against' *Les Troyens à Carthage.* The 'for' team included in varying degrees of conviction, A. de Rovray (Fiorentino) in *Le Moniteur Universel,* Léon Kreutzer in *L'Union,* A. de Gasperini in *Le Ménestrel,* Joseph d'Ortigue in *Le Journal des Débats,* Franck-Marie in *La Patrie,* Johannès Weber in *Le Temps* and Léon Durocher in *Revue et Gazette Musicale.* Against them stood the phalanx of Paul Scudo in *Revue des Deux Mondes,* Alexis Azevedo in *L'Opinion Nationale,* B. Jouvin in *Le Figaro,* Edmond Rack in *La France* and Nestor Roqueplan in *Le Constitutionnel.*

The public sided with the latter group, but even apparently unbiased opinions indicate that the work was woefully under-rehearsed. Berlioz in his *Memoirs* confirms that it needed another three or four general rehearsals. He and his friends also expected hostile demonstrations but with the exception of a solitary boo there were none. One writer who was present stated that, apart from two items, to be noted presently, it was received 'with a silence more cruel than boos.'[23]

The new 'prologue explicatif', an oratorio-like introduction intended to elucidate the missing two acts of *La Prise de Troie—* recited by a 'rhapsodist' before, and sung by a chorus from behind a curtain depicting Troy in flames, failed either to inform or impress the audience. In the main work most of the principal singers were uncertain in their roles, watching the prompter rather than the conductor and dragging the time of the music. Intervals between the acts seemed endless, one taking 55 minutes. The famous 'Royal hunt and storm' failed to make any effect. Of the entire work the septette, 'Tout n'est que paix et charme', which was encored, and the duet 'Nuit d'ivresse et d'extase infinie!' were the only two items which were favourably received. Yet the innate power of the opera made its effect, particularly as might be expected, among musicians. Both Meyerbeer and Bizet attended several performances. But from official France there was not the slightest acknowledgement.

Neither Emperor nor Empress, not even Minister Vaillant showed any interest or attended a single performance. Officially it was left to Berlioz' musical colleague, the Grand Duke Ernest of Saxe-Coburg-Gotha to rectify the omission with a letter of good wishes for the opera's success.[24]

The result was inevitable. Although Carvalho had charged higher admission prices in an attempt to cover the increased costs (he would not receive his first subvention until 1 January 1864) the opera still ran for 21 performances. But receipts were never satisfactory, an average of 3,400 francs for the first ten performances, [25] about half houses. Economic exigencies combined with a loss of interest by the artists and stage hands who recognised that at best they had achieved only a succès d'estime, then led to a rapid introduction of cuts. The 'Royal hunt and storm' did not survive the first performance. Soubies relates that not only had it had an unfriendly reception but it could have been the cause of a serious accident. Berlioz wanted several real waterfalls in the scene (at least so he says in his *Memoirs*. He got a painted stream instead) and the proximity of the Seine to the theatre inspired Carvalho to provide them. 'But, a wrongly given signal caused a real flood [presumably during a final rehearsal] and it was judged prudent not to repeat the experiment.'[26]

Berlioz lists ten pieces which were cut, some during rehearsals, others following the first performance. He approved the excision of Iopas' air 'O blonde Cérès' because de Quercy was not up to singing it properly, and the duet for Aeneas and Dido 'Errante sur tes pas', because he considered that following it Charton-Demeur had not the necessary reserves of voice left for her final big scene. It was of this scene at the first performance that Scudo reported—'She was obliged to emit the cries of a hyena.'[27] Hylas' charming song sung by Edmond Cabel was, however, another matter. This disappeared while Berlioz was away from the theatre through illness. Cabel's contract required him to sing not more than 15 times a month but he now had to sing in a revival of *La Perle de Brésil* as well as *Les Troyens à Carthage* which meant that he had to be paid 200 francs for each additional performance. Cabel and Hylas' song were consequently removed together in the interests of economy.

These cuts were undoubtedly creating their own vicious

circle. The more cuts made and the less interest taken in the presentation of the opera, the less interest was there from the public. A fall in receipts reflects this, 1,700 francs a performance, then 1,600, until on 16 December it reached 1,300. Cutting losses was cutting audiences as well. An announcement that the production was ending brought a slight improvement, 1,800 francs for the 20th performance, 2,300 francs for the 21st and final on Sunday 20 December.[28] Berlioz states that Carvalho agreed to cancel Charton-Demeur's contract and that she left for Madrid. *Le Ménestrel* announced her probable engagement at the Théâtre Italien[29] where, in fact, she would appear the following year.

But, it is an ill wind . . . ! Berlioz received royalties from the production which he described as 'considerable'. He had also sold the vocal score in Paris and in London. He calculated that the interest on the amount received (said to be 50,000 francs) would equal his annual income from *Le Journal des Débats* and enable him to retire from musical criticism. His place would be taken by Joseph d'Ortigue. In all it was well said of Berlioz under the Second Empire—'He did not have success, but he had the glory.'[30]

Carvalho tried to come to terms with the situation, which undoubtedly was causing him grave financial concern, by presenting Verdi's *Rigoletto*. As happily as it was unexpected it had an enormous success, and after *Faust* and *Richard Cœur de-Lion* it would be the most performed opera to be produced at the Théâtre Lyrique, having a total of 243 performances. The first performance was given on Christmas Eve when receipts came to 6,500 francs and the first 25 performances would bring in 148,000 francs.[31] By the end of January 1864 it was having four performances in one week and 200 to 300 people were being turned away each evening.[32] It is easy to believe that it had been produced 'to the chagrin and mortification of M. Bagier' of the Théâtre Italien where the opera was also in the repertoire. The new ensemble was said to 'be remarkably good' although readers were warned, 'whoever goes to hear the opera at the Théâtre Lyrique should, if possible, disremember Mario and Ronconi.'[33] Go they did, in droves. During 1864 *Rigoletto* would have 83 performances at the Théâtre Lyrique, while at the Théâtre Italien there would be only 12.

There is a similarity here with the vogue for opera in the vernacular which Carl Rosa created in the British Isles during the 1870s. For Carvalho it was also an innovation since up to that time works in translation which he had presented at the Théâtre Lyrique were either forgotten operas or operas rarely performed. With *Rigoletto* new ground was broken in Théâtre Lyrique policy. The translation, which was from Piave's adaptation of Victor Hugo's original play, was by Edouard Duprez. The same translation had been used when *Rigoletto* was performed for the first time in French at Brussels in 1858. This version contains an air for Madeleine inserted into act three after the duke has gone upstairs and before Gilda returns in man's clothes. Madeleine here sings, 'Prends pitié de sa jeunesse,' four stanzas where she pleads with Sparafucile for the life of the handsome young stranger. It is impossible to discover if this air was ever sung on the French stage.*

The production seems to have reached an exceptional standard and Léon Durocher announced flatly, 'The performance will rank among the most brilliant of the Théâtre Lyrique.'[34] The final duet in act two (Si, vendetta, tremenda vendetta), which created 'violent enthusiasm',[35] 'Comme la plume au vent' (La donna è mobile) and the quartette were all encored. The 'Ah! veglia, o donna' duet was curtailed, which *Le Figaro*, rightly, considered 'a mutilation.'[36] As for the singers: Never before had Monjauze sung with such taste and charm. Léontine de Maësen as Gilda displayed brilliant qualities which she had only hinted at in *Les Pècheurs de Perles.* Her romance was delightfully sung.[37] Ismaël, the Rigoletto, who like de Maësen had made his Théâtre Lyrique debut in *Les Pècheurs de Perles* was a remarkable artist. He was born Jean-Vital-Ismaël Jammes at Agen in 1827, the son of a poor tailor. His family was too poor to help him, so with neither money nor education, but evidently with a superb baritone voice he set out from his native town as a strolling singer, walking first to Bordeaux and then to Nantes. In Nantes he was engaged as a chorister at the theatre and shortly after was called upon to sing the role of Max in *Le Chalet.* He was then only 16. He next set off for Paris, where he

*

See Appendix F.

was said to have been refused admission to the Conservatoire, but taking lessons from a little known teacher he landed an engagement in a minor Belgian theatre. Musically and scholastically he educated himself and in time began to find engagements among French provincial opera houses. His reputation at length reached Paris where Carvalho engaged him for the Théâtre Lyrique.[38] The last role he would create would be Le Marquis in Planquette's *Le Chevalier Gaston* at Monte Carlo in 1879.

Although he enjoyed a long and successful career Ismaël seems all the time to have suffered from defects of voice production. In 1863 at the age of 36 when he should have been in his vocal prime, we read that as Rigoletto, in the first act of the opera 'he was not master of his voice. His intonation was uncertain and he was often too loud.' Later, he offended by singing the beginning of the 'Cortigiani' scene ('La ra, la ra') in full voice, but from then on his performance demonstrated strength and pathos. Yet, he was advised that his faults of production should be quickly remedied. The voice was 'placed' too far back and so it took from his role 'part of the tone which the role should have.'[39] Notwithstanding these imperfections *Rigoletto* brought the year 1863 to a close with exceptional success. It was a year in which one could mark up a double score for the work done. Alas, financially, it was otherwise.[40] It would seem that Carvalho had spent his subvention even before he received it.

What was popularly known as the liberty of the theatres was promulgated by imperial decree on 6 January 1864[41] to come into force on the following 1 July. It repealed earlier decrees commencing with two of Napoleon I from 1806 and 1807. Anyone could now build and exploit a theatre upon making a declaration to the Minister of the Imperial Household and Fine Arts, to the Préfecture of the Paris police, or to the Préfecture of the départements. Moreover anyone could now present any class of entertainment in any theatre without restraint. Previously the repertory of each theatre was restricted to a certain type of work—tragedy, farce, opera—to which the director was bound to adhere. Now, there was nothing to prevent Carvalho, for example, from producing *Faust* with a tragedy by Voltaire, a farce by Labiche and with horn pipes danced between the acts, all in the one evening.

Certain police ordinances were introduced during the same year. They regulated walking about and speaking in auditorium corridors during performances, requests for songs or music not advertised on the playbills, the removal of hats at the rise of the curtain, restrictions on smoking both in the auditorium and behind stage, the arrival and departure of carriages by approved ways, and the time of theatre closing, which was again firmly fixed at midnight for all occasions. There were also conditions to cover the materials used in the construction of theatres and even such details as the minimum amount of space to be allotted to seat places.[42] It represented an early version of modern planning permission and the opening of no new theatre could take place until the conditions were fulfilled. One wonders how energetically these statutes were enforced.

Coincidentally, late in 1863 new billposting arrangements for theatres and concerts had been introduced into Paris and the recently annexed suburbs whereby the walls would no longer be defaced. Instead 200 special kiosks, lit by gas in the evening would be allotted to all the districts.[43] Police regulations also existed concerning the size of posters. Their size could not exceed 63 centimetres high or 43 centimetres wide. This rule at least was rarely adhered to. The administration, recognising the diverse public at whom the bills were directed, was tolerant. Besides, large supplementary posters were seldom used except to advertise new productions, or by theatres presenting spectacular entertainments.[44]

Throughout January there was an epidemic of influenza which made 'sad havoc among the singers, and at all the musical theatres a change in performance [was] almost nightly necessitated.'[45] Fortunately all was well by 23 February and the Théâtre Lyrique could join forces with the Opéra Comique to give the first four of the annual lenten concerts at the Tuileries. Artists and chorus from both companies took part in excerpts from the Théâtre Lyrique repertory of *Philémon et Baucis, La Reine Topaze, Faust, Peines d'amour perdues, La Perle du Brésil, Joseph*, and *Richard Cœur-de-Lion*.[46] Socially there was also news of Prince Poniatowski's forthcoming opera, *L'Aventurier*, which, in an excess of irony a Paris correspondent of *The Musical World* petitioned, 'Please circulate this important piece of intelligence as far and wide as you can.'[47]

The most important piece of musical intelligence circulating in Paris during the early part of 1864 concerned Charles Gounod's new opera *Mireille*. Although Gounod was suffering from one of his frequent episodes of ill health he had finished it during the previous November. From then it was said to be in continuous rehearsal under his direction. The libretto by Michel Carré was based on Frédéric Mistral's Provençal poem which had appeared as recently as 1859. *The Musical World* made a prescient observation when it noted: 'The lyric pastoral of *Mirèio*, written in the Provençal dialect, by M. Fréderic Mistral, though little known abroad, is esteemed by literary judges in France as one of the poetic masterpieces of the age . . . Nevertheless, the poem has been considerably more talked about than read, even in Paris, the seat of learning, science and the arts,—notwithstanding, too, the existence of what is pronounced by those who have examined it, a very good translation into the received vernacular—and it is very probable that M. Mistral will find more readers, through his unanticipated connection with M. Gounod, than under any circumstances might otherwise have fallen to his lot.'[48]

Relations between Gounod and Mistral remained courteous throughout the adaptation (they were even described as courtly) and Mistral would eventually arrive in Paris to attend the final rehearsals.[49] As early as January it was also announced that 40 seats in the stalls had been taken up for the first performance 'by inhabitants of Arles and St. Rémy [de Provence]',[50] Gounod continued to rehearse indefatigably, although the preparation of the opera was not without its periods of crisis. In February Madame Carvalho finding part of the score too dramatic for her voice 'declined the honour of interpreting it'. This no doubt was Madame's way of demanding more vocalises. For a while Gounod dug in his timid heels. Madame remained obdurate. Then it was recollected that a similar situation had arisen over *Faust*, which, thanks to concessions made by both parties was happily resolved. Reciprocal concessions were consequently made again to the satisfaction of both sides, 'and above all in the interest of the public.'[51]

It was a most distinguished public that attended the first performance on 19 March. 'The theatre' we read, 'offered the most brilliant coup d'œil and all our beautiful warriors were under arms. Duchesses, baronesses, bankers were all contending for the best boxes and if tickets could have been auctioned... the direction would have recovered part of its expenses from that very first evening.'[52]

Yet, *Mireille* was not a success with the public. Neither was it a success with the critics, although Prosper Pascal in *Le Ménestrel* believed that the score would 'remain one of M. Gounod's claims to celebrity,'[53] while even Rossini was reported to have placed *Mireille* above all of Gounod's works.[54] But Scudo in the *Revue des Deux Mondes* was scathing. This hybrid work, he gibed, which is neither opera nor opera comique and in which there are only six pieces that one could call dramatic music... 'On leaving the auditorium of the Théâtre Lyrique after the first performance I was not able to prevent myself from crying out, "Vive Verdi! there is more dramatic music in *Rigoletto* than in all the works of M. Gounod."'[55] Paul Smith [-Wilhelm] (Edouard Monnais) in the *Revue et Gazette Musicale* thought that the opera began better than it ended, but added 'One must say and say again that it is mounted with exceptional care, that all the decors [by Rubé] are as effective as dioramas and that the singing and dancing of the chorus charms both the ear and the eyes.'[56] Conversely, *The Orchestra* stated, 'The mise en scène is poor and indifferent in the extreme.'[57] It was *The Orchestra* too which judged the situation astutely when it reported, '*Mireille* abounds in true musical gems but is not destined to be a stage success. So convinced has been M. Carvalho of this, that since its first representation various changes in the 4th act have been rehearsed and abandoned, without ever being submitted to the public. The opera in fact, as an opera, terminates with Act 2nd and the rest is a concert. One scenic change for the better has been made. The farm-scene before the Desert of the Crau has been changed to a pretty landscape, which rises immediately on the desert-scene, thus saving the necessity of an entr'acte.'[58]

In spite of its lack of success the opera continued to attract audiences until the end of May, but before this we read, 'It has been much curtailed, and the last acts now contain not half the music composed for them.'[59] Much of Vincent's music had to be cut because the tenor Morini was incapable of singing it,[60] but neither was Miolan-Carvalho at her best. We are told, she 'cannot succeed in interesting the audience in the heroine she so indifferently represents. Added to that she sings so out of tune, that sometimes it is an absolute affliction to listen to her.'[61] Vocally, she may have been passing through a bad phase for on 10 April it was announced that performances had been suspended because she was ill.[62]

Mireille was revived at the Théâtre Lyrique on the following 15 December, but now 'arranged in three acts and with an entirely new dénouement ... The third act has entirely disappeared, and, consequently, the attempted murder of Vincent by Ourrias and the apparitions in the Rhône (who always made a rattling sound in crossing the stage, totally unconnected with spirits or water) are done away with, much to our satisfaction. [This latter scene had been universally disliked, although it contains melodious and evocative music, and provoked both 'unexpected hilarity'[63] and the critical opinion that Eugène Sue 'could not beat it.'][64] Nothing remains of Act IV but the chanson du Pâtre and Mireille's couplets "Heureux petit berger" and instead of dying at the end of the piece, as in the first edition, the heroine is united to Vincent.'[65] A new duet, originally composed for Tietjens and Giuglini when an Italian version of the opera (with the happy ending) was presented in London during the previous July, and now sung by Miolan-Carvalho and Michot, was also added to this last act. Miolan-Carvalho at least took her revenge on those who had recorded that she sang out of tune, for the ever-complaisant Gounod had included for her in act one 'a very difficult air de bravoure in three-four time [the well known 'O légère hirondelle'] which she sings with the greatest effect, terminating with a wonderful shake on D in alt.'[66]

Notwithstanding the new D in alt, the winter revival with its happy ending succeeded no better than the spring inauguration with its sad one. During 1864 *Mireille* had had only 30 performances at the Théâtre Lyrique. In 1865 it would have a further 11; the last would take place in late January or early February, and that would be all.*

*

Mireille never achieved success until it was staged at the Opéra Comique, where, as at the Théâtre Lyrique it passed through a number of different arrangements. Since 1939 the version performed there is one scrupulously reconstituted by Gounod's pupil, Henri Busser and Reynaldo Hahn. This is the version which was produced at the Aix-en-Provence Festival in 1954 and at the Wexford Festival in 1961.

Two extra-theatrical anecdotes associated with *Mireille* can be recorded. The first was of a reception at Princess Mathilde's where Miolan-Carvalho sang airs from her new role accompanied by Gounod, and then, with Gounod still at the piano was joined by Vicomtesse de Grandval (who was an accomplished singer as well as a composer) in the letter duet from *Les Noces de Figaro* 'which electrified the assembly.'[67] The second tells how Nestor Roqueplan thanked Carvalho in *Le Constitutionnel* for having notified him, as he had the other critics, that the revival of *Mireille* had had to be postponed owing to Michot's illness—by telegram! It had saved him a vexatious journey and was a novel use of the private telegraph which he commended to the other directors.[68]

Holy Week was celebrated at the theatre with two grand sacred concerts on Holy Thursday and Easter Saturday. All the artists, chorus and orchestra headed by Miolan-Carvalho took part, which was understandable, since the concerts were for their own benefit![69] Regrettably for the beneficiaries, they were poorly attended.[70]

It was planned that the next new production to take place in April would be an opera by Félicien David and Michel Carré. Originally in two acts and called *L'Esclave* it was now extended to three acts with a ballet and retitled *La Captive*. This and Ernest Reyer's *Érostrate* originally performed at Baden-Baden in 1862 were to alternate for the remainder of the season. Neither was ever publicly performed at the Théâtre Lyrique. *La Captive* with Mlles Sannier and Ebrard and MM. Monjauze and Petit in the cast was withdrawn following the dress rehearsal, a decision reached jointly by director, composer and librettist. It was reported that changes in the libretto were necessary but that Carré was ill just then.[71] David was said to be altering *La Captive* for production at the Opéra when he died in 1876,[72] but it was never staged.

This failure was to be followed by a much more serious disappointment for Carvalho. His next new production, which did not take place until 14 June, was Bellini's *Norma*. This might be considered a continuation of his policy to revive well known works in French from the Italian repertory following his success with *Rigoletto*, had not the opera been so hastily mounted—in just eight days![73] Both Soubies[74] and Lasalle[75] state that the hurried presentation was caused by the liberty of the theatres coming into force on 1 July and explain that the Théâtre de la Porte-Saint-Martin was preparing the same opera for performance on that date. This was true, but Carvalho's reason for producing *Norma* ahead of a rival theatre was somewhat more complicated. He was indeed pursuing his policy of presenting successful Italian operas in translation yet the opera he had originally decided upon was not *Norma*, but *Don Pasquale*. Then shortly before production date, Ismaël, the Don Pasquale, 'suffered a violent throat infection with all the characteristics of angina.'[76] Carvalho, by now pretty desperate found he could engage two singers, Mme Andrieux-Charry from Rouen and M. Puget, who had already sung Etienne Monnier's translation of the roles of Norma and Pollione in the provinces. The cast was completed more satisfactorily with Leontine de Maësen as Adalgise and Petit as Orovèse. But even de Maësen seems to have failed to repeat her success as Gilda. (By ironic coincidence the Adalgise at the Porte-Saint-Martin was Ismaël's wife.) Mme Charry lacked both strength of voice and physical stature 'to represent the inspired druidess' while Puget's voice had become 'too worn to allow him to sing Pollion.'[77] As with all such improvised productions the decor was inadequate, the costumes shoddy.[78]

Léon Durocher introduced an important principle concerning the revival of familiar operas in translation when he wrote that the project was 'not without danger.' 'A successful work,' he pointed out 'is a known work. One is aware in advance of the style, the character, the sensation it creates, the effect it produces. So much the worse for you if the programme does not come up to expectations, if the spectator shakes his head in disappointment as he leaves the theatre and says, "That's it, but it is not right." The score can lose nothing and the failure is blamed entirely on the performers ... In brief, at the Théâtre Lyrique they sing *Norma* as if it were an opera by M. Verdi. One could not imagine a more utter misinterpretation.'[79]

Withal, financially, affairs cannot have been too disastrous for it was late in May when Carvalho decided to prolong his season until the end of June.[80] Unless, like the gambler who is broke, with *Don Pasquale* then in view, he was hazarding a last throw to recoup his losses. The latter situation seems unlikely,

for the return of Michot from the Opéra to the Théâtre Lyrique
in the coming season was forecast about the same time. The
current season ended on 30 June with *Rigoletto*.[81] (Adelaide
Ristori and her company had given a performance of *Medea* on
27 June and would perform *Maria Stuarda* two days later.)
Miolan-Carvalho had to be in London by 27 June where she was
singing Catherine in *L'Etoile du Nord* at Covent Garden—at a
reputed fee of 15,000 francs a month.[82]

The music critic, Pier Angelo Fiorentino (A. de Rovray), who
had once fought a duel with swords with his colleague Amédée
Achard leaving him dangerously wounded,[83] had died on 31
May, while early in July Mme Anne Gabriele Orfila, the wife of
Matéo José Buenaventura Orfila, a distinguished Spanish-
Parisian physician and amateur buffo-bass, who in her own
right was a singer, pianist and renowned leader of a Paris salon
where academics, writers and the most famous singers met, also
died.[84] But, as ever, life too pressed on. Charles Réty was about
to marry Amélie Faivre[85] and, as in the previous year, the closed
Théâtre Lyrique was occupied with rehearsals for the forthcoming
season at Baden-Baden.[86]

1864—1865

The 1864—65 season would demonstrate considerably more
activity on Carvalho's part, but with one or two exceptions
neither artistically nor financially would it be any more
rewarding. Some theatre repairs were found necessary which
delayed the opening from the customary 1 September until two
evenings later when *La Reine Topaze* with Miolan-Carvalho*
was revived. About the same time it was confidentially announced
'that Mr. Benedict's *Lily of Killarney*, under the title of *La Rose
d'Erin* will be positively brought out at the Théâtre Lyrique . . .
about the first or second week of December.'[1] It was not,
although Miolan-Carvalho was cast for Eily O'Connor and
Benedict would arrive in Paris early in October to consult with
his translators. They were MM d'Ennery and Crémieux who
had 'altered and nearly entirely reconstructed [the libretto] in
order to suit the French taste'—to such an extent 'that Mr
Boucicault with difficulty could recognise the Colleen Bawn.'[2]

A more important non-performance, advertised in July, was Bizet's Ivan IV which eventually had its first production as recently as 1946.

What *was* 'brought out' was the postponed *Don Pasquale*. (The libretto recommended that the name be pronounced 'à l'italienne: Pascouâlé' to help the musical prosody). Although it was not destined to remain long in the repertory it was nevertheless a successful production, much of its success being due to Ismaël in the title role. Norina and Malatesta's duet at the end of act one was encored, as, inevitably, 'with a veritable frenzy'[3] was the Pasquale—Malatesta duet. Norina seems to have been undersung and much over-acted by de Maësen. A new tenor, Gilland (lately arrived from a Café-Concert near the Palais-Royal) was almost useless as an actor, while as a singer, his voice seemed tired, the timbre throaty. Troy lacked some of the gaiety needed for Malatesta but he sang with grace and elegance. Of the quartette, Ismaël alone seems to have been completely successful. Not since Lablache had there been his equal. Unfortunately his voice was not deep enough to produce the full effect of the role, but this was not entirely his fault since Deloffre had allowed the orchestra to play out as if it were Lablache it was accompanying.[4]

An innovation in the production was the alteration of the setting to the Louis Quinze period. The first production at the Théâtre Italien in 1843 had employed contemporary costumes and settings. Moreover, act one now took place in a garden with Pasquale making a grand entry in a sedan chair, while the 'scene of the creditors' (perhaps the recitative and duet between Pasquale and Norina at the beginning of act three, with the preceding chorus) was replaced by a 'scène de bal'.[5]

A one act opéra comique called *L'Alcade* by a debutant composer, Uzepy had preceded *Don Pasquale*. Apart from the

---

*

Artists engaged for this season were: Mmes Miolan-Carvalho, Faure-Lefebvre, de Maësen, Nilsson, Gravière-Ebrard (she had lately married, hence the Gravière), Wilhème, Estagel, Albrecht, Duclos, Michot, Fonti, Renaudy. MM Monjauze, Michot, Ismaël, Troy, Petit, Lutz, Froment, Legrand, Wartel, Gabriel, Peront, Guyot, Bach, Gilland, Huet, Caillaud, Colomb, Mortier, Devrieux, Gerpré. Chef d'orchestre: Deloffre; Chef de chœurs, Bleuse. M. 4 Sept 1864.

overture and a pretty romance for tenor both music and libretto were said to fall below mediocrity.[6]

If *Don Pasquale* was only a semi-success there can be no question of the success of Verdi's *La Traviata*, translated by Édouard Duprez and now produced under the title of *Violetta*. Once again the work was set in the Louis Quinze period, then seemingly the fashionable epoch for 19th century opera settings. Perhaps it created a satisfactory sense of Second Empire opulence.

As in all productions of *La Traviata* the attraction was the soprano singing Violetta, here Christine Nilsson at the very outset of her great career. Born in 1843 in Sweden, the daughter of a small farmer, she had been befriended by Baroness Leuhusen herself a former singer, (Adelaide Valerius), who gave her some early lessons and then brought her to Paris where she became a pupil of Wartel. She is said to have auditioned for Carvalho by singing Rode's 'Variations' with their exhausting passages and staccati, and Meyerbeer's 'Robert, toi que j'aime', then considered the touchstone for sopranos aspiring to reach the first flight. He engaged her at once for three years at a salary which increased progressively from 2000 to 3000 francs a month.[7]

Violetta was an audacious role to choose for a début, yet she triumphed resplendently. Among the crowded audience at the first performance were Adelina Patti, Mmes Miolan-Carvalho and Duprez-Vandenheuvel and Mme Doche the actress who played Marguerite Gautier when *La Dame aux Camélias* was first staged at the Théâtre du Gymnase.[8] Little wonder that 'she was nervous, painfully so at first'[9] but 'she plucked up increasing courage as she went along.'[10] Her French pronunciation was reported both as 'better than good'[11] and 'worse than indifferent,'[12] so the truth must be somewhere between. We read that 'The Second "Swedish Nightingale" does not in the least resemble the first [Jenny Lind] except in complexion. She is tall and handsome, with fair hair and light blue eyes, elegant and engaging in manner, and possessing a voice eminently pure, flexible, and true in the upper range, though decidedly weak and deficient in the lower register. [It should be remembered that she was then just 21 years old] ... there is a certain dreamy tenderness in her look and a pathetic melody in the tones of her voice which impart a great charm to her rendering of the part.'[13] Lutz, too, was very highly praised, but Monjauze, although his singing was satisfactory, 'no longer had the physique' for the role of Rodolphe (Alfredo). 'How can he expect anybody to take him for the son of Lutz?' enquires Léon Durocher. 'I admit that M. Lutz ought to have had his hair grey, but even that would have been fruitless while the abdominal question remained unresolved.'[14] The staging of the opera was described as dazzling, the costumes, of a marvellous luxury.[15]

That was how it looked from the auditorium, but an interesting letter from an experienced member of the audience who saw a performance from an unusual position back-stage tells a different story. The writer was Lillie de Hegermann-Lindencrone*, wife of the Danish Minister to France and previously wife of the American banker, Charles Moulton. She was a good amateur singer having studied under Delle Sedie and Garcia. Her seat was in a 'box behind the curtain and very small and very dark—(I think it was the director's box)— . . . If ever I thanked my stars that I was not a star myself it was then. Everything looked so tawdry and claptrap: the dirty boards, the grossly painted scenery, the dingy workmen shuffling about grumbling and gruff, ordered and scolded by a vulgar superior. Of course the stars do not see all these things because they only appear when the heavens are ready for them to shine in.

'The overture, so it sounded to us, was a clash of drums, trumpets and trombones all jumbled together. After the three knocks of the director, which started up the dust of ages into our faces until we were almost suffocated, the curtain rose slowly with great noise and rumbling. The audience looked formidable as we saw it through the mist of cloudy gas-light, a sea of faces, of colour and vagueness. The incongruity of the costumes was a thing to weep over. If they had tried they could not have made it worse. The lady guests, walking and chatting, in a *soi-disant* elegant salon, were dressed, some in Louis XV splendour, some in dogesses' brocades, some in modern finery, with bows and ribbons and things looped up any way. Nilsson was dressed in

*

By coincidence some 40 years ago her descendant Knud de Hegermann-Lindencrone and the writer corresponded about gramophone records of old singers. Nilsson, although six months younger than Patti, never recorded.

quite modern style—flounces, laces, and fringes, and so forth, while Alfredo had donned a black velvet coat à la something, with a huge jabot which fell over a frilled shirt-front. He wore short velvet trousers, and black-silk stockings covered his thin legs without the least attempt at padding. The "padre" was in a shooting-jacket, evidently just in from a riding-tour. He held a riding-stick, and wore riding-gauntlets which he flourished about with such wide gesticulations that I thought he was going to hit Nilsson in the face. We could not hear the singing so well from where we sat; but the orchestra was overpowering, and the applause deafening, like peals of thunder.

'I laughed when the gang of workmen rushed on to the stage as soon as the curtain came down, and began sweeping and taking down one set of furniture and putting on another; especially in the last act, when Violetta's bed came on and the men threw the pillows from one to the other, as if they were playing ball. They hung up a crucifix, which I thought was unnecessary, and brought in a candlestick. I wondered if they were going to put a warming-pan in the bed. A mat was laid down with great precision. Then Nilsson came in, dressed in a flounced petticoat trimmed with lace, a "matinée", and black slippers and got into bed.

'After the performance was over, the curtain was raised and the artists came forward to bow; the stage was covered with flowers and wreaths. And Nilsson, in picking up her floral tributes, was wreathed in smiles; but they faded like mist before the sun the minute the curtain was lowered, and she looked tired and worn out.'[16]

Paul Scudo, the failed singer turned music critic, had died on October 14, at Blois, where he was in the habit of visiting friends during the summer. His death was due to some mental condition, and it now appeared that for some time previously at the theatre and in conversation, changes in his personality had caused concern. It was remarked that the passion which he had brought to his criticism of even the best works had indicated the beginnings of a deranged mind.[17] One report even went so far as to announce that he was always eccentric.[18] In October also the engagement was reported of Mme Amélie Rey-Balla for some performances of *Norma* and for an important new production of Verdi's *Macbeth*.[19] Wagner's *Lohengrin* was promised, but never materialised.[20]

The high standard of the current Théâtre Lyrique company was commented upon as was the change in artistic direction which Carvalho had brought about by introducing translations of well known Italian and German operas 'to induce the public to patronise his theatre.'[21] This policy had nevertheless produced its critics and Carvalho was forced to defend his position through the press. He pointed out that even from the time of the Sevestes' management the theatre had brought out works such as *Il Barbiere di Siviglia*, *La Gazza Ladra*, and *Otto Mesi in Due Ore* in French translation without protest, and that the new regulations even extended that privilege, so enabling a much increased music loving public to enjoy works hitherto inaccessible to 99 per cent of the population. The only new condition imposed when the subvention was granted was that one new French opera composed by a Prix de Rome lauréat must now be presented annually. Accordingly he had produced *Les Pêcheurs de Perles*, but he had also presented *Mireille* and *Les Troyens*. He also called attention to the fact that the Théâtre Italien did not pay authors' rights, all the operas performed there being in the public domain, whereas he was paying Verdi 12 per cent of the gross receipts of his works at the Théâtre Lyrique.[22]

In an oblique way he got support from Henri Blaze de Bury (Castil-Blaze's son and Scudo's successor on the *Revue des Deux Mondes*) who asked, 'Of what use is it to encourage them [young and untried composers] and their efforts when the public refuses to pay any attention to them? If an act is commissioned from one of them it fails to go. Two or three years later the same thing is tried again, with the same result. No theatre, even if it were four times as heavily subsidised as the Théâtre Lyrique, could continue to exist on such resources. So the result is that they turn to accredited talent and call on such men from outside as Gounod, Félicien David and Victor Massé. The younger composers at once shout treason and scandal. Then they select masterpieces by Mozart or Weber and there are the same outcries, the same recriminations. So, finally, where are these young composers of genius? Let them be named. "There are in the world only two places" said Prince Metternich "the stage or the loge." On the stage I cannot see them. Let them go therefore to the orchestra and hear *Le Nozze di Figaro*, *Oberon*, *Der Freischütz* and *Orphée*. The lesson there is indeed as good as another and again we are doing something for them by placing such models before them.'[23]

Blaze de Bury ignores entirely the purpose for which Adolphe Adam founded the 'third lyric theatre'. Although greatly weakening his case by overstating it, yet he justifies Carvalho, and all theatre managers who can remain in management only as long as they can keep their theatres viable.

Mme Ugalde now suddenly decided to relinquish her soprano roles and instead undertake contralto parts. It was maliciously remarked, 'Some unkind persons suggest that Madame Ugalde undertakes characters with low notes because her voice has no longer any high ones,'[24] Then just before Christmas Carvalho tried to deflect his critics by producing two one act pieces. These were *Bégaiements d'Amour* by Grisar and *Le Cousin Babylas* by Henri Caspers. The music of the latter was reported to be 'light, airy, agreeable, thoroughly French in character,'[25] but there was more hyperbole than discrimination in ascribing to Grisar 'among musicians, a corresponding place to that assigned by painters to Watteau.'[26]

The new year of 1865 began with Carvalho demonstrating his customary activity. 'M. Carvalho will not be caught napping,' reported *Le Ménestrel.* 'He makes more provision for the end of the season than others would make for the entire year.'[27] This was so with *La Flûte enchantée* being rehearsed in the main foyer, while in the small foyer rehearsals of *Macbeth* were taking place at the same time. His immediate concern however was for Poniatowski's three act opera comique *L'Aventurier.* 'The prince senator will thus be named on the playbill'[28] it was snobbishly announced. Nor will it come as a surprise to read that the first performance was 'brilliant', although the brilliance seems to have inclined more towards the auditorium than the stage. Princess Mathilde occupied Miolan-Carvalho's box, (on their way to the performance the carriage conveying the Carvalho family had been overturned by a wagon, but luckily no one was hurt)[29] and also present were numerous members of the Senate and of the Circle de Union Artistique, of which Poniatowski was the president. But it was at the general rehearsal that Poniatowski was paid his greatest compliment, when Rossini, who never went to the theatre any more, occupied a box facing the stage until the very end, which was at one in the morning. At the same rehearsal were the Duc and Duchesse de Morny, (the Duc would die in less than two months, a momentous loss to the Emperor and to France) Prince von Metternich and similar social figures, besides a gathering of artists, Gounod, Roger, Alexandre Dumas, and others.[30] As a singer Poniatowski knew how to write for the voice, but the overall effect was no better than 'agreeable' and benevolently it was recorded, 'A little more originality and more fire would have been acceptable in certain parts.'[31] The libretto, by de Saint-Georges bore a resemblance to *Les Diamants de la Couronne* which, with Scribe, he had written for Auber almost a quarter of a century before. Instead of Portugal the scene was now set in Mexico. There could scarcely have been a less opportune locale just then, for the Emperor Maximilian, having accepted the crown at the instance of Napoleon III, and sustained by French troops, was already involved in guerilla warfare which would end with his execution. At the time that Poniatowski and de Saint-Georges had first decided on their subject the future had appeared much brighter. The failure of Maximilian's expedition was matched by the failure of Poniatowski's score. All Paris society could not sustain it for more than ten performances.

A singular production was now projected, (in consequence of the liberty of the theatres) a play by Ernest Legouvé with choral and symphonic music and recitatives by Gounod. It was entitled *Les Deux Reines de France*, the two queens being Ingeburge and Agnès de Méranie who were to be played by Adelaide Ristori and Mlle Rousseil. The third principal role of King Philippe-Auguste was to be taken by Jouanni. Although the period in which the play was set was as long ago as 1200 it nevertheless presented a controversial historical subject which had involved a king of France and two popes, one of whom, Innocent III had placed France under interdict. In the delicate political situation then existing between France and the Vatican, and which Legouvé seems to have ignored (how Gounod could have ignored it is more difficult to understand) the outcome was inevitable: the play was banned. Legouvé wrote a letter of protest to the Minister, Vaillant, but the censorship remained. He had some consolation in being able to read the entire drama before an audience of writers, ladies and gentlemen of quality in the hospitable salon of Mme Lafont de la Vernède.[32] Gounod, too, had his music performed privately when M. and Mme Bertin opened their salon to him. The audition was attended by amateurs and connoisseurs of distinction. Legouvé, book in hand gave a commentary on the situations in relation to the music, and also read some extracts. For chorus there were four singers from the Opéra and Vicomtesse de Grandval sang the womens' solo parts. Gounod both directed and sang the male solos while the accompanists were Bizet and Saint-Saëns. 'An enthusiastic success greeted the new work.'[33] It would eventually have its first public performance at the Théâtre Ventadour in 1872 when the Napoleonic rein had passed away for ever.

A production of Mozart's *La Flûte enchantée* more than compensated for any disappointment caused by the suppression of *Les Deux Reines.* The history of most of Mozart's operas in Paris is repeated here yet again. It had been performed first at the Opéra in 1801 under the title of *Les Mystères d'Isis* with text by E. Morel de Chédeville and recitatives and mutilations (taken from *La Clemenza di Tito, Le Nozze di Figaro* and *Don Giovanni* and even snatches of a Haydn symphony)[34] by Ludwig Wenzel Lachnith, a horn player and arranger of operas who had migrated from Prague to Paris. Fétis called it 'a monstrous compilation' and it was jocularly named 'Les Misères d'ici'.[35] Yet by 1827 it had had 134 performances. Lachnith became so elated at the success of his workmanship that he is recorded as bursting from the theatre one evening after a performance, exclaiming, 'That's it. I don't want to compose any more operas. I will never do anything better.'[36] In 1829, 12 performances of *Die Zauberflöte* were given at the Théâtre Italien in German (with other German operas) by a company from Aachen under Joseph August Roeckel. It was there received with enthusiasm.

The translators for the present production were Nuitter and Beaumont 'who respected the score while modifying scenes which might have appeared somewhat bizarre to the public.'[37] These modifications were sometimes a little drastic. For example, Tamino becomes a young fisherman of Memphis, and instead of falling in love with Pamina on seeing her portrait, has been in love with her all the time. He is also loved by the Queen of the Night who consequently becomes her daughter's rival. The serpent is replaced by evil minded gnomes, the padlock

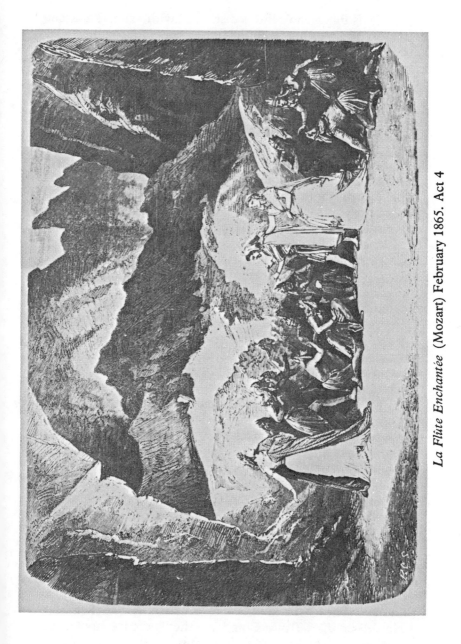

La Flûte Enchantée (Mozart) February 1865. Act 4

which seals Papageno's lips is dispensed with, while Papagena wears no disguise, but from the first appears as a young girl.[38] Instead of translating the duet of the two priests, 'Bewahret euch vor Weibertücken', Nuitter and Beaumont seem rather to have sent it up, for the verse now reads:

'When through misfortune a loving soul
Permits itself to be deceived in love
What is one to do? One can either hang oneself,
Or deceive someone in turn.'

The most significant alteration of all was to change the opera into four acts as had earlier happened with *Les Mystères d'Isis*. This needed the addition of two short pieces to serve as introductory music to the new second and fourth acts. One of these interludes was arranged from Monostatos' air 'Alles fühlt der Liebe Freuden', the other seems to have been a page from some Mozart symphony. The trio, 'Soll ich dich, Theurer, nicht mehr seh'n?' was placed before the chorus 'O Isis und Osiris' and with this chorus the third act ended. Lastly, the chorus 'Triumph, Triumph, Triumph!' occurring in the finale was suppressed.[39]

Some minor changes were also introduced by the singers, passages altered by Depassio (Sarastro) to show that he could descend to low E and E flat, and liberties taken by Michot as much to avoid an awkward interval as to introduce some high notes of which Mozart would never have dreamt. Nilsson (Queen of the Night) sang her two airs without alteration or transposition.[40] During rehearsals, certain of the singers believing that they should be given more to do had sought to have airs from other Mozart operas included in their roles, but Carvalho retorted—rather pompously if the report is correct— 'that Mozart's work will be given with integrity and unadorned.'[41] A chorus of 100 voices was announced, and a group of 'orphéonistes' had been recruited from M. Delafontaine's choir to swell the numbers.[42]

The scenery for the opera was advertised as by Cambon and Despléchin[43] but it seems to have been mainly a rehash of settings used in *L'Ondine*, *Les Pêcheurs de Perles* and *Les Troyens*.[44] The decor in the temple of Isis had earlier been deployed in *Les Troyens*, and as the audience applauded Depassio for his singing of 'Isis! c'est l'heure' ('O Isis und Osiris') it is recorded that someone leant towards Berlioz who was present and asked him, 'Well, what do you think?' 'They are a remarkable people, the Parisians,' replied Berlioz, 'they applaud the decor this evening in *La Flûte enchantée*, but they did not applaud the very same decor in *Les Troyens*.'[45] One interesting detail in connection with the production is the announcement of stage lighting by electricity, although whether it was actually used or not remains uncertain. We read prior to the first night, 'What may be accomplished by means of the mise-en-scène, scenery, decorations, appointments, costumes, machinery and lights, electric, bude* and other . . .'[46] In general however the work appears to have been well presented and exceptionally well received. One reviewer wrote, 'Were I to mention all the pieces which pleased I should tear the catalogue thématique out of my score and send it to you in order to save time.'[47]

Among the singers taking part, Nilsson and Depassio stood out because of their spectacular roles. Depassio, late of the Opéra was a 'real basso profondo' whose voice if 'not of the finest quality' could 'sing the music of Sarastro without alteration.' The same reviewer records, 'Mdlle Nilson [sic] is hardly equal to the prodigious demands of the Queen of the Night; but she goes at the music courageously and at least seems to achieve all that is required.'[48] One has to turn again to Mme de Hegermann-Lindencrone to gain the most colourful description of Nilsson's singing of this role. 'She has some phenomenal high notes, which are clear as bells,' we read. 'She makes that usually tedious grand aria which every singer makes a mess of, quite lovely and musical, hovering as she does in the regions above the upper line like a butterfly and trilling like a canary-bird. A Chinese juggler does not play with his glass balls more dexterously than she plays with all the effects and tricks of the voice.'[49]

The greatest affirmation of *La Flûte enchantée*'s success lay perhaps in the fact that with capacity takings at the Théâtre Lyrique then amounting to 6,700 francs, the average receipts for the first 20 performances reached 6,200 francs.[50]

In March 1865 the secretary of the Théâtre Lyrique was M.

---

*

Bude-light or lime-light. From Bude in Cornwall where Gurney, the inventor of the light, lived.

Delore.[51] During the same month Miolan-Carvalho, de Maësen and Troy (with artists from the Opéra Comique) took part in the first lenten concert at the Tuileries. There were duets from *La Flûte enchantée* and *Les Noces de Figaro*, and Miolan-Carvalho sang the *Mireille* waltz song and the Gounod-Bach 'Ave Maria'. The concert took place at 9.30 in the evening before an audience which included the Empress, Prince Napoleon and Princess Mathilde.[52] These concerts were very grand affairs as the following account makes clear. 'The invités were admitted by the private entrée. Ascending the staircase celebrated for the balustrade in oxydised silver, you find yourself in the salon vert whose pale sea-green draperies form so admirable a background for the graceful chefs-d'œuvre of Chaplin's brush. Thence into the petit salon gris. A long appartment usually devoted to card tables, separates these private drawing-rooms from the Salle des Maréchaux where the company assembled . . .'[53] 'The Hall of Marshals—always a fine room—is excessively pretty when filled with a parterre of ball-dresses; and now these dresses all seem to be made of gossamer soufflé, so light, you would easily believe that the wearer could, if she pleased, fly, instead of walk, up into the gallery.'[54] An admonitory sign was displayed over the entrance to the hall on these occasions. It read, 'Il ne faut pas lorgner sa Majesté'[55]—or 'Don't quiz the Emperor.' It was in March too that Marie Sax was summoned before the Seine tribunal by Adolphe Sax who as earlier recorded enjoined her to change her assumed name within 24 hours. She did so, within a month, by the clever expedient of now spelling it Saxe which prompted *Le Ménestrel* to ponder if she might not now be sued by 'le Roi de Saxe, le duc de Saxe-Cobourg-Gotha, le duc de Saxe-Meiningen' and others for assuming this distinguished patronymic.[56]

Two one act operas were also produced in March. *Les Mémoires de Fanchette* (mémoires here meaning account or bill) by Nicolò Gabrielli, a count much patronised by the court. The plot was founded on a supposed incident in the life of Dufresny, a descendant of Henry IV, who fell so deeply into debt that on his laundress presenting her 'mémoire', and having no money to pay her, he proposed himself instead, was accepted, and married her. Henri Moreno (Henri Heugel) in *Le Ménestrel* described the music as facile and agreeable.[57] The second work, *Le*

Mariage de Don Lope was by Edouard de Hartog, a Dutch expatriate well known in Paris musical circles. [He] 'has not disappointed his friends' was one reviewer's verdict 'while the public has received him in the most flattering manner. Fortunately for the enhancement of his music M. de Hartog has been provided with a very merry, intelligible and interesting book.'[58] Gabrielli's influence appears not to have extended beyond the court, for his opera had a mere three performances. De Hartog's friends, and the public, were more appreciative for he had a respectable run of 27.

April would bring news of the death of old Mme Vadé, who from the very beginning had performed the 'duenna' roles at the Théâtre Lyrique. Her last appearance on any stage had been at the little Théâtre de la Tour d'Auvergne, where some months before she had sung in a concert given by her daughter Caroline Vadé. 'The bravos of that evening which seemed to rejuvenate her, were for her the last bravos.'[59]

April also brought Verdi's *Macbeth* to the Théâtre Lyrique. The alterations which Verdi made for this production in his original score as presented at the Teatro della Pergola, Florence in 1848, have already been recounted in detail* and so do not need comment here. In brief it was announced that *Macbeth* would be performed in four acts and 12 scenes and 'should be considered as a work specially composed for the Théâtre Lyrique. It contains not less than twelve new pieces. In the third act there is a fantastic ballet for which Verdi has also written music.'[60] More spectacularly it was reported that 'the grand march of *Macbeth* will be performed by a military band under the direction of M. Paulus, the excellent conductor of the Musique de la Garde de Paris. The new family of instruments of Adolphe Sax will make their debut there and the opera will end with a hymn which M. Carvalho intends to have sung by 100 choristers.'[61] (It was not the first opera of *Macbeth* to be produced in Paris. Hippolyte Chélard had had an opera of that name with text by Rouget de Lisle of 'La Marseillaise' and Auguste Hix performed at the Opéra in 1827).

*

See *The Complete Operas of Verdi* by Charles Osborne, *The Operas of Verdi* Vol. I by Julian Budden, and an article 'Verdi's two Macbeths' by George Badacsonyi in *Opera*, February 1976.

Verdi had wanted Edouard Duprez to make the French translation and the matter had advanced to the stage where it was announced that Duprez was being helped by Georges Hainl (conductor at the Opéra) 'with the rhythmic application of the words to the music,'[62] but Carvalho had already entrusted the work to Nuitter and Beaumont. On 22 October 1864 Verdi had written from Busseto to Léon Escudier advising him that because of the number of alterations which he wished to make, including the new ballet, 'Carvalho had better abandon the idea of producing *Macbeth* this winter.' Eleven days later on November 2 he wrote again, following the success of *La Traviata*, (*Violetta*) asking Escudier 'to thank warmly in my name, ciear-sighted, brave Carvalho, the noble artists, the chorus and M. Deloffre, who, from what I hear did wonders with his orchestra.' He now hoped to have the necessary alterations to *Macbeth* finished by 10 January, 1865, for which Escudier is to pay him 10,000 francs for all countries outside Italy, at the same time allowing him to retain his author's rights for the entire French Empire. By 2 December he is having difficulty with the ballet. 'It can only be put at the beginning of act three after the chorus,' he writes. 'There are only witches on the stage, and to make these amiable creatures dance for a quarter of an hour or twenty minutes will be a furious *divertissement*. One couldn't even introduce sylphs or spirits or anything else, because we have them when Macbeth swoons. If you have anything to suggest write to me at once.' On the following 23 January the ballet was still troubling him, and included in a letter giving many directions, he writes, 'Please ask the conductor of the orchestra to superintend the study of the dances from time to time, and to point out the *tempi* that I have marked. Ballet dancers always alter the time; if that is done in this case the ballet will lose its character entirely and will fail to produce the effect which I think it should.'*

*

In view of the problems created by the ballet, for which 26 dancers were reported to have been engaged (M 26 March 1865) the names of those who took part deserve to be recorded. They were:

M. Theòdore, Mlles Ricois, Haisler.

Coryphées. Mlles Boisserie, Vattone, Bultiau, Bélisson, Lhostellier, Brach.

Corps de ballet. Mlles Dauvergne, Verbigier, Guyonneau, Dubosc, Van Dieghen, Monroy, Carray, Damand, Davenne.

Quatorze Sorcières (*Macbeth* libretto, Paris 1865)

He also gives instructions about the instrumentation and positioning of the small off-stage orchestra for the apparition of the kings—'They should be placed under the stage near an open trap-door big enough for the sound to rise and spread through the theatre, but mysteriously, and as in the distance.' The effect that Banquo's ghost will make also concerns him. He explains, 'I have seen *Macbeth* played many times in France, in England and in Italy, and everywhere Banquo is made to appear from behind a side-scene; he turns round and moves about in an agitated manner and inveighs against Macbeth, and then goes quietly away behind another side-scene. In my opinion this produces no illusion and causes no sensation and one doesn't understand whether he is a ghost or a man. When I put *Macbeth* on the stage in Florence, I made Banquo appear (with a long wound in his forehead) from a trap-door exactly in Macbeth's place. He did not move about, but only shook his head at the right moment. He was terrifying.'[63]

One reviewer describes the first Paris performance as follows: 'Verdi's *Macbeth* has at length been produced at the Théâtre Lyrique with all the requisite pomp of splendid and picturesque scenery, decorations, groupings and costumes, and has, in consequence pleased the Parisians mightily. I do not think the music has made a profound impression, and the acting would cause much surprise in an English audience. Nevertheless to my thinking, the opera contains some of the composer's finest pieces, and one scene of the witches is surpassingly grand . . . [Rey-Balla] possesses some tragic instincts and has a powerful voice, which, however, reveals a good deal of wear and tear. In appearance Madame Rey-Balla is singularly unsuited for the character of Lady Macbeth. M. Ismaël shows much talent in Macbeth but his notion of a Scottish thane is greatly distorted and MM. Monjauze and Petit appear to have "killed, not Scotch'd" their parts.'[64] Care at least seems to have been taken with the settings although perhaps not always with the happiest results, for Macbeth's room in the last act 'was literally copied after a design by M. Viollet-le-Duc in the dictionary of furniture.'[65]

Although, following the first performance, Carvalho and Escudier would both send telegrams to Verdi announcing 'an immense success' this was obviously first night euphoria, for a week later Verdi was writing, 'In some French papers I have noticed sentences which would admit of doubt [as to how *Macbeth* had gone]. Some draw attention to one thing, some to another. One finds the subject is sublime and another that it is not suited for music, while another says that I did not know Shaspeare [sic] when I wrote *Macbeth*. But in this they are quite wrong. I may not have rendered *Macbeth* well, but that I do not know, do not understand and feel Shaspeare [sic], no, by heavens no!' That Carvalho, who had produced, had as usual altered the score, is apparent from a subsequent letter. 'M. Carvalho's device of having the drinking song sung by the tenor [Macduff] is certainly ingenious, but I am still of the opinion that this spoils the complete effect of the finale.'

The opera had only 14 performances, the last announced to take place on 29 May, and on 3 June Verdi would dejectedly conclude, 'When everything has been properly reckoned, weighed and summed up, *Macbeth* is a failure. Amen. I confess however, that I did not expect it. I did not think I had done too badly but it seems I was wrong.'[66] With the passing of a century it is now too easy to recognise that it was the Théâtre Lyrique public, (or Carvalho's production) that was wrong. Time has proved Verdi to have been triumphantly right.

Two further operas, one a creation, the other a revival ended the season. The creation was a first work called *Le Roi Candaule* by Eugène Diaz (de la Pena) son of the celebrated Barbizon-school painter. It came in for much criticism because of Michel Carré's libretto. What is the use, asked one reviewer, 'of dragging in classical personages by the ears, and trying to induce people to come and listen to an absurd piece which has no more to do with Candaule and Gyges than a silk purse with the ear of. . . ?'[67] Another declared it to be 'more suited for the Bouffes or Varietés, being written in the . . . Belle-Hélène style, without, however, the genuine form of [the latter].'[68] Diaz was received more sympathetically, and it was considered 'that, without having written a *chef d'œuvre*, which few people do when they begin, there is enough serious thought and good writing in his opera to make us think that we shall hear of him again, and under more favourable circumstances.'[69] It was a belief that would be realised.

The revival was exceptional in that it was an opera by

Mendelssohn, or rather an adaptation of Mendelssohn's opera *Die Heimkehr aus der Fremde.* The opera's history commenced with Mendelssohn's first visit to England and Scotland in 1829. While in London he seriously injured his knee which incapacitated him for two months. During this time he wrote the opera as a silver-wedding gift for his parents, his friend Karl Klingemann, then secretary to the Prussian Legation in London writing the libretto. It was not performed publicly until 1851, after Mendelssohn's death. Later in that year it was produced in London, translated by H.F. Chorley as *Son and Stranger.* The Théâtre Lyrique production was called *Lisbeth ou La Cinquant- aine* with the libretto altered 'to suit the exigencies of the popular taste by M. Jules Barbier, but I cannot say therefore' adds the reviewer 'that the opera has been benefitted.'[70] The score was evidently much modified as well and the opinion of Paul Smith in the *Revue et Gazette Musicale* was that the composition (which Mendelssohn called Liederspiel and not opera) while not out of place in the theatre, did not seem destined to produce much effect there.[71] Charles Potier, one of the artists taking part was not a singer but a well known actor late of the Théâtre des Variétés, but Petit the bass playing Kautz, sang 'I'm a roamer' 'gloriously',[72] as basses still do today.

Although not directly concerning the Théâtre Lyrique, an application from members of the Opéra orchestra to their then director Emile Perrin for an increase of salary has passing interest since fees paid to instrumentalists must have been more or less the same at the principal Paris theatres. Undoubtedly players at the Opéra could command rather higher amounts, for which reason one can only feel all the more sympathy for their lesser endowed colleagues at the Opéra Comique and Théâtre Lyrique. It was said of the memorandum sent to Perrin that figures spoke more eloquently than words. They surely did, for, of the 84 musicians employed in the Opéra orchestra, 34 were paid less than 1,200 francs *a year,* the players of the side drum and triangle were each paid as little as 950 and 750 francs, while the maximum paid to the six principal soloists was only 2,500 francs. It does not seem unreasonable, therefore, that they should seek a maximum of 3,500 francs, with an increase for most members to 1,800 francs and a minimum rate of 1,200 for the lowly side drum and triangle players.[73] Reaction from the

Opéra was predictable for the period, Perrin suggested that all dissatisfied members should resign. (More impartially *Le Ménestrel* pointed out that choristers would also seek an increase if instrumentalists were granted one, and argued that choristers were obliged to attend many more rehearsals. This would increase costs not only by 64,000 francs as estimated for the orchestra, but by 120,000 francs.[74]) Negotiations having failed, the instrumentalists set about resolving their problem in individual fashion. On one evening they played the entire five acts of *Les Huguenots* right through, fortissimo. Then, 'two days after, the entire band seemed to be suffering—the wind instruments from disease of the chest, and the strings from general debility, and nothing louder than a piano could be noticed even in the most dashing parts of *Guillaume Tell*.' These tactics continued for a time until the administration offered an annual increase of 16,000 francs (£640) for the entire orchestra of 95 or 96 players*! Their parsimonious attempt at conciliation did not succeed. Shortly afterwards the Opéra ceased to be attached to the Emperor's Household and the administration, backed by the customary subvention was assigned to a manager at his own 'risques et péril'.[75]

It may be pointed out that the instrumentalists, especially string players could earn extra fees by teaching. In practice therefore members of the Opéra orchestra—and by extension, of the Théâtre Lyrique—were more likely to have an annual income of 6,000 to 10,000 francs, by no means a fortune, and they certainly had to work for it.

The theatre closed for the season on 30 June with a performance of *La Flûte enchantée*. On the previous Wednesday there had been a benefit performance for 'an artist' when *Le Roi Candaule* and *Lisbeth* were played. Roger and Mme Meillet appeared and sang the act four duet from *Les Huguenots*. Roger also sang an air from *La Dame blanche*.[76] At this special performance all eyes were on Mme Miolan-Carvalho's box, where conspicuous with the celebrated singer was the new chevalier of the Légion d'honneur, the painter Rosa Bonheur, wearing the decoration of the order.[66]

---

*

There is a discrepancy in the number of musicians given here with the number recorded above.

1865-1866

The summer of 1865 turned out to be exceptionally warm and dry, and even as late as October a correspondent was writing, 'the heat has been so intense that in these latter days the fountains have stopped their supplies; the boulevards have remained unwashed; and even the Seine, showing its Thames-like bed, has been obliged to borrow of its neighbours, we are by chance thankful in due season, and don't complain when it rains as it has done today. People were rubbing their hands with delight as the water rushed down the sides of the streets.'[1] In such prolonged warm weather infection was inevitable and an outbreak of cholera in South West France, particularly in Marseille was awaited with fear in Paris. It arrived in due course and the same correspondent reported 'We suck parasol handles hollowed out and stuffed with camphor (supposed to be an efficient preventative against cholera, but isn't) and accost each other savagely with, "Quoi de nouveau?" The other answers sadly, "Rien." '[2] Not surprisingly theatre attendance was lowered since people were remaining in the country and we find that all four opera houses were 'doing but small business'.[3]

The Théâtre Lyrique had reopened on 1 September with *La Flûte enchantée*, 'still the pièce de résistance and ... as successful as anything can be in the present state of affairs.'*
In October, Napoleon III and Otto von Bismarck were meeting in Biarritz, ostensibly to discuss plans for peace, actually laying plans for the Austro-Prussian war. Bismarck had brought in his train the band of the 34th Prussian Regiment (from his child-

---

*

Artists engaged for this season were:
Mmes Miolan-Carvalho, de Maësen, Nilsson, Tual, Wilhème, Estagel, Albrecht, Daram, Michot, Demay, Ladois, Duclos.
MM. Monjauze, Michot, Ismaël, Depassio, Troy *aîné*, Lutz, Puget, Froment, Wartel, Barré, Gabriel, Legrand, Gilland, Peront, Guyot, Gerprè, Troy *jeune*, Caillaud, Blum, Bosquin, Pons, Stroheker, Duchesne, Anselme.
Chefs d'Orchestre: Deloffre, Mangin, Sarrazin.
Chef de Chœurs: Bleuse *Accompagnateurs:* Salomon, Mangin.
Régisseur Général: Arsène (*Almanach de la Musique*, 1866, 21)

hood province of Pomerania) which gave six concerts at the Cirque d'Impératrice. He attended one of them with his daughter.[4] The occasion inspired a fraternal hymn, words by Baron Taylor. The chorus went as follows:

'O noble sons of Germany
Greetings to you, messengers of peace
Here are the times dreamt of by Charlemagne,
No longer is it Germans, no longer French.'

Seemingly not content with this gesture of friendship the Baron next approached the Emperor to have one of the bands of the Grenadier Guards sent to Berlin on a reciprocal visit.[5] Few then appeared to realise that the Austro-Prussian encounter would be merely the prelude to the Franco-Prussian disaster. In five years' time the band of the Grenadier Guards would indeed set out for Berlin, only to be stopped short at Sedan.

In the meantime, a new opera, with a quasi-historico-political plot, *Le Roi des Mines* by Edmond Chérouvrier, had reached the Théâtre Lyrique stage. The king of the mines was Gustavus Vasa, King of Sweden, who, after the fashion of Peter the Great of Russia working incognito as a shipwright, was here found working as a miner. The libretto by Dubreuil was poor, the score equally so. The latter was judged to be too long and was cut, trimmed and mutilated,[6] until, in spite of it being a work of three acts and four scenes, it lasted no longer than an hour and a half in actual playing time.[7] What was left of it contained too much dialogue. Besides it was presented with old and dusty scenery and costumes from earlier productions. Little wonder that it had only five performances and that Armand Gouzien in the *Revue et Gazette Musicale* should reserve judgement on Chérouvrier until he had seen his second opera.

The work that followed, *Le Rêve*, with music by Edmond Savary, another 'maiden-speech theatrical'[8] was no more successful. 'Here is one of those librettos to which debutant composers are exposed,' wrote Gustave Bertrand in *Le Ménestrel*, 'they can console themselves in realising that their elders are no better served. As for the music, it is well formed but entirely lacking in originality.'[9] It was original, in fact, only in lacking trombones in the scoring, especially, we are told, since the action passes in Germany, where 'this instrument is cultivated with passion.'[10]

The critic, Gustave Héquet (Léon Durocher) of the *Revue et*

Gazette Musicale died on October 26.[11] Wednesday, 15 November being the feast day of Sainte-Eugénie, the Empress's patron saint, all the theatres were beflagged and illuminated.[12] The Court then departed for Compiègne where a theatrical review was staged. The little Prince Imperial played a grenadier, the Austrian ambassador, Prince von Metternich, 'a great friend of music' played the piano.[13]

It was December before the first worthwhile production of the season was given, when Paris saw Flotow's *Martha* for the first time in French. The story of this opera is said to have had its origin in a certain *Ballet des chambrières à louer* performed at the court of Louis XIII in 1617.[14] A more likely source perhaps is a comedy by Ancelot and Decomberousse, *Madame d'Egmont ou Sont-elles deux?* performed at the Théâtre des Variétés in 1833.[15] The first confirmed source is a ballet, *Lady Henriette ou La Servante de Greenwich* with scenario by de Saint-Georges, choreography by Mazilier and music by Flotow (first act only), Burgmüller and Deldevez, first performed at the Opéra on 21 February 1844. This story was adapted by Friedrich Wilhelm Riese who wrote under the pseudonym of W. Friedrich and who, like Flotow was a German living in Paris. Riese translated and adapted many French plays and operas including Flotow's *Alessandro Stradella* and though German by birth, his style of writing like Flotow's style of composition was much influenced by his years spent in France.

Martha was first performed in Paris in Italian at the Théâtre Italien on 11 February 1858, and it is recorded that translated into French it was well known throughout the French provinces before Carvalho presented it in 1865.[16]* It is also recorded that it had been offered to him for production before the Théâtre Italien during his first term at the Théâtre Lyrique but that he had turned it down.[17] For the present production it was widely advertised that three pieces from Flotow's earlier opera, *L'Âme en Peine* would be introduced into the score. All editions of

*

There is a French score in the British Library, presumed to have been published in 1858 with translation by C[revel] de Charlemagne, and RGM, 12 December 1858 announces performances at Toulouse, Bordeaux, Angers, and Montauban.

'Kobbé' in their resumé of *Martha* record, 'Paris, Théâtre Lyrique, December 16, 1865, when was interpolated the famous air "M'appari" from Flotow's two-act opera, *L'Âme en Peine.*' Two details need correction here. Firstly, the date of production was December 18, not 16,[18] secondly, 'M'appari' had been already 'admirably sung by Mario and rapturously applauded by the public' in the production at the Théâtre Italien in 1858.[19] Certainly this air was not one of the three introduced, as will be shown. Moreover there is no evidence to indicate that it was not in the *Martha* score from the beginning, and a score in the British Library published in Vienna and *assumed* to be an 1848 edition includes the air, 'Ach! so fromm' which strongly suggests that it was always part of it.

The confusion may have arisen because one of the airs introduced, 'Depuis le jour j'ai paré ma chaumière' had been very popular in *L'Ame en Peine*, but this was a baritone air and had been inserted into Act 4 of *Martha* for Plunkett.[20] De Saint Georges had written new words for it beginning 'Depuis l'instant où de votre visage.' The other pieces introduced were a grand bravura air, 'C'est une fille du village' also in act 4 to show off Nilsson's high notes,[21] and a 'fanfare vocale',[22] 'Le cor résonne' for the chorus, added to the hunting songs in act 3. Carvalho's meddling with opera scores has frequently been commented upon, but here at least he had the sanction of both librettist and composer, for de Saint-Georges had written new appropriate verses for the airs and Flotow had arrived in Paris about the first week of December to be present at the final rehearsals.[23] He would remain for the first two performances.[24]

The production was enormously successful and would remain in the theatre's repertory almost to the end. 'The last rose of summer', the 'spinning wheel quartette', Plunkett's 'porter song' (transferred to act 1) and Nancy's 'hunting song' in act 3, were all encored. Strangely enough, Michot does not appear to have received the most expected encore of all, for 'M'appari', here translated to 'Lorsque mes yeux enchantés'.* He may have

*

If Michot sang these words as quoted by Armand Gouzien in the *Revue et Gazette Musicale*, he was using a combination of Charlemagne's and de Saint Georges' translations!

been off form at this time. Earlier the opera had had to be postponed because he was ill, and of his first night performance one critic recorded that 'he roared lustily when the opportunity was afforded him.'[25] Gustave Bertrand, while noting that he sang the romance very well nevertheless reports that he tired his voice singing high B's and C's from the chest.[26]

Nilsson was almost entirely successful, although there were reservations about her singing of 'The last rose of summer'— 'the sentimental cantabile is not her style.'[27] Neither did her interpolated air in act 4 have its expected effect. She succeeded, however, with the triplets which ended the spinning wheel quartette, in which d'Ortigue considered she rivalled Patti.[28]

Great care had been taken with the production, the Richmond fair scene was particularly animated. The costumes were rich and in good taste. The decor (by Rubé) was picturesque, especially the setting for act 3, the hunting scene, which was excellent.[29] At the end of this act a great theatrical impression was created by having Queen Anne carried in on a palanquin, but at the finale of act 2 although much money had been squandered on electric light, the effect was spoiled by this lavishness.[30] Whatever the effect, we have here the first recorded use of electric light on the stage of the Théâtre Lyrique.

The first performance was graced by Princess Mathilde, the Minister for Public Works and Mme Béhic, Baron Haussmann, and a crowd of other notabilities,[31] not forgetting Flotow. Receipts for performances which followed would reach 6000 francs a night, and for the first 15 nights would amount to 84,000 francs.[32]

Less than two weeks after *Martha* was produced it was followed by the prize-winning opera which had been commissioned by Carvalho from Prix de Rome laureates. The successful candidate among five who competed was Gratien-Norbert (Adrien) Barthe who had been unanimously chosen by a jury which included Auber and Gounod. Today, his name is not even to be found in 'Grove'.

The opera was *La Fiancée d'Abydos*, an adaptation of Byron's *The Bride of Abydos* by Jules Adenis, with a drastically altered ending. The alteration was insisted upon by Carvalho, who had a fourth act added. In this instance he may have been influenced by his wife for when Barthe sent in his score, 'it was straight discovered that Madame Carvalho had not been sufficiently minded in the apportioning of the music, so that the composer was enforced to add two or three pieces more.' It was admitted however that 'it would have been difficult to preserve the dénouement of the poem, there being nothing dramatic in the death of Selim and Zuleika' and in justification of this adaptive approach it was decided, 'at a grand theatre a serious termination might be desirable; but the Théâtre Lyrique suffers no dolorous ending, and Madame Carvalho is altogether more attractive when smiling than when sobbing.'[33]

Every effort was made to present the opera as a major event (Miolan-Carvalho's name in the programme testifies to that) settings were by Rubé and Chaperon, and, most exceptional for an unknown opera in Paris, Choudens had published the score and had it on sale in the music shops concurrently with the first performance. Although it would not succeed the work was well received by the critics. Yet amongst the indulgent reviews there is more than a hint of eclecticism, derived, let it be said, from all the best masters. We read of 'a certain phrase very reminiscent of the finale of *Le Comte Ory*,' a very sensitive reflection of Félicien David, a third act ending exactly like the final trio in act 2 of *La Juive*, a rhythm in act 4 reminiscent of act 5 of *Robert-le-Diable*—'in truth it is the second hand of Meyerbeer.'[34] For good measure there was 'a love duet rather "Faustish" in character, which produced a great effect.'[35]

This did not seem like a work of originality likely to stand the test of time. In fact it did not survive the season. Its failure had consequences far beyond Barthe. Carvalho's financial position, already unsound, now became precarious. In the following July he would publicly deny that he was trying to sell shares in his theatre, yet he seems to have been seeking a loan of 100,000 francs.[36] Artistically it turned him towards the revival of well known operas, as more likely to be box-office successes, and for a time at least, he would curtail his presentation of new operas. Bizet's *Ivan IV*, earlier referred to, would probably be the greatest casualty of this policy.

This unanticipated change of plans presented its own problems. The translation of the classics into French and their production on stage took time, consequently it would be May, over four months away before the next new opera would be performed. Happily Carvalho had a number of successful operas in the repertory on which he could rely. *La Flûte enchantée* would be performed 58 times during the season, *Martha,* 55 times, *Rigoletto* 46 times and with this help he would survive.

In the interim there was news that Wagner intended to spend the winter in Paris (he went to Triebschen instead), and that *Lohengrin* might be produced at the Théâtre Lyrique[37] (it was not). Who did arrive in Paris in the early spring of 1866 was Balfe, to discuss once again in vain the production of *La Bohémienne* with Carvalho.[38] *Faust* had its 200th performance at the Théâtre Lyrique on 19 February,[39] and in the following May Gounod would be elected to the Académie des Beaux Arts, to replace Clapisson, gaining 19 votes to Félicien David's 16, Victor Massé's one, and Antoine Elwart's none.[40] Miolan-Carvalho, Nilsson, Michot and Troy were among the artists who took part in the first Tuileries lenten concert that year.[41] About the same time Léon Carvalho in association with Hostein, then manager of the Théâtre de la Gaîté, had obtained permission to build an immense theatre in the Champ de Mars for the Exhibition of 1867. It was intended to present opera, comedy, tragedy, vaudeville and concerts in every language in 'this dramatic Babel.'[42] Yet again the ungallant Adolphe Sax proceeded against the now Marie Saxe insisting that her name was not Saxe but Sasse, and claiming that his 'individuality would suffer if she were allowed to continue to use the name of Saxe.'[43] She may have disliked her name because the word sasse in French means bailing scoop. Whatever her reason she would have the unusual distinction of singing under four names during her career, Sasse, Sax, Saxe and Sass. In May, Count Baciocchi, superintendent of the imperial theatres was appointed Senator[44] and in the same month Emile Balanqué, the first Méphistophélès would die at the early age of 38. He had lost his voice about three years previously and in an attempt to make a living had become producer at the theatre in Angers. Even then, luck was against him for the theatre burned down soon after. So, 'he returned to Paris to a wife and five children and died "literally" of grief.'[45]

Very early in the year it had been announced that Gluck's *Armide* was in course of preparation. Mme Charton-Demeur had been engaged expressly—'impossible to make a better choice'—and was already working on her role with Berlioz,[46] but the project was abandoned in March.[47] The next opera to be produced (on 8 May), consequently, would be Mozart's *Don Giovanni* and since de Maësen, now Mme de Maësen-Gradine was 'in a state of health that would render her appearance in the part of Donna Anna impossible,'[48] the role was taken over by Charton-Demeur.

The story of earlier mutilated versions produced in Paris conforms to the experience of Mozart's other works produced there. It was first performed at the Opéra on 17 September 1805. The translators and adapters of the libretto were J. Thuring, a 'général de brigade' and D. Baillot, assistant librarian at the Château of Versailles. The music was arranged by Christian Kalkbrenner, then coach and chorus master at the Opéra. He would be associated with Lachnith (the perpetrator of *Les Mystères d'Isis*), in some extraordinary pastiche oratorios, but the musical destruction of *Don Giovanni* he achieved on his own. Helped by his literary colleagues scarcely a scene or musical piece was left untouched culminating in the trio of the masks being sung by three basses![49] Castil-Blaze had his turn too, at the Odéon on 24 December 1827 when the opera was produced using his adaptation of Molière's play, and with dialogue instead of recitatives. Dialogue was again used instead of recitative by the present translators and one source at least described it as 'borrowed from the immortal Molière.'[50] A few recitatives remained. 'The short recitative which follows the introduction,' (very difficult to identify), some bars which connect the two phrases sung by the Commandeur in the graveyard scene', while 'only two bars of Donna Anna's great recitative [?'Don Ottavio, son morta' ?'Crudele? ah no, mio, bene'] were cut.' The new translation was not always exact, characteristics of some of the roles had been altered, but on the whole it was a faithful version.[51]

Musically, the off-stage orchestra had been retained for the first act finale, but the effect of the orchestra on stage—apparently, just some violins on a platform—was so insignificant it would have been better to have abolished it.[52] There were some cuts, an aria for Don Juan, perhaps 'Metà di voi qua vadano', Leporello's second act aria, 'Ah, pietà, Signori miei' and the duet for Zerline and Leporello, 'Per queste tue manine', seldom if ever performed, even today.

The production was not elaborate. In the finale of the opera following the supper and the entrance of the Commandeur the scene changed back to the graveyard where the Don's damnation took place. It then changed to the outside of his château where Donna Anna, Donna Elvire, Ottavio and the others are found waiting to surprise him on his return.[53] Gustave Bertrand reported that things did not go too well in the 'damnation scene' on the first night. Some accident happened to the mask and draperies of the Commandeur which prevented him coming forward on stage, neither was there sufficient light on him. But by the second performance the matter had been put right and the effect was excellent. By the second performance there was also more mastery of stage machinery and production and so an interval was avoided which previously had disrupted the action and the opera ended before midnight! Bertrand also recommended that the dialogue should be curtailed and that much of the comedy should be suppressed, (we may be certain that at the Théâtre Lyrique Leporello was allowed a very loose rein) also that recitatives should be restored in certain parts, at least in the graveyard scene.[54]

The general rehearsal on 1 May had gone badly. Troy, the Leporello, was ill, and towards the end of the evening, Barré, the Don, had become very hoarse.[55] By 8 May he had recovered and so it was decided to present the opera at once. In Paris it was a year of *Don Juans*, for almost concurrently there were three productions, at the Opéra, the Théâtre Italien and the Théâtre Lyrique. Of the three it was generally conceded that the Théâtre Lyrique production was the best and the following review in *The Orchestra* fairly reflects this opinion.

'The house was crowded,' we read, 'and the effect (save some little hitches in the scenery without which no première représentation which respects itself can possibly pass off), was most satisfactory. The opera is stated to be in two acts; but if we count the number of times the "rideau de service" was lowered, we may look on it as a five-act work. (This has since been modified and I hear that all goes on smoothly). With this exception ... the opera was a remarkable and well-deserved success ... certainly the best of the three editions with which we have been favoured this season ... I doubt whether it would be possible to find three more remarkable representatives of Anna, Elvire and Zerline, than Mdmes. Charton-Demeur, Nilsson and Carvalho. M. Barré, the Don, [who like M. Geffroy playing Molière's Don Juan at the Comédie Française wore five different costumes, 'the emblem of the diversity of his amours']⁵⁶ was not our beau ideal of the character; but he is young and it was a début; so we must be indulgent. If he did not give all the fire to the 'Finch' han del vino', the casse-cou of all the baritones, he at all events deserves a good mark for the charming manner in which he sang the serenade. Troy was a capital Leporello, not coward enough perhaps in the last scene. Michot sang the charming airs 'Dalla sua pace' and 'Il mio tesoro', like a real artist; taking Rubini's famous trait* in the latter. Lutz was a good Masetto and Depassio a handsome and big-voiced Commandeur: only he ought to learn to keep still in the tomb scene.'⁵⁷

There were encores for 'Là ci darem' and 'Batti, batti', and the trio of the masks 'was so well executed that the whole house rose as one man and insisted on its repetition ... Without going so far as to say, like the musical critic of a highly distinguished journal here, that "the body of Mozart must have jumped for joy in its tomb" ... I have no doubt that had he been still alive he would have been delighted with the remarkable performance of this part of his chef-d'œuvre. I noticed old musicians present who were quite taken aback; amongst others Levasseur, [a famous bass, and Leporello] and Berlioz (a great man, whatever

---

*

An allusion to Rubini's singing of the aria in which very unethical things were done to Mozart. As with all such stories there is more than one version extant. Ernest Legouvé records: 'It was he who one day, at a rehearsal of *Don Giovanni* and during the opening bars of 'Il mio tesoro' leant towards the orchestra and said to the clarinettist who had just executed a brilliant variation, "Monsieur, would you be good enough to lend me this?" And to the stupefaction of the prompter and amid frantic applause of band and public he introduced the variation at the end of his aria'. (Ernest Legouvé, Trans. Albert D. Vandam, *Sixty Years of Recollections.* London 1893. 2V. I. 210). According to Jouvin, editor of *Le Figaro*, 'The famous trill of Don Ottavio, Mozart had entrusted to his first violins and not to his first tenor. Rubini ... decided, at the time, to take what was to his advantage where he could find it.' (M. 27 May 1866)

our private opinion of *Les Troyens* may be), who covered his face and cried like a child. The mise en scène is very good, and the orchestra under the order of M. Deloffre deserves high praise.'[58]

Although the reviewer in *The Orchestra* omits mention of it there was also general agreement that the final moralising scene should be cut. At this period it was never performed, and neither the Opéra nor the Théâtre Italien productions had included it. D'Ortigue in the *Journal des Débats* blamed this 'appendage' on Da Ponte and considered that it would be as well 'to end the second act conforming to the custom followed everywhere else both in the interest of the public and of the work itself.'[59] Armand Gouzien in the *Revue et Gazette Musicale* agreed with him.[60]

A more virulent attack appeared in the *Revue des Deux Mondes* written by F. de Lagenevais. 'With Don Juan dead all interest is lost' he proclaimed 'and the characters brought back purposelessly do nothing but pour cold water on the spectator and benumb in him the impression of the great performance which he has seen—a drama of colour, of vengeance, of love, especially of love in all its forms ... In Germany they don't bother you with this ridiculous epilogue, but it means nothing to the Théâtre Lyrique that others are content with the normal, for them the spirit of a great work is not sufficient, they must insist on the letter ... They have Mozart's manuscript.' (The score of *Don Giovanni* which Pauline Viardot had bought in London in 1858 for £200, and which apparently had been examined by all the Paris critics at the time.) Not content with these harsh words, F. de Lagenevais continues, 'It is useless now after everyone else to stress the inadequacy of the orchestra at the Théâtre Lyrique, and the poverty of the chorus there. In the same way the grand finale produced no effect and in the scene with the Commandeur, the renowned dramatic stroke passed unnoticed. Definitely, Mozart's Don Juan is not an opera comique.'[61]

And who was F. de Lagenevais? It was a pseudonym used generally by writers for the *Revue des Deux Mondes*, but very frequently by Henry Blaze de Bury. Blaze de Bury, with Emile Deschamps had had a new five act version of *Don Juan* produced at the Opéra in March 1834. It would have its 100th performance there in 1872 and apparently would remain in use until a new version arranged by Adolphe Boschot supplanted it in 1934. So, almost certainly in this instance de Lagenevais was Blaze de Bury, and Blaze de Bury had an axe to grind. What he wrote mattered little. The house was booked out for the first 18 performances[62] and on Thursday 10 May Princess Mathilde— 'whose salons still remain open during May each Sunday'—was among the audience.[63] In no manner would *Don Juan* equal the success of *La Flûte enchantée,* but it would deserve honorable mention by having 71 performances over three seasons.

Nicolai's *Les Joyeuses Commères de Windsor* (*Die Lustigen Weiber von Windsor*) now had its first Paris performance, although it may have been produced in Bordeaux in 1864. It was intended that it should alternate with *Don Juan* but it was almost a complete failure. Blaze de Bury considered that Nicolai had merited better 'than the cold and scornful reception given to him,'[64] while Armand Gouzien was surprised at the lack of enthusiasm with which even the overture (well known through Pasdeloup's concerts) was greeted.[65] Jules Barbier's translation was recorded as 'not too distorted'[66] although presumably Carvalho alone could explain why Mistress Page's air about Herne the hunter in act 3 should be replaced by 'Rule Britannia'. Adapted to French words it now went:
      'Et l'Angleterre dira encor
      La folle histoire de Windsor'[67]
The weakness of the entire production is evident in that the most notable comic episode of the first performance seems to have been an untimely accident to Falstaff's braces.[68] Musically the most popular piece was the duet in act 2 between Anne and Fenton, in which 'the violin obligato was admirably performed by the soloist M. Vizentini.'[69] As Falstaff, Ismaël was too light of voice and laboured 'under the common belief of all French actors that the character he represents ought to be dressed in red and have red hair.' Mlle Saint-Urbain (Mistress Ford) had had 'a succession of "fiascos": fiasco at the Italiens: fiasco at the Bouffes Parisiens; fiasco at the Théâtre Lyrique.' Mlle Daram (Anne) alone seems to have been completely satisfactory, singing in time and in tune and looking the part admirably.[70] Gustave Bertrand in *Le Ménestrel* emphasising with what enthusiasm his paper had greeted the many masterpieces in translation already presented by Carvalho described *Les*

Joyeuses Commères as worthless. He suggested that principal works only warranted international production, and that genius alone had the right to travel and to survive.[71] In spite of this set-back to the programme, it would still be announced in May that 'The Théâtre Lyrique will not close this year except for one month because of the success of *Don Juan*.'[72]

To end the season two one act operettas were performed. The first, *Le Sorcier* was by 'a lady of quality who employs her leisure in composing romances and salon operas and whose receptions are extolled each winter by the chroniclers of the high life.'[73] Her pseudonym, Anaïs Marcelli shielded the identity of Mme Perrière-Pilté. She was both librettist and composer of *Le Sorcier* which Armand Gouzien summed up by declaring, 'We pity the singers who have had to interpret such incoherence, and the orchestra which has had to repeat these infantile accompaniments and this naive overture.'[74] For reasons best known to Carvalho it would nevertheless remain in the repertory until 1868 receiving a total of 30 performances.

The second, *Les Dragées de Suzette*, was more professional, having been composed by a professional, Hector Salomon, then a répétiteur at the theatre, to a libretto by Jules Barbier—('his worst' according to *The Orchestra*), and Delahaye. It was another episode of the Pompadour period, this time set in the country house of the celebrated ballet dancer, Mlle Sallé. Salomon's work had to combat the boredom created earlier by *Le Sorcier*, but his music gave proof of more energy and originality than is generally to be found in a débutant.[75] Following Ristori's by now customary performances of *Medea* and *Maria Stuarda* on 27 and 29 June,[76] the theatre closed for the season on 30 June with the 24th performance of *Don Juan*.[77]

1866–1867

It re-opened as intended on 1 August with *Martha** and with the promise of a revival of *Faust* for the fête day celebrations on the

*

Artists engaged during this season were: Mmes Miolan-Carvalho, Nilsson, Charton-Demeur, Dubois, Daram, Michot, Demay, Jeanne Devries, Wilhème, Balbi-Verdier, Rouvroy, Regnault, Schroeder, Adelaide Cornelis (from the

15th. A new general stage manager, M. Briet, formerly director of the Théâtre des Arts, Rouen, had been engaged.[1] No announcement can be found explaining the departure of M. Arsène who had held the post for so many years. M. Delore, the secretary-general was also replaced by Jules Ruelle, editor of the *Messager des Théâtres*,[2] and translator of operas, ranging from Donizetti's *Il Campanello di Notte* to Glinka's *A Life for the Tsar*. Earlier in July Carvalho had set out for Italy, to seek a Roméo for Gounod's forthcoming opera.[3] On the casting of this particular role there will be much more, anon.

With the performance of *Faust* on 15 August there was also the usual cantata, this year *Le Génie de la France* with words by Henri d'Erville and music by Hector Salomon, who, sometime later would receive a gold medal and a very flattering letter from the Emperor for his pains.[4] Queues would begin to form for these free performances about 5 a.m. except for the Opéra, the most popular venue, where the public would take up positions as early as midnight. At mid-day the doors would be opened, the floods of people would pour in and within minutes the auditoriums would be filled. The Opéra which normally held 2000 spectators, on these occasions would contain almost 3000, for there would be up to ten people in boxes intended to hold five.[5]

On the fête day there would be celebrations outside the theatres as well. In 1866 the place de la Concorde and the Champs Elysées were illuminated. At the Invalides and the Barrière du Trône there were monster outdoor military parades and acrobatic displays. Regattas were held on the Seine and the celebrations ended with a display of fireworks at the Trocadero. But the celebrations in that year led to tragedy as well as enjoyment. All went well until after the fireworks display. The Pont de la Concorde had been cordoned off to take the crowds crossing from the left bank to the right only. Another bridge further down had been reserved for crowds moving in the opposite direction. But about half past ten a mob broke through

---

Royal English Opera, Covent Garden), Talvo-Bedogni, Ferdinand-Sallard, Mélanie Tedesco, Duclos, Olivier, Lambelé, MM Monjauze, Michot, Ismaël, Lutz, Troy *aîné*, Depassio, Barré, Cazaux, Vitaux, Laurent, Brion d'Orgeval, Berardi, Jamet, Jaulain, Troy *jeune*, Laveissière, Puget, Neveu, Legrand, Guyot, Wartel, Marchot, Bosquin.

from right to left against the oncoming mass which resulted in ten people being crushed to death and some 50 to 60 being seriously injured.[6]

Coincident with this tragic occurrence afflicting the poor of Paris, Gustave Chadeuil of *Le Siècle* was raising the question of the theatres' poor tax, but in the theatre directors' defence, not in the interest of his less fortunate fellow citizens. Taxes had been levied on fêtes and amusements in France as early as 1407 under Charles VI. In 1541, Francis I, the Renaissance king, had allocated them for the relief of the poor and from that time onwards, with percentages that had altered during the reigns of Kings Louis XIV, XV, and XVI, and later in the year 1848 and again in 1851, these had persisted. Chadeuil showed that in 1861 the poor tax paid by the Paris theatres alone had amounted to 1,600,000 francs, while authors and composers had received only 1,200,000 in royalties. With some truth but showing little compassion it was remarked, 'Theatres cannot get on without authors, but could contrive to manage without the poor.' The amount involved had earlier been levied on the gross receipts. In 1866 it equalled ten per cent of annual profits.[7]

That was not the only trouble theatre directors had to endure from bureaucracy just then. In June a stamp duty on all posters, hence on theatre posters, had been proposed. The duty would be proportionate to the size of the posters, but it would treble the cost. The theatres were naturally displeased. The purpose of the tax seemed directed primarily towards simplifying the format of the posters and, once more towards reducing the huge sheets of paper for which the Paris walls could not find space. On the whole it was considered that it would do no great harm. The public would soon become accustomed to the new scheme and would find it easier to detect the notices which interested them.[8]

It may here be noted that the present season would run entirely on revivals until the beginning of the new year. Those projected were *Faust, La Reine Topaze, Mireille, Violetta, Rigoletto, La Flûte enchantée, Don Juan, Martha, Oberon, Les Noces de Figaro* and *Le Freischütz*. The last opera was to be restaged with 'éclat' and was the revival which was awaited with most interest.

Lohengrin too was 'positively' to be performed but would not be ready until January. The preludes and some choruses had been performed by Pasdeloup at his Champs Elysées concerts, where they had been encored. We read that 'Princess Metternich has promised her influence in the great world towards ensuring the success of this fresh specimen of the "Music of the Future"', and it was hoped that her Excellency might 'fulfil her promise better than she was able to do in the case of the first representation of *Tannhäuser*.'[9] A second interesting production promised was a French translation of Donizetti's *Lucrezia Borgia* with Mlle Saint-Urbain (Lucrèce), Mlle Dubois (Orsini), Monjauze (Gennaro), and Ismaël (Le Duc Alphonse).[10] Finally there were to be revivals of *Philémon et Baucis* and *Le Médecin malgré lui*.

Of these four operas *Le Médecin malgré lui* alone would be performed, on 28 September, but it is highly significant that it had been intended to revive *Philémon et Baucis* reduced to two acts, (that is, with the second act or 'orgy scene' deleted) which, it was said, was the original form in which Gounod had composed it for Baden-Baden. When first produced at the Théâtre Lyrique it was decided to extend it to three acts because of the old prejudice that anything shorter was an inferior work.[11] Although it was never revived at the Théâtre Lyrique, when it was later staged successfully by Emile Perrin at the Opéra Comique in 1876, it was in this fashion with the second act omitted.

Signe Hebbe, a Swedish dramatic soprano who had made her début at the Stockholm opera, had been engaged expressly for *Lohengrin*, having successfully sung Elsa in Germany. In January 1867 she was on the point of making her début in an opera by Joncières when it was decided that the role suited Nilsson better. During the following November she would set off for Warsaw where she had been engaged by the impresario Merelli without Paris ever having heard her.[12]

Faust having returned to the repertory, recitatives were used instead of dialogue for the first time in Paris on Monday 10 September. It was reported that 'at the first hearing these recitatives seemed to slow down both the action and the score; it was true to say that the artists did not seem to have mastered them yet.'[13]

With the passage of years, death amongst old acquaintances was becoming more frequent. Count Baciocchi did not live long to enjoy his rank of senator, for he would die early in October. On his death the post of Superintendent of Theatres was abolished, the position of Director General of Theatre Administration being created in its stead. To this Camille Doucet was appointed. It was thought that Baciocchi's seat in the Senate might be filled by Auber,[14] now a robust veteran of 84. (It would be, on 1 January, 1867.) Joseph Thierry, scene painter and partner of Cambon would also die in October. He had painted settings for *Faust, Orphée* and many other productions at the Théâtre Lyrique.[15] Then late in November, the critic Joseph-Louis d'Ortigue would die in his 65th year.[16] Ernest Reyer would take his place on the *Journal des Débats*.

But not all was mournful. Léopold Ketten, until recently an accompanist at the Théâtre Lyrique, made his debut as a tenor at the Théâtre Italien in *Don Pasquale*, with Patti!, where understandably, 'he was so nervous it would be unfair to pass even the shadow of an opinion.'[17]

The eagerly awaited revival of *Le Freischütz*, newly translated by Trianon and E. Gautier, took place on 8 December. It had been widely advertised as the first authentic version to be performed in Paris—incorrectly—since, as was earlier noted, it had already been given at the Théâtre Italien in German in 1829 and, more particularly at the Opéra in 1841, translated by Emilien Pacini, and with recitatives specially composed by Berlioz. It was for this production that Berlioz had orchestrated Weber's 'Invitation to the Waltz' as ballet music.

The present production had had numerous postponements, the most recent due to the non-arrival of a special 'props' moon from London. The story is related as follows: M. Carvalho, a shrewd director who knows the importance of good stage effects had ordered a superb moon and its operator from London, but in spite of all English assurances the moon failed to appear. A concerned Carvalho sent off telegram after telegram; the moon he was told had departed and had arrived. M. Carvalho was bewildered, he telegraphed again and made other enquiries, but everywhere, there was total eclipse. Finally, after three days of anguished frustration, moon and operator were found contentedly installed at the Théâtre de la Porte-Saint-Martin—the operator not having a word of French.[18] With the moon there were other special effects, a waterfall illuminated by electricity, a weird Wolf's Glen scene (the last set to be painted by Joseph Thierry), all under the care of MM. Delaporte et fils, who presumably helped with the moonlight as well. Thierry's partner Cambon had painted the remainder of the scenery.[19]

Carvalho's efforts to make this a production of consequence did not stop at the visual. The orchestra was augmented and 150 choristers (recruited mainly from Orphéonistes) sang the well known Huntsmen's Chorus.[20] In the auditorium too it was quite a gala occasion and two rows of fauteuils had been incorporated into the parterre. Nevertheless the audience seemed to receive this fine work coldly—'it did not have the success of [Offenbach's] *La Vie parisienne* and *Barbe-bleue*.[21] Even the choir of 150 lacked warmth and spirit and the traditional encore for the Huntsmen's Chorus was called for by very few voices. Only Miolan-Carvalho as Agathe, and the orchestra under Deloffre, were irreproachable.[22]

The opera was performed 11 times to full houses during December. Yet it was not an entirely propitious production for Carvalho, apart altogether from the ambiguous reviews. There were complaints from the public, about the increase of prices from 8 to 10 francs for fauteuils in the balcony,[23] but above all about queueing arrangements on the first night, in cold mid-December. Sixteen letters were received by the editor of *Le Figaro*. The following from 'Em. Laurent, law student' speaks for all.

'Sir. I am neither millionaire, nor man of letters, nor stage-hand, nor fireman. No theatre director is under any obligation to invite me to a first performance, so when I wish to attend at the birth of any dramatic work, I modestly queue up. Therefore on Saturday I queued for *Le Freischütz*. Two hours before the box-office was due to open I was at my post: 30 people at most were there before me so I could be sure of getting a seat. Of course I did not dream of getting into the parterre; not content with filling it with the claque, they tend to reduce it more and more [by introducing fauteuils], but the amphitheatre, I reminded myself, contains about 300 seats and even if M. Carvalho has placed 200 claquers there, 100 seats still remain. About eight o'clock up to 30 people were allowed to pass in, and those who remained [some 200 to 300] were discourteously told to disperse as quickly as possible. I addressed an opinion to a gentleman

Le Freischütz (Weber) 1866, Main Centre Illustration; Act 2. Scene 2. (The Wolf's Glen) surrounded by other stage settings from the same opera

wearing a white tie, a member of the staff, who pointed out a policeman to me. I understood and withdrew.

'Now sir, I ask your help. That first performances should be reserved for the press is only just. That a director should want applause for his moon, his waterfall, even for Weber (who must have been singularly flattered from the depths of his last resting place)—nothing better. But would it not improve things if the same director had the courtesy to say to those who stood shivering at his door "Go home and warm yourselves. We will not be able to admit you." '[24]

It might have been better after all, if, as was projected, Gluck's *Armide* had been produced instead.[25]

1867 was to be Carvalho's Indian summer. It would also allot him his last throw of the Théâtre Lyrique dice. It was a good year for a gamble for it was the year of the Exposition Universelle, the last great exhibition of the Second Empire. In fact, as early as September 1866 it had been announced that the theatre would remain open throughout the following summer[26] to take advantage of the crowds that were expected to throng Paris.

Yet his first production of the year could hardly have been less successful. It was a three act opéra comique, *Deborah*, composed by Devin-Duvivier who paid the costs himself of having his work performed. (And why not? Meyerbeer had done much the same at the Opéra for years.) Unfortunately Devin-Duvivier had neither Meyerbeer's money nor his talent, and so the opera received a very perfunctory production. '*Deborah* is a Leah and the music is "bosh",'[27] declared *The Orchestra*. The libretto was derived from Walter Scott's 'The Highland Widow', a matriarch who urges her son to remain with his clan and rise against the house of Hanover. He refuses. 'The mother curses him in D minor and is sustained in her blasphemous mood by the choristers who, in opera are always interested in quarrels between parents and children, husbands and wives etc..'[28] The plot moreover included a masked ball, staged 'in a smoky setting, lit by three candles planted sadly in a meagre candelabrum set on a rickety table',[29] following which principals and chorus were supposed to set off to attack a castle still wearing their fancy dress. This provoked roars of laughter and whistles* not because of the incongruity of the situations but because members of the audience recognised the costumes as coming from old productions in the repertory. Poor Devin-Duvivier had a short run for his money, only three performances.

Joncières' *Sardanapale*, with a libretto based on Byron's *Sardanapalus* which followed fared somewhat better with 16 performances, although with Christine Nilsson in the cast this could scarcely be considered a success either. *Galignani's Messenger* records 'that it elicited from M. Théophile Gautier [who rarely wrote an ill word about anyone] one of the most charming articles that ever dropped from his prolific pen. He talks much about Georges Sand, Ingres, Gavarni, and says but little about *Sardanapale*, and in truth, the least said about it the better.'[30] Gustave Bertrand found in it echoes of various masters, German, Italian and French with impressions of Donizetti and Verdi leading to the most glaring imitations of Wagner. Nevertheless, he considered the production, in spite of some Carthagenian reminiscences, not unworthy of the luxury and richness of the Babylonian subject.[31] 'Carthagenian reminiscences' is undoubtedly a reference to scenery previously used in *Les Troyens à Carthage*, and emphasises again how Carvalho's financial difficulties were forcing him into artistic retrenchment.

Something of a crisis had occurred in January when the Emperor and Empress were due to attend a performance of *Le Freischütz*. Michot took ill suddenly and Carvalho decided to replace the advertised opera with *Martha*. But Monjauze the Lyonel, refused to sing; he was occupied rehearsing the role of Sardanapale at the time, so, the performance had to be cancelled. Carvalho threatened Monjauze with massive damages,[32] but their majesties did not take offence and returned for a performance of *Faust* in March.[33] The vogue for the latter opera was indeed far from exhausted, but it was for Gounod's new opera, *Roméo et Juliette* that a vogue was about to begin since it would have its first triumphal performance on 27 April.

As can be understood it was a very major production and like so many major productions, from the beginning it generated trouble. Carvalho returned from Italy without having found a

In 19th Century Paris besides hisses and boos audiences expressed displeasure by stridently whistling through their street door keys. O. 16 Feb. 1867.

tenor to sing Roméo. Two young tenors in the company (one was Jaulain) were said to have studied the first act so that Gounod could audition them.[34] Victor Capoul, then a rising young tenor at the Opéra Comique was next sought. This led to complications since Carvalho was unable to come to terms with de Leuven and Ritt, the Opéra Comique directors who had refused a forfeit of 40,000 francs to release Capoul to sing the role. This sum had been offered, not by Carvalho but by Choudens, Gounod's publisher who had entered into a separate agreement for six years with Capoul whereby the latter would sing in Gounod's operas, both in Europe and America at a fee of 2000 francs a month.[35] There was even a suggestion that reciprocal arrangements could exist between the two theatres and that Miolan-Carvalho would perform at the Opéra Comique.[36] Gounod eventually resolved the problem, when in an exchange of letters with Capoul he explained (at great length) that he really wanted Michot all the time.[37] Such an opportune solution did not fool everyone and it was generally believed that Gounod had decided upon this compromise because he was afraid of offending the direction of the Opéra Comique. This would be in character. Besides it was no time for him to make enemies since Ambroise Thomas' *Mignon* was about to be produced at the Opéra Comique, an event which, *The Orchestra* smirked, would probably decide the question of pre-eminence between the two composers—'the great success of one will certainly be a "coup de bas" for the other.'[38] As we now know the contest ended in a very successful draw.

Not only finding a suitable tenor, but finishing the opera seems to have given Gounod trouble. He is said to have composed the last act twice. The difficulty appears to have been another apotheosis scene,[39] two of which he had already composed, in *La Reine de Saba* and in *Faust*. Yet another would have been intolerable, but the opera ended once again with very few on the stage, seemingly a predilection of Gounod's.

Interest in *Roméo et Juliette* reached a peak by the end of March 1867 and it was reported unofficially that for the general rehearsal, seats would be on sale to the public at 20 francs each. The press too would be there without prejudicing their usual invitation to first performances, but having a paying public there as well was thought to be 'a curious innovation'.[40*] The first performance would also be the first immediate success that

Gounod had ever enjoyed, and while a correspondent of *The Musical World* might write ironically, 'The majority of French critics assert that the new *Romeo* will not only snuff out all the other *Romeos*,** but all M. Gounod's operas to boot, not ignoring *Faust* or *Mirella* to say nothing of snuffing out all other operas ever written,'[41] that was the situation in Paris, at the time, where opera was concerned.

The correspondent of *The Orchestra* agreed with 'the majority of French critics'. '*Roméo et Juliette* is fame for the composer and a fortune for the Théâtre Lyrique,' he wrote. 'Out of the chaos of remembrance which is left by a single hearing, one recollection is distinct enough—the recollection of the breadth and grandeur of the whole... [Following the love duet] scarcely would the audience hear the scene out; the house rose; bravos and cries interrupted the artists; enthusiasm gave place to order, and all regard for unity of action and consecutiveness of effect broke down in the long tumultuous plaudits... As a

*

It would not have been an innovation since the first rehearsal in Paris for which there was an admission charge had taken place at the Opéra either for a ballet, *Les Sauvages* by Maximilien and Pierre Gardel, first performed on 31 October 1786, or for the opera, *Phèdre* by F.B. Hoffman and J.B. Lemoyne, performed on 21 November 1786. This had come about following a decree of Louis XVI enacted on 24 October which permitted entry to rehearsals at a price of three livres each, the money collected to be shared among the artists. Previous to this, attendance at rehearsals had been rigidly controlled, and apart from Ministers of State, not more than 80 special invités selected from artists and connoisseurs who would be able to proffer advice, could be present. But, whereas to be one of the 80 invited was an honour eagerly sought after, when the Opéra doors were thrown open to anyone willing to pay, interest plunged. Three public rehearsals (or previews!) had been planned, but the first having produced a mere 627 livres, the others were cancelled. On 24 November 1787 a further ordinance permitted three editors to attend general rehearsals free of charge, but on the strict understanding that no information would appear in their newspapers concerning libretto or music, decor or artists. The first editors to be admitted came from the *Petites-Affiches*, the *Mercure* and the *Journal de Paris*. Article by E.M. de Lyden in *Le Figaro*. Reported M 8 Mar. 1868.

**

At that time there had been at least nine, from Georg Benda's, produced at Gotha in 1776 and Dalayrac's, produced at the Opéra Comique in 1792 up to Richard Yrvid's (The Marquis Richard d'Ivry) presented privately about this period but not professionally until 1878.

work of art we believe *Roméo* will live; for it stands on its own merits; it will neither gain nor lose by comparison with what has gone before.'[42] The duel scene in act 3 arranged by Ad. Desbarolles was 'thrillingly realistic',[43] the costumes, settings (eight scenes painted by Cambon and Despléchin) and production, splendid. Miolan-Carvalho as Juliette insisted on her waltz song, 'Je veux vivre dans ce rêve' which she sang 'with a rare perfection', although rather patronisingly it was recorded that it was modelled in the style of which ' "Il Bacio" had set the taste.' 'The orchestra [under Deloffre] was on a level with the work which it interpreted, and that says sufficient.'[44]

Naturally some parts were not entirely successful. On the first night 'the two first acts were received only tepidly.'[45] A cavatina for Frère Laurence with an off-stage chorus and tenor solo accompanied by organ, was quickly cut.[46] The orchestral passage at the beginning of act 5 while Juliette lies in her drugged sleep was considered too long for the advanced hour . . . 'Half at least of this music will have to be ruthlessly shorn.'[47] But these were small defects and by mid-May places had long been booked in advance for the 25th performance (with receipts of up to 8,000 francs a night) and Choudens had sold the English and German rights for 30,000 francs.[48]

Its success was unquestionably helped by the many royal visitors to the Exhibition. The Queen of Belgium came and praised Gounod and Miolan-Carvalho equally,[49] the Crown Prince and Princess of Prussia came and remained until the end of the performance,[50] the composer—Duke of Saxe Coburg-Gotha came accompanied appropriately by Gounod,[51] there was even a visit from their Imperial Highnesses of the Ottoman Empire.[52] Parisian celebrities also attended. At the first performance, Patti occupied a box in the second tier, applauding frequently. On the same evening Nilsson sat in a modest fauteuil in the orchestra stalls, but was absent for the third and fourth acts since she was singing in a benefit concert at the Odéon, while one noticed the Duchess Colonna (the noted sculptress, Marcello) seated in the balcony.[53] Perhaps the opera received the highest mark of success of all when a parody called *Rhum et eau en Juillet* was presented at the Théâtre Déjazet.[54] By the end of the year 89 performances had been given. There would be only one more in 1868, but that is another story.

The last new production during the 1866–67 season was Bellini's *La Sonnambula*, in a translation by Monnier, which had been in use for a long time in the provinces. To accompany *La Sonnambula*, Félicien David's 'ode-symphonie', *Le Désert* was announced for production in operatic form,[55] but this did not materialise. In March it had been published that either Donizetti's little known *Maria di Rohan* or *La Sonnambula* would be performed, maintaining the policy of producing translated Italian operas. The latter work was chosen. It was also to be the vehicle for the début of a new soprano, Jeanne Devries.[56] It was not a success and had only 12 performances. Unwisely Devries had been promoted as a new Malibran. Gustave Bertrand praised her performance, but pithily observed, 'She is only 17 and at that age Malibran was not a Malibran either.'[57] F. de Lagenevais also spoke well of her, but spoke very ill of everything else in the opera. 'This Elvino' he declares, 'good Gods!, and the Count, and those choristers who beat time on stage, and who sing invariably out of tune, and that orchestra, fluctuating, alternating, out of time with the singers, either hurrying or slowing the movements and by continual inattention focussing the spectator's ear on the shortcomings of Bellini's instrumentation, imperfections which with a more discriminating hand could be covered by a veil.'[58] Historically, the only point of note in the production was that costuming, as in the successful *Don Pasquale* of three years previously was from an earlier period, and no longer was the Count dressed, as at the Théâtre Italien in the contemporary uniform of the infantry of the line.[59]

Besides the royal visitors already mentioned, Prince Oscar of Sweden, a distinguished writer and musical amateur was present at a performance of *Martha*, which had then been played 100 times. During the interval he was brought to the artists' foyer where he had a long chat with his compatriot Christine Nilsson, after which he visited her at her appartments.[60] Socially it was a most exhilarating time for the young soprano. For taking part in Rossini's *Stabat Mater* on Holy Thursday and singing an 'O Salutaris' composed by Auber in the Tuileries Chapel on Easter Sunday she was rewarded with a pair of diamond ear-rings by the Emperor and Empress.[61] Later in May she was complimented for her singing in *La Flûte enchantée* by the King and Queen of Belgium.[62] It may have been with relief that she set off for the more simple theatrical life at Her Majesty's Theatre, London early in June, pledged to return to the Théâtre Lyrique from 15 August to 15 November.

The Exhibition also inspired an innovation at the Théâtre Lyrique, the engagement of Carlotta Patti (Adelina's second eldest sister) for a series of 12 concerts. These were arranged as 'spectacles coupés'. For example, the evening of 16 June offered the last two acts of *Rigoletto*, followed by Carlotta Patti with Wieniawski and Jaëll (violinist and pianist) and ending with the second act* of *La Flûte enchantée*.[63] Carlotta had the double disadvantage of living in the shadow of her very famous younger sister and of suffering from a limp. The latter made an opera career impossible, but in 1863 Frederick Gye had engaged her for similar concert performances at Covent Garden. In London the attempt had proved unsuccessful. In Paris the result was the same, since, of her first concert at least, on 2 May we read, 'the house had a rather poor attendance.'[64] She pleased the Paris critics nonetheless, one of whom wrote, 'all speculation was at an end as soon as Carlotta opened her mouth to sing the rondo finale from *La Sonnambula*. She literally [!] electrified the audience. Carlotta's voice was compared to a lark, soaring higher and higher until it became a point of light, and then melted into air.'[65]

There was also Miolan-Carvalho's annual benefit on 31 May, which this year, for whatever reason, would produce only 14,000 francs.[66] All the more surprising since originally it had been intended to present an abbreviated version of *Don Juan* with a cast made up of Faure, Obin, David and Mme Sass from the Opéra and with Miolan-Carvalho as Zerline, and Nilsson as Elvire.[67] Unfortunately the project could not be realised because the artists from the Opéra were unable to cope with the French dialogue in the time available, so acts one and two were performed instead, sung entirely by Théâtre Lyrique artists. The programme also included act one of *Violetta*, act two of *Faust*, act two of *La Flûte enchantée*, and two short plays,

---

*

As performed at the Théâtre Lyrique when the opera was performed in four acts.

Octave Feuillet's *Un Cas de Conscience* and a comedy, *Après le Bal*.[68]

The last of the many musical events associated with the Exhibition took place at the Théâtre Lyrique on 2 September. Baron Taylor had organised a series of international choral contests in various Paris theatres during the month of August and ten thousand choristers from France, Germany, Belgium, Norway, Sweden, Denmark and Switzerland had arrived to compete for a large gold medal presented by the Empress. The winners were a Swedish students choir from Uppsala University under their conductor Oscar Arpi and at this final concert given by the pick of the choirs, French and foreign, they 'again bore off the palm.'[69]

Earlier in June a most extraordinary incident had occurred. On Tuesday 25, just before midnight the composer Lucien Dautresme burst into the Théâtre Lyrique in a rage and attacked Léon Carvalho.

The drama was enacted as follows:

Scene 1. The Théâtre Lyrique.

Carvalho is on stage with members of the company discussing a rehearsal of *Faust* which has just taken place with a new Marguerite, Mme Duprez-Vandenheuvel. Enter Dautresme who approaches Carvalho menacingly.

D. 'So you won't fight?'

C. 'It is a business matter, not an affair of honour.'

D. 'Then I must thrash you to force you to fight.'

C. 'If anyone struck me I should know what to do.'

D. 'You would fight?'

D. then assaults C. and the combatants are separated by MM Gounod, Deloffre, Legrand, Duchesne and Salomon. Tableau!

Scene 2. A Police Station.

Dautresme is brought before the Commissioner of Police and a charge is laid against him by Carvalho.

Scene 3. A Courtroom.

Dautresme (in witness-box) states that three years previously he had composed an opera, *Cardillac* which M Carvalho had undertaken to produce in his theatre, but this promise he had not kept. He eventually lost patience and believing himself wronged challenged M Carvalho to a duel, which this gentleman refused on the grounds that it was not an affair of honour but an affair of commerce. He believed differently and so went to the Théâtre Lyrique where he found M Carvalho conducting a rehearsal. He admitted to calling M Carvalho a coward and to spitting in his face. A scuffle ensued during which he broke his umbrella over M Carvalho's head.

The Tribunal sentences M Dautresme to six months imprisonment and to payment of all costs.[70] Fin!

The real action of the period however, although it pervaded all Paris, was far from the court-room or even the theatre. It centred on the Tuileries, or on those places where the occupants and intimates of the Tuileries assembled. Countess Perrière-Pilté (Anaïs Marcelli) gave a fancy dress ball at her mansion in the rue de Monsieur.[71] At Princess Mathilde's, Mlle Schroeder, a new soprano engaged for the Théâtre Lyrique sang the cavatina from *Semiramide*, a song by Schumann, and the duet from *Les Noces de Figaro* with Miolan-Carvalho, who in turn sang Cherubin's air. At one of Rossini's 'Saturdays', Barré sang the chansonnette 'Le Lazzarone' composed by his host.[72] Such was the irrepressible gaiety of the time that 'though they had only left off their deep mourning for the Emperor Maximilian the day before,' the Emperor and Empress visited the Théâtre Italien to see Mr. Sothern play in *Our American Cousin*. 'Their Majesties appeared to enjoy the performance thoroughly and stayed till the end.'[73]

The apex of the action and of the Exhibition itself was probably reached on 1 July when prizes were distributed to the winning exhibitors. Fourteen thousand people were said to have gathered in the gigantic Palais de l'Industrie for the occasion and among the 150 guests who crowded the colourful platform there were Emperors and Empresses, Kings and Queens, Princes and Princesses, the Sultan of Turkey, the Khedive of Egypt and Lord Mayors and municipal representatives from London, Edinburgh and Dublin.[74] Rossini's recently composed 'Hymn to Napoleon III and his valiant people' resounded from hundreds of voices and instruments, ending, as instructed by the official programme with 'a general cry of "Vive l'Empereur!" — repeated three times. The cannon are to thunder, all the bells are to ring out, and the drums are to beat, to arms.'[75]

They called the Exhibition the Fête of Peace and had built a palace to house it on the Champ de Mars! Did no one in Paris in that grandiloquent year foresee the outcome? Probably many, but just then it was an unpopular prediction to make and anyhow who wanted to rock so fair-sailing a boat. Yet ominous murmurings could be heard if one were prepared to listen. A few evenings before this diverting deification occurred they were performing *Hernani* at the Théâtre Français. In the scene before Charles V's election to the imperial throne of Germany, where Hernani tells him that he might crush the imperial eagle before it is hatched, these lines applied by a quick witted audience to Prussia, 'were cheered to the echo.'[76]

1867–1868

As earlier explained the Théâtre Lyrique remained open this year throughout the entire summer. Obviously it was a good commercial proposition, confirmed by the amounts taken at the combined Paris theatres during the period of April to August. Receipts for these five months had reached over 7,000,000 francs, an increase of 2,500,000 francs over the same period in 1866.[1]

In August, in connection with the Exhibition, the three opera houses announced competitions for new operas. Works entered at the Opéra and Opéra Comique had to be composed to predetermined libretti, but for the Théâtre Lyrique composers were free to choose whatever book they liked best, irrespective of style or length. The closing date was fixed for 16 August 1868,[2] but this would later be extended to 30 October.

During the summer there had been the usual minor problems of resignations of artists. Monjauze had tendered his earlier at the end of March. Not entirely surprising in view of the contretemps over the cancelled performance, but it was reported that he and Carvalho had parted amicably.[3] The bass, Cazaux would leave in June. Edouard Mangin's resignation was announced at the same time. He would be replaced by Adolphe Blanc who was composer, violinist and conductor[4] and who in turn would resign in the following February (when Mangin would be re-engaged), taking with him a letter from Carvalho thanking him for 'his artistic and devoted cooperation.'[5] Albert Vizentini, the solo violinist would also leave the orchestra.[6] In a subsequent varied career he would for a time direct the Grand Théâtre at Lyon where he would give the first French production of *Die Meistersinger von Nürnberg* in 1896.

On the positive side, Christine Nilsson made her re-entry to the theatre in *Martha* on Saturday 17 August. Two evenings earlier the annual cantata had been sung in the Emperor's honour. It had been written this year by Jules Adenis with music by Jules Massenet.[7] Nilsson gave three further performances of *Martha* during the following week, when the audience 'covered her with flowers, and recalled her after each act, almost after each scene.'[8] It was in the following month that she complimented her friend and rival Adelina Patti by attending a performance of *Lucia di Lammermoor* at the Théâtre Italien, when 'she applauded with true enthusiasm.' On the very next evening Patti returned her visit and came to see *Martha*.[9]

Among the operas listed by Carvalho for future production were some capricious choices—Flotow's *Alessandro Stradella*,[10] Pedrotti's *Tutti in Maschera* and Federico Ricci's *Il Marito e l'Amante*, the latter two to be translated by Nuitter and Beaumont.[11] None of these was ever presented there. Neither was *Lohengrin* which was in actual rehearsal in November, but unfortunately, lacking a capable tenor.[12]

The first new opera to be performed this season was Jules Cohen's *Les Bleuets*. Cohen was an ex-prize winning student of the Conservatoire. He was also the son of a wealthy banker who had died in 1863 leaving 10,000,000 francs, and a brother-in-law of Desiré Pollonais director of the Paris newspaper *La France.* His widowed mother would in 1868 marry Emilien Pacini, the translator and librettist. None of these factors was a disadvantage to him as an opera composer, whatever the standard of his music.

His opera was mounted with a cast headed by Nilsson and with scenery painted by Cambon. It was a four act work, set in the sixteenth century in the realm of Castile. Cormon and Trianon, the librettists, were said to have got the idea of their story from Victor Hugo's poem, 'Les Bleuets' and at least two critics quoted the refrain:

    'Allez, allez, ô jeunes filles,
      Cueillir des bleuets dans les blés!'

According to Gustave Bertrand much of Cohen's music was

copied from the best hands as well. In the overture there were reminiscences of *Guillaume Tell*, in act one a chorus bore a resemblance to the soldiers' chorus from *Faust*, in act three a ritournelle from act five of *L'Africaine* could be heard, while a song for Sœur Dorothée was modelled on an air from the last act of Auber's *Le Domino Noir*. There was also a mad scene—à la Donizetti—which Nilsson sang 'with marvellous grace and originality and which was encored.'[13] Armand Gouzien considered it was the weakness of the role of Estelle which prevented Nilsson from creating a more memorable effect, but confirmed that the production was good, especially in the last act where a deployment of crowns, ermine and purple effaced the soldiers' drab costumes in act three.[14]

The performance cannot have been helped by a hilarious mishap which occurred. The last act of *Les Bleuets* was divided into two scenes, a rustic interior set downstage changing by a transformation scene in view of the audience into the interior of a cathedral. Up to that time transformation scenes in all the Paris theatres from the Opéra down to the most modest stages were signalled by a sharp whistle from the stage manager. Such a situation inevitably led to ingenious gallery-goers giving a similar whistle in the midst of scenes with predictable results. To resolve the problem a large bell was fixed above the inside of the proscenium arch, and the signal was henceforth given by striking it. Everyone was satisfied that this would end the annoyance, since gallery-goers bringing large bells into the theatre were likely to be noticed, but they had not reckoned on the unintentioned ingenuity of stage hands. It happened that the new arrangement was introduced for the first time at the Théâtre Lyrique at the première of *Les Bleuets*. Everybody back-stage had been instructed and warned beforehand. So, the curtain rose on act four disclosing a cottage in which a couple commenced to sing a duet. The opera now called for an off-stage chorus to break in on the duet. Unfortunately it also called for a tam-tam (a large gong-like instrument) to interrupt the chorus.

The chorus master who was in charge here continues the story of the unhappy episode.

'I hold the score in my left hand,' he relates, 'and am armed with a bass drum stick in my right with which to conduct the chorus and from time to time strike the tam-tam which a man holds suspended in front of me. The author [Cormon] is by my side, the director, [Carvalho] is giving the final touches to the staging. Exactly on cue I strike the tam-tam and the stage hands thinking it is the new signal, make the scene change! Now surrounding us there is a cathedral thronged with artists in Renaissance costume, while downstage, amidst a table and stools, pitchers and pewter goblets, the duet, nonplussed, stops, as does the orchestra.

'The author, director and I throw ourselves down behind some scenery to avoid being seen. The audience explodes in laughter. The stage manager utters profanities that would make a guardsman blush. [Carvalho] yells, "Curtain! Curtain!" [Cormon] his arms raised to heaven, cries "That's it! We are [expletive deleted] lost! The piece is ruined."'

The curtain had to be lowered and when calm was restored and the rustic scene reset, they began the last act again. This time it went without a hitch, but when the sound of the tam-tam was heard the laughter was renewed, undoubtedly more isolated, enough however to envelop the sombre drama in which the opera ends with 'a marvellously gay atmosphere.'[15]

Throughout it all—and the eight subsequent peformances— Nilsson reigned supreme. The Archduke Ludwig Victor of Austria attended her performance on Monday 28th October.[16] (The Emperor Franz Joseph accompanied by his brothers, had come on a visit to Paris in late October. It had been convened by Napoleon III perturbed at the new North German Confederacy and the growing imperialism of Prussia.) She would soon leave for the Opéra where she would create Ophélie in Ambroise Thomas' *Hamlet*, and so on 16 November* she gave her last performance at the Théâtre Lyrique in *Les Bleuets*. She was saluted with a shower of bouquets and crowns fashioned from bleuets and laurels. Later, as she left the theatre, the throng, eager to honour her formed a procession and accompanied her carriage to her home.[17]

Shortly before *Les Bleuets* had been produced, Bleuse, the chorus master had resigned at very short notice to become choir master at the church of St. Sulpice. His place was assigned to a

*

RGM 17 November 1867 gives 'last Friday', 15 November, but 16 November seems the more probable date.

newcomer, Henri Maréchal, the agent of the tam-tam catastrophe at the first performance.[18] Aristide Volgnier, the assistant chorus master, piqued no doubt by having an outsider promoted over his head, resigned shortly afterwards.[19] Although performances of *Les Bleuets* ended in mid-November it was not until a month later that a new opera reached the stage. It was Dautresme's *Cardillac*. Earlier Dautresme had taken Carvalho's advice (although he had left it very late) and had brought his case before the Tribunal of Commerce. The tribunal gave judgement that Carvalho must produce the opera under forfeit of 20,000 francs within two months of receiving a completed score.[20] Acts of God such as the illness of Mlle Daram had however caused unavoidable postponements.[21]

The story of the opera was taken from yet another of E.T.A. Hoffmann's tales, 'Das Fräulein von Scuderi'* which some 40 years earlier had been dramatised by Antony Béraud and staged at the Ambigu-Comique as a vehicle for the famous actor Frédérick Lemaître. It was from this dramatisation, the story of a mad jeweller so in love with his creations that whenever he sold one he would set about recovering it, even by murder, that Nuitter and Beaumont had derived their libretto. Henri Moreno in *Le Ménestrel* reported that Dautresme lacked individuality and advised him to shun vulgarities such as the use of polka rhythms and coarse accompaniments by three trombones in his future operas. The central role of Cardillac was played by Ismaël but to Barré went 'the honours of the evening'.[22]

It will be remembered that Dautresme had been sentenced to six months imprisonment for attacking Carvalho, but it would seem that his incarceration was neither very penal nor very prolonged. Following the first performance of *Cardillac*, he and Carvalho had shaken hands in the best theatrical tradition, and Carvalho had generously offered to try to have his sentence remitted.[23] Nevertheless he entered the Sainte-Pélagie prison on 20 December.[24] It was surely uncharitable that two days later Moreno would recount Dautresme's difficulties and energy in getting his opera staged, energy which had also begot him six months in goal, difficulties which had brought him no greater

---

* Last set as an opera by Paul Hindemith.

reward than a fifth [and final] performance which had taken 'a paltry 326 francs and some centimes at the box-office.'[25]

Dautresme sent a letter in reply to *Le Ménestrel* from Sainte-Pélagie explaining that while he did not receive newspapers there, yet, certain echoes had reached him. His collaborators, Nuitter and Beaumont had brought him word of the fifth performance producing a mere 326 francs. This was entirely wrong, the correct figure was 1074 francs. He adds, 'My present situation is none too good, but I do not complain.'[26] His forbearance was rewarded for he would be released in a month on 20 January 1868.[27]

About the same time Carvalho also had his problems. On 8 December the very existence of the Théâtre Lyrique was threatened, and we read that, 'One cannot conceal that the withdrawal of M. Carvalho will be a fatal blow to our third lyric theatre which he has raised to such heights during these latter years. Let us hope that everything will be satisfactorily arranged, especially that the Municipality of Paris will appreciate the general interest which the Théâtre Lyrique inspires at so many levels.'[28] This advocacy was intended presumably as an appeal to the municipality not to press too hard for the rent of their theatre. In confirmation of this Moreno would write an article in early January 1868 strongly criticising the municipality for their stinginess. 'Efforts are being multiplied to make up the budgetary deficit which excites everyone's sympathy except that of the municipal coffers of the city of Paris.' he declared. 'Thus—very strange—the individual creditors of the Théâtre Lyrique have agreed to the moratorium sought by an administrator who has done so much for opera, whereas, it is the good city of Paris which shows itself to be intractable.' Moreno concludes by asking if there is not someone else close to the municipal administration who could be petitioned.[29]

By then Carvalho was beyond anyone's help, municipal or national, but, like the good showman he was, when his time would come he would go down in dramatic fashion with all flags flying. Meanwhile he had one more opera to produce and it was surely no more than justice that it should happen to be a work which posterity would acknowledge, for it was Bizet's *La Jolie Fille de Perth.*

The fully documented story of this production has already

been written.* Briefly it can be said that the role of Catherine was intended for Christine Nilsson, but the work suffered so many postponements that by the time it was performed she had left the company and Catherine was sung by Jeanne Devries instead. The delays were due, first either to Carvalho's dilatoriness or to his financial dilemma, but later Bizet himself had the production deferred until after the Exhibition. The allegation, frequently encountered, that Nilsson had broken her contract with Carvalho in order to create Ophélie at the Opéra cannot be sustained, since as early as May it had been announced that following her London engagement she would be returning to the Théâtre Lyrique from 15 August to 15 November only, prior to leaving for the Opéra.[30] In fact, Bizet had written to his friend and pupil Edmond Galabert in January 1867, 'We commence rehearsals in March until the end of May. Nilsson will be two months in London and will return on 15 August in *La Jolie Fille de Perth*.'[31] The same news was announced in the daily press,[32] so her plans were well known in advance both to Bizet and to Carvalho. Nowhere can evidence of a broken contract be discovered and it is much more likely that she merely found Jules Cohen's *Les Bleuets* to be socially more desirable, as, with Cohen to back it, Carvalho certainly had found it pecuniarily more rewarding.

Whatever the reasons for the various postponements a general rehearsal took place on 23 September, following which, (although the first performance had been already advertised for both 24 and 27 September[33]) 'it was unanimously agreed that the score was too unusual to be staged during the Exhibition and that it should await the return of the Parisians—which means the month of November.'[34] Other motives were given for deferring the production, at least one of them—'the imminent departure of Mlle Nilsson to the Opéra which makes the performance of M. Jules Cohen's *Les Bleuets* urgent'[35]— confirming the opinion expressed above. From this press announcement it is clear also that adjourning the first performance came as a marked surprise to the Paris opera world.

*

See Mina Curtiss, *Bizet and His World*, and Winton Dean, *Georges Bizet, His Life and Work*.

La Jolie Fille de Perth had been read through for the first time late in June when the cast was recorded as Mlles Devries, Ducasse and MM Ismaël and Lutz, with a new tenor from Bordeaux taking the role of Henri Smith.[36] By August we find that Barré had taken over Ismaël's role of the Duc de Rothesay, while Wartel had joined the cast as Simon Glover.[37]

In his review of the first performance Armand Gouzien described it as 'the only one which was truly successful at the Théâtre Lyrique since *Roméo et Juliette.*'[38] Although favourably meant, this was hardly eloquent praise in view of the productions in between. Among certain defects he noted uncertainty in the singing of Devries and Massy in the love duet in act one, and in the singing of the duet in act three by Barré and Ducasse, a strange occurrence for an opera so long in rehearsal. Strangely too, he thought little of the now well known Serenade* sung by Massy in act two, but praised highly Ralph's air, 'Quand la flamme de l'amour'** which followed, sung by Lutz. By far the most popular item in the opera (agreed by all the critics) was the 'Danse bohémienne', which was encored.

Although Bizet seemed perfectly content with the performance and would write elatedly to Galabert, 'my work obtained a genuine and serious success. I was not hoping for so enthusiastic a reception which was at the same time so severe,'[39] yet Gouzien introduces a dissident note. 'The new piece merited better as to production', he reports, 'we see yet again on the noblemen's backs and on the grand ladies of the Duc de Rothesay's court, the purple, the ermine and the brocades which for a long time have acquired rights of retirement through length of service.'[40] So once again we learn of Carvalho's lack of money. Gouzien did add however, that 'apart from some minor criticism of the orchestra in the "Danse bohémienne", it deserved nothing but praise.'[41]

*

A different arrangement to the one in the current score.

**

Curiously, Ralph's serenade has always been more popular than Henri Smith's in France. *The World's Encyclopaedia of Recorded Music*, a good criterion of operatic aria taste during the '78' record period, lists nine versions of the former but only three of the latter. Of these, one is by the English tenor, Heddle Nash, while another is an orchestral arrangement by Sir Thomas Beecham.

In spite of this, in less than a month it would be reported that 'M. St. Georges' [librettist with Adenis] opera at the Lyrique, *La Jolie Fille de Perth* is a failure, and the Fair Maid sings to houses as deserted as the street in which they chopped off the recreant knight's hand.'[42] It would have only 18 performances, by coincidence, the same number as *Les Pêcheurs de Perles.*

During September, auditions had been held to fill the post of first violin solo left vacant by Albert Vizentini.[43] About the same time Michot's resignation was announced and on 13 October Massy took over the role of Roméo.[44] Three evenings later during a performance of *Roméo et Juliette* 'several bits of burning canvas were seen to fall upon the stage. The curtain was lowered and the audience rightly thought that some of the scenery must have caught fire. Wild cries of "Fire! Fire!" instantly arose, and there was a general rush to the doors. In a few minutes, balcony, boxes and pit were nearly empty. Only a few individuals of greater presence of mind had preferred remaining in the house to facing the much greater danger of a terror-stricken crowd. In the meantime, the fire had been quickly extinguished, and most of the audience returned to their seats, [though hardly their original ones] when the opera continued as if nothing had happened.'[45] Such episodes (when danger has passed) always prompt a flurry of amusing if unlikely tales. This time it was a story of the man who had taken a 'cocotte' to a stage box and presented her with an enormous bouquet. When the fire began she rushed out leaving him and bouquet behind, whereupon with great presence of mind he retrieved the bouquet and brought it home to his wife to make amends for his lateness.[46]

The last performance of *Roméo et Juliette* for 1867 took place on 21 December, 'Mme Carvalho [having] been compelled by fatigue temporarily to quit the Lyrique.'[47] Instead *Faust* and *Rigoletto* were performed on alternate evenings. Léon Carvalho had been in negotiation with Monjauze however, and it was now announced that the latter would soon return to the Théâtre Lyrique to join Miolan-Carvalho in their old success of *La Fanchonnette.*[48]

The new year of 1868 brought the surprising news that Maréchal Vaillant had authorised M. Bagier, director of the

Italian Opera to sub-let the Théâtre Ventadour to Léon Carvalho for French opera on those evenings of the week when Italian performances were not given, that was, on Mondays, Wednesdays and Fridays.* Carvalho would retain the direction of the Théâtre Lyrique, and its subvention, and would continue to present operas at that theatre each evening but these now would be almost exclusively simple productions, or operas by young composers. Elaborate works, such as *Faust, Roméo et Juliette* and translations such as *Le Freischütz* would be transferred to the more prestigious stage of the Théâtre Ventadour.[49]

'The old Théâtre des Italiens is about to be converted into a species of chapel-of-ease to the Lyrique'[50] is how *The Orchestra* described the arrangement. Bagier was insistent that confusion between the two companies occupying the same theatre should not arise, and so Carvalho's company had to perform there under the title of Théâtre de la Renaissance. Moreover no translation of an Italian opera currently in performance there could be given, but Carvalho had the right to introduce translations of other operas besides new scores. The Commission of the Society of Dramatic Authors had decreed that royalties payable should be ten per cent both on new works and on translations.** Works in the public domain would continue to be performed free.[51] In order to avoid competition it was intended

---

*

Some confusion exists here. Octave Fouque in *Histoire du Théatre-Ventadour*, p.134, gives the evenings as Tuesdays, Thursdays and Saturdays. The *Revue et Gazette Musicale*, 6 September 1868 states that Carvalho held the lease for the odd numbered (impair) days of the week, but omits to add on which day it considered the theatrical week began. The first performance of *Faust* there certainly took place on a Monday and other evidence strongly suggests that the French performances were given on Monday, Wednesday and Friday.

**

In France at this time librettist and composer held equal rights. For example, Scribe and Meyerbeer each received the same royalties for *L'Africaine* or *Le Prophète*. In Italy the arrangement was quite different. There the composer purchased a libretto outright from an author, usually for as little as £50 to £150. In Italy also the librettist frequently simplified his task by taking a successful poem or drama, often from the French, and, having cut it to a practical length introduced the rhymes of his cavatinas, duets, concerted pieces and choruses.

that performances by the Renaissance company should take place on evenings when productions of the least consequence were being given at the Théâtre Lyrique.

This new project was to be launched on 15 March and a number of new works announced for production by the Théâtre de la Renaissance included Saint-Saëns' *Le Timbre d'Argent.* The most anomalous member of the cast for this opera was the ballet dancer Coralie Brach (from the Opéra) who had been engaged to mime the role of Circé and for whom Carvalho, at his most flamboyant had planned 'a ballet under water, an aquarium ballet.'[52] Deloffre would be placed in charge of the new orchestra, while Edouard Mangin would return to the Lyrique as principal conductor. Seat prices for the Renaissance would be the same as they had been at the Lyrique, but at the latter theatre it was promised that prices would be reduced, as they were, from 12 April.[53]

Faust was the first opera to be performed—on Monday, 16 March. The theatre was full and while it did not match the grandeur of the Italian performances, yet the boxes created a brilliant spectacle. The performance was advertised for eight o'clock, but did not commence until eight-thirty. 'An unpunctuality all too frequent at the Théâtre Lyrique' it was declared, 'about which the public has every reason to complain, it is not so at the Opéra or at the Théâtre Français.' In addition the theatre was unheated so everyone shivered with cold. Then, the singers unused to the new theatre found difficulty in projecting their voices, especially in the beginning. The scenery had been repainted and rebuilt to fit the new stage, and the costumes had been renovated,[54] but these were the only satisfactory features in what was hardly the happiest of inaugural performances. In fact Carvalho's intention to bring 'the choice pieces of his repertory within reach of the elegant society of Paris who have an opportunity three times a week of conveniently witnessing these performances'[55] was nothing more than his ultimate gamble. It would not succeed.

At the Théâtre Lyrique from January onwards the repertory had included *La Fanchonnette* (later transferred to the Renaissance), *La Flûte enchantée, La Jolie Fille de Perth, Le Freischütz, Martha,* and *Richard Cœur-de-Lion.* But there were ominous signs that all was not well. In January cold weather and snow had drastically reduced receipts at all the theatres.[56] Later both Bertrand and Moreno had expressed reservations about the Renaissance enterprise.[57] Then in April it was announced that Miolan-Carvalho was eagerly awaited in Brussels where she had been commanded by the Queen of the Belgians to sing Juliette at a fee of 2000 francs a performance.[58] She set off immediately after her last performance of this role at the Renaissance, on Friday 1 May, when there were renewed bouquets and bravos.

On the same date of 1 May it was unexpectedly announced that Carvalho was giving up the Théâtre Lyrique in order to devote all his time to the Théâtre de la Renaissance. Since the Italian season had just ended he would now give performances each evening there instead of three times a week. Three new operas were said to be ready for production but time had run out for Carvalho; on 4 May the Théâtre Lyrique closed[59], on 6 May he was declared bankrupt,[60] and on 7 May activity ceased in his Théâtre de la Renaissance.[61] His liabilities were said to reach one million francs.[62] The sad business was finally resolved the following August when it was reported, 'M. Carvalho has succeeded in effecting an amiable adjustment of his financial difficulties. He had 200 creditors of whom 185 consented to take five per cent of their claims, as well as the stage property, scenery, etc., of the Lyrique, which will bring them in another fifteen per cent.'[63] As for the unfortunate out-of-work choristers (in the 1860s neither Equity nor the Welfare State had yet emerged) Henri Maréchal approached the Director General, Camille Doucet, who sought the sum of 2000 francs from Vaillant. This was granted and was shared equally among them.[64]

The stigma of bankruptcy did not harm Carvalho either professionally or socially and during the annual Corps Législatif debate on theatre subventions which took place in July he was highly praised, and it was declared that his ruin had come about because he had tried to maintain too high a standard.[65] His forced resignation from the Théâtre Lyrique did open the way for a new appointment. Nestor Roqueplan, sometime director of the Opéra Comique was mentioned, but he quickly denied the rumour.[66] A more likely candidate was Louis Martinet of the Fantaisies-Parisiennes.[67] Ultimately the selection was as surprising as it was laudable, for the director chosen was Paris's leading advocate of Wagner's music, then ironically (when not patronisingly) known as 'the music of the future'. His name was Jules Etienne Pasdeloup and his appointment was officially confirmed on 22 August 1868.[68]

Chapter 6

Pasdeloup, and the end 1868–1870

1868–1869

Pasdeloup was born in Paris in 1819 and studied at the Conservatoire as a pianist and composer. In the political changes of 1848 he had the good fortune to be appointed governor of the Château of Saint Cloud which placed him among persons of influence and gave him leisure for composition. But his compositions went unperformed by the musical societies in Paris which impelled him to form his own orchestra, the Société des Jeunes Artistes du Conservatoire. Through these young instrumentalists he found his true vocation, that of a successful conductor who made it his mission to introduce the works of modern composers both native and foreign in performances at the Salle Herz in the rue de la Victoire. In 1861 he moved to the much larger Cirque Napoléon where he gave his Concerts Populaires each Sunday afternoon.

He was an ardent admirer of Wagner although his efforts to promote Wagner's works were not always well received. When his orchestra rehearsed the overture to *Die Meistersinger* for the first time, 'the musicians hissed noisily as soon as the work was done'[1] to show their displeasure and, coincidentally, to reveal an extraordinary lack of discipline. Later when a *Lohengrin* prelude was performed, part of the audience called for an encore. The majority protested so vehemently, however, that following a number of unsuccessful attempts to recommence the piece, Pasdeloup could restore quiet only by announcing that he would give the encore at the end of the concert.[2] But matters improved rapidly. Shortly afterwards both the Pilgrims'

Chorus from *Tannhäuser*[3] and the 'beautiful religious march from *Lohengrin*'[4] [?Procession to the Minster ?Bridal Chorus] were encored.

His appointment as director of the Théâtre Lyrique was undoubtedly helped by influential patrons from the Saint Cloud days, Baron Haussmann, who earlier had appointed him organiser and conductor of concerts at the Hotel de Ville and Count de Nieuwerkerke, Surintendant des Beaux-Arts who frequently had him conduct official concerts at the Louvre. Whoever first contemplated the idea it would do nothing to advance Pasdeloup's career, and in less than two years he would leave the theatre a ruined man, like so many before him.

There were a number of reasons for this. Firstly, while the notion of replacing Carvalho with a director who would present a completely contrasting programme may have had something to commend it, in practice it never worked, for during his period of office Pasdeloup presented only one opera that Carvalho had not earlier promised, Wagner's *Rienzi*. The trouble was that, although a highly successful concert organiser and an excellent conductor Pasdeloup was totally inexperienced as a theatre man, and he even seemed to lack interest in the undertaking. Moreover he was hampered as Réty had been eight years earlier by having economies imposed on him immediately he took over, which led to the same reduction in artistic standards, and, as a consequence, in box-office receipts. Carvalho might grandiosely lose a million francs, but creditors were not forthcoming to enable Pasdeloup to do the same. Later Paris would make amends by naming the square after him on which stood the Cirque Napoléon.

Meanwhile there was much for him to do in the early autumn of 1868. A delay had been caused by Carvalho's creditors (including the Ville de Paris) demanding that Pasdeloup take over the scenery, costumes and properties in the theatre at their valuation of 336,000 francs. Since Pasdeloup's repertory was to be entirely different to Carvalho's he took the advice of *The Orchestra*, which declared, 'it would be sheer madness of him to sink such a sum in tinsel lumber,' postponed signing his contract and instead, accompanied by Hainl, Perrin and de Leuven, set off for Baden-Baden where *Lohengrin* was being performed.[5]

Within a short time concessions were made. The official

receiver, M. Copin agreed to an offer made by Pasdeloup whereby he would take only what stage material he needed for the operas he was about to present, at the same time depositing a sum equal to their value. The Tribunal decided accordingly and ordered another valuation since the first seemed exaggerated,[6] but the Ville de Paris appealed the decision, which meant that a final judgement was not reached until the following April. Once again, *The Orchestra* would report, 'difficulties have been smoothed away. He entered into possession of his theatre more than a week ago . . . The first fortnight was paid in advance and not less than sixty thousand francs have been deposited by M. Pasdeloup in a "caisse particulière" towards paying up the arrears of salaries due by the former director to the artists.[7] Whatever *The Orchestra* might report, Pasdeloup's difficulties had not been smoothed away but he had at least entered into possession of the Théâtre Lyrique.

There were various announcements at the same time that Carvalho was about to re-open the Théâtre de la Renaissance. Deloffre was said to be loyally supporting him and reorganising a chorus and orchestra. The first two operas announced for production were *Le Timbre d'Argent* and *Lohengrin*.[8] His chances of presenting *Lohengrin* were remote as the following extract of a letter from Wagner to a Paris friend makes clear. 'There must be some way to make this man understand that he will never obtain either from me or from Bülow consent to put on my *Lohengrin* with a group of artists which he might casually gather together,' wrote the enraged Master. 'He may nag me but he won't get it. How did we ever get into such a dilemma?'[9] Whatever the ultimate reason, on 8 November Carvalho withdrew from his impossible position with the following brief announcement, 'It is decided that the Théâtre de la Renaissance will not re-open,'[10] and with that dejected adieu he actively disappears from this story.

Conversely Pasdeloup was forging ahead much more success-fully, but then unlike poor Carvalho he had Wagner for an ally. In the same letter in which he wrote so irascibly about Carvalho, Wagner speaks of Pasdeloup with casual consideration. 'Pasdeloup has proposed a provisional agreement which would immediately attract us whenever I would be freed from Carvalho' he observes. 'As for the premium it would have to be remitted to me on the day I would be released from Carvalho, and if I wanted an advance before that I would only have to send him word and he would reply as a devoted friend. These are his very words. I do not know what to say. All this is so painful and once again has the same substance as my usual experiences of Paris affairs . . . In any event I am inclined to give preference to Pasdeloup over any other entrepreneur, even Pollini,* Escudier, etc., who offer me all the performances I wish for in Paris modelled on German productions. I am quite eager, for to tell you the truth I have faith in the zeal of this poor old conductor, but if the matter remains as it is now I will not know what to say and I think it might be better to say nothing more and to leave everything as it is in the mire of the Parisian Jews—of which I know a little. Please tell Pasdeloup that I thank him for his letter, but really I would not know how to answer him today. If he takes the Théâtre Lyrique he should engage Eckert, that at any rate is good advice. Excuse my very bad mood.' Some two months earlier he had written to Alexandre Flaxland, 'I give M. Pasdeloup full authority to perform my operas in the Théâtre Lyrique, over-ruling the Opéra.'[11]

Encouraged no doubt by this concession Pasdeloup called the members of the orchestra and choristers to a meeting at the school attached to the Church of Saint-Laurent** in the faubourg Saint-Martin on Thursday 3 September, and informed them that money owing to preferential creditors, the orchestra and the chorus would be paid over forthwith. He further arranged a meeting for the following Thursday, this time at the theatre so that contracts could be signed and everyone could get back to work right away. Understandably this news was received with considerable pleasure.[12]

He then set about organising his administration. M. Benou, who for a long time had managed the business affairs of the Palais-Royal and Vaudeville theatres became his general administrator. Jules Ruelle remained as secretary. No final

*

Bernhard Pollini of the Hamburg Opera.
**

Not so inappropriate a place to summon a theatre company as it might seem, since for a hundred and fifty years the annual Foire de Saint Laurent had once been held close by.

decision was taken about conductors except that Edouard Mangin was retained. (Apparently he would be later joined by Vandenheuvel). Hector Salomon also remained as principal répétiteur. Eugène Vast, organist at Saint-Germain-l'Auxerrois was appointed chorus master, and Augustin Vizentini, also from the Vaudeville, and Albert Vizentini's father, became stage manager.[13]* He seems to have taken Wagner's advice and engaged Carl Eckert to superintend the preparation of *Rienzi* when that opera went into rehearsal. Many Paris journalists in fact stubbornly insisted that he was being brought in as a new conductor.[14]

Inspired by the success which his policy of lower prices had enjoyed at the Concerts Populaires he adopted the same plan for the opera performances. Henceforth orchestra fauteuils would cost five francs, balcony seats, six francs, second tier boxes, four francs and pit (parquet), two francs.[15] He also introduced the innovation of having opera performances at the Théâtre Lyrique on Sunday evenings.[16]

Concurrently the chorus had been rehearsing Halévy's *Le Val d'Andorre* with which the theatre would re-open on Saturday 24 October. Outside, the theatre was illuminated for the occasion, but inside 'it was cold, gloomy; the music of Halévy awakened only muted echoes.'[17] Such a depressing opinion did not augur well for Pasdeloup's new enterprise.

Fidès Devries, Jeanne Devries' younger sister made her début as Rose-de-Mai in *Le Val d'Andorre* which was conducted by Mangin.[18] She was a pretty, blond girl who within two years would become a member of the Opéra where she would have a highly successful career.

A revival of *Martha* followed on 26 October. Jeanne Devries took over the role of Martha and shortly after, the role of Rosine when *Le Barbier de Séville* re-entered the repertory. Rossini had died on Friday 13 November (he was always superstitious) and
*

His singers included: *Sopranos and Mezzo-sopranos* Mmes Orgeni, Schroeder, Daram, Gilbert, Jeanne Devries, Fidès Devries, Formi, Ducasse, Duval, Wilhème, Guerin, Denizet.

Tenors MM. Monjauze, Massy, Raoul Delaspre, Blum, Bosquin, Coëlho, Verdellet, Berti, Legrand.

Baritones and Basses: Lutz, Meillet, Caillot, Aubéry, Géraizer, Labat, Wartel, Gabriel, Bacquié, Girardet, Grignon.

was buried with appropriate pomp in Père Lachaise cemetery on 21 November. On the following evening Pasdeloup arranged a special memorial concert at the theatre. The programme consisted of the overture to *Semiramide*, followed by some dedicatory verses recited by Monjauze, 'Inflammatus' from the *Stabat Mater* sung by Mlle Schroeder and the chorus 'La Charité'. Most inappropriately the evening then ended with a performance of *Le Barbier de Séville*.[19] One doubts the good faith of Pasdeloup's intentions even more when we read that he repeated the identical programme two evenings later. Homage, it seems, was being paid to the box-office rather than to Rossini. To many artists in Paris the death on 27 October of Count Walewski may have been a greater tragedy for he had always been a good friend and his exalted position had lent that friendship the greatest importance.

Le *Maître de Chapelle* and Grisar's *Bégaiements d'Amour* were subsequently added to the repertory towards the end of 1868. Pasdeloup's first new production, *L'Irato* by Méhul and Marsollier passed almost unnoticed, for so unsuccessful was it that among all the Théâtre Lyrique productions it shared the unhappy distinction, with one other, of having only one performance. It had been composed in 1801 in the commedia dell'arte style to amuse Napoleon I, then First Consul to whom the score was dedicated. Théophile Gautier wrote of this revival, 'After *L'Œil Crevé* [Hervé], *La Belle Hélène* and *La Grande Duchesse de Gérolstein* one cannot but acknowledge that *L'Irato* seemed a little pallid.'[20] Daniel Bernard in *L'Union* was much more direct. 'It was positively massacred by M. Pasdeloup's artists who are the "clairs de lune" of the last company which we have seen perform on the same stage' he reported. 'The new director declares that he does not want stars. Very good! but that is not sufficient reason for leaving us completely in the dark.'[21]

The first important production by Pasdeloup was Gluck's *Iphigénie en Tauride* which was staged on 26 November. Mme Gaston-Lacaze was brought specially from Lyon to sing Iphigénie but she accomplished 'nothing that raised it above the ordinary.' The outstanding artist of the performance was Pasdeloup himself, standing at his desk in the manner of a Kapellmeister from across the Rhine. Ensemble and execution were excellent.[22] The chorus, considerably augmented by students from the

Conservatoire sang in time and in tune.[23] The principals alone
were disappointing. 'Pasdeloup's company still needs artists "di
primo cartello"' observed Théophile Gautier, 'he has not got a
"diva" nor a tenor with an exceptional top C.'[24] Even more
disappointing, indeed, almost unbelievable was Pasdeloup's
solecism in introducing the larghetto from Mozart's quintette in
A major in the interval before the last act, although Gustave
Bertrand admitted 'it was played so ravishingly, one could not
help applauding.'[25] Hector Berlioz, then extremely ill, having
attended one of the last performances was, according to Ernest
Reyer, very satisfied.[26]

Reyer also recorded that on the following Sunday (29
November) Pasdeloup conducted a second performance of
Iphigénie, having 'directed in the morning the beautiful Mass of
Mme la Vicomtesse de Grandval at the Panthéon, and, in the
afternoon the concert at the Cirque [Napoléon].'[27] Since he had
also retained his appointment as conductor of the Orphéonistes
one can begin to understand why he had so little time to devote
to the theatre. The production did not succeed and had only 15
performances. Its failure may have been due to poor singing, but
partly it may have been due to the cultural atmosphere of the
time. Francisque Sarcey was probably right in his summing up
that 'this is a little serious for our generation accustomed to the
antics of Offenbach's buffooneries. Tragedy, with or without
music, seems to have gone out of fashion.'[28]

His next effort was much more successful, but then it was
Adolphe Adam's *Le Brasseur de Preston*, one of the operas which
formed part of the repertory of Adam's Opéra National when he
had first founded it more than twenty years before. It seems to
have been a rough and unready performance conducted by
Mangin, ('M. Pasdeloup reserves his arm for the solemn
occasions,'[29] Reyer observed tartly) which nevertheless would
hold the stage until the theatre closed in 1870.

Apart from these few productions very little was happening as
the year ended. Eugène Vast, the recently appointed chorus
master had resigned from the company,[30] while Deloffre had
been appointed conductor to the Opéra-Comique where he was
assured of a warm welcome by the orchestra.[31] There was a
suggestion that Rossini's *Otello* would be presented with Mme
Brunet-Lafleur, borrowed from the Opéra-Comique, as

Desdemona. 'Why?'[32] Henri Moreno enquired with some justification. In fact, it never reached the Théâtre Lyrique stage. What did reach the stage was a revival of *Rigoletto* on 8 January 1869 with Schroeder, Bosquin and Lutz, but it was later reported, 'it has not filled the house to overflowing.'[33] In an effort to fill the house at any cost a new arrangement had been introduced on 1 January whereby monthly season tickets could be purchased for 30 francs. They admitted the holder every evening except for first performances when seats had to be bought at normal box office prices.[34] In effect this meant that seats were now being sold for as little as approximately one franc each. It may have been this uncertain situation which persuaded Jules Ruelle to resign from his post of secretary general.[35] Some months later he would be reported to be writing a libretto for a five act opera, *Manfred*, borrowed from Byron for which Massenet was to compose the score.[36]

On 15 January there was a new production of sorts, though not a new opera. A Premier Prix de Rome of 1868 named Wintzweiller had a cantata titled *Daniel* performed. Mlle Gilbert and MM Massy and Giraudet dressed in black occupied three presidential arm chairs on stage; but the biblical subject 'did little to captivate the hearer.' Nevertheless there was a very fashionable artistic audience headed by the venerable Auber, although unwell, and Baron Taylor, whom Napoleon III would shortly nominate as senator. What made some amends was the addition of the tomb scene from Nicola Vaccai's *Giulietta e Romeo*, translated by Adolphe Larmande[37] and sung by Mme Wertheimber and Mlle Priola. Wertheimber, whose voice by then was very worn, still electrified the entire theatre as Romeo and 'reminded us of the great days of Mme Viardot.' There was a second performance of these two pieces.[38]

Don Juan was next revived on 24 January but, like *Rigoletto*, did not succeed in 'filling the treasury.'[39] Once again Pasdeloup's failure to provide an adequate cast was commented upon. 'He does not want stars, but one cannot perform the classics, above all, unless with artists of the first order,' wrote Henri Moreno.[40] A writer in the *Revue et Gazette Musicale* concurred: 'Unfortunately he does not work on the same principles as M Carvalho, the production is therefore diminished as, consequently, is the success, in spite of all the care given elsewhere to the orchestral part.'⁴¹ Neither was a revival of *Violetta* on 1 February any more successful. The principal role was taken by Aglaja Orgeni, or to give her her full name, Anna Maria Aglaja Görger von St. Jörgen, a Hungarian recommended to Pauline Viardot by Clara Schumann. In 1866 she had been a successful Violetta at Covent Garden, but at the Théâtre Lyrique, singing in poor French and probably considered to be German by the audience, (anti-German feeling was rapidly rising just then) her success was not repeated. Gustave Bertrand recorded with regret the deplorable marks of disapproval with which she was greeted. 'Under the pretext of protesting against the bravos of the claque, or of over-enthusiastic friends (justifiable in the beginning),' he explains, 'they ended by showing themselves to be as unjust as they were brutal. In short, Mlle Orgeni is an artist of merit.'⁴² The situation was not helped by her wearing an ill-fitting dress 'which required continual "hitching up"' and 'once or twice her nervousness became so painfully apparent that she was moment-arily inaudible.'⁴³ Orgeni's most successful days were to come later perhaps, when she became a singing teacher, first in Dresden and then from 1914 in Vienna.

She has left a description of a rehearsal at the Théâtre Lyrique which is interesting for the information it gives of the preparation which an opera received there, at a time when in many theatres operas were presented with scarcely any prepara-tion at all.

'At last—I had my first stage rehearsal yesterday—pour la mise en scène, as they call it here. Every movement is dictated and must be followed as from an oracle. Every chair must remain on exactly the same spot, every step we take is plotted. Throughout the first and second acts I submitted to it all calmly, accepted their orders, and allowed them to push me from place to place. But in the end, my patience snapped at their lack of logic and over-production. During the farewell scene I simply said: "I will not play it like that, production is to have regard for order but it should not tie the artist's hands. I do not feel the farewell in this manner, I am not able to do it that way." At first they stared in amazement at this open revolt, then Pasdeloup said: "Well then, let us see you play the scene in your fashion. We will see if it is possible."'

It was of course possible and according to Orgeni the

rehearsal ended with everyone 'moist-eyed', and quite astonished at her 'German sensitivity'. Like a true prima donna she got her priorities right, for having arranged the production she then set about arranging her costumes—to the soprano singing this role, always as important as Verdi's music. 'They promise to be charming,' she enthused. 'The first: [the ill-fitting one!] crimson silk with tulle, fully puffed, covered with silver and camellias; the second: lilac silk, covered with delicate muslin, lilac bow; the third: completely white, set with pearls, camellias and green sprays—and finally, a négligé.'[44]

Apparently the only success which the Théâtre Lyrique was having at the time was with, of all things, a Swedish quartette! It consisted of four men, two tenors and two basses who had been members of the choir from Uppsala University which had visited the Théâtre Lyrique in 1867. (They seem to have resembled the Mills Brothers or the Ink Spots of the 1930s.) They performed in the intervals between the acts of the operas singing Swedish songs, and so popular did they become that they were invited to sing at numerous private concerts, including one at Princess Mathilde's.[45] Whatever their success they were scarcely part of Adolphe Adam's original plan to present unpublished operas by young French composers.

Even when Pasdeloup did present a new French work he showed little imagination in his choice. It was a one act opera comique, *En Prison*, by Ernest Guiraud, which had been gathering dust on the Théâtre Lyrique shelves for upwards of ten years. Guiraud is remembered today as the composer of the recitatives to *Carmen* following Bizet's death and for having completed *Les Contes d'Hoffmann*. He was born in New Orleans where his father, also a musician, had settled, and his first opera was performed in that city when he was only 15. He protested strongly against the staging of *En Prison*, an immature work by the standards of 1869, which he believed would not help his reputation, but Pasdeloup insisted on his rights. Before the first performance Legrand gave a long explanation of the controversy from the stage to 'a cold if not hostile audience.' There were whistles when the librettists' names were mentioned, but Guiraud's name was greeted with prolonged applause. There was also 'some whistling at the end, but the piece passed without interruption.'[46] 'An "opéra de salon" lost on a very large stage'[47] seems to have been a fair assessment of the result. A revival of *La Poupée de Nuremberg* ended the evening's entertainment, 'and this time there was no need for M. Legrand to say anything to the public, its success was inviolable.'[48]

Berlioz died, a lonely and dispirited man, on 8 March. The artistic world, as nearly always, would make amends later. His seat at the Institut was filled by Félicien David, who received 18 of the 32 votes cast.[49]

During all this time Pasdeloup was striving to make a successful assault on musical Paris with his production of *Rienzi.* In this he was helped by his new secretary-general, Léon Leroy who had succeeded Jules Ruelle. Leroy had been a disciple of A. de Gasperini, the Paris critic and advocate of Wagner's music who had died during the previous April. On 26 January 1868, Leroy had reported in *La Liberté* that Carvalho had signed a contract with Nuitter (Charles Truinet) to produce *Lohengrin* at the Théâtre Lyrique. Nuitter had translated the work and was acting as Wagner's agent. The rehearsals were to be supervised by Hans von Bülow and the première had been fixed for May. (Carvalho's contract had given him exclusive rights to *Lohengrin* provided it was staged before 26 January 1869, but this was revoked on 22 August 1868.[50] It was this muddle which had provoked Wagner's outburst against Carvalho, recorded earlier.) The production of *Lohengrin* having fallen through, Wagner's approval of Pasdeloup becomes much more understandable. However he might boast about offers from Pollini and Escudier, Wagner was well aware that Pasdeloup was his only hope of having one of his operas performed in Paris just then.

Pasdeloup was approaching his task with great care. In March when rehearsals were well advanced he set off for Lucerne to discuss details of production with the Master.[51] Wagner, 'who does not give his approval easily' concurred with his suggestions and seemingly agreed that Pasdeloup should adapt the score accordingly[52] in order to make it more acceptable to the Parisians. There were many cuts, after the first performance there would be more[53] until there was little left save unceasing dialogue between Rienzi and the people of Rome. Apart from this there certainly was no skimping on the presentation. Five new settings were painted by Cambon and

Rubé. The chorus was 120 strong. A number of principal artists in the company had even agreed to join it for this production. Extras were said to number 200. There were two ballets, one for soldiers and knights, the other, a 'feminine divertissement' which was led by Zina Mérante.[54] The costumes by Eugène Lacoste were numerous and very rich.[55] Rienzi would even make an entrance on horseback. Moreover there was continual rehearsal and the Théâtre Lyrique which normally closed for Good Friday only, this year closed for all of Holy Week to allow more time.[56]

The theatre had been permitted to raise its prices for the production,[57] but from 13 May onwards they would be reduced again to normal[58]—a bad sign. Three hundred places had been reserved in the stalls, parterre and amphitheatre for sale to the public on the day of the first performance.[59] Soubies records how he queued with two friends from 11 a.m. to gain seats in the fourth balcony.[60] A brilliant and distinguished audience attended the general rehearsal which lasted until after two in the morning. We learn that on that evening the report was current in the theatre that Wagner would be present on the first night in spite of his avowed intention of staying away, published in La Liberté.[61]

The performance took place and the reviews, although extensive— Le Ménestrel featured it on the front page, three columns long—were almost entirely critical. This is not to suggest that the work was not carefully and convincingly analysed, but the approach was strictly according to contemporary beliefs. To such beliefs Wagner was anathema, and 'the music of the future' was simply a composition of satanic strains played by a blasphemous Pied Piper leading listeners to a cacophonic hell. All were agreed that the production itself was of a high standard, although the cast, with the exception of Monjauze as Rienzi and Mlle Priola as a messenger of peace, was considered inadequate. Charles Bannelier in the Revue et Gazette Musicale had some reservations about the orchestra, conducted, of course, by Pasdeloup,[62] but Gustave Bertrand in Le Ménestrel was more concerned to emphasise that except for Lohengrin no further Wagner was needed in Paris. 'M. Wagner confirmed in a letter that M. Pasdeloup had only taken the direction of the Théâtre Lyrique to perform his six operas,' he reports. 'We hope that M. Pasdeloup will repudiate this bragging. If the Théâtre Lyrique is subventioned it is primarily to assist the French school and M. Pasdeloup must never forget that. One Wagner opera will suffice for our enlightenment.'[63] The element of jealousy seen to intrude here was fanned by members of the press. *Don Juan* was then playing alternately with *Rienzi.* 'A swan to a crow, a nightingale to a screech owl,'[64] was how one reviewer saw it. But even Soubies, a devoted partisan had to admit that the response to the work was indifferent.[65]

Yet for a time it must have had a succès d'estime, for on 12 April we find Princess von Metternich writing to Pasdeloup: 'Monsieur. Are you able to reserve a box for me at *Rienzi* tomorrow, Tuesday, or, if not, on Thursday or Saturday? I am writing directly to you because I am told that all the places have been taken for seven performances, and because I assume that the director alone reserves some little corners for the friends and admirers of Wagner.'[66] The artistic views of that ubiquitous, intolerant bore, 'the man in the street' were on the other hand pungently expressed by *Galignani's Messenger* as follows: 'The mighty noise of hot contention and Wagnerian clangour shakes the winged statue on its pedestal in the place du Châtelet. Curiosity drives however, a compact crowd there every night, and some few converts who went to scoff, remain to pray; but Wagner will not go down in Paris. Nor can he be forced down our throats against the stomach of our sense, either by M Pasdeloup or by any other manager.'[67]

Neither was Pasdeloup's position improved when on 3 April judgement was given against him in the case of the Théâtre Lyrique materials and costumes, and he was ordered to pay the receiver M. Copin, 100,000 francs.[68] He seems to have appealed, for a further judgement was recorded against him in July when he was then obliged to pay the full estimated value of 'about 300,000 francs—a small fortune for Carvalho's creditors.'[69]

Even the succès d'estime which would at least give *Rienzi* 38 performances was not duplicated with Pasdeloup's next production, *Don Quichotte*, a three act opera comique by Ernest Boulanger with libretto by Barbier and Carré after Cervantes. It was intended that it would alternate with *Rienzi* and like *En Prison* it too was said to have remained for ten years without

Interior of the Théâtre Lyrique with a performance of Boulanger's *Don Quichotte* on stage (1869).

being produced.[70] It was received with indulgence but without much enthusiasm for it had neither interest nor movement, nothing but a series of scenes badly strung together which passed before the eyes of the spectator like magic lantern slides.[71] Paul Bernard thought the music charming from beginning to end, but considered Pasdeloup's conducting too Germanic.[72] Gustave Bertrand observed ironically, 'He would not want to show less solicitude for a French composer than for the King of Bavaria's Kapellmeister,'[73] for Pasdeloup conducted relatively few performances.

From all that had taken place in the foregoing season, or rather, because so little had taken place, it is not surprising to read an announcement in June of Pasdeloup's retirement from the Théâtre Lyrique. It was noted that 'his first season has been singularly unfortunate,' but the rumour was immediately denied by *Le Figaro* which asserted that he would remain for another season.[74]

The current season had ended with a performance of *Rienzi* on 31 May when there had been exceptional applause for the artists and especially for 'the enterprising impresario.' Following act four a laurel wreath was thrown from the audience to Monjauze, who was also presented by Pasdeloup with a tie pin set with an emerald surrounded by brilliants. An appreciative letter from Wagner had been hoped for [some hope!] which could be read ceremoniously from the stage. What had arrived was a letter of complaint drawn up by the Société des Auteurs et Compositeurs Dramatiques demanding that the Théâtre Lyrique give a pre-determined number of unpublished works by French composers in the forthcoming year.[75] The season certainly cannot be said to have ended with a flourish, for on Monday, 24 May, *Violetta* had taken only 525 francs at the box-office. Theatre receipts seem to have been generally down, although an exception was *Le Petit Faust* at the Théâtre Folies Dramatiques which on the same Monday evening took in over 3,000 francs.[76]

To reopen his next season Pasdeloup had first threatened a further dusting off of old material, a production of Legouvé and Gounod's *Les Deux Reines*,[77] which, it will be remembered had been withdrawn for political reasons some years before. By August, however, a more symbolic inaugural was announced— a revival of *Rienzi*. Massy would now take the principal role,

Monjauze being incapacitated from having lately broken his arm.[78] In August also Pasdeloup signed a contract with the family of the late Fromental Halévy to produce his unpublished opera *Noé ou le Deluge*.[79] It was an unfinished work which would be completed by Halévy's son-in-law Georges Bizet but would not be performed until 1885 and then in Germany at Karlsruhe as *Noah*. It would never be staged in France. Operas promised with *Rienzi* in the coming season were *La Bohémienne* (at last it would happen!), *La Statue*, *Don Pasquale*, *Le Bal Masqué* (Verdi) and a new opera *Nydia* by Joncières, which in time would be produced under the title of *Le Dernier Jour de Pompéi*.[80]

Two Théâtre Lyrique artists had died in June, the composer Salvatore Sarmiento and his more successful colleague, Albert Grisar. Others would be appointed chevaliers of the Légion d'honneur in August, Henri Meilhac, Auguste Rubé (the scene designer) and Ernest Boulanger. For the fête day on 15 August (this year the centenary of the birth of Napoleon I), *Don Quichotte* was performed at the Théâtre Lyrique, preceded by a cantata, *La Fête de France* written by Nérée Desarbres with music by Edouard Mangin.[81] The latter would in due course receive the time honoured gold medal accompanied by the Emperor's compliments for his pains.[82]

But excitement was lacking. Even the announcement of the names of the successful candidates in the competition for new operas (there were 43 entries) caused little stir, and in retrospect reflects little credit on the discernment of the jury.* The winners were as follows:

First: Le Magnifique. Opéra comique in one act. Libretto by Jules Barbier, taken from Boccaccio, music by Jules Philippot, a pianist-composer, then (as now) unknown in the theatre.

Second: La Coupe et les Lèvres. Grand opera in five acts. Libretto by Ernest d'Hervilly from Alfred de Musset's play,**

*

They deserve to be named as an example of how wrong such juries can be. The members were, for music: MM Benoît, Deloffre, Dupré, Eugène Gautier, Labarre, Massé, Poniatowski, and Johannès Weber; for libretti: Azevedo, Blaze de Bury, Dumas fils, Edouard Fournier, Jouvin, Hippolyte Prévost, Louis Roger and Francisque Sarcey. RGM. 20 Dec. 1868.

**

Puccini would later base his opera, *Edgar* on the same play.

music by Gustave Canoby, a disciple of Fromental Halévy. *Third: Fiesque.* Opera in three acts. Libretto by Charles Beauquier, after Schiller, music by Edouard Lalo.[83]

The winner had been assured of a production at the Théâtre Lyrique, but *Le Magnifique* was not staged until 1876 when it had four performances at the Opéra-National-Lyrique.

Of all the theatrical activities inaugurated in Paris during that season of 1868–69, what has stood the test of time, what still remains? Believe it or not, the 'Café-théâtre des Folies-Bergère,' which had opened its doors in May.[84]

1869–1870

What was to be not only Pasdeloup's last season, but also the last season of the Théâtre Lyrique itself commenced as promised with *Rienzi* on 1 September. A comment made in relation to the performance that 'M. Pasdeloup threatens to produce *Rheingold* whereat there is much consternation in anti-Wagner circles,'[1] was probably more mischievous than serious and assuredly emanated from a visit by Léon Leroy, Pasdeloup's secretary-general to the first performance of the work in Munich on 22 September.[2]

It was a season which began with little activity. Mlle Sternberg had left the company for Brussels[3] to be replaced by Mlle Franchino late of the Monnaie in Brussels while Augustin Vizentini, the stage manager, had departed to become director of the theatre at Lille,[4] but among old hands who remained,* were Mlle Daram and MM Massy, Monjauze, Meillet and Lutz.

The lack of an adequate repertory of operas—an inherent weakness—was revealed when a concert performance of Félicien David's *Le Désert* was given on 12 September, even though the combined chorus and orchestra was said to number 180.[5] It must have had some success since it was repeated four evenings later. On both occasions the performance ended with the first and second acts of *Le Barbier de Séville.*[6] It may have been the

---

*

Among artists newly engaged were Mlles Brunet-Lafleur, from the Opéra-Comique, and Vercken, sopranos, Lombia, mezzo-soprano, and MM Coppel and Mottès, tenors.

ease of production of these concerts which encouraged Pasdeloup to continue with more Félicien David of the same kind, this time the symphonic ode, *Christophe Colomb* for which 200 participants were promised. To *Christophe Colomb* was added the overture to Rossini's *Semiramide*, an air from *Le Freischütz* sung by Mlle Schroeder, a 'Fantaisie-Caprice' by Vieuxtemps, played by M. Mauchin (the solo violinist of the orchestra), the whole ending with a march from *Tannhäuser* for chorus and orchestra, presumably the entrance to the Minstrels' Hall.[7] Two more performances were given, on 10 and 11 October,* but *Christophe Colomb* was not as well received as *Le Désert*.[8]

There were nevertheless some revivals of past successes; on 16 October, *Rigóletto* conducted by Pasdeloup and with a new tenor from Bordeaux, M. Coppel. Three evenings later Monjauze returned to the theatre to take part in *Le Val d'Andorre*,[9] and on 13 November there was a performance of *Le Barbier de Séville* to commemorate the anniversary of Rossini's death.[10] Next, on 25 November the composer and librettist of the prizewinning *Le Magnifique* were given an audition of their opera by the artists provisionally chosen to perform in it,[11] and lastly, in January 1870, *Le Médecin malgré lui*, 'was received with pleasure but without enthusiasm.'[12] Regrettably, by 5 December, *Rienzi* had had to be withdrawn, and in January it would be announced that 'the family of the late M. Halévy acting in conjunction with M. Georges Bizet have withdrawn *Noé* from the Lyrique alleging that M. Pasdeloup's artists are not able to do it justice,'[13] but by then, as will be seen, Pasdeloup would have little interest in the Théâtre Lyrique or the abilities of the artists engaged there. More likely the opera was withdrawn, faute de mieux, to seek a more reliable stage.

Pasdeloup's first new opera of the season, Joncières' *Le Dernier Jour de Pompéï* which was performed on 21 September was no more successful than *Christophe Colomb* had been, nor indeed more successful than most of the works which he had brought to the Théâtre Lyrique. The Wagnerian influence apparent in Joncières' earlier opera, *Sardanapale* had now

---

*

Without giving dates *L'Art Musical* of 10 June 1870 reports that *Le Désert* was performed seven times and *Christophe Colomb* three times.

almost overwhelmed him (he was one of the French faithful who had made the pilgrimage to Munich for *Das Rheingold*) and he had scored a march in act one in the style of the overture of *Tannhäuser.* 'But it is one of those skills which Wagner alone knows how to employ,' warned Lavoix fils, 'and the march we refer to created more noise than effect.' He expressed much the same feelings about a stage orchestra for brass instruments.[14]

The story had been taken from Bulwer-Lytton's novel, but so badly adapted by Nuitter and Beaumont 'to such abominal verse that any opera would have sunk under such a libretto.'[15] The dancers taking part in the ballet headed by a Mlle Rust had been obligingly released from the Opéra by Emile Perrin.[16] It was grandiloquently reported that the scenery would be designed by Robecchi, Cambon, Rubé and Chaperon, no less than four of the best stage artists in Paris, but the reality was that scenery made for other productions was being re-used, as were the costumes.[17] Especially incongruous was the final scene where Vesuvius erupts and which provoked peals of laughter. 'The two or three squibs spit forth by the convulsed volcano are conducive to mirth alone,' reported *Galignani's Messenger,* '. . . we can assure M. Pasdeloup that no country theatre in Italy would have ventured to put off the public with such a wretched apology for an eruption.'[18] Even worse was the boat bearing the lovers to safety, a toy model jerking across the backcloth and manned by finger sized sailors rowing with all the power of their mechanism.[19] Then there were the enthusiastic admirers of Mlle Schroeder who were so impatient to salute her big air in act four that they launched two huge bouquets on to the stage almost before she had begun to sing it.[20]

There was much borrowing in Joncières' score and not only from Wagner. The beginning of one air was remarkably similar to Nelusko's 'Adamastor, roi des vagues profondes' from *L'Africaine*[21] and F. de Lagenevais having remarked on the strong Wagnerian influence also found, 'continual reminiscences of Verdi and Donizetti.'[22] It later transpired that the low standard of performance was because Pasdeloup, who conducted, had suffered what was called some form of cerebral congestion a short time before.[23] His condition had not allowed him to be present at the final rehearsals and after a number of performances he wrote to the press explaining that the work had been given under the most trying conditions and invited the critics to attend again. But even on the second visit the critics could see no reason for changing their poor opinion of the work, and as Gustave Bertrand cogently observed, the meagre receipts trail along at a minimum during these well meaning performances.[24] There would be only 13.

The next card which Pasdeloup played was one which had won Carvalho a couple of games—the translation of a Verdi opera. He now staged the promised Le Bal Masqué, translated, like Rigoletto and La Traviata by Edouard Duprez. One of his problems was to find a suitable soprano for Amelia. This he solved, not entirely successfully, by re-engaging Mme Meillet. The opera was being performed at the Théâtre Italien during the same season which made his casting problems all the more sensitive.

The production was received almost with rapture by most of the critics. Gustave Bertrand found it more satisfactory in every way than either Macbeth or Ernani.[25] (The latter had been frequently performed at the Théâtre Italien.) Lavoix fils agreed, declaring it to be 'of all Verdi's scores one of the most painstaking in style. Less colourful than Il Trovatore, less passionate than Rigoletto, it comes closest of all to La Traviata. This work although inferior to those I have named is however freer than any other from the inequalities of style which mar the most elegant pages of the Master of Busseto.' He goes on to record that Le Bal Masqué was staged with a care deserving every praise. Massy [Richard] sang his role well, although lacking flexibility of voice and showing fatigue in the last act. Amelia was too high for Mme Meillet, but her experience enabled her to triumph over this shortcoming. Borghèse's voice did not always respond to her intentions as Ulrique. Lutz, as Renato, did not seem to make the most of his abilities, he did not produce all that was expected of him. 'The chorus is good, the orchestra excellent and well conducted [by Pasdeloup] and everything augurs a success.'[26] Clearly the casting was substandard and Gustave Bertrand confirms that principal roles were always better sung at the Théâtre Italien, but, on the other hand the ensemble was better at the Théâtre Lyrique.[27] Galignani's Messenger adds, 'the choruses especially are immeasurably superior to those at the Italiens, than which nothing could be worse.'[28]

At the Théâtre Lyrique even the standard of ensemble cannot have been that impressive, neither was the policy adventurous, and as the season commenced, F. de Lagenevais was writing: 'First of all the company is mediocre. Where are the rudiments of production, the means of giving satisfaction without at the same time incurring ruin with the costs of a musical production of the first rank? Then, the Théâtre Lyrique as it is presently constituted has this system, which I do not intend either to praise or to blame, of giving a very large share to the foreign schools in order to serve usefully young [French] composers. I glance over the list of works to be performed this winter and there I see only one new score of M Joncières, *La Bohémienne* by M Balfe, and a posthumous *Noé* by Halévy. Now, if to this translation and this exhumation you add Wagner's *Lohengrin*, I ask you what room is there left for unknown talent?'[29]

Reflecting on the situation it cannot come as a surprise to read as early as 14 November that Pasdeloup, fatigued by all the work he had undertaken, the Orphéon, Concerts Populaires, and the theatre, is said to be retiring from the Théâtre Lyrique.[30] Nevertheless he would play one more hand in this theatrical poker game. Balfe's *La Bohémienne* had been promised so long and so often that it was ironic that it should at last reach the Théâtre Lyrique stage in the last season of the theatre's existence. From his youth Balfe had been a frequent visitor to the Continent and since so little of this part of his career has been recorded it may not be inappropriate here to set down briefly something of his life and times in Paris.

In 1828 from January to May he was engaged as principal baritone at the Théâtre Italien singing Figaro (*Il Barbiere di Siviglia*), Dandini, Masetto, and Il Podestà in *La Gazza Ladra*.[31] He was one of a highly distinguished roster of singers which included Bordogni, Donzelli, (Vincenzo) Graziani, Zucchelli, Galli, Blasis, Sontag and Malibran. With this last great artist he would be associated in later years both as singer and as composer. The marvel of this engagement was not merely that Balfe was singing among such exalted company in Paris, but that having been born in Dublin on 15 May 1808 he was singing there at the incredibly early age of 19!

In later years he would give concerts there. On 16 March 1842, for example, he joined forces with his expatriate fellow countryman, the Limerick pianist George Alexander Osborne, to give a recital in the salon of M. Erard. The programme included Osborne's compositions played by him, and items from Balfe's and Rossini's works sung by Balfe (who included the 'Largo al factotum'), his pupil W.H. Weiss, and Mmes Lina Roser Balfe, Henriette Nissen and Pauline Viardot, who sang the rondo-finale from *The Maid of Artois*, originally composed by Balfe for her sister Maria Malibran.[32]

As a composer he had had three operas with libretti by Scribe, de Leuven, Brunswick and Hippolyte Lucas produced in Paris during the eighteen-forties— *Le Puits d'Amour* in 1843, *Les Quatre Fils Aymon* in 1844, both at the Opéra-Comique, and *L'Étoile de Séville* in 1845 at the Opéra. These works each received 28, 17 and 15 performances respectively, and did little to further Balfe's career. In a representative example of 19th century romantic rhetoric, Berlioz, when reviewing *Les Quatre Fils Aymon*, wrote, 'There are people who are amazed that an Englishman could have written this pretty music, but first of all Balfe is not English, he is a son of Ireland, the green Erin, the sweet country of the harp as Tom Moore called it. The Irish are all improvisers, they improvise whether it be their verse, their prose, their music or their miming. The only thing they do not improvise is revolutions . . . Besides why should not an English-man make good music? There are plenty of Italians, French and Germans who make very bad music . . . M. Balfe's music, it is easy to see is improvised à l'Irlandaise, full of vivacity and verve . . . It is expressive and dramatic and only needs occasionally a little more originality.'[33]

The origins of *La Bohémienne* are involved but begin with de Saint-Georges who wrote a ballet, *La Gypsy* (based on Cervantes' story 'La Gitanella') which, choreographed by Mazilier and with music by François Benoist, Ambroise Thomas, and M.A. Marliani was presented at the Opéra on 28 January 1839. Balfe's two biographers, Barrett and Kenney, although often unreliable, have recorded that much of the music for what was to be *The Bohemian Girl* had been composed by Balfe as early as the summer of 1841. Some of this music he may have used later in *Le Puits d'Amour*. Next, two writers for *Le Figaro*, Gustave Lafargue on 9 July and Jules Prével on 13 July 1869, relate that following the performance of the ballet, which with Fanny

Elssler had had a considerable success, de Saint-Georges and
Balfe had begun to write an opera based on the same story. This
was to be produced at the Opéra, and they further relate that it
even reached rehearsal there with Rosine Stoltz, Duprez and
Barroilhet. The reason they give for its subsequent withdrawal,
the appointment of Léon Pillet as director, is however both
unconvincing and inconsistent. Nevertheless, this in no way
invalidates the fact that de Saint-Georges and Balfe could have
been working on *La Bohémienne*. Where de Saint-Georges is
concerned the similarity of his transformation of *Martha* from
ballet into opera, with a like alteration of *La Gypsy* to *La
Bohémienne* is surely significant. As for Balfe, a little at least of
the text of *La Bohémienne* suggests that it was the French words
which were first set to music, and that the English version came
later. There is some evidence to confirm this from Gustave
Lafargue who writes, 'Balfe took away his score to be translated
into English, and *La Gypsy* was performed in London with
immense success . . . It goes without saying that it is the original
poem of M. de Saint-Georges which will be performed at the
Théâtre Lyrique.'[34] Finally, although less reliably, since the
information may have been gleaned from Lafargue, *The Orchestra*
of 26 November 1869 reports, '*The Bohemian Girl* in becoming
La Bohémienne will also return to its original language, Mr
Bunn's libretto having been translated from a French libretto
prepared for its use by M. St. Georges.' All this conflicts with the
generally accepted belief that the libretto of *The Bohemian Girl*
is an original work written by Alfred Bunn, but a *Bohemian Girl*
partially composed in advance to a text later translated and
arranged by Bunn would at least help to explain how between 20
April 1843 and 17 December 1845, Balfe could manage to have
six operas ready for production, three in Paris, three in London,
besides finding time to undertake an English provincial tour and
to appear on the London stage.

In France, *La Bohémienne* was first performed at the Théâtre
des Arts, Rouen, on 23 April 1862. The French score was
arranged in a prologue and four acts* instead of *The Bohemian*

*

A score had been published by Gérard et Cie, following the Rouen production
in which the opera was arranged in four acts only. In an edition published after
the production at the Théâtre Lyrique, act one became the prologue. There

Girl's three acts. The names of the characters were mainly retained as they had appeared in *La Gypsy*, but the setting was altered from the Edinburgh of King Charles II to Hungary. There were recitatives instead of spoken dialogue and the emphasis on the leading female roles had altered, La Reine Mab (The Gipsy Queen) had now become the principal character, superseding Sarah (Arline). This change may have come about through the availability in Rouen of Galli-Marié, later the first Carmen, who sang the role of the Queen. Jules Laurent Duprato, a scarcely remembered composer from Nîmes supplied the recitatives and also composed two new airs for Galli-Marié.[35] It is unlikely that these remain, for the French vocal score, published after the Théâtre Lyrique production, refers to 'The pieces added by the authors of the music and the libretto, the recitatives, duets and airs written specially for the Théâtre Lyrique.'[36] The airs (if the legend in the score is correct) included one composed especially for Marie Roze[37] who had been the original choice for Sarah in the Paris production. De Saint-Georges helped with the staging at Rouen and was present at the first performance, but Balfe did not attend. The opera was very successful there and was given 13 successive performances, a remarkable number for a provincial production.[38]

De Saint-Georges produced the work at the Théâtre Lyrique as well,[39] and although Balfe was in Paris throughout the time of the later rehearsals, he appears to have been confined to bed, ill for most of the period. Late in February 1870 he would write from 154 Avenue des Champs Elysées to a friend in London, 'I have been for four months confined to the house with an attack of bronchitis which would have killed many a finer fellow than M.W.B. Heureusement, ni la mort, ni le Diable would have anything to do with me.'[40] As the time for performance approached we read that, 'the orchestral rehearsals under Pasdeloup are proceeding not without difficulty. The irascible director does not allow comments from anyone—not even the composer. And instead of following the singers he is here just as stubborn as with the musicians.'[41] The artists however were

were other changes, mainly the addition of a quartette, a duet, two airs for Sarah ('A peine puis-je y croire!' and 'La grandeur, l'opulence'), and the deletion of an air for La Reine, all of which made Sarah the leading female role once again.

delighted with their costumes. It was reported grudgingly that Pasdeloup had done the thing well but with little enthusiasm. He believed in the motto of the Paris 'bohémien', that 'since a man has only one body he needs only one suit.'[42]

On 30 December the opera passed off well, 'despite the injudicious intemperate zeal of the claquers who provoked two conflicts with the public which at one time threatened to be a very "bianchi e neri" affair since they insisted on giving more plaudits for their money than were bargained for; the public as on many previous occasions resented this insolent interference... And after the audience had sternly silenced the claque, they turned to the cordial enjoyment of the opera and to the sincere and hearty recognition of its many beauties... '[43] Lavoix fils found 'the principal qualities' of *La Bohémienne* to be 'a great melodic facility and a certain elegance in the orchestra, and above all in the arrangement for the voice.' The overture and 'Quand une voix bien tendre' ('When other lips') were known from concerts, Sarah's 'romance du rêve' ('I dreamt that I dwelt'), well sung by Brunet-Lafleur was encored, as surprisingly, was the quartet, 'Le beau jour, la belle fête!' ('From the valleys and hills'); 'Doux ange de ma vie' ('The heart bowed down') passed unnoticed—Le Comte d'Arnheim was considered rather a bore—and the finale of act three was coldly received. Monjauze was very hoarse; he would be replaced by Coppel in later performances, Wertheimber as the Gipsy Queen displayed a rich contralto voice in the lower register, but had difficulty with her higher notes. The success of the evening seems to have been Brunet-Lafleur. Pasdeloup conducted, the orchestra and ensembles went well, the scenery was satisfactory, and the ballet costumes, particularly those in act two, were warmly applauded.[44]

In all, only one thing was at fault and that was a question of timing, for by 1869, in France, *La Bohémienne* was a musical anachronism. As *La Presse* pointed out, 'Our generation neither knows nor applauds the Maestro Balfe.'[45] To have a real success the opera had come to Paris nearly thirty years too late. Still, it was far from being a failure and on New Year's Eve there was a party after the performance at which Balfe and de Saint-Georges 'addressed their thanks to MM the orchestra [where were the stage artists?!]. Champagne was opened and the health of the new opera was drunk in chorus. Balfe, to show his appreciation of Edouard Mangin for the care he had taken with rehearsals, 'presented him with a magnificent chronometer.'[46] Some evenings later Mlles Galli-Marié, Marie Roze, Revilly and Moisset, all from the Opéra-Comique attended a performance. Galli-Marié, the Rouen Gipsy Queen, 'congratulated Mlle Wertheimber on the manner in which she had sung her role.' Another distinguished visitor on that evening was M. le Vicomte de Laferrière, who, from his box applauded 'the pure and sympathetic voice of Mme Brunet-Lafleur.'[47]

For Balfe, an ill and aging man, although, as his letter shows, still confident and young in heart, there was also acknowledgement. M. Maurice Richard, the new Ministre des Beaux Arts of Emile Ollivier's cabinet wrote to him: 'Monsieur. I have the honour to inform you that by a decree of the 18 of this month the Emperor has graciously decided to appoint you Chevalier de la Légion d'honneur...'[48] It was a belated but well deserved tribute. In England musicians who had brought far less honour to their country had been knighted. It came just in time, for Balfe would die on 20 October, only eight months later.

For Pasdeloup, this operatically was also the end. Having offered his resignation to Maurice Richard some weeks before, he would retire on 31 January 1870. In a defiant gesture, symbolic of the man, he was to conduct *Rienzi* on that evening for his last performance, when the receipts would amount to only 2000 francs.[49] This stiff-necked integrity in the cause of Wagner, especially amidst the political climate existing in Paris in 1870 made him many enemies. He even seemed to provoke enmity deliberately, and much of the antagonism at his Concerts-Populaires may have been due not so much to his introduction of Wagner's music, as to his allowing a small aggressive minority in the audience to insist on encores. Enemies he had in spite of his profound influence on the musical life of Paris—or more likely because of it. There was Gustave Lafargue, who, when a stage foreman died suddenly of apoplexy during a performance of *La Bal Masqué*, maliciously reproached him in *Le Figaro* for not attending the man's funeral and for refusing to allow artists required for rehearsal to attend.[50] Following his resignation, Thomas Sauvage, President of the Society of Authors, Composers and Music Publishers and joint director of the Odéon would write vindictively, 'with the temerity of inexperience M. Pasdeloup plunged into this abyss, of which he did not know the depth. M. Pasdeloup has a musical passion to satisfy: with a passion of the heart one is blind, with the passion of the ear, one is deaf.'[51]

Like all men who have enemies, Pasdeloup equally had friends, some, as we have noted in high places. Indeed his decision to resign may ultimately have hinged on the formation on 2 January of Emile Ollivier's new liberal cabinet with the consequent fall of his patron, le Grand Préfet, Baron Haussmann. Before he resigned he called his company together to explain to them contritely, why, in modern parlance, he was obliged to make them redundant. He was reported to be making the most honourable efforts so that his resignation would not close the theatre or suspend the performances. The means of livelihood of almost 200 people (artists, musicians, choristers) depended on him, and the new Minister, Maurice Richard, was much concerned about the situation.[52] He would retire with personal losses of 80,000 francs, having mortgaged the profits of his Concerts-Populaires for two years.[53] But as Marie Escudier (a staunch friend) would write in *La France Musicale*, 'He leaves with his head high and his hands clean. Everyone has been paid from the highest to the lowest, no one is at the loss of a centime— except one. Discouraged and ruined after two years of incessant fatigue and dogged efforts, it is he.'[54]

With the departure of Pasdeloup there were a number of contenders for the vacant post, among them, amazingly, Carvalho. Since negotiations with the Préfet de la Seine, the Commission Municipale and the Ministre des Beaux Arts were bound to be protracted, the artists and musicians took matters into their own hands and formed a commonwealth after the fashion of the Comédie Française. This body of 'artistes en société' sought a double subvention from the Minister as a preliminary. It was an over-optimistic approach which did not succeed, but as an indication of the Minister's concern he did find an extra 10,000 francs which gave them a subsidy of 60,000 francs for the four months until the end of May. The Société further hoped to receive the theatre from the Municipality free of all rent and with a reduction of lighting and running costs. In the circumstances the Municipality had little opportunity for bargaining.[55] Pasdeloup seems to have been generous enough to have agreed to allow them to retain scenery and costumes without charge.[56] The question of a lease and the vexed 'droit des pauvres' (lately reduced to five per cent) appears to have been left in abeyance.

Each artist was to receive a basic salary of 100 francs a month. Anything over that amount would depend entirely on what was taken at the box-office and would be shared equally among all, from principal singers and conductors to stage hands.[57] Offers of support came from all sides. Gounod and de Saint-Georges promised their active cooperation. Miolan-Carvalho and Nilsson announced that in memory of their old theatre they would take part in a benefit performance.[58] There were some disagreements and defections: Mme Wertheimber refused to sing except for a fee, Monjauze announced that he would leave at the end of the season to seek a career in Italian opera, but Léon Leroy remained as secretary-general with Benou as administrator, while MM. Meillet and Gabriel took over production.[59]

Following Pasdeloup's final performance on Monday 31 January the theatre re-opened on the following Thursday with *La Bohémienne*. The Sociétaires then turned their attention to selecting a new production. Their choice fell on Halévy's *Charles VI*, first performed at the Opéra in 1843 and not heard in Paris since 1850. Emile Perrin, currently director of the Opéra had given permission for its staging at the Théâtre Lyrique.[60] Likewise from de Leuven at the Opéra-Comique permission had come to present a new opera by de Saint Georges and Flotow called *L'Ombre*, originally intended for his theatre.[61] The cast was to consist of Marie Cabel, Monjauze, Meillet and a young soprano from the Opéra-Comique and Opéra, later to become well known in England, named Marie Roze. She too had been ceded to the Société by the helpful Perrin.

His reasons for granting the rights of *Charles VI* to the Théâtre Lyrique may not have been as magnanimous as they seem. The opera had been viewed with disfavour for political reasons during the Second Empire and there was a report then current that a revival at the Opéra had lately been rejected because of its rousing air, 'Guerre aux tyrans! Jamais en France, jamais l'Anglais ne régnera.'[62] By 1870 France was having sufficient problems with Germany to wish to avoid wounding

English feelings from the stage of its foremost state opera house. Nevertheless the time was ripe for some well judged jingoism to be instilled into the plain people of Paris. Away from the official Opéra it need not cause offence to England and with the transgressing country having become Germany in the minds of the audience, the sentiment was just what was then needed.

From the beginning the production had run into difficulties. First Brunet-Lafleur became ill, upsetting the rehearsal schedule. Then, scenery promised by the Opéra was thought to have been destroyed in a fire necessitating the building of new sets.[63] Fortunately this was found to be untrue, the scenery was undamaged with the exception of one salon scene which the Odéon generously replaced.[64] The opera was then announced for 19 March but next Mlle Schroeder became ill and her role of Isabeau had to be taken over by Mlle Daram, 'who accepted it to help her comrades since the role was not in her style.' Brunet-Lafleur now left the cast and once again Emile Perrin came forward releasing Rosine Bloch to undertake the role of Odette, but right away Rosine Bloch went down with influenza and there was a further postponement.[65] *Charles VI* eventually reached the Théâtre Lyrique stage on Tuesday 5 April and from all accounts did not warrant this amount of effort. Nestor Roqueplan describes it simply as 'a fiasco.'[66]

A quasi-historical episode in the life of Charles VI presented a situation sufficiently full of colour and intrigue to attract an audience, with patriotic overtones as an added allure. Patriotism was certainly in the ascendant just then, but it was a confused patriotism although this was scarcely recognised, and loyalties were weaker than they seemed. On 16 March the theatres had been illuminated and beflagged to celebrate the anniversary of the birth of the young Prince Imperial.[67] It was to be the last occasion for celebration in the life of the Second Empire. As for *Charles VI*, Lavoix fils paid the sociétaires a rather left-handed compliment by congratulating them for having got it on the stage at all. He then went on to recount the many cuts which had been made for reasons of economy, the ballet in the second act, the march and big finale in the third. They amounted to almost 140 pages of the orchestral score. In spite of this he still found the opera a little long in places. Mangin conducted valiantly but the orchestra was below the standard of the Théâtre Lyrique.

The famous refrain 'Guerre aux tyrans!' with Massy as Charles
VI accentuating the phrase, 'Réveille-toi, France opprimée'
brought the house down.[68] This was in act one and the opera
ends with a similar defiant flourish, this time, 'Mort aux tyrans!'
A number of items in the work were obviously well known and
popular but this was essentially a sentimental revival which,
artistically, had no more relevance to the year 1870 than had the
recent production of La Bohémienne. Sentiment and patriotism
alone gained it 22 performances.

The second projected work, L'Ombre did not reach the stage
at all. It had gone into rehearsal about mid-February and
Flotow had arrived in Paris to take charge on 3 March.[69] On 6
March it was reported, 'Cabel's role in L'Ombre is written so
high that she asks for some alterations,' to which was added the
mischievous comment, 'Nevertheless one knows that it is not
the high tessitura of the singing which troubles her.'[70] The latter
suggests rivalry between her and the young Marie Roze, almost
20 years her junior. Yet, a week later all seemed well and Flotow
was said to be 'enchanted with Cabel' and to have paid 'the most
flattering compliments to the pretty Marie Roze.'[71] This
satisfactory position seemed to continue and by 20 March
orchestral rehearsals had commenced.[72] Early in April Cabel
was stricken with bronchitis and rehearsals had to be 'momen-
tarily' suspended.[73] Then, suddenly on 17 April it was announced
that the production was abandoned,* Cabel having had to
resign her role for health reasons, and that Flotow had returned
to Germany.[74] It may be noted in passing that Cabel's health
had recovered sufficiently by the second week of May to permit
her to sing her celebrated 'Air des Fraises' in a benefit
performance at the Odéon.[75]

The season continued to limp along until on 22 May a notice
appeared stating that 'the sudden heat-wave has caused the
Association of Artists of the Théâtre Lyrique to end their
exploitation with a grand performance in which all the theatres
of Paris and the élite of their artists will take part.'[76] It was held

---

*

It was eventually produced at the Opéra-Comique on 7 July 1870 when
Cabel's role was taken by Priola.

on Tuesday 31 May* when receipts reached 7440 francs. The Emperor had sent 1,000 francs for his box.[77] It was a 'concert panaché' made up of pieces from the most popular works in the repertory. So, the Théâtre Lyrique closed, defeated but not dishonoured, for in the five months of its last year the curtain had risen on most evenings. Within that time 150 performances of 13 different operas had been given. These were *Le Barbier de Séville*, 3; *Le Maître de Chapelle*, 2; *Le Brasseur de Preston*, 12; *Rienzi*, 1; *Charles VI*, 22; *La Bohémienne*, 28; *Le Val d'Andorre*, 6; *Rigoletto*, 8; *La Poupée de Nuremberg*, 11; *Le Médecin malgré lui*, 12; *Le Bal Masqué*, 41; *En Prison*, 3; and *Les Dragées de Suzette*, 1.

The precariousness of the Société's operation had been obvious not only to officialdom and the public but to the artists themselves. At the time of its formation it was noted, 'all these elements, we say, seem sufficient to keep open the doors of the third lyric theatre until a more responsible arrangement arrives to ensure its future.'[78] A proposal for such an arrangement had been made to the Minister, Maurice Richard, by Pasdeloup, before he resigned. It planned to place the Opéra, the Opéra-Comique and the Théâtre Lyrique under the general control of Emile Perrin with directors at the two latter theatres to act in conjunction with him. Marie Escudier of *La France Musicale* was all for the idea,[79] as were Gustave Bertrand and Henri Moreno.[80] It was pointed out that as matters stood the Théâtre Lyrique was not viable. If standards were lowered in an attempt to economise, the public merely stayed away. If an effort was made to improve them by engaging better artists the director went bankrupt. Indeed, it could be truly said of every director who had held office since the theatre's inception that he had left it broke—or dead. However, the committees of both Dramatic Authors and Composers promptly rejected the plan, fearing that it would give a monopoly of all subventioned French opera in Paris to Perrin and his associate directors.[81]

*

RGM, 5 June 1870 reports: 'The Théâtre Lyrique closed its doors on Wednesday,' which would make it 1 June, but all other sources, including Soubies give 31 May. It is possible that while the last official performance took place on 31 May, this benefit was held on the evening after the regular season had ended.

In the circumstances, as has been earlier noted there were several applicants for Pasdeloup's post. With Carvalho, the following were announced: Roux, an ex-director of many French provincial theatres and currently a theatre correspondent, Léon Sari[82] sometime director of the Délassements-Comiques and subsequently impresario of the Folies-Bergère, Théodore Letellier, late of the Monnaie Theatre, Brussels, and Louis Martinet.[83] The competition quickly narrowed between Carvalho, much favoured by the artists, and Martinet.

Carvalho submitted a memorandum of his plans to the Minister which seems to have been considered favourably.[84] His real difficulty lay with the Commission Municipale headed by the Préfet de la Seine to whom on 11 April he presented his plans and offered ways and means of carrying them out. His figures included a sum of 70,000 francs as an annual rent to cover running expenses, lighting and heating. In addition he offered to pay ten per cent of all receipts over 750,000 francs, the net amount which he estimated was needed to manage the theatre successfully.[85] By 24 April negotiations between him and the Préfecture de la Seine had broken down and he withdrew his candidature.[86] His case was immediately taken up by his loyal friends, the Théâtre Lyrique artists who, addressing themselves to the Préfet, earnestly prayed that he would use his influence with the Commission Municipale on Carvalho's behalf, for they believed him to be the only candidate 'capable of saving this unfortunate theatre.'[87] A petition had also been addressed to the Minister on his behalf, signed by Auber, Thomas, Gounod, David, Reyer, Massé and others. Then on 28 May after a flurry of conflicting statements it was announced. 'It is decided. M. Louis Martinet has signed the lease of the Théâtre Lyrique and consequently is director. A proverb says, "God tempers the wind to the shorn lamb." We hope that the old adage will hold good for the new director.'[88] His nomination was made official on 1 July when the decree was signed by the Minister.[89] A report circulating at the same time that Carvalho was now having talks with wealthy capitalists to build him a new opera house may safely be discounted.[90] A second, that he was hoping to succeed de Leuven at the Opéra-Comique is more credible.[91]

Louis Martinet was originally a painter, a pupil of Gros. He next turned picture dealer and, having founded the Société Nationale des Beaux Arts, opened a gallery in leased premises at 28 boulevard des Italiens in 1861. Edmond and Jules de Goncourt went to see a 'Jesus among the doctors' by Ingres which was hanging there with paintings by Delacroix, Flandrin, Fantin-Latour, Carolus-Duran and others in May 1862.[92] His most notable exhibition was probably one of the recently deceased Eugène Delacroix' paintings in 1864. In the autumn of 1862 he constructed a small concert room there in which recitals were given, at first occasionally, but later under the direction of the tenor Roger and the composer Debillemont, daily. When the liberty of the theatres was proclaimed in 1864 Martinet built a theatre on a large open space which occupied part of his property. His architect, Charpentier, was a well known Parisian theatre architect of the period. Martinet engaged the novelist Champfleury to act as co-director with him, and since it was proposed to present various forms of entertainment the theatre was named, Les Fantaisies-Parisiennes. Late in 1865 Champfleury resigned and Martinet became in name what he had been in fact from the beginning, sole director. In 1866 he resolved to produce musical pieces only, either unpublished works or works which had been dropped from the repertories of the large theatres. The Exhibition of 1867 brought the same benefits to him as it did to the other theatres. He rose to the occasion commercially, if not entirely artistically, by producing Mozart's *L'Oca del Cairo* in a version orchestrated by his conductor Charles Constantin, to which three other pieces by Mozart were added by the translator, Victor Wilder. In 1868 Francisque Sarcey would record, 'Les Fantaisies-Parisiennes continues under the excellent direction of M. Martinet to merit the name of second Opéra-Comique.'[93]

Martinet's lease of the boulevard des Italiens property (which he held from the fourth Marquess of Hertford, the first begetter of the Wallace Collection) cannot have been as secure as he imagined, for early in 1869 he was obliged to demolish his recently built theatre and surrender a completely cleared area where it had stood, by 15 April of that year.[94] So on 1 April he transferred his company to the Théâtre de l'Athénée in the rue Scribe.[95] This was an underground theatre, in the literal sense of the word, for it was a small theatre laid out in stalls, two rows of private boxes and a dress circle and was built in a cellar. To reach all parts of the auditorium one walked downstairs.[96] Here, until the summer of 1870, he produced works as varied as the Ricci brothers' *Crispino e la Comare (Le Docteur Crispin)* and Verdi's *I Masnadieri*, translated by Jules Ruelle as *Les Brigands*, with Mlle Marimon as Amalia.

Having won control of the Théâtre Lyrique he set off with his conductor, Charles Constantin to seek singers in Germany.[97] He intended to inaugurate his first season with a new opera, *L'Esclave* by Edmond Membrée,[98] and among works mentioned for revival was a first French performance of Wallace's *Maritana*.[99] On 30 July there was an audition of a three act opera *Frédéric Barberousse* by the Portuguese composer Miguel Angelo Pereira.[100] It was the last performance, public or private ever to take place in the Théâtre Lyrique as it then stood for on 16 July France declared war on Germany, during the first days of September all theatres were closed by police decree, and on 19 September the siege of Paris began. The theatre remained closed throughout the siege. As in most of the Paris theatres the foyer was turned into an ambulance station, beds were set up, and the lady artists helped to nurse the wounded.[101]

As soon as the Armistice was signed on 28 January 1871, Martinet reassumed his full rights. He reassembled a company and put into rehearsal *L'Esclave, Les Brigands, La Dame Blanche* and *Si j'étais Roi.* The season was to commence on 2 April when yet again history stepped in, for on Tuesday 28 March the Commune installed itself in the Hotel de Ville. It would seem that Louis Martinet was to be the Louis XVII of the Théâtre Lyrique. During the time of the Commune the Fédération Artistique gave a number of concerts at the theatre. Then on Sunday 21 May Thiers' Versaillais troops re-entered Paris. They had entered at Auteuil and by Wednesday morning, three columns of regular troops had reached the first and fourth arrondissements in the general area of the Place du Châtelet approaching the Hotel de Ville. A column under General de Cissey had converged by the left bank and now stood opposite Notre Dame, troops under General Vinoy had advanced beyond the Louvre, while General Douay's contingent had reached the Pointe Saint-Eustache. Luck might have saved the building as it had saved the Bibliothèque Nationale, but just then the Théâtre Lyrique's luck was out. Missiles had been falling around it all morning and then, about nine o'clock thick smoke curled from the last window on the right of the façade. The wind was blowing from the south west that morning and flames soon spread, first through the foyer, and then, crossing the corridor of the first tier of boxes, they reached the auditorium, destroying it and the stage completely. For Martinet it was a doubly unlucky day as he had recently furnished his office and his library and many valuable paintings went up in the flames. By chance the wind kept the fire from the upper part of the building on the side facing the river. Here were stored costumes, music, administrative papers and the archives of the theatre which consequently escaped.[102]

Neither as a building nor as a company was this the end of the Théâtre Lyrique. A new theatre, the Théâtre des Nations would rise from the ruins in 1874. (In 1899 it would become the Théâtre Sarah Bernhardt). But it was the end of an era. Coincidentally the Théâtre Lyrique had arrived with the Second Empire, and it and the Empire and all that the period symbolised vanished together, for as the flames took hold of the Théâtre Lyrique they were beginning to die down on the embers of a burnt out Tuileries. Nothing now remained but a Second Empire silhouette.

APPENDICES

Notes of Sources

Introduction
pp 1 to 12

1   Albert de Lasalle *Mémorial du Théâtre Lyrique* Paris 1877 2, 3
2   Albert de Lasalle *Les Treize Salles de l'Opéra* Paris 1875 201
3   RGM 3 July 1842
4   *Almanach de la Musique* Paris 1866 23
5   *Ibid.   Ibid.*
6   Arthur Pougin *Adolphe Adam, sa vie, sa carrière, ses mémoires artistiques* Paris 1877 182–184
7   Lasalle *Mémorial du Théâtre Lyrique* 4
8   Pougin 187
9   Lasalle *Mémorial du Théâtre Lyrique* 4, 5
10 JD 21 Nov. 1847
11 Lasalle *Mémorial du Théâtre Lyrique* 7
12 MW 22 Jan. 1848
13 Pougin 193
14 L-Henry Lecomte *Le Théâtre Historique* Paris 1906 46
15 *Ibid.* 2–4
16 *Ibid.* 4–6
17 ILN 27 Feb. 1847
18 Lecomte 6–15
19 *Ibid.* 51, 52
20 *Ibid.* 114
21 MW 29 July 1848
22 Albert Soubies *Histoire du Théâtre Lyrique 1851–1870* Paris 1899 2
23 M 25 May 1851
24 F 17 and 24 July 1856
25 M 1 June 1851
26 *Ibid.* 13 July 1851
27 Lasalle *Mémorial du Théâtre Lyrique* 13–16
    RGM 7 Sept. 1851
    C 30 Sept. 1851
    Jules Massenet *Mes Souvenirs 1848–1912* Paris 1912 32
    Lecomte 5–7, 10, 11
28 E & J de Goncourt & Cornelius Holff *Mystères des Théâtres 1852* Paris 1853 66
29 M 17 Aug. 1851
30 RGM 14 Sept. 1851 (M of same date gives a somewhat different list)

Chapter 1

The brothers Seveste as directors 1851–1854

1851–1852
pp 13 to 28

1　M 5 Oct. 1851
2　JD 30 Sept. 1851
3　MU 8 Oct. 1851
4　Alfred Loewenberg *Annals of Opera 1597–1940* London 1978 Col. 643 (Reported)
5　*Ibid.* I Col. 571 (Reported)
6　M 26 Oct. 1851
7　RGM 26 Oct. 1851
8　JD 1 Nov. 1851
9　I 1 Nov. 1851
10　M 26 Oct. 1851
11　JD 27 Nov. 1851
12　*Ibid. Ibid.*
13　MW 22 Nov. 1851
14　*Ibid.* 20 Dec. 1851
15　*Ibid.* 22 Nov. 1851
16　RGM 18 Jan. 1852
17　MW 24 Jan. 1852
18　JD 13 Jan. 1852
19　MW 24 Jan. 1852
20　RGM 1 Feb. 1852
21　Goncourt & Holff 67
22　RGM 15 Feb. 1852
23　*Ibid. Ibid.*
24　*Ibid. Ibid.*

25　Emile Humblot *Un Musicien Joinvillois de l'époque de la Révolution: François Devienne 1759–1803* St-Dizier 1909 41
26　Pougin 209, 210
27　RGM 29 Feb. 1852
28　M 29 Feb. 1852
29　JD 25 Feb. 1852
30　M 7 March 1852
31　RGM 7 March 1852
32　M 18 Jan. 1852
33　F J Fétis *Biographie Universelle des Musiciens (Supplément & Complément)* Paris 1878 V. I. 293, 294
34　*Ibid.* V. II 367, 368
35　Goncourt & Holff 138
36　RDM March 1852
37　M 14 March 1852
38　*Ibid.* 28 March 1852
39　M 18 April 1852
40　Goncourt & Holff 203
41　M 18 April 1852
42　RGM 8 Feb. 1852
43　M 18 April 1852
44　*Ibid.* 2 May 1852
45　RGM 2 Jan. 1853

1852–1853
pp 28 to 39

1　M 30 May 1852
2　*Ibid.* 11 July 1852
3　RGM 23 May 1852
4　Goncourt & Holff 347
5　RGM 10 Oct. 1852
6　*Ibid.* 17 Oct. 1852
7　Goncourt & Holff 429
8　RGM 31 Oct. 1852

9　*Grove's Dictionary of Music & Musicians* (3rd Edition) London 1928 I 630
10　RGM 7 Nov. 1852
11　JD 10 Nov. 1852
12　RGM 12 Dec. 1852
13　JD 7 Jan. 1853
14　Soubies 7

15 RGM 2 Jan. 1853
16 M 26 Dec. 1852
17 RGM 12 Dec. 1852
18 JD 7 Jan. 1853
19 RGM 13 Feb. 1853
20 RDM Feb. 1853
21 Ivor Guest *The Ballet of the 2nd Empire 1858–1870* London 1953 128
22 *The Times* 12 March 1841 (Reported by Cyril W. Beaumont *Complete Book of Ballets* London 1951 214)
23 Lasalle *Mémorial du Théâtre Lyrique* 26
24 RGM 20 Feb. 1853
25 M 30 Jan. 1853
26 *Ibid.* 27 Feb. 1853
27 *Ibid.* 6 March 1853
28 *Ibid.* 1 May 1853
29 *Ibid.* 22 May 1853
30 *Ibid.* 6 March 1853
31 *Ibid.* 20 March 1853
32 *Ibid.* 16 Jan. 1853
33 *Ibid.* 1 May 1853

34 Louis Engel *From Mozart to Mario* London 1886 2 V. V. I. 91
35 A.D. Vandam *An Englishman in Paris* London 1900 307
36 Ferdinand Bac *Intimités du Second Empire* Paris 1932 3 V. V. 3 *Poètes et Artistes* 129–131.
37 Maxime Du Camp *Souvenirs d'un Demi-Siècle* Paris 1949 2 V. V. I. 130
38 Alfred Leroy (Trans. Anne Cope) *The Empress Eugénie* London 1969 41
39 JD 17 March 1853
40 *Ibid. Ibid.*
41 *Ibid.* 6–7 May 1853
42 M 17 April 1853
43 Pougin 222
44 Lasalle *Mémorial du Théâtre Lyrique* 55
45 RGM 1 May 1853
46 M 22 May 1853
47 *Ibid.* 5 June 1853
48 *Ibid. Ibid.*

1853–1854
pp 39 to 50

1 M 17 July 1853
2 C 6 Sept. 1853
3 Adam Carse *The Orchestra from Beethoven to Berlioz* Cambridge 1948 339
4 JD 11 Oct. 1854
5 M 21 Aug. 1853
6 *Ibid.* 11 Sept. 1853
7 RGM 11 Sept. 1853
8 M 11 Sept. 1853
9 RGM 25 Sept. 1853
10 JD 10 Oct. 1853
11 Walter Dexter [Ed.] *The Letters of Charles Dickens* London 1938 3 V. V. II. 703
12 RGM 9 Oct. 1853
13 JD 10 Oct. 1853
14 MW 22 Oct. 1853

15 M 16 Oct. 1853
16 C 25 Oct. 1853
17 RGM 25 Dec. 1853
18 *Ibid.* 30 Oct. 1853
19 M 20 Nov. 1853
20 RGM 4 Dec. 1853
21 M 8 Jan. 1854
22 Lasalle *Mémorial du Théâtre Lyrique* 30
23 MW 22 July 1854
24 JD 5 Jan. 1854
25 M 12 Feb. 1854
26 Soubies 17
27 M 12 Feb. 1854
28 MW 4 March 1854
29 JD 2 March 1854
30 *Wagner writes from Paris . . .* Ed. and trans. R.L. Jacobs &

     Geoffrey Skelton London 1973
     158

31   M 26 Feb. 1854

32   RGM 24 March 1866

33   MW 2 June 1866 (Reported)

34   *Ibid.* 25 March 1854

35   Lasalle *Mémorial du Théâtre Lyrique* 31

36   MW 3 June 1854

37   M 23 April 1854

38   *Ibid.* 28 May 1854

39   ILN 10 June 1854

40   M 4 June 1854

41   *Ibid.* 21 May 1854

42   *Ibid.* 9 July 1854

43   Soubies 10, 11

Chapter 2

Perrin and Pellegrin 1854–1856

1854–1855
pp 51 to 63

1	Richard Wagner *Mein Leben*	20	JD 11 Oct. 1854
	Munich 1915 210, 211	21	MW 3 Feb. 1855
2	RGM 30 July 1854	22	JD 26 Jan. 1855
3	MW 12 Aug. 1854	23	RDM Feb. 1855
4	*Ibid.* 19 Aug. 1854	24	MW 24 Feb. 1855
5	RGM 3 Sept. 1854	25	*Ibid. Ibid.*
6	MW 16 Sept. 1854	26	*Ibid.* 3 Feb. 1855
7	*Ibid.* 23 Sept. 1854	27	RDM March 1855
8	RGM 1 Oct. 1854	28	MW 21 April 1855
9	Ibid. 15 Oct. 1854	29	*Ibid.* 26 May 1855
10	JD 11 Oct. 1854	30	*Ibid. Ibid.*
11	RGM 15 Oct. 1854	31	*Ibid. Ibid.*
12	MW 11 Nov. 1854	32	*Ibid.* 30 June 1855
13	JD 9 Jan. 1855	33	*Ibid. Ibid.*
14	RDM Jan. 1855	34	*Ibid.* 19 May 1855
15	MW 6 Jan. 1855	35	*Ibid.* 31 March 1855
16	*Ibid.* 30 Dec. 1854	36	*Ibid.* 28 April 1855
17	RGM 31 Dec. 1854	37	*Ibid. Ibid.*
18	MW 30 Dec. 1854	38	*Ibid.* 1 Sept. 1855
19	*Ibid.* 29 July 1854	39	*Ibid.* 19 May 1855
		40	*Ibid.* 15 Sept. 1855

1855–1856
pp 63 to 68

1	MU 23 Sept. 1855	12	MW 10 Nov. 1855
2	GF 9 Oct. 1855	13	*Ibid.* 15 Dec. 1855
3	MU 14 April 1855	14	RGM 16 Dec. 1855
4	RGM 22 Feb. 1845	15	MU 23 Dec. 1855
5	Victor Combarnous *L'Histoire*	16	U 18 Dec. 1855
	du Grand-Théâtre de Marseille.	17	M 11 Nov. 1855
	1787–1919 Marseille 1927 71–	18	*Ibid.* 16 Dec. 1855
	76	19	*Ibid.* 23 Dec. 1855
6	Soubies 14	20	*Ibid.* 4 March 1855
7	RGM 7 Oct. 1855	21	MW 26 Jan. 1856
8	MU 6 Jan. 1855	22	A 23 Dec. 1855
9	MW 6 Oct. 1855	23	RGM 3 Feb. 1856
10	*Ibid.* 10 Nov. 1855	24	Soubies 15
11	JD 31 Dec. 1855	25	RGM 24 Feb. 1856

Chapter 3

Léon Carvalho 1856–1860

1856–1857
pp 69 to 82

1   Mina Curtiss *Bizet & His World* London 1959 193 (Reported)
2   *Richard Wagner's Letters* Sel. & Ann. Wilhelm Altmann Leipzig 1925 2 V. V. I. 347 V. II. 90, 105
3   *Lettres Françaises de Richard Wagner* Ed. Julien Tiersot Paris 1935
4   Reynaldo Hahn *Thèmes variés* Paris 1946 105, 106
5   GM 25–26 Feb. 1856
6   RDM 15 March 1856
7   RGM 9 March 1856
8   Soubies 16
9   RGM 4 May 1856
10 JD 29 March 1856
11 RGM 30 March 1856
12 *Ibid.* 20 April 1856
13 Lasalle *Mémorial du Théâtre Lyrique* 41
14 RGM 18 May 1856
15 *Ibid.* 25 May 1856
16 Louise Parkinson Arnoldson *Sedaine et les Musiciens de son temps* Paris 1934 11.
17 M 23 March 1856
18 *Ibid.* 22 June 1856
19 *Ibid. Ibid.*
20 *Ibid.* 29 June 1856
21 M 6 July 1856
22 JD 29 March 1856
23 M 15 June 1856
24 *Ibid. Ibid.*
25 *Ibid.* 14 Sept. 1856
26 Soubies 18
27 RDM Oct. 1856
28 *Ibid. Ibid.*
29 Albert Soubies & Charles Malherbe *Histoire de l'Opéra Comique* Paris 1892 V. I. 282, 283
30 M 19 Oct. 1856
31 RDM Feb. 1857
32 Lasalle *Mémorial du Théâtre Lyrique* 41
33 M 4 Jan. 1857
34 RDM 1 Feb. 1857
35 MW 17 Jan. 1857
36 RDM Feb. 1857
37 MW 17 Jan. 1857
38 M 18 Jan. 1857
39 *Ibid.* 1 Feb. 1857
40 *Ibid.* 21 Dec. 1856
41 MW 17 Jan. 1857
42 M 15 March 1857
43 RDM 1 April 1857
44 James Robinson Planché *Recollections and Reflections* London 1872 2 V. V. I. 75, 76
45 RGM 1 March 1857
46 JD 6 March 1857
47 RGM 1 March 1857
48 JD 6 March 1857
49 MW 7 March 1857
50 M 22 March 1857
51 RGM 14 June 1857
52 *Ibid.* 12 April 1857

1857–1858
pp 82 to 92

1	Lasalle *Mémorial du Théâtre Lyrique* 44	23	*Ibid.* 7 Feb. 1858
2	RGM 6 Sept. 1857	24	*Ibid. Ibid.*
3	GM 6 Sept. 1857	25	JD 3 April 1858
4	RGM 18 Oct. 1857	26	*Ibid.* 23 April 1858
5	*Ibid.* 6 Sept. 1857	27	M 18 April 1858
6	M 30 Aug. 1857	28	JD 23 April 1858
7	MW 12 Sept. 1857	29	M 4 April 1858
8	M 27 Sept. 1857	30	*Ibid.* 11 April 1858
9	JD 24 Oct. 1857	31	*Ibid.* 25 April 1858
10	RGM 8 Nov. 1857	32	*Ibid.* 2 May 1858
11	JD 17 Nov. 1857	33	Lasalle *Les Treize Salles de l'Opéra* 170
12	M 8 Nov. 1857		
13	MW 19 Dec. 1857	34	RGM 16 May 1858
14	C 11 Oct. 1858	35	*Ibid. Ibid.*
15	JD 6 Jan. 1858	36	JD 16 May 1858
16	RDM 1 Feb. 1858	37	M 16 May 1858
17	F 11 Feb. 1858	38	RGM 16 May 1858
18	RGM 17 Jan. 1858	39	Lasalle *Mémorial du Théâtre Lyrique* 47
19	Lasalle *Mémorial du Théâtre Lyrique* 45	40	RGM 13 June 1858
20	M 17 Jan. 1858	41	JD 19 June 1858
21	JD 22 Jan. 1858	42	M 13 June 1858
22	M 17 Jan. 1858	43	RGM 25 July 1858
		44	JD 20 July 1858

1858–1859
pp 92 to 110

1	MW 30 Oct. 1858	16	Lasalle *Mémorial du Théâtre Lyrique* 48
2	M 12 Sept. 1858	17	M 17 March 1859
3	*Ibid. Ibid.*	18	Albert Soubies & Henri de Curzon *Documents inédits sur le Faust de Gounod* Paris 1912
4	JD 15 Sept. 1858		
5	RGM 3 Oct. 1858		
6	JD 9 Oct. 1858	8	
7	MW 22 May 1858	19	*Ibid.* 22
8	M 17 Oct. 1858	20	Louis Pagnerre *Charles Gounod, sa vie et ses œuvres* Paris 1890 142
9	*Ibid.* 28 Nov. 1858		
10	Lasalle *Mémorial du Théâtre Lyrique* 47	21	Soubies & de Curzon 52
11	M 16 Jan 1859	22	*Ibid.* 51
12	RGM 12 Dec. 1858	23	M 25 Sept. 1859
13	*Ibid.* 25 July 1858	24	*Ibid.* 30 Oct. 1859
14	M 16 Dec. 1894	25	*Ibid.* 16 Dec. 1894
15	RGM 6 March 1859	26	Soubies & de Curzon 26

27 *Ibid.* 31
28 M 16 Dec. 1894
29 Soubies & de Curzon 42
30 *Ibid.* 53
31 *Ibid.* 33
32 James Harding *Gounod* London 1973 49
33 Curtiss 25
34 RDM 15 Sept. 1859
35 M 20 Feb. 1859
36 *Ibid.* 27 Feb. 1859
37 Curtiss 83, 84
38 Pagnerre 146
39 Fétis (Supp. et Comp.) V. I 47
40 M 16 Dec. 1894
41 *Ibid.* 20 March 1859
42 Soubies & de Curzon 8–10
43 FM 27 March 1859
44 Pagnerre 147
45 RGM 27 March 1859
46 M 27 March 1859
47 RDM 1 April 1859
48 MW 2 April 1859
49 RDM 1 April 1859

50 MW 24 Sept. 1859
51 Curtiss 88
52 JD 19 May 1859
53 RDM 1 June 1859
54 JD 19 May 1859
55 RGM 15 May 1859
56 *Ibid. Ibid.*
57 RGM 17 April 1859
58 Soubies & de Curzon 8
59 M 29 May 1859
60 Soubies & de Curzon 9
61 RGM 29 May 1859
62 *Ibid.* 22 May 1859
63 M 26 June 1859
64 *Ibid.* 10 July 1859
65 RGM 12 June 1859
66 M 24 July 1859
67 RGM 12 June 1859
68 *Ibid.* 26 June 1859
69 M 3 July 1859
70 Soubies & de Curzon 9
71 M 3 July 1859
72 *Ibid.* 4 Sept. 1859
73 *Ibid.* 21 Aug. 1859

1859–1860
pp 110 to 122

1 M 2 Oct. 1859
2 C 30 Sept. 1859
3 RDM 15 Oct. 1859
4 M 6 Nov. 1859
5 *Ibid. Ibid.*
6 RGM 2 Oct. 1859
7 M 16 Oct. 1859
8 April Fitzlyon *The Price of Genius* London 1964 345
9 MW 26 Nov. 1859
10 JD 22 Nov. 1859
11 Henry F. Chorley *Thirty Years' Musical Recollections* New York 1926 V. II 236, 237
12 M 27 Nov. 1859
13 RGM 11 Dec. 1859
14 MW 15 Oct. 1859
15 Fétis (Supp. et Comp.) V. II 487
16 RGM 18 Dec. 1859

17 MW 4 Feb. 1860
18 JD 16 Feb. 1860
19 Lasalle *Mémorial du Théâtre Lyrique* 52
20 MW 3 March 1860
21 JD 23 Feb. 1860
22 RDM 15 March 1860
23 MW 31 March 1860
24 M 5 Feb. 1860
25 MW 17 March 1860
26 RGM 8 April 1860
27 M 12 Feb. 1860
28 RGM 15 April 1860
29 M 22 April 1860
30 *Ibid.* 11 March 1860
31 *Ibid.* 29 April 1860
32 *Ibid.* 15 April 1860
33 MW 14 April 1860
34 JD 14 April 1860
35 MW 14 April 1860

36 Lasalle *Mémorial du Théâtre*
 Lyrique 52
37 M 8 April 1860
38 *Ibid* 22 April 1860
39 F 8 April 1860
40 *Ibid* 15 April 1860
41 M 15 April 1860
42 MW 12 May 1860

Chapter 4

Charles Réty takes over 1860–1862

1860 continued
pp 123 to 129

1	RGM 16 March 1856	18	Lasalle *Mémorial du Théâtre Lyrique* 54
2	F 2 July 1895		
3	RGM 13 May 1860	19	RGM 10 June 1860
4	JD 19 May 1860	20	MW 23 June 1860
5	RGM 13 May 1860	21	M 17 June 1860
6	*Ibid. Ibid.*	22	*Ibid.* 24 June 1860
7	M 13 May 1860	23	RGM 8 July 1860
8	Lasalle *Mémorial du Théâtre Lyrique* 52	24	M 17 June 1860
9	RGM 13 May 1860	25	*Ibid.* 22 July 1860
10	*Ibid. Ibid.*	26	RGM 26 Aug. 1860
11	RDM 15 May 1860	27	MW 1 Sept. 1860
12	JD 22 May 1860	28	M 19 Aug. 1860
13	MW 19 May 1860	29	*Ibid.* 26 Aug. 1860
14	Soubies 28	30	MW 14 July 180
15	M 3 June 1860	31	RGM 1 July 1860
16	*Ibid.* 13 May 1860	32	*Ibid.* 5 Aug. 1860
17	*Ibid.* 10 June 1860	33	M 26 Aug. 1860
		34	F 9 Sept. 1860

1860–1861
pp 130 to 138

1	MU 9 Sept. 1860	18	Soubies 30
2	M 9 Sept. 1860	19	MW 2 Feb. 1861
3	*Ibid. Ibid.*	20	JD 19 Feb. 1861
4	*Ibid.* 30 Sept. 1860	21	RDM 15 Feb. 1861
5	MW 10 Nov. 1860	22	F 10 March 1861
6	M 21 Oct. 1860	23	JD 26 March 1861
7	RGM 21 Oct. 1860	24	M 14 April 1861
8	M 21 Oct. 1860	25	RGM 14 April 1861
9	RGM 4 Nov. 1860	26	*Ibid.* 21 April 1861
10	M 2 Dec. 1860	27	*Ibid.* 27 Jan. 1861
11	*Ibid.* 16 Dec. 1860	28	F 24 March 1861
12	RGM 23 Dec. 1860	29	*Ibid.* 31 March 1861
13	JD 29 Dec. 1860	30	JD 20 March 1860
14	RDM 1 Feb. 1861	31	RGM 5 Nov. 1871
15	F 9 Dec. 1860	32	MU 18 Oct. 1844
16	M 30 Dec. 1860	33	Franco Abbiati *Giuseppe Verdi* Milan 1959 4 V. V. III. 333.
17	MW 26 Jan. 1861		

34	Luigi Arditi *My Reminiscences*	38	M 12 May 1861
	London 1896 110	39	*Ibid. Ibid.*
35	RDM 15 June 1861	40	Lasalle *Mémorial du Théâtre*
36	MW 25 May 1861		*Lyrique* 58
37	*Ibid* 6 July 1861	41	*Ibid* 19 May 1861
		42	*Ibid* 12 May 1861

1861–1862
pp 139 to 147

1	M 26 May 1861	30	M 23 Feb. 1862
2	*Ibid* 21 July 1861	31	RGM 23 March 1862
3	RGM 1 Sept. 1861	32	M 23 March 1862
4	RGM 28 July 1861	33	GM 19 April 1862
5	*Ibid* 1 Sept. 1861	34	Lasalle *Mémorial du Théâtre*
6	MW 14 Sept. 1861		*Lyrique* 61
7	Soubies 28	35	RGM 27 April 1862
8	MW 30 Nov. 1861	36	*Ibid* 6 July 1862
9	*Ibid* 2 Nov. 1861	37	M 27 April 1862
10	M 27 Oct. 1861	38	*Ibid* 11 May 1862
11	JD 12 Nov. 1861	39	RGM 1 June 1862
12	RDM 15 Dec. 1861	40	M 1 June 1862
13	RGM 24 Nov. 1861	41	*Ibid* 29 June 1862
14	Lasalle *Mémorial du Théâtre*	42	RGM 3 Aug. 1862
	Lyrique 59	43	M 30 March 1862
15	RDM 15 Dec. 1861	44	*Ibid* 29 June 1862
16	*Ibid. Ibid.*	45	*Ibid* 6 July 1862
17	JD 21 Dec. 1861	46	*Ibid* 13 July 1862
18	Lasalle *Mémorial du Théâtre*	47	*Ibid* 22 June 1862
	Lyrique 59	48	*Ibid* 3 Aug. 1862
19	M 15 Dec. 1861	49	*Ibid* 24 Aug. 1862
20	MW 4 Jan. 1862	50	*Ibid* 10 Aug. 1862
21	RGM 27 Oct. 1861	51	*Ibid* 14 Sept. 1862
22	*Ibid* 20 Oct. 1861	52	RGM 14 Sept. 1862
23	M 22 Dec. 1861	53	Lasalle *Mémorial du Théâtre*
24	RGM 22 Dec. 1861		*Lyrique* 95
25	I 8 Feb. 1862	54	Soubies 34
26	JD 28 Jan. 1862	55	F 9 Oct. 1862
27	RGM 2 Feb. 1862	56	*Ibid* 12 Oct. 1862
28	M 26 Jan. 1862	57	*Ibid* 5 Oct. 1862
29	GM 31 Jan. 1862	58	RGM 12 Oct. 1862

Chapter 5

Carvalho at the place du Châtelet 1862–1868

1862–1863
pp 149 to 162

1	Brockhaus Enzyklopädie, Wiesbaden	30	MW 15 Nov. 1862
		31	GM 13 Nov. 1862
2	B 25 Oct. 1862	32	Lasalle *Mémorial du Théâtre*
3	Lasalle *Mémorial du Théâtre Lyrique* 64		*Lyrique* 66
		33	RGM 7 Dec. 1862
4	RGM 2 Nov 1862	34	M 21 Dec. 1862
5	MW 16 Aug 1862	35	*Ibid. Ibid.*
6	RGM 2 Oct. 1859 and 15 June 1862	36	*Ibid.* 28 Dec. 1862
		37	RGM 14 Dec. 1862
7	B 1 Nov 1862	38	RDM 15 Nov. 1862
8	RGM 2 Nov. 1862	39	RGM 9 Nov. 1862
9	B *Ibid.*	40	M 11 Jan. 1863
10	Lasalle *Mémorial du Théâtre Lyrique* 64	41	RDM 1 Feb. 1863
		42	Otto Jahn *W.A. Mozart.*
11	MW 8 Nov. 1862		Leipzig. 1856–59 4 v. v. IV.
12	BN 31 Oct. 1862		767
13	(B 25 Oct. and 1 Nov. 1862	43	M 11 Jan. 1863
	(BN 31 Oct. 1862	44	*Ibid.* 25 Jan. 1863
	(Lasalle *Mémorial du Théâtre Lyrique* 64, 65	45	*Ibid.* 12 Apr. 1863
		46	*Ibid.* 15 Feb. 1863
14	GM 6 Sept. 1857	47	*Ibid.* 1 Feb 1863
15	Mikhail Ivanovich Glinka. *Memoirs* (Trans R.B. Mudge) Oklahoma 1963 235	48	*Ibid.* 22 Mar. 1863
		49	*Ibid. Ibid.*
		50	AM 5 Feb. 1863
16	B 1 Nov. 1862	51	M 8 Feb. 1863
17	M 27 July 1862	52	*Ibid.* 5 Apr. 1863
18	Soubies and Malherbe V.II 34, 35	53	*Ibid. Ibid.*
		54	MW 11 Apr. 1863
19	RGM 2 Nov 1862	55	*Ibid. Ibid.*
20	M 2 Nov. 1862	56	RDM 15 Apr. 1863
21	UL 12 Nov. 1862	57	RGM 5 Apr. 1863
22	M 12 Oct. 1862	58	MW 11 Apr. 1863
23	*Ibid.* 19 Oct. 1862	59	M 19 Apr. 1863
24	RGM 26 Oct. 1862	60	RGM 10 May 1863
25	*Ibid.* 12 Oct. 1862	61	M 1 Feb. 1863
26	M 26 Oct. 1862	62	RGM 3 May 1863
27	RGM 12 Oct. 1862	63	*Ibid. Ibid.*
28	MW 25 Oct. 1862	64	*Ibid.* 26 Apr. 1863
29	M 2 Nov. 1862	65	M 14 June 1863

66	*Ibid.* 7 June 1863
67	*Ibid.* 26 July 1863
68	RGM 5 July 1863
69	M 26 July 1863
70	RGM 26 Apr. 1863
71	M 28 June 1863

1863–1864
pp162 to 180

1	M 28 June 1863
2	*Ibid.* 12 July 1863
3	RGM 19 July 1863
4	M 5 July 1863
5	*Ibid.* 2 Aug 1863
6	*Ibid.* 23 Aug. 1863
7	*Ibid. Ibid.*
8	*Ibid.* 4 Oct. 1863
9	*Ibid. Ibid.*
10	F 8 Oct. 1863
11	RGM 4 Oct. 1863
12	MW 3 Oct. 1863
13	JD 8 Oct. 1863
14	Henry Davison (Ed.) *From Mendelssohn to Wagner.* London 1912 271–2
15	M 25 Oct. 1863
16	RGM 26 Apr 1863
17	M 12 Apr. 1863
18	RDM 1 May 1862
19	M 25 Oct. 1863
20	A. de Pontmartin. *Souvenirs d'un vieux critique* Paris 1882 320
21	Davison 274
22	M 8 Nov. 1863
23	Pontmartin 320
24	RGM 29 Nov. 1863
25	Adolphe Boschot. *Une Vie Romantique: Hector Berlioz.* Paris 1919 372
26	Soubies 39
27	RDM 15 Nov. 1863
28	Boschot 373
29	M. 20 Dec. 1863
30	Comte Fleury and Louis Sonolet *La Société du Second Empire* Paris 1924 4 V. Vol. IV 390
31	AM 7 Jan. 1864
32	*Ibid.* 21 and 28 Jan. 1864

33	MW 2 Jan. 1864
34	RGM 27 Dec. 1863
35	M. 27 Dec. 1863
36	F. 27 Dec. 1863
37	RGM 27 Dec. 1863
38	Fétis (Supp. et Comp.) V.II. 13, 14
39	RGM 27 Dec. 1863
40	*Ibid.* 3 Jan 1864
41	M 10 Jan. 1864
42	Hippolyte Hostein. *La Liberté des Théâtres.* Paris 1867 22–23
43	M 15 Nov. 1863
44	Hostein, 33–34
45	MW 30 Jan. 1864
46	M 28 Feb. 1864
47	MW 19 Dec. 1863
48	*Ibid.* 2 Apr. 1864
49	M 21 Feb. 1864
50	*Ibid.* 3 Jan. 1864
51	*Ibid.* 7 Feb. 1864
52	MW 2 Apr. 1864
53	M 20 Mar. 1864
54	A. Carel. *Histoire Anecdotique des Contemporains.* Paris 1885 40
55	RDM 15 Apr. 1864
56	RGM 27 Mar. 1864
57	O 30 Apr. 1864
58	*Ibid.* 9 Apr. 1864
59	*Ibid.* 30 Apr. 1864
60	*Ibid.* 4 June 1864
61	*Ibid.* 30 Apr. 1864
62	RGM 10 Apr. 1864
63	Soubies 63
64	MW 2 Apr. 1864
65	O 24 Dec. 1864
66	*Ibid. Ibid.*
67	M 22 May 1864
68	C 12 Dec. 1864
69	RGM 20 Mar. 1864

70 M 3 Apr. 1864
71 *Ibid.* 1 May 1864
72 Léon Aubin *Le Drame Lyrique.* Tours 1908 61
73 M 19 June 1864
74 Soubies 40
75 Lasalle *Mémorial du Théâtre Lyrique* 70
76 RGM 12 June 1864
77 U 22 June 1864

78 Lasalle *Mémorial du Théâtre Lyrique* 70
79 RGM 19 June 1864
80 *Ibid.* 22 May 1864
81 M 3 July 1864
82 RGM 26 June 1864
83 ILN 22 June 1850
84 M 10 July 1864
85 *Ibid. Ibid.*
86 *Ibid.* 3 July 1864

1864–1865
pp 180 to 199

1   MW 17 Sept. 1864
2   *Ibid.* 22 Oct. 1864
3   M 11 Sept. 1864
4   RGM 11 Sept. 1864
5   Lasalle *Mémorial du Théâtre Lyrique* 72
6   M 11 Sept. 1864
7   Louis Engel. *From Mozart to Mario.* London 1886 2.v. vol. II 311
8   MW 5 Nov. 1864
9   *Ibid. Ibid.*
10 RGM 30 Oct. 1864
11 *Ibid. Ibid.*
12 MW 5 Nov. 1864
13 GM 4 Nov. 1864
14 RGM 30 Oct. 1864
15 M 30 Oct. 1864
16 Lillie de Hegermann-Lindencrone. *In the Courts of Memory 1858–1875* New York, 1912, 73–75
17 M 13 Nov. 1864
18 O 29 Oct. 1864
19 *Ibid.* 1 Oct. 1864
20 MW 1 Oct. 1864
21 O 5 Nov. 1864
22 GM 13 Nov. 1864
23 RDM 1 Dec. 1864
24 MW 3 Dec. 1864
25 GM 23 Dec. 1864
26 O 17 Dec. 1864
27 M 22 Jan. 1865
28 *Ibid. Ibid.*

29 O 4 Feb. 1865
30 M 29 Jan. 1865
31 O 4 Feb. 1865
32 M 12 Mar. 1865
33 *Ibid. Ibid.*
34 M 22 Jan. 1865
35 *Grove.* v. 8 (Fifth Edition)
36 RGM 26 Feb. 1865
37 M 12 Feb. 1865
38 Georges Servières. *Épisodes d'Histoire Musicale.* Paris 1914 156
39 RGM 6 Apr. 1879
40 T 8 Mar. 1865
41 M 12 Feb. 1865
42 *Ibid.* 5 Mar. 1865
43 *Ibid.* 8 Jan. 1865
44 Lasalle. *Mémorial du Théâtre Lyrique* 75
45 F 5 Mar. 1865
46 MW 21 Jan. 1865
47 O 11 Mar. 1865
48 MW 4 Mar. 1865
49 Hegermann-Lindencrone 72
50 O 8 Apr. 1865
51 F 12 Mar. 1865
52 M 12 Mar. 1865
53 O 14 Mar. 1868
54 *Ibid.* 28 Mar. 1868
55 *Ibid.* 6 Apr. 1867
56 M 5 Mar. and 2 Apr. 1865
57 *Ibid.* 26 Mar. 1865
58 MW 8 Apr. 1865
59 F 9 Apr. 1865

60 M 9 Apr. 1865
61 *Ibid.* 5 Mar. 1865
62 U 14 June 1864
63 ML Jan. 1923 ('Verdi's letters to Léon Escudier', Trans. L.A. Sheppard)
64 MW 29. Apr. 1865
65 C 24 Apr. 1865
66 ML (Verdi's letters) Apr. 1923
67 O 17 June 1865
68 GM 23 June 1865
69 O 17 June 1865
70 MW 17 June 1865
71 RGM 11 June 1865
72 O 17 June 1865
73 M 30 July 1865
74 *Ibid.* 13 Aug. 1865
75 O 31 Mar. 1866
76 RGM 2 July 1866
77 M 2 July 1866

1865–1866
pp 199 to 211

1 O 14 Oct. 1865
2 *Ibid.* 28 Oct. 1865
3 *Ibid.* 11 Nov. 1865
4 *Ibid. Ibid.*
5 M 29 Oct. 1865
6 RGM 1 Oct. 1865
7 T 3 Oct. 1865
8 RGM 22 Oct. 1865
9 M 22 Oct. 1865
10 Lasalle. *Mémorial du Théâtre Lyrique* 77
11 RGM 29 Oct. 1865
12 RGM 19 Nov. 1865
13 M 3 Dec. 1865
14 Margaret M. McGowan *L'Art du Ballet de Cour en France 1581–1643* Paris 1963 282
15 JM 27 Jan. 1877
16 M 24 Dec. 1865
17 RGM 21 Feb. 1858
18 T 16 Dec. 1865
19 RGM 21 Feb. 1865
20 F 28 Dec. 1865
21 MW 30 Dec. 1865
22 F 28 Dec. 1865
23 RGM 10 Dec. 1865
24 MW 30 Dec. 1865
25 *Ibid. Ibid.*
26 M 24 Dec. 1865
27 MW 30 Dec. 1865
28 JD 25 Dec. 1865
29 RGM 24 Dec. 1865
30 T 27 Dec. 1865
31 RGM 24 Dec. 1865
32 *Ibid.* 21 Jan. 1866
33 MW 13 Jan. 1866
34 M 7 Jan. 1866
35 O 13 Jan. 1866
36 RGM 15 July 1866
37 M 7 Jan 1866
38 *Ibid.* 11 Mar. 1866
39 O 24 Feb. 1866
40 *Ibid.* 26 May 1866
41 M 25 Feb. 1866
42 O 24 Feb. 1866
43 *Ibid.* 21 Apr. 1866
44 M 13 May 1866
45 O 12 May 1866
46 M 21 Jan. 1866
47 *Ibid.* 1 Apr. 1866
48 O 21 Apr. 1866
49 Lasalle. *Mémorial du Théâtre Lyrique* 79
50 AM 17 May 1866
51 T 16 May 1866
52 *Ibid. Ibid.*
53 O 12 May 1866
54 M 13 May 1866
55 *Ibid.* 6 May 1866
56 C 14 May 1866
57 O 19 May 1866
58 *Ibid. Ibid.*
59 JD 19 May 1866
60 RGM 13 May 1866
61 RDM 15 May 1866
62 O 19 May 1866

63	M 13 May 1866	71	M 27 May 1866
64	RDM 15 June 1866	72	RGM 20 May 1866
65	RGM 27 May 1866	73	*Ibid* 17 June 1866
66	*Ibid. Ibid.*	74	*Ibid. Ibid.*
67	O 2 June 1866	75	O 23 June 1866
68	*Ibid. Ibid.*	76	M 24 June 1866
69	*Ibid. Ibid.*	77	RGM 8 July 1866
70	*Ibid. Ibid.*		

1866–1867
pp 212 to 227

1	RGM 15 July 1866	37	*Ibid* 11 Nov. 1866
2	*Ibid* 22 July 1866	38	O 10 Nov. 1866
3	M 22 July 1866	39	*Ibid* 14 Apr. 1866
4	*Ibid* 14 Oct. 1866	40	M 31 Mar. 1867
5	*Ibid* 19 Aug. 1866	41	MW 18 May 1867
6	O 18 and 25 Aug. 1866	42	O 4 May 1867
7	*Ibid* 25 Aug. 1866	43	M 5 May 1867
8	M 10 June 1866	44	RGM 5 May 1867
9	MW 1 Sept. 1866	45	*Ibid. Ibid.*
10	RGM 19 Aug. 1866	46	MW 4 May 1867
11	M 2 Sept. 1866	47	O 4 May 1867
12	RGM 1 Dec. 1867	48	*Ibid* 18 May 1867
13	M 16 Sept. 1866	49	M 19 May 1867
14	O 6 Oct. 1866	50	RGM 9 June 1867
15	*Ibid* 20 Oct. 1866	51	PM 6 July 1867
16	M 25 Nov. 1866	52	RGM 14 July 1867
17	O 10 Nov. 1866	53	F 29 Apr. 1867
18	M 9 Dec. 1866	54	RGM 21 July 1867
19	C 10 Dec. 1866	55	M 2 June 1867
20	M 28 Oct. 1866	56	RGM 3 Mar. 1867
21	MI 15 Dec. 1866	57	M 16 June 1867
22	RGM 16 Dec. 1866	58	RDM 1 July 1867
23	F 10 Jan. 1867	59	Soubies 41
24	*Ibid* 14 Dec. 1866	60	M 28 Apr. 1867
25	Soubies 47	61	*Ibid* 12 May 1867
26	M 2 Sept. 1866	62	*Ibid* 2 June 1867
27	O 26 Jan. 1867	63	F 16 June 1867
28	*Ibid. Ibid.*	64	*Ibid* 3 May 1867
29	JD 27 Jan. 1867	65	MW 11 May 1867
30	GM 18/19 Feb. 1867	66	RGM 9 June 1867
31	M 10 Feb. 1867	67	M 26 May 1867
32	AM 31 Jan. 1867	68	*Ibid* 2 June 1867
33	M 10 Mar. 1867	69	O 7 Sept. 1867
34	*Ibid* 19 Aug. 1866	70	*Ibid* 29 June 1867
35	MW 10 Nov. 1866	71	F 9 Feb. 1867
36	M 4 Nov. 1866	72	M 3 Feb. 1867

73 O 10 Aug. 1867
74 *Ibid* 6 July 1867
75 *Ibid* 13 July 1867
76 *Ibid* 29 June 1867

1867–1868

pp 227 to 239

1   M 15 Sept. 1867
2   RGM 22 Dec. 1867
3   M 31 Mar. 1867
4   F 9 July 1867
5   RGM 1 Mar. 1868
6   F 13 June 1867
7   RGM 4 Aug. 1867
8   *Ibid* 25 Aug. 1867
9   M 22 Sept. 1867
10 RGM 24 Nov. 1867
11 *Ibid* 25 Aug. 1867
12 F 29 Nov. 1867
13 M 27 Oct. 1867
14 RGM 27 Oct. 1867
15 Henri Maréchal. *Paris-Souvenirs d'un Musicien 185-. –1870.* Paris 1907, 217–218
16 RGM 3 Nov. 1867
17 M 24 Nov. 1867
18 RGM 3 Oct. 1867
19 F 29 Oct. 1867
20 M 18 Aug. 1867
21 RGM 20 Oct. 1867
22 M 15 Dec. 1867
23 F 14 Dec. 1867
24 *Ibid* 20 Dec. 1867
25 M 22 Dec. 1867
26 *Ibid* 29 Dec. 1867
27 *Ibid* 26 Jan. 1868
28 *Ibid* 8 Dec. 1867
29 *Ibid* 5 Jan. 1868
30 *Ibid* 26 May 1867
31 *Georges Bizet, Souvenirs et correspondance par Edmond Galabert,* Paris 1877. 6
32 M 13 and 20 Jan. 1867
33 *Ibid* and RGM 22 Sept. 1867
34 *Ibid* 29 Sept. 1867
35 *Ibid. Ibid.*
36 *Ibid* 30 June 1867
37 *Ibid* 18 Aug. 1867
38 RGM 5 Jan. 1868
39 Winton Dean, *Georges Bizet. His Life and Work.* London 1965. 72. (Reported)
40 RGM 5 Jan. 1868
41 *Ibid. Ibid.*
42 O 25 Jan. 1868
43 RGM 13 Sept. 1867
44 *Ibid* 22 Sept. and 6 Oct. 1867
45 O 26 Oct. 1867
46 F 17 Oct. 1867
47 O 21 Dec. 1867
48 RGM 22 Dec. 1867
49 *Ibid* 16 Feb. 1868
50 O 21 Mar. 1868
51 M 1 Mar. 1868
52 *Ibid. Ibid.*
53 RGM 12 Apr. 1868
54 *Ibid* 22 Mar. 1868
55 O 28 Mar. 1868
56 M 19 Jan. 1868
57 *Ibid* 22 and 29 Jan. 1868
58 *Ibid* 26 Apr. 1868
59 Soubies 51
60 Winton Dean, 73
61 Soubies 49
62 M 21 June 1868
63 GM 3 Sept. 1868
64 AM 28 May 1868
65 M 26 July 1868
66 GM 16 July 1868
67 RGM 31 May 1868
68 O 5 Sept. 1868

Chapter 6

Pasdeloup, and the end 1868–1870

1868–1869
pp 241 to 257

1	O 14 Nov. 1868		37	RGM 24 Jan. 1869
2	M 13 Dec. 1868		38	M and RGM 17 Jan. 1869
3	O 19 Dec. 1868		39	O 6 Mar. 1869
4	M 17 Jan. 1869		40	M 31 Jan. 1869
5	O 5 Sept. 1868		41	RGM 31 Jan. 1869
6	RGM 13 Sept. 1868		42	M 7 Feb. 1869
7	O 19 Sept. 1868		43	O 6 Feb. 1869
8	M 23 Aug. 1868		44	Erna Brand. *Aglaja Orgeni*:
9	*Lettres Françaises de Richard*			Das Leben einer grossen
	Wagner. ed. J. Tiersot, Paris			Sängerin. Munich 1931, 249
	1935, 282		45	M 14 Feb. 1869
10	M 8 Nov. 1868		46	RGM 7 Mar. 1869
11	*Lettres Françaises de Richard*		47	Lasalle *Mémorial du Théâtre*
	Wagner, 280, 283–284			*Lyrique* 85
12	M 6 Sept. 1868		48	RGM 7 Mar. 1869
13	*Ibid.* 20 Sept. 1868		49	MW 22 May 1869
14	*Ibid.* 13 Sept. 1868		50	Georges Servières. *Richard*
15	RGM 11 Oct. 1868			*Wagner jugé en France.* Paris
16	M 13 Dec. 1868			1886. 134, 139
17	RDM 1 Nov. 1868		51	F 19 Mar. 1869
18	M 1 Nov. 1868		52	M 28 Mar. 1869
19	*Ibid.* 22 Nov. 1868		53	RGM 11 Apr. 1869
20	MU 30 Nov. 1868		54	*Ibid.* 21 Mar. and 4 Apr. 1869
21	U 23 Nov. 1868		55	M 14 Mar. 1869
22	M 29 Nov. 1868		56	*Ibid.* 28 Mar. 1869
23	RGM 29 Nov. 1868		57	GM 8 Apr. 1869
24	MU 30 Nov. 1868		58	JD 13 May 1869
25	M 29 Nov. 1868		59	*Ibid.* 6 Apr. 1869
26	JD 28 Dec. 1868		60	Soubies 55
27	*Ibid.* 6 Dec. 1868		61	O 9 Apr. 1869
28	JI 6–13 Dec. 1868		62	RGM 11 Apr. 1869
29	JD 28 Dec. 1868		63	M 11 Apr. 1869
30	RGM 15 Nov. 1868		64	MW 1 May 1869
31	M 27 Dec. 1868		65	Soubies 55
32	*Ibid. Ibid.*		66	Maxime Leroy. *Les Premiers*
33	O 23 Jan. 1869			*Amis Français de Wagner.*
34	M 3 Jan. 1869			Paris 1925, 227
35	AM 14 Jan. 1869		67	GM 15 Apr. 1869
36	F 9 May 1869		68	M 18 Apr. 1869

69	*Ibid.* 11 July 1869
70	M 16 May 1869
71	Lasalle *Mémorial du Théâtre Lyrique* 86
72	RGM 16 May 1869
73	M 9 May 1869
74	MW 5 June 1869
75	M 6 June 1869

76	*Ibid.* 30 May 1869
77	*Ibid.* 16 May 1869
78	*Ibid.* 29 Aug. 1869
79	RGM 22 Aug. 1869
80	MW 4 Sept. 1869
81	RGM 22 Aug. 1869
82	MS 16 Oct. 1869
83	M 27 June, 4 and 11 July 1869
84	*Ibid.* 9 May 1869

1869–1870
pp 257 to 275

1	MW 18 Sept. 1869
2	M 5 Sept. 1869
3	*Ibid.* 15 Aug. 1869
4	RGM 16 May 1869
5	*Ibid.* 12 Sept. 1869
6	*Ibid.* 19 Sept. 1869
7	*Ibid.* 10 Oct. 1869
8	*Ibid.* 17 Oct. 1869
9	*Ibid.* 24 Oct. 1869
10	*Ibid.* 14 Nov. 1869
11	*Ibid.* 28 Nov. 1869
12	FM 23 Jan. 1870
13	MW 15 Jan. 1870
14	RGM 26 Sept. 1869
15	GM 14 Oct. 1869
16	M 5 Sept. 1869
17	*Ibid. Ibid.*
18	GM 30 Sept. 1869
19	Lasalle *Mémorial du Théâtre Lyrique* 87
20	M 26 Sept. 1869
21	RGM 26 Sept. 1869
22	RDM 1 Nov. 1869
23	M 26 Sept. 1869
24	*Ibid.* 3 Oct. 1869
25	*Ibid.* 21 Nov. 1869
26	RGM 21 Nov. 1869
27	M 21 Nov. 1869
28	GM 25 Nov. 1869
29	RDM 1 Sept. 1869
30	M 14 Nov. 1869
31	F 29 Jan., 27 Feb., 6 Mar., 10 Apr., 1 May, 1828
32	RGM 13 Mar. 1842
33	JD 23 July 1844

34	F 9 July 1869
35	M 22 May 1892
36	E. Gérard et Cie, Paris
37	F 9 July 1869
38	MU 25 May 1862
39	RGM 5 Dec. 1869
40	Joseph Bennett. *Forty Years of Music 1865–1905.* London 1908, 104
41	F 22 Dec. 1869
42	*Ibid.* 2 Dec. 1869
43	GM 6 Jan. 1870
44	RGM 2 Jan. 1870
45	P 2–3 Jan. 1870
46	F 11 Jan. 1870
47	*Ibid.* 13 Jan. 1870
48	M 27 Feb. 1870
49	FM 6 Feb. 1870
50	F 26 Dec. 1869
51	RGM 27 Feb. 1870
52	F 21 Jan. 1870
53	*Ibid.* 16 Jan. 1870
54	FM 23 Jan. 1870
55	M 23 Jan. and 6 Feb. 1870
56	RGM 30 Jan. 1870
57	*Ibid. Ibid.*
58	FM 6 Feb. 1870
59	RGM 30 Jan. and 6 Feb. 1870
60	*Ibid.* 30 Jan. 1870
61	M 15 May 1870
62	MW 18 Dec. 1869
63	RGM 13 Feb. 1870
64	M 13 Mar. 1870
65	RGM 13 Mar. 1870
66	C 11 Apr. 1870

67	RGM 20 Mar. 1870
68	*Ibid.* 10 Apr. 1870
69	*Ibid.* 6 Mar. 1870
70	M 6 Mar. 1870
71	*Ibid.* 13 Mar. 1870
72	RGM 20 Mar. 1870
73	*Ibid.* 3 Apr. 1870
74	M. 17 Apr. 1870
75	*Ibid.* 15 May 1870
76	RGM 22 May 1870
77	*Ibid.* 5 June 1870
78	*Ibid.* 30 Jan. 1870
79	FM 23 Jan. 1870
80	M 23 and 30 Jan. 1870
81	FM 6 Feb. 1870
82	F 6 Apr. 1870
83	M 15 May 1870
84	RGM 10 Apr. 1870
85	*Ibid.* 17 Apr. 1870
86	*Ibid.* 24 Apr. 1870
87	M 1 May 1870
88	RGM 28 May 1870
89	*Ibid.* 10 July 1870
90	*Ibid.* 5 June 1870
91	M 19 June 1870
92	*Edmond and Jules de Goncourt Journal (Ed. Robert Ricatte) Monaco 1956. 5 v. v. V. 107*
93	JI 8–15 Sept. 1868
94	C 20 Mar. 1869
95	L-Henry Lecomte *Histoire des Théâtres de Paris. Les Fantaisies–Parisiennes 1865–69,* Paris 1912
96	O 18 Feb. 1870
97	RGM 26 June 1870
98	M 19 June 1870
99	RGM 28 May 1870
100	*Ibid.* 31 July 1870
101	*Ibid.* 1 Oct. 1870/71
102	Lasalle *Mémorial du Théâtre Lyrique* 97–99

Appendix A

List of operas performed at the Théâtre Lyrique, Paris, during the years 1851 to 1870

Each work is described either as opera, opera-comique or opera-ballet (op., op-c., op-bt.). The number of acts in the production follows the title (1 a., etc.). Most of the works listed were creations of the Théâtre Lyrique and where works were first performed at other theatres this is indicated by the symbol†. Cast lists, not always complete, have been compiled mainly from *Le Ménestrel*, *Revue et Gazette Musicale*, *Bibliothèque Dramatique*, and *Théâtre Contemporain Illustré*. The year in which each opera was first performed, the number of performances it received in a particular year and the total number of performances for the years 1851 to 1870 are recorded as follows: 1851 (10), '52 (5), '63 (7). *Total 22*, etc.

1851

Director: Edmond Seveste

Sept. 27
MOSQUITA LA SORCIÈRE op-c. 3 a (Scribe and Vaëz) Boisselot
Mosquita, Rouvroy; *Benita*, Mendez-Loustauneau; *Dolorès*, Vadé; *Don Manoël*, Michel; *Peblo*, Menjaud; *L'Alcade Gallardo*, Grignon père; *Carasco*, Bordier; *Morellos*, Wilhem.
1851 (21), '52 (4). *Total 25.*

Sept. 28
LE BARBIER DE SÉVILLE† op-c. 4 a. (Castil-Blaze) Rossini
Rosine, Duez; *Almaviva*, Biéval (Lourdel); *Figaro*, Meillet; *Bartholo*, Dumonthier; *Bazile*, Prouvier.
1851 (19), '52 (10), '53 (4), '54 (15), '55 (6), '56 (14), '58 (8), '68 (21), '69 (26), '70 (3). *Total 126*
LE MAÎTRE DE CHAPELLE† op-c. 1 a. (Gay) Paër
Gertrude, Guichard; *Barnabé*, Ribes; *Benetto*, Soyer.
1851 (29), '52 (33), '53 (8), '54 (34), '55 (43), '56 (11), '57 (1), '68 (8), '69 (13), '70 (2). *Total 182.*

Oct. 17
LES RENDEZ-VOUS BOURGEOIS† op-c. 1 a. (Hoffmann) Niccolò
Isouard
Julie, Guichard; *Reine*, Guillard; *Louise*, Vallet; *Dugravier*, Grignon père;
Jasmin, Ribes; *Charles*, Menjaud; *Bertrand*, Neveu; *César*, Fosse.
1851 (21), '52 (21). *Total* 42

Oct. 18
MA TANTE AURORE OU LE ROMAN IMPROMPTU† op-c. 2 a (Lon-
champs) Boieldieu
Tante Aurore, Vadé; *Julie*, C. Vadé; *Marton*, Guichard; *Valsain*, Biéval
(Lourdel); *Frontin*, Meillet; *Georges*, Leroy.
1851 (27), '52 (19), '53 (14), '56 (10). *Total* 70.

Oct. 23
MURDOCK LE BANDIT op-c. 1 a. (de Leuven) Gautier
Arabelle, Mendez-Loustauneau; *Arthur*, Dulaurens; *Murdock*, Ribes;
Marquis, Neveu.
1851 (24), '52 (13). *Total* 37.

Nov. 9
MAISON A VENDRE† op-c. 1 a. (Duval) Dalayrac
1851 (11), '52 (9). *Total* 20.

Nov. 16
AMBROISE, OU VOILÀ MA JOURNÉE† op-c. 1 a. (de Monvel) Dalayrac
1851 (5). *Total* 5.

Nov. 22
LA PERLE DU BRÉSIL op. 3 a. (Gabriel and Saint-Etienne) David
Zora, Duez; *La Comtesse de Cavallos*, Guichard; *Lorenz*, Philippe; *Don
Salvador*, Bouché; *Rio*, Soyer; *Un Brésilien*, Junca.
1851 (17), '52 (47), '53 (4), '58 (39), '59 (9), '63 (15), '64 (13).
Total 144.

Nov. 30
LES TRAVESTISSEMENTS† op-c. 1 a. (Deslandes) Grisar
Josephine, Guichard; *Victor*, (?) Daudé
1851 (6), '52 (2). *Total* 8.

1852

Directors: Edmond Seveste. From April, Jules Seveste

Jan. 6
LA BUTTE DES MOULINS op-c. 3 a. (Gabriel and Deforges) Adrien
Boieldieu
Comtesse de Séran, Vadé; *Marielle*, Rouvroy; *Roger, Comte de Séran*, Fosse;
Eloi, Meillet; *Dorliton*, Neveu; *Monthabor*, Junca; *Brichard*, Dumonthier;
Pierre Martin, Willems, *Joseph*, Prouvier; *Un Garçon de café*, Gastineau; *Un
Commissaire de police*, Andrieux.
1852 (17). *Total* 17.

Jan. 26
LE MARIAGE EN L'AIR op-c. 1 a. (de Saint-Georges and Dupin) Déjazet
Colombine, Guichard; *Léandre,* Biéval (Lourdel); *Pierrot,* Grignon fils;
Cassandre, Grignon père.
1852 (22). *Total* 22.
Feb. 11
LE PENSIONNAT DE JEUNES DEMOISELLES† (LES VISITANDINES)
op-c. 2 a (Picard and Vial) Devienne
Amélie, Guichard; *Victorine,* Petipa; *Mme Wanderven,* Vadé; *Melfort,* Biéval
(Lourdel); *Frontin,* Ribes; *Grégoire,* Leroy.
1852 (16). *Total* 16.
Feb. 21
LES FIANÇAILLES DES ROSES op-c. 2 a. (Jules Seveste and Deslys)
Villeblanche
Youla, Mendez-Loustauneau; *Gretchen,* Vallet; *Frédérique,* Guillard; *Berthe,*
Dupont; *Van Schalg,* Leroy; *Wilhem,* Dulaurens; *Nicodème,* Neveu; *Pifpaf,*
Grignon; *Vantruck,* Andrieux.
1852 (24). *Total* 24.
LA POUPÉE DE NUREMBERG op-c. 1 a. (de Leuven and de Beauplan)
Adam
Berthe, Rouvroy; *Miller,* Meillet; *Cornélius,* Grignon père; *Donathan,*
Menjaud.
1852 (47), '53 (16), '54 (2), '69 (22), '70 (11). *Total* 98.
March 11
JOANITA† op. 3 a. (Ed. Duprez and Oppelt) Gilbert Duprez
Joanita, Caroline Duprez; *Pauline,* Guichard; *Stéphano,* Duprat; *Chevalier
de Romuald,* Balanqué; *Léonce de Bongard,* Poultier.
1852 (15). *Total* 15.
April 23
LA PIE VOLEUSE† op. 3 a. (Castil-Blaze) Rossini
Ninette, Duez; *Petit Jacques,* Rouvroy; *Claudine,* Vadé; *Philippe,* Dulaurens;
Villebelle, Bouché; *Le Bailli,* Ribes.
1852 (7). *Total* 7.
Sept. 4
SI J'ÉTAIS ROI op-c. 3 a. (d'Ennery and Brésil) Adam
Néméa, Colson; *Zélide,* Rouvroy; *Une Bayadère,* Garnier; *Mossoul,* Laurent;
Kadoor, Junca; *Zéphoris,* Tallon; *Pifear,* Menjaud; *Zizel,* Leroy;
Atar, Lemaire.
1852 (66), '53 (19), '54 (5), '56 (19), '57 (6), '58 (15), '59 (10), '60 (19), '61 (2), '63
(15). *Total* 176.
Oct. 2
FLORE ET ZÉPHIRE op-c. 1 a. (de Leuven and Deslys) Gautier
Mariette, Guichard; *Mme Vertbois,* Vadé; *Saturnin,* Ribes; *M. Vertbois,* Leroy.
1852 (41), '53 (33), '54 (32), '55 (20). *Total* 126.
Oct. 14
CHOISY-LE-ROI op-c. 1 a. (de Leuven and Carré) Gautier
Mme de Pompadour, Petit-Brière; *Perrette,* de Corcelles; *Colas,* Grignon fils;
Baron de Montchenu, Grignon père.

1852 (16), '53 (6). *Total* 22.
Oct. 27
LA FERME DE KILMOOR op-c. 2 a. (Deslys and Woestyn) Varney
Suzannah, Rouvroy; *Leghy,* Guichard; *Edith,* Vadé; *Sir Francis MacYvor,*
Biéval (Lourdel); *Bob,* Grignon fils; *Turneps,* Neveu; *Radcliff,* Willems.
1852 (5). *Total* 5.
Nov. 3
LE POSTILLON DE LONJUMEAU† op-c. 3 a (de Leuven and Brunswick)
Adam
Madeleine, Guichard; *Chappelou,* Chollet; *Marquis de Corcy,* Leroy; *Biju,*
Grignon père.
1852 (19), '53 (8), '54 (1). *Total* 28.
Nov. 8
LES DEUX VOLEURS† op-c. 1 a. (de Leuven and Brunswick) Girard
Adeline, Renaud; *Jean de Beauvais,* Colson.
1852 (31), '53 (6). *Total* 37.
Dec. 8
GUILLERY LE TROMPETTE op-c. 2 a. (de Leuven and de Beauplan)
Sarmiento
Guillery, Guichard; *Zina,* Rouvroy; *Léonarde,* Vadé; *Fabrice,* Carré; *Taillefer,*
Ribes; *Rebolloso,* Grignon père.
1852 (6), '53 (19). *Total* 25.
Dec. 22
TABARIN op-c. 2 a. (Alboize and Andrel) Bousquet
Francesquine, Colson; *Petit-Pierre,* (Mlle) Renaud; *Primerose,* Vadé; *Tabarin,*
Laurent; *Pansurot,* Grignon; *Mondor,* Leroy.
1852 (4), '53 (18). *Total* 22.

1853

Director: Jules Seveste

Jan. 5
LE ROI D'YVETOT† op-c. 3 a. (de Leuven and Brunswick) Adam
Jeanneton, Guichard; *Marguerite,* Garnier; *Josselin,* Chollet; *Adalbert,* Carré;
Daniel, Menjaud; *Reginald d'Houdeville,* Junca.
1853 (8). *Total* 8.
Jan. 22
LE LUTIN DE LA VALLÉE op-bt. 2 a. (Alboize and Carré) Gautier
Kathy, Térésa, Mme Brigitte, Le Lutin, Comte Ulric, Mlles Guy-Stéphan,
Renard, Lisereux, Millet, Kohlenberg, MM. Saint-Léon, Frappart (dancers);
Mme Petit-Brière, M. Biéval (Lourdel) (singers).
1853 (33). *Total* 33.
March 11
LES AMOURS DU DIABLE op-c. 4 a. (de Saint-Georges) Grisar
Urielle, Colson; *Lilia,* Renaud; *Phoebé,* Noël; *Thérésine,* Vadé; *Goth,* Larcena;
Le Comte Frédéric, Tallon; *Belzébuth,* Coulon; *Le Gouverneur Hortensius,*

Leroy; *Bracaccio,* Junca; *Paternick,* Colson; *Le Grand Visir,* Grignon; *L'Eunique,* Neveu.
1853 (48). *Total* 48.
April 11
LE ROI DES HALLES op-c. 3 a. (de Leuven and Brunswick) Adam
Marielle, Guichard; *Mme Bourdillat,* Vadé; *Une Jeune Fille,* Garnier; *Duc de Beaufort (Jean),* Chollet; *Planchet,* Laurent; *Martineau,* Grignon; *Bourdillat,* Junca; *Dandinelli,* Colson.
1853 (35), '54 (4). *Total* 39
April 28
COLIN-MAILLARD op-c. 1 a. (Carré and Verne) Hignard
Pélagie Bonneau, Vadé; *Collette,* Larcena; *Florine,* C. Vadé; *Brigitte,* Garnier; *Le Baron de la Verdure,* Grignon; *M. Bonneau,* Neveu; *Léonidas,* Cabel; *Cyprien,* Biéval (Lourdel); *Cotylédon,* Menjaud.
1853 (39), '54 (6). *Total* 45.
May 17
L'ORGANISTE DANS L'EMBARRAS op-c. 1 a. (Alboize) Weckerlin
Berthe, Larcena; *Albert,* Carré; *Klussmann,* Grignon; *Coppélius,* Leroy; *Un Huissier,* Lemaire.
1853 (11), '54 (26). *Total* 37.
May 28
LE PRÉSENT ET L'AVENIR Epilogue. 1 a. 'Divers auteurs'
Mmes Renaud, Guichard, Colson, Petit-Brière.
MM. Tallon, Laurent, Sujol, Cabel, Ribes, Junca, Grignon.
1853 (1). *Total* 1.
Sept. 3
LA MOISSONNEUSE op. 4 a. (Bourgeois and Masson) Vogel
Michelma, Colson; *Zerline,* C. Vadé; *Balsamo,* Laurent; *Juliani,* Tallon; *Mathéo,* Junca; *Gaëtan,* Colson; *Le Barigel,* Leroy; *Carpagnole,* Menjaud; *Un Brigadier,* Léon; *Un Guide,* Quinchez.
1853 (26). *Total* 26.
Sept. 4
LA PRINCESSE DE TRÉBISONDE Prologue. 1 a. 'Divers auteurs'
Mmes Garnier, Petit-Brière, Girard, Vadé, Chevalier.
1853 (11). *Total* 11.
Sept. 20
BONSOIR, VOISIN op-c. 1 a. (Brunswick and de Beauplan) Poise
Louisette, Meillet-Meyer; *Digonard,* Meillet.
1853 (31), '54 (15), '55 (23), '56 (10), '57 (1). *Total* 80.
Oct. 6
LE BIJOU PERDU op-c. 3 a. (de Leuven and Deforges) Adam
Toinon, Cabel; *Marotte,* Garnier; *Le Marquis d'Angennes,* Sujol; *Coquillière,* Leroy; *Le Chevalier,* Menjaud; *Pacôme,* Meillet; *Bellepointe,* Cabel; *Le Vicomte,* Quinchez; *Le Baron,* Adam; *Le Comte,* Andrieux.
1853 (40), '54 (27), '55 (12), '56 (8), '61 (33), 62 (12). *Total* 132.
Oct. 15
LE DIABLE À QUATRE† op-c. 4 a. (Creuzé de Lesser) Solié
Margot, Girard; *La Comtesse,* Petit-Brière; *Maître Jacques,* Grignon;

1853 (16), '54 (7). *Total* 23.

Oct. 22

LE DANSEUR DU ROI op-bt. 3 a. (Alboize and Saint-Léon) Gautier
La Duchesse de Chevreuse, (Nathalie) Fitz-James; *Cramoisi*, Saint-Léon;
Mlles Yella, Arányváry, Lilienthal, Lisereux, Nathan, Lequine, Godefroi
(dancers); C. Vadé, Ribes, Grignon (singers).
1853 (11). *Total* 11.

Nov. 28

GEORGETTE OU LE MOULIN DE FONTENOY op-c. 1 a. (Vaëz)
Gevaert
Georgette, Girard; *Corbin*, Cabel; *Clovis*, Grignon; *Maître Renard*, Leroy;
André, Sujol.
1853 (16), '54 (27). *Total* 43.

Dec. 31

ELISABETH OU LA FILLE DU PROSCRIT† op. 3 a. (de Leuven and
Brunswick) Donizetti
Elisabeth, Colson; *La Comtesse*, Petit-Brière; *Marie*, Vadé; *Nizza*, Girard; *Le
Comte Vanikof*, Tallon; *Michel*, Laurent; *Le Grand Duc*, Colson; *Ivan*, Junca;
Ourzac, Cabel; *Kisolof*, Leroy.
1853 (1), '54 (34). *Total* 35.

1854

Directors: Jules Seveste. From 26 July, Emile Perrin

Feb. 6

LES ÉTOILES op-bt. 1 a. (Clairville) Pilati
L'Étoile, Lemonnier; *Phosphoriël*, Chapuy; Mlle Lequine (dancers); *Une
Française*, Petit-Brière; *Une Espagnole*, Garnier; *Une Anglaise*, Chevalier
(singers).
1854 (17). *Total* 17.

Feb. 24

LA FILLE INVISIBLE op-c. 3 a. (de Saint-Georges and Dupin) Adrien
Boieldieu
Hermance, Meillet; *Lisbeth*, Girard; *Brijitte*, Vadé; *Everard*, Tallon; *Conrad*,
Meillet; *Le Docteur Servatius*, Cabel; *Le Caporal Kokmann*, Menjaud.
1854 (19). *Total* 19.

March 16

LA PROMISE op-c. 3 a. (de Leuven and Brunswick) Clapisson
Marie, Cabel; *Simonette*, Girard; *Mme Hubert*, Vadé; *Petit-Pierre*, Laurent;
Giromon, Junca; *Théodore*, Colson; *Guillaume*, Legrand.
1854 (57), '55 (3). *Total* 60.

March 26

LE PANIER FLEURI† op-c. 1 a. (de Leuven and Brunswick) Thomas
Angélique, Petit-Brière; *Roland*, Grignon; *Beausoleil*, Sujol.
1854 (23). *Total* 23.

April 16
UNE RENCONTRE DANS LE DANUBE op-c. 2 a. (G. Delavigne and de Wailly) Henrion
Hélène, Petit-Brière; *Le Prince Hermann,* Colson; *Le Peintre Hermann,* Meillet; *Waldorf,* Grignon; *Carl,* Leroy; *Fritz,* Adam. *Verner,* Quinchez; *Albert,* Andrieux.
1854 (17). *Total* 17.

April 25
LA REINE D'UN JOUR† op-c. 3 a. (Scribe and de Saint-Georges) Adam
Francine, Meillet; *Lady Pekinbrook,* Vadé; *Simone,* C. Vadé; *Marcel,* Rousseau de Lagrave; *Trumbell,* Grignon; *Comte d'Elvas,* Legrand; *Le Shérif,* Leroy.
1854 (25), '55 (2). *Total* 27.

May 20
MAÎTRE WOLFRAM op-c. 1 a. (Méry) Reyer
Hélène, Meillet; *Frantz,* Tallon; *Wolfram,* Laurent; *Wilhelm,* Grignon.
1854 (13), '55 (4), '57 (6). *Total* 23.

June 1
LE TABLEAU PARLANT† op-c. 1 a. (Anséaume) Grétry
Isabelle, C. Vadé; *Columbine,* Girard; *Cassandre,* Leroy; *Léandre,* Colson; *Pierrot,* Sujol.
1854 (3). *Total* 3.

Oct. 7
LE BILLET DE MARGUERITE op-c. 3 a. (de Leuven and Brunswick) Gevaert
Marguerite, Deligne-Lauters; *Dorothée,* Chevalier; *Berthe,* Meillet; *Tobias,* Achard; *Reinhold,* Meillet; *Jacobus,* Colson.
1854 (31), '55 (10). *Total* 41.

Oct. 31
SCHAHABAHAM II op-c. 1 a. (de Leuven and Carré) Gautier
Olivette, Girard; *Valentin,* Allais; *Schahabaham II,* Junca; *Agobar,* Leroy; *Curtius,* Ribes.
1854 (23), '55 (18). *Total* 41.

Nov. 29
LE ROMAN DE LA ROSE op-c. 1 a. (Barbier and Delahaye) Pascal
Marguerite, Meillet; *Christine,* Girard; *Daniel,* (Mlle) Bourgeois; *Walter,* Grignon.
1854 (11), '55 (9). *Total* 20.

Dec. 16
LE MULETIER DE TOLÈDE op-c. 3 a. (d'Ennery and Clairville) Adam
Elvire, Cabel; *Carmen,* Garnier; *La Camarera Mayor,* Vadé; *Manoël,* Sujol; *Don Pèdre,* Cabel; *Don Salluste,* Ribes; *Don César,* Legrand; *Pablo,* Adam; *Un Huissier,* Andrieux; *Un Officier,* Quinchez.
1854 (7), '55 (47). *Total* 54.

Dec. 24
A CLICHY op-c. 1 a. (d'Ennery and Grangé) Adam
Hector, Legrand; *Prosper,* Ribes; *Ducormier,* Leroy.
1854 (4), '55 (72), '56 (13). *Total* 89.

Dec. 31
DANS LES VIGNES op-c. 1 a. (Brunswick and de Beauplan) Clapisson
Gros Pierre, Meillet; *Nicolas,* Colson.
1854 (1), '55 (18). *Total* 19.

1855

Directors: Emile Perrin. From 29 September, Pellegrin.

Jan. 24
ROBIN DES BOIS† (*) op. 3 a. (Castil-Blaze and Sauvage) Weber
Annette (Agathe), Deligne-Lauters; *Nancy (Aennchen),* Girard; *Tony (Max),*
Rousseau de Lagrave; *Richard (Kaspar),* Marchot; *Robin des Bois (Samiel),*
Junca; *Reynold (Kuno),* Grignon; *Dick (Kilian),* Colson.
1855 (59), '56 (15), '57 (8), '59 (7), '60 (7), '62 (10), '63 (22), '66 (11), '67 (49), '68 (13). *Total* 201.

March 7
LES CHARMEURS op-c. 1 a. (de Leuven) Poise
Georgette, Meillet; *Mère Michel,* Vadé; *Julien,* Achard; *Bobin,* Grignon.
1855 (44), '56 (16), '58 (6). *Total* 66.

April 10
LISETTE op-c. 2 a. (Sauvage) Ortolan
Lisette, Girard; *La Comtesse,* Chevalier; *Germain,* Crambade; *Marquis de
Fonville,* Colson; *Comte de Terburg,* Legrand.
1855 (11). *Total* 11.

May 14
JAGUARITA L'INDIENNE op-c. 3 a. (de Saint-Georges and de Leuven)
Halévy
Jaguarita, Cabel; *Eva,* Garnier; *Maurice,* Monjauze; *Hector van Trump,*
Meillet; *Mama-Jumbo,* Junca; *Le Sergent Pétermann,* Colson; *Tobie,* Adam.
1855 (84), '56 (8), '61 (18), '62 (14). *Total* 124.

June 6
LES COMPAGNONS DE LA MARJOLAINE op-c. 1 a. (Carré and Verne)
Hignard
Marceline, Girard; *Monique,* Vadé; *Simplice,* Achard; *Guerfroid,* Marchot;
Landry, Cabel; *Boniface,* Leroy.
1855 (24). *Total* 24.

June 13
L'INCONSOLABLE op-c. 1 a. (de Saint-Georges and de Leuven) Halévy
1855 (20). *Total* 20.

(*)
First performed at the Théâtre Lyrique as composed by Weber and called *Le Freischütz*
on December 8, 1866. The translation was by Trianon and E. Gautier and the cast was
as follows: *Anne (Agathe),* Miolan-Carvalho; *Nancy (Aennchen),* Daram; *Eveline,*
Cornélis; *Berthe,* Demay; *Emma,* Griselli; *Anna,* Regnault; *Max,* Michot; *Gaspard
(Kaspar),* Troy; *Ottokar,* Legrand; *Le Prieur (L'Ermite),* Berardi; *Herman (Kuno),*
Neveu; *Kilian,* Troy jeune; *Samiel,* Wartel; *le Piqueur,* Guyot; *2e Piqueur,* Gabriel.

June 19
LA SIRENE† op-c. 3 a. (Scribe) Auber
Zerlina, Pannetrat; *Mathéa,* Vadé; *Scopetta,* Dulaurens; *Duc de Popoli,*
Prilleux; *Scipion,* Achard; *Bolbaya,* Grignon; *Pecchione,* Quinchez.
1855 (16), '56 (1). *Total* 17.
Sept. 14
UNE NUIT A SÉVILLE op-c. 1 a. (Nuitter and Beaumont) Barbier
Inès, Girard; *Zéphora,* Garnier; *Don Zapatéro,* Grignon; *Rodriguez,* Colson;
Fernand, Legrand; *Julio,* Allais.
1855 (26). *Total* 26.
MARIE† op-c. 3 a. (de Planard) Hérold
Marie, Bourgeois; *Emilie,* Pannetrat; *Suzette,* Girard; *La Baronne,* Vadé;
Adolphe, (Ernest) Leroy; *Henri,* Achard; *Le Baron,* Grignon; *Lubin,* Girardot;
Georges, Prilleux.
1855 (26), '56 (12). *Total* 38.
Oct. 25
LES LAVANDIÈRES DE SANTAREM op-c. 3 a. (d'Ennery and Grangé)
Gévaert
Margarita, Deligne-Lauters; *Teresa,* Bourgeois; *Don Luiz,* (Mlle) Girard;
Manoël, Dulaurens; *Duc d'Aguilar,* Grignon; *Pablo,* Prilleux; *Jean V, Roi de
Portugal,* Marchot; *Baron de Casilhas,* Legrand.
1855 (21), '56 (2). *Total* 23.
Nov. 21
ROSE ET NARCISSE op-c. 1 a. (Nuitter and Beaumont) Barbier
Rose, Garnier; *Narcisse,* Legrand.
1855 (11). *Total* 11.
Nov. 24
LE SECRET DE L'ONCLE VINCENT op-c. 1 a. (Boisseaux) de Lajarte
Thérèse, Caye; *Marcel,* Meillet; *Boivin,* Quinchez.
1855 (11), '56 (31), '57 (3). *Total* 45.
Dec. 14
LE SOLITAIRE† op-c. 3 a. (de Planard) Carafa
Élodie, Pannetrat; *Marie,* Girard; *Marceline,* Vadé; *Le Solitaire,* Bauche;
Palzot, Marchot; *Charlot,* Allais; *Alberti,* Cabel; *1er Soldat,* Beaucé; *2me
Soldat,* Adam.
1855 (6), '56 (9). *Total* 15.
Dec. 29
L'HABIT DE NOCE op-c. 1 a. (d'Ennery and Bignon) Cuzent
Catherine, Bourgeois; *Nina,* Garnier; *Reynold,* Achard; *Schlawag,* Marchot;
Jean, Girardot; *Matheus,* Leroy; *Un Piqueur,* Adam.
1855 (1), '56 (19). *Total* 20.

1856

Directors: Les artistes en société. From 20 February, Léon Carvalho.

Jan. 18
FALSTAFF op-c. 1 a. (de Leuven and de Saint-Georges) Adam
Mistress Martyn, Mistress Margaret, Miss Polly, Bourgeois, Vadé, Garnier; *Falstaff,* Hermann-Léon; *Simpron,* Legrand; *Bardolf, Pistol, Nyms,* Allais, Leroy, Adam.*
1856 (23). *Total* 23.

LE SOURD OU L'AUBERGE PLEINE† op-c. 3 a, (de Leuven and Langlé) Adam
Mlle Josephine Doliban, C. Vadé; *Mlle Isidore d'Orbe,* Garnier; *Mme Legras,* Vadé; *Pétronille,* Girard; *Doliban,* Prilleux; *Dasnières,* Girardot; *Le Chevalier d'Orbe,* Legrand.
1856 (45), '57 (16), '58 (12), '60 (12), '61 (18), '62 (9), '63 (20), '64 (1). *Total* 133.

March 1
LA FANCHONNETTE op-c. 3 a. (de Leuven and de Saint-Georges) Clapisson
Fanchonnette, Miolan-Carvalho; *Hélène Boisjoli,* Brunet; *Marchande de fleurs,* Vadé; *Marchande de plaisirs,* C. Vadé; *Marchande de fruits,* Emma; *Gaston de Listenay,* Monjauze; *Don José d'Apuntador,* Hermann-Léon; *Monsieur Boisjoli,* Prilleux; *Candide,* Girardot; *Père Bonheur,* Grignon; *Chevalier de Soyecourt,* Legrand; *Marchand de Coco,* Adam; *Officier,* Quinchez; *Marchand de Gateaux,* Beaucé; *Majordome,* Andrieux.
1856 (112), '57 (9), '58 (2), '59 (38), '68 (31). *Total* 192.

March 22
MAM'ZELLE GENEVIÈVE op-c. 2 a. (Brunswick and de Beauplan) Adam
Geneviève, Meillet; *Marie,* Garnier; *Mme Basilic,* Vadé; *Pornic,* Meillet; *M. Pontorson,* Grignon.
1856 (12). *Total* 12.

April 16
LE CHAPEAU DU ROI op-c. 1 a. (Fournier) Caspers
Jeannette, Garnier; *Loys,* Pannetrat; *Olivier,* Achard; *Landry,* Meillet.
1856 (10). *Total* (10).

May 23
RICHARD COEUR-DE-LION† op-c. 3 a. (Sedaine) Grétry
Marguerite, Brunet; *Laurette,* Pouilley; *Antonio,* Girard; *Mathurine,* Vadé, *Colette,* C. Vadé; *Beatrix,* Caye; *Richard,* Michot; *Blondel,* Meillet; *Florestan,* Legrand; *Williams,* Cabel; *Le Sénéchal,* Quinchez; *Mathurin* and *Un Paysan,* Leroy; *Guillot,* Girardot; *Urbain,* Adam.
1856 (42), '57 (28), '58 (17), '59 (45), '60 (31), '61 (17), '62 (6), '63 (15), '64 (9), '65 (24), '66 (31), '67 (24), '68 (13). *Total* 302.

*
Precise casting uncertain.

Sept. 19
LES DRAGONS DE VILLARS op-c. 3 a. (Cormon and Lockroy) Maillart
Rose Friquet, Borghèse; *Georgette*, Girard; *Sylvain*, Scott; *Thibaut*, Girardot;
Bellamy, Grillon; *Un Pasteur*, Adam; *Un Dragon*, Quinchez; *Un Lieutenant*,
Garcin.
1856 (47), '57 (26), '58 (20), '60 (25), '61 (16), '62 (19), '63 (3). *Total* 156.
Dec. 27
LA REINE TOPAZE op-c. 3 a. (Lockroy and Battu) Massé
La Reine Topaze, Miolan-Carvalho; *La Comtesse Filomèle*, Pannetrat; *Une
Hoteliere*, C. Vadé; *Rafaël*, Monjauze; *Annibal*, Meillet; *Francatrippa*,
Balanqué; *Fritellino*, Froment; *Zeno*, Serène; *Gritti*, Lesage; *Lorédano*,
Beaucé; *Manfredi*, Legrand; *Bembo*, Cabel.
1856 (2), '57 (113), '58 (7), '60 (9), '64 (17), '65 (7), '66 (15). *Total* 170

1857

Director: Léon Carvalho

Feb. 27
OBERON† op. 3 a. (Nuitter, Beaumont and de Chazot) Weber
Rézia, Rossi-Caccia; *Fatime*, Girard; *Puck*, Borghèse: *Oberon*, Froment;
Huon, Michot; *Sherasmin*, Grillon; *Sadack*, Leroy; *Aboulifar*, Girardot; *Le
Bey*, Bellecour.
1857 (68), '58 (15), '63 (17). *Total* 100.
May 26
LES NUITS D'ESPAGNE op-c. 2 a. (Carré) Semet
Barbara, Vadé; *Carmen*, Moreau; *Inésille*, Girard; *Franck Owen*, Grillon;
Major Robinson, Lesage; *Gil Nünez*, Girardot; *Docteur Moreto*, Bellecour;
Scipion, Froment.
1857 (22), '58 (24). *Total* 46.
June 10
LE DUEL DU COMMANDEUR op-c. 1 a. (Boisseaux) de Lajarte
Louise, Brunet; *Diane*, Caye; *Le Commandeur de Tréville*, Leroy; *Le
Chevalier Armand*, Beaucé; *Le Marquis Roger*, Legrand; *Un Exempt*,
Quinchez.
1857 (4). *Total* 4.
LES COMMÈRES op-c. 1 a. (de Leuven and Grandvallet) Montuoro
Signora Cocomera, Girard; *Lorenza*, Brunet; *Christine*, Caye; *Pasquale*,
Froment; *Le Podestà*, Leroy; *Gregorio*, Cabel.
1857 (4). *Total* 4.
Sept. 1
EURYANTHE† op. 3 a. (de Leuven and de Saint-Georges) Weber
Euryanthe, Rey; *Zarah*, Borghèse; *Bernerette*, A. Faivre; *Odoard*, Michot;
Reynold, Balanqué; Girardot; Gabriel, Lesage, Serène.*
1857 (28). *Total* 28.
*

Roles of last four artists uncertain.

Oct. 3
MAÎTRE GRIFFARD op-c. 1 a. (Mestépès) Delibes
Isabelle, Moreau; *Jeanette*, Faivre; *Léandre*, Froment; *Griffard*, Leroy.
1857 (31), '58 (26), '59 (7). *Total* 64.
Nov. 5
MARGOT op-c. 3 a. (de Leuven and de Saint-Georges) Clapisson
Margot, Miolan-Carvalho; *Nanette*, Girard; *La Présidente Artemise*, C. Vadé;
Gervaise, Caye; *Le Marquis de Brétigny*, Monjauze; *Landriche*, Meillet;
Jacquot, Froment; *Le Vicomte de Tréfeu*, Legrand.
1857 (25), '58 (5). *Total* 30.
Dec. 30
LA DEMOISELLE D'HONNEUR op-c. 3 a (Mestépès and Kauffmann)
Semet
Elizabeth, Moreau; *Dona Hélène*, Rey; *Dona Florinde*, Vadé; *Reinette*,
Marimon; *Une Paysanne*, Faivre; *Un Page*, Caye; *Jean de Tavannes*, Audran;
Monsieur de Pardaillan, Grillon; *Le Marquis de Mendoza*, Balanqué;
Tremblet, Gabriel; *Monsieur de Canillac*, Potel; *Monsieur de Vaudreuil*,
Beaucé; *Jean-Pierre*, Serène.
1857 (1), '58 (33), '59 (2). *Total* 36.

1858

Director: Léon Carvalho

Jan. 15
LE MÉDECIN MALGRÉ LUI op-c. 3 a. (Barbier and Carré) Gounod
Lucinde, Caye; *Martine*, Faivre; *Jacqueline*, Girard; *Géronte*, Lesage; *Léandre*,
Froment; *Sganarelle*, Meillet; *Monsieur Robert*, Leroy; *Valère*, Wartel; *Lucas*,
Girardot.
1858 (58), '59 (22), '60 (4), '62 (15), '66 (6), '67 (21), '68 (4), '70 (12). *Total* 142.
April 16
PRECIOSA† op-c. 1 a. (Nuitter and Beaumont) Weber
Preciosa, Borghèse; *Lorenzo*, Froment; *Testaferrata*, Serène; *Truxillo*, Gabriel;
Marphurius, Leroy; *Un Capitaine*, Quinchez.
1858 (34), '59 (27). *Total* 61.
DON ALMANZOR op-c. 1 a. (Ulbach and Labat) Renaud de Vilbac
Dona Clorinde, Vadé; *Dona Isabelle*, Moreau; *Jacinthe*, Girard; *Don Almanzor*,
Wartel; *Don Félix*, Potel; *Pédrille*, Cibot.
1858 (16). *Total* 16.
May 8
LES NOCES DE FIGARO† op-c. 4 a. (Barbier and Carré) Mozart
La Comtesse, Duprez-Vandenheuvel; *Suzanne*, Ugalde; *Chérubin*, Miolan-
Carvalho; *Marceline*, Faivre; *Barberine*, Girard; *Almaviva*, Balanqué; *Figaro*,
Meillet; *Bartholo*, Wartel, *Basile*, Legrand; *Antonio*, Lesage.
1858 (89), '59 (47), '60 (9), '63 (38), '64 (12), '65 (5). *Total* 200.

May 21
GASTIBELZA† op. 3 a. (d'Ennery and Cormon) Maillart
Dona Sabine, Borghèse; *Paquita*, Faivre; *Gastibelza*, Michot; *Le Roi*, Lesage;
Don Alvar, Legrand; *Le Comte de Saldagne*, Cibot; *Mattéo*, Potel.
1858 (14), '59 (1). *Total* 15.

June 9
L'AGNEAU DE CHLOÉ op-c. 1 a. (Clairville) Montaubry
Chloé, Caye; *Myrtile*, Girard; *Lysandre*, Wartel.
1858 (10). *Total* 10.

Sept. 8
LA HARPE D'OR op-c. 2 a. (Jaime fils and Dubreuil) Godefroid
Cinthia, Wilhème; *Corella*, C. Vadé; *Horatio*, Michot; *Sbrighella*, Serène;
Ascanio, Beaucé; *Gambara*, Wartel; *Matteo*, Bellecour.
1858 (9). *Total* 9.

Sept. 29
BROSKOVANO op-c. 2 a. (Boisseaux) Deffès
Hélène, Marimon; *Michaëla*, Girard; *Joritza*, Lesage; *Basile*, Girardot;
Constantin, Froment; *Hassan*, Gabriel;
1858 (29), '59 (5). *Total* 34.

1859

Director: Léon Carvalho

Feb. 28
LA FÉE CARABOSSE op-c. 3 a. (Lockroy and Cogniard) Massé
Carabosse Mélodine, Ugalde; *La Comtesse Rosalinde*, Vadé; *Gisette*, Faivre;
Albert, Michot; *Daniel*, Meillet; *Ghislain*, Froment; *Le Comte Magnus*, Leroy;
Pharamond, Gabriel.
1859 (25). *Total* 25.

March 19
FAUST op. 5 a. (Barbier and Carré) Gounod
Marguerite, Miolan-Carvalho; *Siebel*, A. Faivre; *Marthe*, Duclos; *Faust*,
Barbot; *Méphistophélès*, Balanqué; *Valentin*, Raynal; *Wagner*, Cibot; *Un
Mendiant*, Serène.
1859 (57), '62 (7), '63 (53), '64 (68), '65 (7), '66 (51), '67 (56), '68 (7). *Total* 306.

May 11
ABOU HASSAN† op-c. 1 a. (Nuitter and Beaumont) Weber
Fatime, Marimon; *Kadoudja*, Vadé; *Zobeide*, C. Vadé; *Abou Hassan*, Meillet;
Omar, Wartel; *Le Calife*, Bellecour.
1859 (21). *Total* 21.

L'ENLÈVEMENT AU SÉRAIL† op-c. 2 a. (Pascal) Mozart
Constance, Meillet; *Blondine*, Ugalde; *Belmont*, Michot; *Pédrille*, Froment;
Osmin, Bataille.
1859 (55), '60 (17), '62 (9), '63 (6). *Total* 87.

Sept. 30
LES PETITS VIOLONS DU ROI op-c. 3 a. (Scribe and Boisseaux) Deffès
Lulli, (Mlle) Girard; *Mme de Beauvais*, Amélie Faivre; . . . . . , Marie Faivre;
Béchamel, Gabriel; *Philippe de Beauvais*, Froment; *Agent de Cardinal
Mazarin*, Wartel; *Commissionaire de Police*, Leroy.
1859 (23), '60 (5). *Total* 28.

Nov. 3
MAM'ZELLE PÉNÉLOPE op-c. 1 a. (Boisseaux) de Lajarte
Catherine, Faivre; *Landry*, Potel; *Bobinus*, Girardot; *Lorrain*, Gabriel.
1859 (9), '60 (13). *Total* 22.

Nov. 18
ORPHÉE† op. 3 a. (Moline) Gluck
Orphée, Viardot; *Eurydice*, Sax; *L'Amour*, Marimon; *L'Ombre*, Moreau.
1859 (20), '60 (76), '61 (28), '62 (12), '63 (2). *Total* 138.

1860

Directors: Léon Carvalho. From April, Charles Réty

Jan. 21
MA TANTE DORT op-c. 1 a. (Crémieux) Caspers
Martine, Ugalde; *La Marquise d'Ambert*, C. Vadé; *Gabrielle*, Durand; *Scapin*,
Meillet; *Le Chevalier de Kerpry*, Legrand.
1860 (22), '64 (40), '68 (5). *Total* 67.

Feb. 18
PHILÉMON ET BAUCIS op. 3 a. (Barbier and Carré) Gounod
Baucis, Miolan-Carvalho, *Une Bacchante*, Sax; *Jupiter*, Battaille; *Vulcain*,
Balanqué; *Philémon*, Froment.
1860 (13). *Total* 13.

March 24
GIL BLAS op-c. 5 a. (Barbier and Carré) Semet
Gil Blas, Ugalde; *Aurore*, A. Faivre; *Laure*, Girard; *Florimonde*, C. Vadé;
Léonarde, Vadé; *Perrette*, Moreau; *Melchior Zapata*, Meillet; *Don Vincent*,
Lesage; *Don Cléophas*, Legrand; *Le Docteur Sangrado*, Wartel; *Quinola*,
Girardot; *Rolando*, Serène; *Nunez*, Potel; *Chinchilla*, Leroy; *Corquelo*,
Gabriel; *Domingo*, Bénié.
1860 (37), '61 (19), '62 (5). *Total* 61.

May 5
FIDELIO† op. 3 a. (Barbier and Carré) Beethoven
Isabelle, Duchesse d'Aragon (*Leonore*), Viardot; *Marceline*, A. Faivre; *Jean
Galéas* (Florestan), Guardi; *Ludovic Sforza* (*Pizarro*), Serène; *Stefano*
(*Jaquino*), Froment, *Le Roi Charles VIII* (*Fernando*), Vanaud; *Rocco*,
Battaille.
1860 (11). *Total* 11.

June 2
LES VALETS DE GASCOGNE op-c. 1 a. (Gille) Dufresne
Blanche, A. Faivre; *Le Marquis de Bassegoulaine,* Girardot; *Le Marquis de Panillac,* Wartel; *Blondel,* Potel.
1860 (33). *Total* 33.

June 5
LES ROSIÈRES† op-c. 3 a. (Théaulon) Hérold
Eugénie, A. Faivre; *Florette,* Girard; *Cateau,* M. Faivre; *Mme Brigitte,* Vadé; *Le Comte d'Ennemont,* Delaunay-Ricquier; *Le Commandeur d'Apremont,* Lesage; *Le Sénéchal,* Gabriel; *Bastien,* Froment; *L'Olive,* Martin.
1860 (25), '61 (5). *Total* 30.

June 17
MAÎTRE PALMA op-c. 1 a. (Gille and Furpille) Rivay
Marta, Moreau; *Palma,* Lesage; *Lorenzo,* Legrand; *Giletti,* Potel.
1860 (3). *Total* 3.

Sept. 1
L'AUBERGE DES ARDENNES op-c. 1 a. (Carré and Verne) Hignard
Claudine, Durand; *Le Père Richard,* Wartel; *Julien,* Verdellet; *Monsieur Petit Pont,* Girardot.
1860 (16), '61 (4). *Total* 20.

CRISPIN, RIVAL DE SON MAÎTRE op-c. 2 a. (Berthoud) Sellenick
Lisette, A. Faivre; *Angélique,* Durand; *Mme Oronte,* Duclos; *Crispin,* Froment; *Labranche,* Balanqué; *Valère,* Legrand; *Monsieur Oronte,* Wartel; *Monsieur Orgon,* Leroy.
1860 (11). *Total* 11.

Oct. 15
LE VAL D'ANDORRE† op-c. 3 a. (de Saint-Georges) Halévy
Rose-de-Mai, Meillet; *Georgette,* Roziès; *Thérèse,* Zévaco; *Stéphan,* Monjauze; *Jacques Sincère,* Battaille; *Lejoyeux,* Meillet; *Saturnin,* Froment; *L'Endormi,* Leroy; *Le Grand Syndic,* Serène.
1860 (34), '61 (44), '62 (1), '68 (28), '69 (22), '70 (6). *Total* 135.

Dec. 17
LES PÊCHEURS DE CATANE op. 3 a. (Cormon and Carré) Maillart
Nella, Baretti; *Dona Carmen,* A. Faivre; *Dame Andréa,* Vadé; *Cecco,* Balanqué; *Fernand,* Peschard; *Le Capitaine Barbagallo,* Wartel; *Nazoni,* Girardot.
1860 (9), '61 (14). *Total* 23.

1861

Director: Charles Réty

Jan. 16
LA MADONE op-c. 1 a. (Carmouche) Lacombe
Catarina, Orwil; *Matéo,* Vanaud; *Un Peintre,* Legrand.
1861 (4). *Total* 4.

Jan. 25
ASTAROTH† op-c. 1 a. (Boisseaux) Debillemont
Thécla, Gilliess; *Ulrich,* Delaunay-Ricquier; *Magnus* and *Astaroth,* Wartel.
1861 (27). *Total* 27.

Feb. 8
MADAME GRÉGOIRE op-c. 3 a. (Scribe and Boisseaux) Clapisson
Mme Grégoire, Rozies; *Mme d'Assonvilliers,* Moreau; *Lucette,* Faivre; *M. de Vaudreuil,* Delaunay-Ricquier; *Gaston,* Froment; *Zurich,* Lesage; *M. d'Assonvilliers,* Wartel; . . . . , Gabriel.
1861 (17). *Total* 17.

March 8
LES DEUX CADIS op-c. 1 a. (Gille and Furpille) Ymbert
Amine, A. Faivre; *Badroulboudour,* Wartel; *Bakbarok,* Girardot; *Hassan,* Grillon.
1861 (41), '62 (10). *Total* 51.

April 11
LA STATUE op-c. 3 a. (Barbier and Carré) Reyer
Margyane, Baretti; *Sélim,* Monjauze; *Amgyad,* Balanqué; *Kaloum,* Wartel; *Mouck,* Girardot; *Ali,* Martin.
1861 (44), '62 (9), '63 (6). *Total* 59.

May 8
AU TRAVERS DU MUR op-c. 1 a. (de Saint-Georges) Poniatowski
Blanche, Moreau; *Juliette,* A. Faivre; *Mme Gambetta,* M. Faivre; *Thomassin,* Battaille; *Gambetta,* Wartel; *Léon,* Legrand; *Pascal,* Grillon.
1861 (5). *Total* 5.

May 15
LE BUISSON VERT op-c. 1 a. (Fonteille) Gastinel
Louisa, Moreau; *Belmann,* Petit; *Gustave III,* Legrand; *Le Chambellan,* Serène; *Cornélius,* Leroy.
1861 (21). *Total* 21.

Oct. 22
LE NEVEU DE GULLIVER op-bt. 3 a. (Boisseaux) de Lajarte
Soudha-Jari, (dancer) Clavelle; *Rebecca,* A. Faivre; *Vieux-Quartier,* Vadé; *Pivoine,* Duclos; *Marcassite,* C. Vadé; *Aventurine,* M. Faivre; *John Gulliver,* Lefort; *Tom Sheep,* Surmont.
1861 (12), '62 (15). *Total* 27.

Nov. 16
LE CAFÉ DU ROI† op-c. 1 a. (Meilhac) Deffès
Le Baron de Gonesse/Louis XV, Girard; *Gilberte,* Baretti; *Le Marquis,* Wartel.
1861 (12), '62 (18). *Total* 30.

Nov. 19
LA NUIT AUX GONDOLES op-c. 1 a. (Barbier) Pascal
Rosalinde, Moreau; *Bettine,* A. Faivre; *Franz,* Peschard; *Le Prince Juliani,* Grillon; *Stéfano,* Legrand; *Placidus,* Wartel.
1861 (5). *Total* 5.

Dec. 6
LA TYROLIENNE op-c. 1 a. (de Saint-Georges and d'Artois) Leblicq
Suzanne, Baretti; *René*, Grillon; *Ortikoff*, Girardot.
1861 (10), '62 (18). *Total* 28.
Dec. 13
LA TÊTE ENCHANTÉE op-c. 1 a. (Dubreuil) Paliard
Isabelle, M. Faivre; *Cardenio*, Bonnet; *Don Gregorio*, Wartel; *Trufaldin*,
Gabriel; *Un Inquisiteur*, Vanaud.
1861 (7), '62 (11). *Total* 18.

1862

Directors: Charles Réty. From 8 October, Léon Carvalho

Jan. 21
JOSEPH† op. 3 a. (Duval) Méhul
Benjamin, A. Faivre; *Jeune Fille*, Durand; *Joseph*, Giovanni (Bazin); *Jacob*,
Petit; *Siméon*, Legrand; *Utobal*, Wartel.
1862 (27), '63 (10). *Total* 37.
March 18
LA CHATTE MERVEILLEUSE op-c. 3 a. (Dumanoir and d'Ennery) Grisar
La Princesse, C. Vadé; *Féline*, Cabel; *Alison*, Moreau; *La Fée aux Perles*,
Dubois; *Urbain*, Monjauze; *Babolin*, Lesage; *Marcel*, Vanaud; *L'Ogre de la
Forêt*, Wartel; *Le Roi*, Leroy.
1862 (62), '63 (10). *Total* 72.
April 11
L'ONCLE TRAUB op-c. 1 a. (Zaccone and Valois) Delavault
M. Faivre; Zévaco; Gabriel; Verdellet.
1862 (10) *Total* 10.
April 23
LA FILLE D'ÉGYPTE op-c. 2 a. (Barbier) Beer
Zemphira, Girard; *Mariquita*, A. Faivre; *Spada*, Balanqué; *Don Coconnas*,
Gabriel; *Nunez*, Leroy; *Pablo*, Peschard; *Diego*, Bonnet.
1862 (13). *Total* 13.
April 25
LA FLEUR DU VAL-SUZON op-c. 1 a. (Turpin de Sansay) Douay
Mignonne, M. Faivre; *Gaston*, Legrand; *Trinqualet*, Guyot; *Nicodeme*,
Girardot; *Un Capitaine*, Garcin.
1862 (9). *Total* 9.
May 24
LE PAYS DE COCAGNE op-c. 2 a. (Deforges) Thys
Violette, Baretti; *Columbine*, M. Faivre; *Le Roi*, Lefort; *Le Premier Ministre*,
Wartel; *Léandre, Gilles*, Verdellet, Surmont.
1862 (2). *Total* 2.

May 28
SOUS LES CHARMILLES op-c. 1 a. (Kauffmann) Dautresme
Henriette, La Comtesse, *Le Chevalier Fabio, Le Chevalier d'Almeida, Le Duc,*
Baretti; Zévaco, Peschard, Petit.*
1862 (3). *Total* 3.

1863

Director: Léon Carvalho

Jan. 7
L'ONDINE op-c. 3 a. (Lockroy and Mestépès) Semet
Ondine, Girard; *Berthe,* Moreau; *Marthe,* Duclos; *Rodolphe d'Aremberg,*
Cabel; *Fraisondin,* Battaille; *Duc d'Aremberg,* Serène; *Ulrich,* Gabriel.
1863 (7). *Total* 7.

March 31
PEINES D'AMOUR PERDUES† op. 4 a. (Barbier and Carré) Mozart
Princesse d'Aquitaine, Faure-Lefébvre; *Rosaline,* Cabel; *Jacquinette,* A.
Faivre; *Papillon,* Girard; *Prince de Navarre,* Léon Duprez; *Biron,* Petit; *Don
Armado,* Wartel; *Niaisot,* Trillet; *Caboche,* Gabriel; *Le Sénechal,* Guyot.
1863 (18). *Total* 18.

May 1
LES FIANCÉS DE ROSA op-c. 1 a. (Choler) Valgrand (de Grandval)
Rosa, Boyer; *Jenny,* A. Faivre; *Halifax,* Legrand; *Nigel,* Girardot; *Maître
Smith,* Wartel.
1863 (7). *Total* 7.

LE JARDINIER ET SON SEIGNEUR op-c. 1 a. (Barrière) Delibes
Petit-Pierre, A. Faivre; *Tiennette,* Estagel; *Margot,* Duclos; *Jean,* Gabriel; *Le
Baron,* Legrand; *Marcasse,* Wartel; *Mathurin,* Girardot.
1863 (11). *Total* 11.

Sept. 11
L'ÉPREUVE VILLAGEOISE† op-c. 2 a. (Desforges) Grétry
Denise, Faure-Lefébvre; *Mme Hubert,* Wilhème; *André,* Cabel; *M. Lafrance,*
Caillot.
1863 (26), '64 (19), '65 (3). *Total* 48.

Sept. 30
LES PÊCHEURS DE PERLES op. 3 a. (Cormon and Carré) Bizet
Leïla, de Maësen; *Nadir,* Morini; *Zurga,* Ismaël; *Nourabad,* Guyot.
1863 (18). *Total* 18.

*
Precise casting uncertain.

Nov. 4
LES TROYENS A CARTHAGE op. 5 a. (Berlioz) Berlioz
Didon, Charton-Demeur; *Anna,* Dubois; *Ascagne,* Estagel; *Enée,* Monjauze; *Narbal,* Petit; *Panthée,* Peront; *Iopas,* De Quercy; *Hylas,* Cabel; *Deux soldats,* Guyot, Teste; *Le Rapsode,* Jouanni;* ....., (Mme) Albrecht; ....., (Mme) Duclos.
1863 (21). *Total* 21.

Dec. 24
RIGOLETTO† op. 4 a. (Ed. Duprez) Verdi
Gilda, de Maësen; *Madeleine,* Dubois; *Le Duc,* Monjauze; *Rigoletto,* Ismaël; *Sparafucile,* Wartel; *Monterone,* Peront.
1863 (3), '64 (83), '65 (53), '66 (31), '67 (24), '68 (9), '69 (32), '70 (8). *Total* 243.

1864

Director: Léon Carvalho

March 19
MIREILLE op. 5 a. (Carré) Gounod
Mireille, Miolan-Carvalho; *Taven* and *Andreloun,* Faure-Lefébvre; *Vincenette,* Reboux; *Azalaïs,* Albrecht; *Norade,* Bayon; *Vincent,* Morini; *Ourrias,* Ismaël; *Maitre Ramon,* Petit; *Ambroise,* Wartel; *Le Passeur,* Peyront.
1864 (30), '65 (11). *Total* 41.

June 14
NORMA† op. 3 a. (Monnier) Bellini
Norma, Andrieux-Charry; *Adalgise,* de Maësen; *Pollione,* Puget; *Orovèse,* Petit.
1864 (8), '66 (5). *Total* 13.

Sept. 9
L'ALCADE op-c. 1 a. (Thierry and Denizet) Uzepy
Juanna Estagel; *Lorenzo,* Ambroselli; *Fabien,* Legrand; *Don José* (*L'Alcade*), Gabriel; *Deux Bandits,* Dervieux, Mortier.
1864 (5), '65 (7), '66 (10). *Total* 22.

DON PASQUALE† op-c. 3 a. (Royer and Vaëz) Donizetti
Louise (*Norina*), de Maësen; *Octave* (*Ernesto*), Gilland; *Le Docteur* (*Malatesta*), Troy; *Don Pasquale,* Ismaël; *Un Notaire,* Bach.
1864 (30), '65 (5). *Total* 35.

Oct. 27
VIOLETTA† op. 4 a. (Ed. Duprez) Verdi
Violetta, Nilsson; *Rodolphe,* Monjauze; *d'Orbel,* Lutz; *Clara,* Wilhème; *Annette,* Estagel; *Le Docteur Germont,* Peront; *Le Vicomte,* Legrand; *Le Baron,* Wartel; *Le Marquis,* Guyot; *Un Domestique,* Garçin.
1864 (25), '65 (26), '66 (20), '67 (9), '68 (8), '69 (14). *Total* 102.

---
*

Jouanni's real name was Juan Pedorlini. Originally he had been a bass singer in Adolphe Adam's ill fated Opéra National. He was a brother of *La Patrie* music critic, Franck-Marie (Franco-Maria Pedorlini).

Dec. 8
LES BÉGAIEMENTS D'AMOUR op-c. 1 a. (de Najac and Deulin) Grisar
Caroline, Faure-Lefébvre; *Polynice,* Froment; *Baptiste,* Guyot.
1864 (9), '65 (10), '68 (10), '69 (7). *Total* 36.
LE COUSIN BABYLAS op-c. 1 a. (E. Caspers) H. Caspers
Isabelle, Albrecht; *Pédrille,* Froment; *Le Docteur,* Wartel; *Babylas,* Gerpré.
1864 (9), '65 (39), '66 (11). *Total* 59.

1865

Director: Léon Carvalho

Jan. 26
L'AVENTURIER op-c. 4 a. (de Saint-Georges) Poniatowski
Dona Fernande, de Maësen; *Anita,* Faure-Lefébvre; *Don Manoël,* Monjauze;
Quirino, Ismaël; *Don Annibal,* Gerpré; *Le Vice-Roi,* Petit.
1865 (10). *Total* 10.
Feb. 23
LA FLÛTE ENCHANTÉE† op. 4 a. (Nuitter and Beaumont) Mozart
Pamina, Miolan-Carvalho; *La Reine de la Nuit,* Nilsson; *Papagena,* Ugalde;
1ère Fée, Albrecht; *2e Fée,* Estagel; *3e Fée,* Fonti; *Sarastro,* Depassio; *Tamino,*
Michot; *Monostatos,* Lutz; *Papageno,* Troy; *Bamboloda,* Gerpré; *Manès*
(*Speaker*), Petit; *1er Prêtre d'Isis,* Froment; *2e Prêtre d'Isis,* Laurent; *Trois*
Génies, Daram, Wilhème, Peyret; *Deux Hommes d'Armes,* Péront, Gilland.
1865 (117), '66 (10), '67 (37), '68 (8). *Total* 172.
March 22
LES MÉMOIRES DE FANCHETTE op-c. 1 a. (Desarbres) Gabrielli
Fanchette, Faure-Lefébvre; *Ursule,* Duclos; *Dufresny,* Froment; *Bournicourt,*
Guyot; *Valentin,* Mortier.
1865 (3). *Total* 3.
March 29
LE MARIAGE DE DON LOPE op-c. 1 a. (Barbier) de Hartog
Lucrèce, Wilhème; *Camille,* Albrecht; *Rosine,* Faure-Lefébvre; *Don Inigo,*
Gabriel; *Don Guzman,* Legrand; *Don Lope,* Gerpré.
1865 (24), '66 (3). *Total* 27.
April 21
MACBETH† op. 5 a. (Nuitter and Beaumont) Verdi
Lady Macbeth, Rey-Balla; *Dame d'honneur,* Meirot; *Macduff,* Monjauze;
Macbeth, Ismaël; *Banquo,* Petit; *Malcolm,* Huet; *Chef des Sicaires,* Cayot;
Officier du Palais, Troy; *Médecin,* Guyot; *1er Fantôme,* Peront; *2e Fantôme,*
Gilland; *3e Fantôme,* Renaudy; . . . . . , Estagel.
1865 (14). *Total* 14.
June 9
LE ROI CANDAULE op-c. 2 a. (Carré) Diaz
Nyssa, Daram; *Gygès,* Puget; *Candaule,* Wartel.
1865 (25), '66 (16). *Total* 41.
LISBETH OU LA CINQUANTAINE† op-c. 2 a. (Barbier) Mendelssohn

Lisbeth, Faure-Lefébvre; *Ursule,* Duclos; *Le Bourgmestre,* Wartel; *Kautz,* Petit; *Hermann,* Froment; *Martin,* Potier.
1865 (8). *Total* 8.
Sept. 22
LE ROI DES MINES op-c. 3 a. (Dubreuil) Chérouvrier
Christel, de Maësen; *La Comtesse Elphège,* Wilhème; *Otto,* Puget; *Le Comte Magnus,* Lutz; *Spiagudry,* Wartel; *Jonas,* Gabriel; *Un Soldat,* Garçin.
1865 (5). *Total* 5.
Oct. 13
LE RÊVE op-c. 1 a. (Chivot and Duru) Savary
Hélène, Estagel; *Le Docteur Walter,* Wartel; *Franz,* Froment.
1865 (7), '66 (1). *Total* 8.
Dec. 18
MARTHA† op-c. 4 a. (de Saint-Georges) Flotow
Lady Henriette, Nilsson; *Nancy,* Dubois; *Lord Tristan,* Wartel; *Lyonel,* Michot; *Plunkett,* Troy; *Un Juge,* Guyot.
1865 (6), '66 (76), '67 (48), '68 (28), '69 (5). *Total* 163.
Dec. 30
LA FIANCÉE D'ABYDOS op. 4 a. (Adenis) Barthe
Zuleika, Miolan-Carvalho; *Medjé,* Gilbert; *Giaffir,* Ismaël; *Selim,* Monjauze; *Haroun,* Lutz.
1865 (1), '66 (18). *Total* 19.

1866

Director: Léon Carvalho

May 8
DON JUAN† op. 2 a. (Trianon, Challamel and E. Gautier) Mozart
Donna Anna, Charton-Demeur; *Zerline,* Miolan-Carvalho; *Donna Elvire,* Nilsson; *Don Juan,* Barré; *Leporello,* Troy; *Don Ottavio,* Michot; *Le Commandeur,* Depassio; *Masetto,* Lutz.
1866 (53), '67 (1), '69 (17). *Total* 71.
May 25
LES JOYEUSES COMMÈRES DE WINDSOR† op-c. 3 a. (Barbier) Nicolai
Mme Ford, Saint-Urbain; *Mme Page,* Dubois; *Anne,* Daram; *Falstaff,* Ismaël; *Ford,* Wartel; *Fenton,* Du Wast; *Page,* Gabriel; *Nigaudin,* Gerpré; *Caius,* Caillaud.
1866 (7). *Total* 7.
June 13
LES DRAGÉES DE SUZETTE op-c. 1 a. (Barbier and Delahaye) Salomon
Suzette, Tual; *Joseph,* Froment; *Van Taff,* Wartel; *Champeaux,* Gabriel; *Germain,* Guyot.
1866 (8), '67 (16), '68 (11), '70 (1). *Total* 36
LE SORCIER op-c. 1 a. (Anaïs Marcelli) Anaïs Marcelli
Martha, Tual; *Jeannette,* Demay; *Françoise,* Ladois; *La Comtesse,* Duclos; *Le*

Sorcier, Wartel; *Raimbaud,* Froment. *Le Comte,* Guyot; *1er Brigand,* Garcin; *2e Brigand,* Berman; *Un Soldat,* Grout.
1866 (6), '67 (8), '68 (16). *Total* 30.

1867

Director: Leon Carvalho

Jan. 14
DÉBORAH op-c. 3 a. (Favre and Plouvier) Devin-Duvivier
Déborah, Talvo-Bedogni; *Diana Honor,* Daram; *Annette,* Demay; *Allan MacDonald,* Puget; *MacHonor,* Lutz; *Robin Chrystal,* Legrand; *Fergus Lorimer,* Troy jeune; *Jonas Piper,* Laurent; *Fallah,* Neveu.
1867 (3). *Total* 3.

Feb. 8
SARDANAPALE op. 3 a. (Becque) Joncières
Myrrha, Nilsson; *Sardanapale,* Monjauze; *Salémène,* Lutz; *Béléses,* Cazaux; *Arbace,* Laurent; *Pania,* Legrand; *Un Soldat,* Guyot.
1867 (16). *Total* 16.

April 27
ROMÉO ET JULIETTE op. 5 a. (Barbier and Carré) Gounod
Juliette, Miolan-Carvalho; *Stéphano,* Daram; *Gertrude,* Duclos; *Capulet,* Troy; *Roméo,* Michot; *Frère Laurent,* Cazaux; *Tybalt,* Puget; *Paris,* Laveissière; *Mercutio,* Barré; *Benvolio,* Laurent? Legrand? *Le Duc de Vérone,* Wartel; *Grégorio,* Troy jeune; *Frère Jean,* Neveu; *Montaigu,* Lutz.
1867 (89), '68 (1). *Total* 90.

June 14
LA SOMNAMBULE† op. 3 a. (Monnier) Bellini
Amina, Devriès; *Lise,* Wilhème; *Thérèse,* Rouvroy; *Elvino,* Vitaux; *Le Comte,* Lutz; *Alexis,* Troy jeune; *Le Notaire,* Guyot.
1867 (12). *Total* 12.

Oct. 23
LES BLEUETS op-c. 4 a. (Cormon and Trianon) Cohen
Estelle, Nilsson; *Sœur Dorothée,* Tual; *Dinarda,* Wilhème; *Béatrix,* Dardenne; *Fabio,* Bosquin; *Mengo,* Troy; *Juan II,* Lutz; *L'Infant,* Legrand; *Don Alvar,* Guyot; *Don Gusman,* Neveu; *Don Pedro,* Boudias; *Don Ruy,* Troy jeune; *Don Sanche,* Baretti; *Un Huissier,* Garçin; *Don Luys,* Fontenay.
1867 (9). *Total* 9.

Dec. 11
CARDILLAC op. 3 a. (Nuitter and Beaumont) Dautresme
Madeleine, Daram *Mme Lamartinière,* Duclos; *Olivier Brusson,* Bosquin; *Maître Cardillac,* Ismaël; *Comte de Moissens,* Barré; *Desgrais,* Wartel.
1867 (5). *Total* 5.

Dec. 26
LA JOLIE FILLE DE PERTH op. 4 a. (de Saint-Georges and Adenis) Bizet
Catherine, Devriès; *Mab,* Ducasse; *Le Duc,* Barré; *Henri,* Massy; *Ralph,* Lutz;

Simon, Wartel; *Un Majordome,* Guyot; *Un Ouvrier,* Neveu; *Un Seigneur,* Boudias.
1867 (3), '68 (15). *Total* 18.

1868

Directors: Léon Carvalho. From 22 August, Jules Etienne Pasdeloup

Nov. 16
L'IRATO† op-c. 1 a. (Marsollier) Méhul
Isabelle, Duval; *Nérine,* Ducasse; *Le Docteur,* Legrand; *Pandolphe,* Wartel; *Scapin,* Caillot; *Lysandre,* Raoult.
1868 (1). *Total* 1.

Nov. 26
IPHIGÉNIE EN TAURIDE† op. 4 a. (Guillard) Gluck
Iphigénie, Gaston-Lacaze; *Diane,* Lisarti; *Une Grecque,* Priola; *Pylade,* Bosquin; *Oreste,* Aubéry; *Thoas,* Caillot; *Le Ministre,* Labat; *Un Scythe,* Grignon.
1868 (11), '69 (4). *Total* 15.

Dec. 23
LE BRASSEUR DE PRESTON† op-c. 3 a. (de Leuven and Brunswick) Adam
Effie, Daram; *Robinson,* Meillet; *Toby,* Wartel; *Jenkins,* Legrand; *Mulgrave,* Giraudet; *Lovel,* Géraizer; *Bob,* Verdellet.
1868 (5), '69 (43), '70 (12). *Total* 60.

1869

Director: Jules Etienne Pasdeloup

March 5
EN PRISON op-c. 1 a. (Chaigneau and Boverat) Guiraud
Formosa, Ducasse; *Trombolino,* Legrand; *Lélio,* Verdellet; *Nigodini,* Gabriel; *Cascaro,* Guyot; *Un Garçon,* Larout; *Un Messager,* Garcin.
1869 (18), '70 (3). *Total* 21.

April 6
RIENZI† op. 5 a. (Nuitter and Guilliaume) Wagner
Irène, Sternberg; *Adriano,* Borghèse; *Le Messager,* Priola; *Rienzi,* Monjauze; *Baroncelli,* Massy; *Cecco,* Bacquié; *Orsini,* Lutz; *Colonna,* Giraudet; *Raimondo,* Labat.
1869 (37), '70 (1). *Total* 38.

May 10
DON QUICHOTTE op-c. 3 a. (Barbier and Carré) Boulanger
La Duchesse, Priola; *Alonza,* Duval; *Thérèse,* Ducasse; *Maritorne,* Denault;

Don Quichotte, Giraudet; *Sancho,* Meillet; *Le Bachelier Carrasco,* Verdellet; *Basile,* Raoult; *L'Hôtelier,* Gabriel; *Un Berger,* Guyot.
1869 (18). *Total* 18.

Sept. 21
LE DERNIER JOUR DE POMPÉI op. 4 a. (Nuitter and Beaumont) Joncières
Ione, Schroeder; *Nydia,* Vercken; *La Saga du Vésuve,* Borghese; *Hermès,* Massy; *Pythéas,* Bacquié; *Diophas,* Jalama; *Claudius,* Brisson; *Diomède,* Grignon; *Milon,* Guyot; *Le Prêteur,* Aubert; *Lydon,* Bryart; *Tetraides,* Gourdon.
1869 (13). *Total* 13.

Nov. 17
LE BAL MASQUÉ† op. 4 a. (Ed. Duprez) Verdi
Amelia, Meillet; *Ulrique,* Borghèse; *Edgard,* Daram; *Richard,* Massy; *Renato,* Lutz; *Sylvano,* Bacquié; *Samuel,* Aubert; *Tom,* Giraudet; *Le Grand Juge,* Auguez; *Un Valet,* Brisson.
1869 (24), '70 (41). *Total* 65.

Dec. 30
LA BOHÉMIENNE† op. 4 a. (de Saint-Georges) Balfe
La Reine Mabb, Wertheimber; *Sarah,* Brunet-Lafleur; *Martha,* Andrieux; *Stenio de Stoltberg,* Monjauze; Le Comte d'Arnheim, Lutz; *Trousse-Diable,* Bacquié; *Narcisse de Krakentorp,* Jalama; *Un Paysan,* Auguez; *Un Bohémien,* Guyot; *Un Officier des troupes de l'Empereur,* Brisson.
1869 (1), '70 (28). *Total* 29.

1870

Directors: Jules Etienne Pasdeloup. From 1 February until 31 May, les artistes en société.

April 5
CHARLES VI† op. 5 a. (C. and G. Delavigne) Halévy
Odette, Bloch; *Isabeau de Bavière,* Daram; *Le Dauphin,* Massy; *Charles VI,* Lutz; *Raymond,* Giraudet; *Le Duc de Bedfort,* Caillot; *L'Homme de la forêt,* Staveni; *Tanguy-Duchâtel,* Labat; *Saintrailles,* Legrand; *Dunois,* Jalama; *La Hire,* Auguez; *Un Soldat,* Copel.
1870 (22). *Total* 22.

Appendix B

List of composers and their operas performed at the Théâtre Lyrique with dates of first performances there. Operas originally performed at other theatres are identified by the symbol †.

ADAM. Adolphe Charles, 1803–1856
La Poupée de Nuremberg	21. 2. '52
Si j'étais Roi	4. 9. '52
† Le Postillon de Lonjumeau	3. 11. '52
† Le Roi d'Yvetot	5. 1. '53
Le Roi des Halles	11. 4. '53
Le Bijou perdu	6. 10. '53
† La Reine d'un Jour	25. 4. '54
Le Muletier de Tolède	16. 12. '54
A Clichy	24. 12. '54
Falstaff	18. 1. '56
† Le Sourd, ou l'Auberge pleine	18. 1. '56
Mam'zelle Geneviève	22. 3. '56
† Le Brasseur de Preston	23. 12. '68

AUBER. Daniel François Esprit, 1782–1871
† La Sirène	19. 6. '55

BALFE. Michael William, 1808–1870
† La Bohémienne (The Bohemian Girl)	30. 12. '69

BARBIER. Frédéric Etienne, 1829–1889
Une Nuit à Seville	14. 9. '55
Rose et Narcisse	21. 11. '55

BARTHE. Gratien-Norbert (Adrien), 1828–1898
La Fiancée d'Abydos	30. 12. '65

BEER. Jules, c. 1835
La Fille d'Égypte	23. 4. '62

BEETHOVEN. Ludwig van, 1770–1827
† Fidelio	5. 5. '60

BELLINI. Vincenzo, 1801–1835
† Norma	14. 6. '64
† La Somnambule (La Sonnambula)	14. 6. '67

BERLIOZ. Louis Hector, 1803–1869
Les Troyens à Carthage   4. 11. '63

BIZET. Alexandre César Léopold (Georges) 1838–1875
Les Pêcheurs de Perles   30. 9. '63
La Jolie Fille de Perth   26. 12. '67

BOIELDIEU. François Adrien, 1775–1834
† *Ma Tante Aurore ou Le Roman impromptu*   18. 10. '51

BOIELDIEU. Adrien Louis Victor, 1816–1883
La Butte des Moulins   6. 1. '52
La Fille invisible   24. 2. '54

BOISSELOT. Dominique François Xavier, 1811–1893
Mosquita la Sorcière   27. 9. '51

BOULANGER. Ernest Henri Alexandre, 1815–1900
Don Quichotte   10. 5. '69

BOUSQUET. Georges, 1818–1854
Tabarin   22. 12. '52

CARAFA DI COLOBRANO. Michele Enrico Francesco Vincenzo
Aloisio Paolo, 1787–1872
† *Le Solitaire*   14. 12. '55

CASPERS. Louis Henri Jean, 1825–1906
Le Chapeau du Roi   16. 4. '56
Ma Tante dort   21. 1. '60
Le Cousin Babylas   8. 12. '64

CHÉROUVRIER. Edmond Marie, 1831–1905
Le Roi des Mines   22. 9. '65

CLAPISSON. Antoine Louis, 1808–1866
La Promise   16. 3. '54
Dans les Vignes   31. 12. '54
La Fanchonnette   1. 3. '56
Margot   5. 11. '57
Madame Grégoire   8. 2. '61

COHEN. Jules Emile David, 1835–1901
Les Bleuets   23. 10. '67

CUZENT. Paul, 1814–1856
L'Habit de Noce   29. 12. '55

DALAYRAC. Nicolas, 1753–1809
† *Maison à vendre*   9. 11. '51
† *Ambroise, ou Voilà ma Journée*   16. 11. '51

DAUTRESME. Auguste Lucien, 1826–1892
Sous les Charmilles   28. 5. '62
Cardillac   11. 12. '67

DAVID. Félicien César, 1810–1876
La Perle du Brésil   22. 11. '51

DEBILLEMONT. Jean-Jacques, 1824–1879
†*Astaroth*   25. 1. '61

DEFFÈS. Pierre Louis, 1819–1900
Broskovano   29. 9. '58
Les petits Violons du Roi   30. 9. '59
†*Le Café du Roi*   16. 11. '61

DÉJAZET. Eugène Joseph, 1819–1880
Le Mariage en l'Air   26. 1. '52

DELAVAULT. Eugène, 1814–1892
L'Oncle Traub   11. 4. '62

DELIBES. Clément Philibert Léo, 1836–1891
Maître Griffard   3. 10. '57
Le Jardinier et son Seigneur   1. 5. '63

DEVIENNE. François, 1759–1803
†*Le Pensionnat de jeunes Demoiselles (Les Visitandines)*   11. 2. '52

DEVIN DUVIVIER. Jean Adolphe Hippolyte, 1827–?
Déborah   14. 1. '67

DIAZ (de la Peña). Eugène Emile, 1837–1901
Le Roi Candaule   9. 6. '65

'DIVERS AUTEURS'
Le Present et l'Avenir   28. 5. '53
La Princesse de Trébisonde   4. 9. '53

DONIZETTI (Domenico) Gaetano (Maria), 1797–1848
†*Elisabeth, ou la Fille du Proscrit (Otto Mesi in due ore, ossia   31. 12. '53
Gli Esiliati in Siberia)*
†*Don Pasquale*   9. 9. '64

DOUAY. Georges, 1840–?
La Fleur du Val-Suzon   25. 4. '62

DUFRESNE. Alfred, 1822–1863
Les Valets de Gascogne   2. 6. '60

DUPREZ. Gilbert Louis, 1806–1896
†*Joanita (L'Abîme de la Maladetta)*   11. 3. '52

FLOTOW. Friedrich Ferdinand Adolf von, 1812–1883
†*Martha (Martha oder Der Markt von Richmond)*   18. 12. '65

GABRIELLI. Nicolo, 1814–1891
Les Mémoires de Fanchette   22. 3. '65

GASTINEL. Léon Gustave Cyprien, 1823–1906
Le Buisson vert   15. 5. '61

GAUTIER. Jean François Eugène, 1822–1878
Murdock le Bandit	23. 10. '51
Flore et Zéphire	2. 10. '52
Choisy-le-Roi	14. 10. '52
Le Lutin de la Vallée	22. 1. '53
Le Danseur du Roi	22. 10. '53
Schahabaham II	31. 10. '54

GEVAERT. François Auguste, 1828–1908
Georgette, ou Le Moulin de Fontenoy	28. 11. '53
Le Billet de Marguerite	7. 10. '54
Les Lavandières de Santarem	25. 10. '55

GIRARD. Narcisse, 1797–1860
† *Les Deux Voleurs*	8. 11. '52

GLUCK. Christoph Willibald, 1714–1787
† *Orphée (Orfeo ed Euridice)*	18. 11. '59
† *Iphigénie en Tauride*	26. 11. '68

GODEFROID. Dieudonné Joseph Guillaume Félix, 1818–1897
La Harpe d'Or	8. 9. '58

GOUNOD. Charles François, 1818–1893
Le Medecin malgré lui	15. 1. '58
Faust	19. 3. '59
Philémon et Baucis	18. 2. '60
Mireille	19. 3. '64
Roméo et Juliette	27. 4. '67

GRANDVAL. Marie Félicie Clémence, [de Reiset] Vicomtesse de, 1830–1907
Les Fiancés de Rosa	1. 5. '63

GRÉTRY. André Ernest Modeste, 1741–1813
† *Le Tableau parlant*	1. 6. '54
† *Richard Cœur-de-Lion*	23. 5. '56
† *L'Epreuve villageoise (Theodore et Paulin)*	11. 9. '63

GRISAR. Albert, 1808–1869
† *Les Travestissements*	30. 11. '51
Les Amours du Diable	11. 3. '53
La Chatte merveilleuse	18. 3. '62
Bégaiements d'Amour	8. 12. '64

GUIRAUD. Ernest, 1837–1892
En Prison	5. 3. '69

HALÉVY. Jacques François Fromental Elie, 1799–1862
Jaguarita l'Indienne	14. 5. '55
L'Inconsolable	13. 6. '55
† *Le Val d'Andorre*	15. 10. '60
† *Charles VI*	5. 4. '70

SAVARY. Edmond, 1835–?
  Le Rêve 13. 10. '65

SELLENICK. Adolphe Valentin, 1820–1893
  Crispin, Rival de son Maître 1. 9. '60

SEMET. Théophile Aimé Émile, 1824–1888
  Les Nuits d'Espagne 26. 5. '57
  La Demoiselle d'Honneur 30. 12. '57
  Gil Blas 24. 3. '60
  L'Ondine 7. 1. '63

SOLIÉ (SOULIÉ, SOULIER). Jean Pierre, 1755–1812
  † *Le Diable à quatre* 15. 10. '53

THOMAS. Charles Louis Ambroise, 1811–1896
  † *Le Panier fleuri* 26. 3. '54

THYS. Pauline, (Mme Sébault) 1836–1909
  Le Pays de Cocagne 24. 5. '62

UZEPY.
  L'Alcade 9. 9. '64

VARNEY. Pierre Joseph Alphonse, 1811–1879
  La Ferme de Kilmoor 27. 10. '52

VERDI. Giuseppe (Fortunino Francesco), 1813–1901
  † *Rigoletto* 24. 12. '63
  † *Violetta (La Traviata)* 27. 10. '64
  † *Macbeth* 21. 4. '65
  † *Le Bal masqué (Un Ballo in Maschera)* 17. 11. '69

VILBAC. Alphonse Zoé Charles Renaud de, 1829–1884
  Don Almanzor 16. 4. '58

VILLEBLANCHE.
  Les Fiançailles des Roses 21. 2. '52

VOGEL. Charles Louis Adolphe, 1808–1892
  La Moissonneuse 3. 9. '53

Wagner. Wilhelm Richard, 1813–1883
  † *Rienzi* 6. 4. '69

WEBER. Carl Maria Friedrich Ernst von, 1786–1826
  † *Robin des Bois (Der Freischütz)* 24. 1. '55
  † *Oberon* 27. 2. '57
  † *Euryanthe* 1. 9. '57
  † *Preciosa* 16. 4. '58
  † *Abou Hassan (Abu Hassan)* 11. 5. '59

WECKERLIN. Jean Baptiste Théodore, 1821–1910
  L'Organiste dans l'Embarras 17. 5. '53

YMBERT. Théodore,
Les Deux Cadis

8. 3. '61

Total creations: 118

Appendix C

Glossary of lesser known opera composers whose works were performed at the Théâtre Lyrique. The list includes only those names not to be found in *Grove's Dictionary of Music and Musicians* (Fifth Edition).

BARBiER Frédéric-Etienne (b. Metz 15 November 1829; d. Paris 12 February 1889). Educated at Bourges where at the same time he studied piano and harmony under an organist in that town. His first stage work a one act opera comique, *Le Mariage de Colombine* was produced there. Went to Paris where he had lessons from Adolphe Adam. Composed up to 80 ephemeral opérettes and ballets. He was conductor at the Théâtre International during the 1867 Exhibition and later at the Alcazar. He also wrote articles and reviews for some unimportant music journals. Besides Théâtre Lyrique had works performed at the Folies-Nouvelles, Déjazet, Folies-Marigny, Bouffes-Parisiens, Fantaisies-Parisiennes, Eldorado, Folies-Bergère, Alcazar, etc., etc., also many chansonnettes for the café-concerts, besides much piano music and opera-fantaisies arranged for orchestra.

BARTHE Gratien-Norbert (Adrien) (b. Bayonne 7 June 1828; d. Asnières 13 August 1898). Studied piano and composition at Paris Conservatoire. Won first Prix de Rome with a cantata, *Francesca de Rimini* in 1854. The Académie thought so highly of his later envoi from Rome, an oratorio, *Judith* that he was awarded the Prix Edouard Rodrigues. Following the failure of *La Fiancée d'Abydos* in 1865 he seems to have ceased composing, at least for the stage.

BEER Jules (b. c. 1835, still living 1902). Fétis describes him as 'a musical amateur with exalted ambitions'. He was also very rich. As a nephew of the great Meyerbeer his position as a composer was at least contentious. With *La Fille d'Egypte* he had two opérettes performed at his home in 1859 and 1861 and a grand opera, *Elisabeth de Hongrie* performed at the Monnaie, Brussels, in March 1871. The latter was received with complete indifference. On the death of his illustrious uncle he composed a funeral march in his honour which, it seems, he insisted on playing to Rossini. Rossini listened attentively and when it had ended murmured, 'Good! Very good! but perhaps it would have been better if you had been the one to die and if the funeral march were by your uncle.'

BOISSELOT Dominique-François-Xavier (b. Montpellier 3 December 1811; d. Paris 10 April 1893). Son of a violin and piano manufacturer established in Montpellier, Marseille and Barcelona. Learned elements of music in the former city and then entered the Conservatoire of Paris. Later studied under Fétis and Lesueur, marrying the latter's daughter. Prix de Rome winner in 1836. Was appointed inspector-general of music schools and theatres in Marseille in 1867. His three act work, *Ne touchez pas à la Reine* was very successful at the Opéra-Comique in 1847.

BOULANGER Ernest-Henri-Alexandre (b. Paris 16 December 1815; d. Paris 14 April 1900). Son of a 'cello professor, attached to the Chapelle du Roi, and of the Opéra-Comique mezzo-soprano, Marie-Julie Boulanger (née Halligner and father of Lili and Nadia Boulanger. His wife was Princess Raïssa Mychetsky which explains Nadia's Russian name). Pupil of Halévy and Lesueur at the Paris Conservatoire. Seven of his works were produced at the Opéra-Comique. Also composed choruses for the Orphéons and songs. He possessed an attractive tenor voice and was professor of singing at the Conservatoire for 22 years.

CASPERS Louis-Henri-Jean (b. Paris 2 October 1825; d. 1906). Son of a Dutch or German piano manufacturer said to have come to Paris during the time of Charles X. Studied at Paris Conservatoire. Besides the Théâtre Lyrique, his stage works were produced at the Opéra-Comique, Bouffes-Parisiens and Porte-Saint-Martin. Cantata for chorus and orchestra, nocturnes, fantaisies and songs. Following his father's death in 1861 he abandoned composition in order to take over the family business.

CHÉROUVRIER Edmond-Marie (b. Sablé-sur-Sarthe 7 February 1831; d. 1905). Was a good pianist by the age of six. Sent to the College of Religious Music in Vaugirard close to Paris where at 14 he composed an 'Ave Maria' without any previous training. Later settled in Le Mans where he composed a number of Masses for the cathedral and some symphonic pieces for the local Société Philharmonique. A wealthy aunt having bequeathed him 300,000 francs he set out for Paris to study at the Conservatoire, but does not appear to have been accepted. Nevertheless he won a second Prix de Rome in 1858. At the time of the Commune was maire-adjoint of the 14th arrondissement of Montrouge, and on the establishment of the regular government was appointed maire. He did not neglect composition entirely, however, and composed a Mass for the church at Montrouge in 1876, and a four-act opera, *Gilles de Bretagne* which does not seem to have been ever performed.

CUZENT Paul (b. 1814; d. St. Petersburg 5 July 1856). Amateur musician and celebrated bare-back horse rider. His mother came of a travelling circus family, his father was a sailor but after a time joined the troupe. Cuzent early became a noted equestrian. At the same time he had learned to play several instruments. In 1844, with his brother-in-law he formed an equestrian team which toured Holland, Prussia and Russia with considerable success. (Another brother-in-law was the tenor, Monjauze). The Emperor Nicholas I invited him to establish a circus in St. Petersburg. Having found fame and fortune he returned to France where he settled at Meulan on the Seine and gave his time to composition. Besides *L'Habit de Noce*, he composed an opera, *Le Démon des Bois*, staged at the Salle Bonne-Nouvelle in 1853. He composed the music for almost all the equestrian exercises at the Cirque as well as a number of melodies.

DAUTRESME Auguste-Lucien (b. Elbeuf 21 May 1826; d. 18 February 1892). First music studies at the Royal College, Rouen. In 1846 entered the Ecole Polytechnique from which he graduated as a naval officer. Found he did not like the sea so he returned to Elbeuf for a business career. His early interest in music had persisted, however, and he now took lessons in composition from the pianist, Jean Amédée Méreaux, then teaching in Rouen. Méreaux encouraged him to enter the Paris Conservatoire to prepare for the Prix de Rome. His dispute with Carvalho and subsequent prison sentence have been recorded. On his release from gaol, for a time he contributed articles on music to the *Paris-Magazine*. As early as 1848 he had shown political awareness taking the liberal side in the revolution of that year, and in 1876 he would be elected to the National Assembly of the Third Republic, becoming Minister for Commerce in 1888. His purely musical compositions included two madrigals in the style of Orlande de Lassus, a sonata, some melodies and choruses for the Orphéons.

DEBILLEMONT Jean-Jacques (b. Dijon 12 December 1824; d. Paris 15 February 1879). Commenced study of the violin at the age of nine and came to Paris to enter the Conservatoire at the age of 15. Some time later joined the orchestra of the Opéra-Comique. Concurrently studied composition under Leborne and Carafa, winning a Prix de Rome. The Municipal Theatre of Dijon presented his first operas. In Paris subsequent works were given at the Théâtre Lyrique, Bouffes-Parisiens, Porte-Saint-Martin, Folies-Marigny, Fantaisies-Parisiennes, etc. In 1876 he became conductor at the Porte-Saint-Martin. He wrote numerous reviews for the Paris musical press.

DEFFÈS Pierre-Louis (b. Toulouse 25 July 1819; d. Toulouse 10 June 1900). First music studies at the Conservatoire of his native city. At age 20 was admitted to the Paris Conservatoire where he was a pupil of Halévy. Prix de Rome winner in 1847. His first stage work was performed at the Opéra-Comique. Operas also given at Théâtre Lyrique, Bouffes-Parisiens, Menus-Plaisirs, Athénée and at the Kursaal in Bad-Ems. A Mass by him was given at Notre-Dame in 1857 but in the theatre his style echoed Offenbach and Lecocq. Appointed director of the Conservatoire of Toulouse in 1883 in which city his name survives as the composer of 'La Toulousaine', the regional anthem.

DÉJAZET Eugène-Joseph (b. Lyon 11 February 1819; d. February 1880). Son of a very popular Paris actress at the Théâtre des Variétés for whom he wrote a great number of songs. Directed the Théâtre du Vaudeville, Brussels, during 1852–53. In 1859 his mother, then aged 61 took over the Théâtre des Folies-Nouvelles which was re-named Théâtre Déjazet, for which he wrote several slight opérettes.

DELAVAULT Eugène (b. Niort (Deux Sèvres) 8 April 1814; d. Niort 24 September 1892) A rich dilettante, the son of a well known amateur painter. He was a professor of mathematics who entered politics. In all, he composed six operas, an oratorio and a Pontifical Mass, for which Pope Pius IX rewarded him with the Cross of St. Gregory the Great.

DEVIN-DUVIVIER Jean-Adolphe-Hippolyte (b. Liverpool 22 May 1827). Son of a music teacher, Eugène Devin. At the age of 12 went with his parents to Berlin where he remained until 1847 receiving music lessons from Professor Dehn. Coming to Paris he entered the Conservatoire under Halévy. Also studied piano with Moscheles and singing with Manuel Garcia. Set some poems by Théophile Gautier to music. Became a church organist and also conducted the orchestra of the Théâtre Délassements-Comiques during the brief sojourn of that theatre in the rue de Provence. An orchestral work by him, 'Le Triomphe de Bacchus', was given at a Saturday Popular Concert in the Alexandra Palace in 1875. Other compositions were a symphony and an overture, 'Over hill, over dale'.

DIAZ (de la Peña), Eugène-Emile (b. Paris 27 February 1837; d. Colleville (Calvados) 12 September 1901). Son of the Barbizon painter Narciso Virgilio Diaz de la Peña (1808-1876). Entered Reber's class in the Paris Conservatoire in 1852, later coming under Halévy. In 1868 he became leader of the orchestra at the Théâtre du Prince Impérial. His best known work La Coupe du Roi de Thulé was produced at the Opéra in 1873. In 1886 he is described as a 'painter-inventor-musician' who has devised a method for stopping run-away horses! An obituary notice mentions that he cultivated painting at the same time as music, finding in it part of his livelihood. Towards the end of his life he seems to have turned to painting entirely. His last stage work, *Benvenuto* was produced at the Opéra-Comique in 1890, and shortly before he died is said to have remarked, 'I paint pictures for America, that yields more than the composition of operas'.

DOUAY Georges (b. Paris 7 January 1840). Wealthy amateur composer. Wrote numerous one act opérettes for Théâtre Lyrique, Folies-Marigny, Bouffes-Parisiens, Délassements-Comiques, Alcazar, Cluny, etc., etc., and composed a great number of chansons and chansonnettes for the café-concerts.

DUFRESNE Alfred (b. 1822; d. 4 March 1863). Pupil of Halévy at the Paris Conservatoire. Had one act opérettes performed at Théâtre Lyrique and Bouffes-Parisiens. Also composed songs.

GASTINEL Léon-Gustave-Cyprien (b. Villers-les-Pots (Côte-d'Or) 1 August 1823; d. Fresnes-Lès-Rungis 20 October 1906). Composer and violinist. Another pupil of Halévy at the Paris Conservatoire and a Prix de Rome winner. Stage works also performed at Opéra-Comique and Bouffes-Parisiens. Composed oratorios, church music, symphonies, chamber music, and choruses for the Orphéons and songs.

GAUTIER Jean-François-Eugène (b. Vaugirard, near Paris 27 February 1822; d. Paris 1 April 1878). Admitted to Paris Conservatoire, December 1831, where he studied violin with Habeneck and composition with Halévy. Won second Prix de Rome. Successively, a leading violinist in the orchestras of the Opéra and Sociétés des Concerts du Conservatoire, and in 1846, 'Chef du Chant' at the Théâtre Italien. For several years was 'maître de chapelle' at the church of Saint-Eugène. Became professor of history of music at the Conservatoire in 1872. Helped to translate a number of Mozart's operas and Weber's *Der Freischütz* into French. Was a well-known Paris music critic. Composed about 15 stage works mostly performed at the Théâtre Lyrique and Opéra-Comique, besides an oratorio and a few minor pieces.

GIRARD Narcisse (b. Nantes 28 January 1797; d. Paris 16 January 1860). Pupil of Reicha. Conductor at the Opéra Italien 1830–32, at the Opéra-Comique 1837–46, and at the Opéra (having taken over from Habeneck), 1846 until his death. Was also violin professor at the Conservatoire. Stage works (including *Les Deux Voleurs*) performed at the Opéra-Comique. Died suddenly on the podium of the Opéra while conducting a performance of *Les Huguenots.*

GRANDVAL Marie-Félicie Clémence [de Reiset] Vicomtesse de (b. Chateau de La Cour-du-Bois, Mamers (Sarthe) 21 January 1830; d. Paris 15 January 1907). At about age 12 became a pupil of Flotow who was a family friend. Later placed herself under Camille Saint-Saëns with whom she studied composition uninterruptedly for two years. Composed under the pseudonyms—among others—of 'Caroline Blangy' and 'Clemence Valgrand.' Operas produced at Théâtre Lyrique, Opéra-Comique, Théâtre Italien, Bouffes-Parisien, Baden-Baden and Bordeaux. Also a symphonic poem, an oratorio, a Mass (performed at St. Eustache) and some pieces played at the Concerts Colonne.

HARTOG Edouard de (b. Amsterdam 15 August 1829; d. The Hague 8 November 1909). Son of a banker and intended for commerce but his vocation was so genuine that his father placed no obstacle in his way to becoming a musician and he received a good artistic education. Travelling to Paris he became a pupil of Elwart and Litolff. Later studied composition with Gustave Heinze, a pupil of Mendelssohn who had settled in Holland. A second stage work at the Fantaisies-Parisiennes, a symphonic prologue for Schiller's *Maid of Orleans* a symphony, a Mass, instrumental and vocal music and choruses.

HENRION Paul (b. Paris 20 July 1819; d. Paris 24 October 1901). At age 11 was apprenticed as a watch-maker to his elder brother but soon left to become a strolling player through the small towns of France. After four years returned to his family in Paris and commenced study of piano and harmony. Composed first under pseudonym of Charlemagne. He would write over a thousand popular songs and his 'Un jour' had a great vogue about 1840. As well as the Théâtre Lyrique production, composed an opérette for the Théâtre des Variétés, many chansons and chansonnettes for café-concerts and piano music for dances.

HIGNARD Jean-Louis-Aristide (b. Nantes 20 May 1822; d. Vernon March 1898). Entered Paris Conservatoire in 1845 as a pupil of Halévy. Second Prix de Rome in 1850. First opera comique performed at Nantes in 1851. Later works at the Théâtre Lyrique and Bouffes-Parisiens. Composed a five act 'drame-lyrique', *Hamlet.* This was a melodrama consisting of spoken dialogue accompanied symphonically by the orchestra. Apart from its unorthodox form, it had the added disadvantage of appearing in 1868 the year Ambroise Thomas' *Hamlet* was produced at the Opéra and so was not performed until 1888 in his native city. Also composed songs, waltzes and a great number of choruses. Was one of Emmanuel Chabrier's teachers.

LEBLICQ Charles-Théodore (b. Brussels 15 August 1833; d. Schaerbecklez-Bruxelles 8 October 1875). Entered Conservatoire of his native city in 1851 where he was a pupil of Fétis for composition. Composed a Mass, sung by the choir of Sainte Gudule in 1856, also an overture, 'Gustave Wasa'.

MARCELLI Anaïs (d. Paris December 1878). Pseudonym of Mme Anaïs de Perrière-Pilté whose wealth and social position gained her an entry to the theatre. Usually was her own librettist. Had a theatre built in her home in the rue Monsieur where her three act opera comique, *Les Vacances de l'Amour* was performed in 1867. Previous to *Le Sorcier* had an earlier opérette *La Contagion* produced at the Beaumarchais in June 1859, and later, another, *Jaloux de soi*, at the Athénée in 1873, as well as a three act play, *Le Talon d'Achille* at the Ventadour in 1875.

MONTAUBRY Jean-Baptiste-Edouard (b. Niort 27 March 1824). First lessons from his father, also a musician. Later, Paris Conservatoire in Habeneck's class. Appointed first, deputy, later, principal conductor at the Théâtre du Vaudeville. Composed many successful operas for this theatre, and especially, a play with music, *Les Filles de Marbre* in which Marco's rondo captured all Paris. Also composed opérettes for the Folies-Nouvelles. Encouraged by the success of his brother, the well-known tenor Achille-Félix, he then trained as a tenor himself, and as such sought engagements in the provinces. Since he was then almost forty years old it was scarcely a judicious change. Subsequently returned to composition with works for the Théâtre Séraphin and Folies Marigny between 1869 and 1875.

MONTUORO Achille (b. Naples, ?1836). May have been the same artist who was appointed director of the Teatro San Carlo Naples in 1862. He certainly returned to Italy from Paris and in 1869 had an opera *Fieschi* produced at the Scala, Milan which was coldly received. In 1874 another opera, *Re Manfredi* was whistled off the stage of the Teatro Regio, Turin.

ORTOLAN Eugène (b. Paris 1 April 1824; d. Paris, 11 May 1891). Son of a distinguished professor of law, he too studied law, eventually entering the Ministry of Foreign Affairs. At the same time he attended the Paris Conservatoire where he was a pupil of Berton and Halévy. Second Prix de Rome in 1847. For 20 years was secretary of the Société des Compositeurs de Musique and used his official position in the Ministry to work for the protection of composers' foreign rights. With *Lisette* also had opérettes produced at the Bouffes-Parisiens and at the theatre in Versailles. He also composed an oratorio, *Tobie*.

PALIARD Léon (b. Lyon 1826; d. Lyon 1 November 1907). A business man who had some lessons from Adolphe Adam and on 28 February 1833 had a one act opera comique, *L'Alchimiste* performed at the Grand Théâtre in his native city. As already noted this was probably the same work as *La Tête Enchantée* but with the title changed. Wrote words and music of a patriotic song, 'Deliverance', given at the same theatre in February 1872 (presumably to commemorate the end of the industrial disturbance of the previous years), and several choruses for the Orphéons.

PASCAL Prosper (b. c. 1825; d. 1880). Stage works also produced at the Opéra-Comique and at Baden-Baden. Composed some vocal melodies. Was music critic of the *Courrier de Dimanche* and translated *Entführung aus dem Serail* for the Théâtre Lyrique. Persuaded Choudens to publish *Faust*.

PILATI (Auguste Pilate) (b. Bouchain (Nord) 29 September 1810; d. Paris 1 August 1877). Commenced music studies at the École Communale of Douai. Paris Conservatoire, 1822. Appointed conductor at Porte-Saint-Martin in 1840 and later at the Beaumarchais. Occasionally used the pseudonyms A.P. Juliano and Wolfart. Composer, with Eugène Gautier, of *Les Barricades de 1848* at the Opéra National. Stage works also at Théâtre Lyrique, Renaissance, Variétés, Porte-Saint-Martin, Folies-Nouvelles, Déjazet, Bouffes-Parisiens, Palais-Royal etc. and at Lille. Many vocal and piano pieces. He composed the music for the romance sung in Victor Hugo's *Ruy Blas* and in 1837 had a burletta, *The King of the Danube*, produced at the Adelphi Theatre, London.

SALOMON Hector (b. Strasbourg 29 May 1838; d. Paris 28 March 1906). At age 9 began to study violin, at age 11, piano. Entered Paris Conservatoire in 1850 with Bazin for harmony and Halévy for composition. Came of a poor family, and the necessity of earning a living forced him to leave the Conservatoire early to become an accompanist at the Bouffes-Parisiens. Here in 1856 he composed music for a ballet. In 1863 became accompanist at the Théâtre Lyrique. Joined Opéra in 1870 as second chorus master, later becoming 'chef du chant'. Resigned this post in 1891. Besides *Les Dragées de Suzette* composed two symphonies, instrumental music, church music, almost 200 songs and an unpublished and unperformed four act opera, *Les Contes d'Hoffmann*.

SARMIENTO Salvatore (b. Palermo 1817; d. Naples 13 May 1869). Pupil of Zingarelli and Donizetti at the Conservatorio di San Pietro e Marella, Naples. Had an 'azione melodrammatica', *Alfonso d'Aragona* performed without success at the Teatro San Carlo in 1838. Later, operas in same theatre. Then, apparently successful career at the Teatro Regio, Parma. Left Parma for Paris in 1851. Returned to Naples in less than two years where in 1854 King Ferdinand II appointed him 'maestro di cappella' during which period he composed much music for the Chapel Royal.

SAVARY Edmond (b. Sedan 1835). Entered Paris Conservatoire in 1848 where he distinguished himself as a pianist. Also composed sonatas for violin and piano and some organ pieces and songs. Subsequently became music teacher at St. Helier on the island of Jersey.

SELLENICK Adolphe-Valentin (b. Strasbourg 1820; d. Les Andelys (Eure) 26 September 1893). Son of a musician. Family originally came from Styria. At an early age became first a violinist then a horn player in the Strasbourg theatre orchestra, later graduating to assistant conductor. Becoming a military band master when élite cavalry regiments were created under the Second Empire, he was appointed to direct the band of the 2nd Voltigeurs. Took part in the Italian campaign of 1859 and in the Franco-Prussian war when he was taken prisoner following the surrender of Metz. On his return to France was appointed bandmaster of the second regiment of the Garde Républicaine. Composed much military band music.

THYS Pauline (Mme Sebault) (b. 1836; d. 1909). Daughter of a minor opera composer, Alphonse Thys (1807–1879). Modelled her style on Offenbach and Gounod according to circumstances and wrote all her own libretti. Opérettes produced at Bouffes-Parisiens (one, *Le Mariage de Tabarin* later given in Naples as *La Congiura di Chevreuse*) and at the Salle Herz. Composed many songs and chansonnettes.

YMBERT Théodore His father was a composer of vaudevilles during the Restoration and at the same time a higher civil servant in the Ministry of War. Ymbert fils was a composer who was also a barrister, but Lasalle records that he soon left Paris and returned to the provinces where he became maire of Bourbonne-les-Bains, (Haute-Marne). He also composed a group of songs, *Sept Fables de La Fontaine*, and a choral work called *Bethléem*.

Nothing can be discovered of the composers, Mlle RIVAY, or MM UZÈPY and VILLEBLANCHE.

Appendix D

Glossary of Librettists and Translators

ADENIS Jules (Jules-Adenis Colombeau) (b. Paris 1823; d. 1900). Educated Collège Bourbon (Lycée Condorcet). On leaving school turned to journalism and the theatre but also worked in an office until 1851. From 1847 until 1849 helped to edit *Le Corsair*. Was secretary of the Société des Artistes Dramatiques. Alone and in collaboration wrote many plays, libretti (*La Jolie Fille de Perth* is the best known) and vaudevilles.

ALBOIZE DE PUJOL Jules-Edouard (b. 1805; d. Paris 9 April 1854). Alone and in collaboration wrote historical romances, plays, libretti and vaudevilles. In 1852 Jules Seveste transferred his privilege regulating Paris suburban theatres to him.

ANSEAUME LOUIS (b. Paris 1721; d. Paris 7 July 1784). First entered community of 'Pères de la Doctrine chrétienne' but quickly left and was successively schoolmaster and tapestry worker. Next joined Opéra-Comique where he was assistant director from 1758 until 1761. With the amalgamation of the Opéra-Comique and Comédie Italienne in 1762 he became secretary, repetiteur and prompter combined. Wrote a great number of libretti for Grétry, Duni, Gluck, Philidor and others.

ARTOIS Achille d' (Louis-Charles-Achille d'Artois de Bournonville) (b. Noyon (Oise) 17 March 1791; d. Versailles 1868). The name is frequently found spelt Dartois. Set out to become a notary, but with his two brothers (with whom he is often confused) was among the remnant of the Scottish company of the Gardes du Corps which accompanied Louis XVIII to Ghent, during Napoleon I's 'hundred days'. Alone and in collaboration wrote vaudevilles, 'féeries' and libretti.

BARBIER Jules-(Paul) (b. Paris 8 March 1825; d. Paris 16 January 1901). Son of the genre and landscape painter Nicolas Alexandre Barbier (1789–1864). Began to write for the theatre at the age of 13. Plays produced at the Comédie-Française and Odéon including *La Loterie du Mariage* in which Sarah Bernhardt appeared. With Michel Carré (his usual collaborator) furnished successful libretti for Massé, Gounod, Thomas, Meyerbeer, Offenbach and others. Also published collections of poetry. Provisional director of the Opéra-Comique in 1887, and for a long time president of the Société des Auteurs Dramatiques.

BARRIERE Théodore (b. Paris 16 April 1821*; d. Paris 15 October 1877). A dramatist who rejected the Scribe formula in favour of realism. Wrote over 80 plays ranging from farce to serious drama, mostly in association with others, but very few opera libretti. Collaborated with Murger in a well known dramatisation of *La Vie de Bohème.*

BATTU Léon (b. Paris 1829; d. Paris November 1857). Son of Pantaléon Battu (1799–1870), (assistant conductor at the Opéra) and brother of the singer, Marie Battu. Dramatist. Libretti for Offenbach, Adam, and (in collaboration) Massé. With Ludovic Halévy translated Mozart's *Der Schauspieldirektor* for the Bouffes-Parisiens in 1856, and again with Halévy wrote *Le Docteur Miracle*, the operetta which won a prize and performance for Bizet and Lecocq at the same theatre in 1857.

BEAUMONT Alexandre (Louis-Alexandre Beaume) (b. Paris 1 August 1827; d. Paris 11 March 1909). Barrister and writer of both novels and legal works, mainly on copyright law. Librettist, almost always in collaboration with Nuitter with whom he also translated *Oberon, Preciosa* and *Die Zauberflöte.*

BEAUPLAN Victor-Arthur Rousseau de (b. Paris 1823; d. Paris 1890). Son of a musician, painter and writer, Amédée-Louis-Joseph Rousseau de Beauplan (1790–1853). Wrote plays and libretti, among which Adam's *La Poupée de Nuremberg* is the best remembered, mostly in collaboration. His associates included Labiche. The anti-democratic sentiments of his plays found favour with the imperial government and he was appointed supervisor of the Odéon in 1868. Towards the end of his life published some collections of poetry.

BECQUE Henry (b. Paris 18 April 1837; d. Paris 12 May 1899). Educated Lycée Condorcet. Theatre début 1867 with libretto of Joncières' opera *Sardanapale.* Plays in realistic style at Vaudeville and Théâtre Français. Contributed to many Paris newspapers.

BERTHOUD Samuel-Henri (b. Cambrai 9 January 1804; d. 1891). Educated Douai College. Edited a newspaper published by his father in that town, later founded his own, *La Gazette de Cambrai.* In 1832 came to Paris where he was associated with many newspapers occasionally using the pseudonym, Sam. Wrote widely on scientific or pseudo-scientific subjects and formed an ethnographic collection which he presented to the city of Douai. Wrote a play and collaborated in a vaudeville for the Variétés. One libretto only can be traced.

BIGNON Eugène (Louis-Thomas) (b. Paris 1812; d. Paris 6 December 1858). Actor and dramatist. Was first apprenticed to a shoemaker, later becoming a stonemason. He began his acting career in the suburban theatres but entered the Odéon in 1841, passing to the Théâtre-Historique in 1845 (where he took part in the opening production of *La Reine Margot*) and to the Comédie-

---

*

Dissertation by Edwin Colby Byam. *Johns Hopkins Studies in Romance Literatures and Languages.* Extra Vol. XIII. 1938.

Française in 1850. Wrote a vaudeville in 1847 and a drama for the Théâtre de la Gaîté in 1857. Collaborated with d'Ennery in the libretto of *L'Habit de Noce.*

BOISSEAUX, Henri (b. 1821; d. Paris 20 November 1863). Dramatist and journalist. Plays at Odéon, Gymnase, Beaumarchais. Libretti, some in collaboration with Scribe for Théâtre Lyrique, Opéra-Comique and Bouffes-Parisiens.

BOURGEOIS,Auguste Anicet- (b. Paris 25 January 1806; d. Pau 12 January 1871). Studied law for a time but the success of his first play (written in collaboration, as were all his stage works) enabled him to retire from the legal profession. Wrote plays, some with Dumas père, vaudevilles and spectacular pieces for the Cirque Olympique, as well as libretti. Is said to have had some part in over 200 works. Was vice-president of the Société des Auteurs Dramatiques.

BOUTET DE MONVEL, Jacques-Marie (b. Lunéville 25 March 1745; d. Paris 13 February 1812). Son of a musician-actor-theatre director, François Boutet, called de Monvel. Jacques-Marie began his career as an actor at the Comédie-Française in 1770, but in 1781 left Paris and settled in Stockholm as reader to Gustave III. The king ennobled him and gave him a pension of 20,000 livres. He returned to Paris in 1789 and performed at a number of theatres. In spite of his Swedish ennoblement was an ardent upholder of the revolution. Wrote libretti for Dalayrac and Dezède. Was father of the noted Comédie-Française actress, Mlle Mars.

BOVERAT, Charles. Ten works by this dramatist are listed by Charles Beaumont Wicks in *The Parisian Stage* Pt IV (1851–75) (*University of Alabama Studies No. 17.* September 1967).

BRÉSIL, Jules-Henri (b. Paris 8 May 1818; d. Bois-Colombes near Paris 22 October 1899). Primarily a highly successful actor who performed in all the principal Paris theatres while at the same time writing for them. Libretti (in collaboration with d'Ennery) for Adam's *Si j'étais Roi* and Gounod's *Le Tribut de Zamora.*

BRUNSWICK, Léon-Lévy (b. Paris 20 April 1805; d. Le Havre 29 April 1859). Wrote over 100 plays and vaudevilles, mainly in collaboration and mostly with his friend Adolphe de Leuven, with whom he worked for more than 20 years. Many of his plays were politically inclined which apparently helped their success. Wrote libretti (all with de Leuven) for Adam, Balfe, Clapisson and others.

CARMOUCHE, Pierre-François-Adolphe (b. Lyon 18 April 1797; d. Paris December 1868). Was in turn, painter, goldsmith and clerk. Had a vaudeville performed in Lyon. Went to Paris where, with assistance from others he wrote almost 300 pieces, dramas, comedies, libretti, parodies, revues. His collaborators included Scribe. Director of the Porte-Saint-Martin and later of the theatres at Versailles and Strasbourg. Established a French company at the St James's Theatre, London.

CARRÉ, Michel-Florentin (b. Besançon 21 October 1822; d., Argenteuil 28 June 1872). Went to Paris to become a painter and for a time studied with Delaroche. In 1841 published poems. He next turned to the stage and wrote many plays, both light and serious—all now forgotten. Best remembered as a librettist with Jules Barbier. Their collaboration included *Mignon* and *Hamlet* (Thomas), *Faust*, *Philémon et Baucis*, *La Colombe* and *La Reine de Saba* (Gounod), *Les Contes d'Hoffmann* (Offenbach), *Galatée* and *Les Noces de Jeannette* (Massé), and *Le Timbre d'Argent* (Saint-Saëns). Less commendable was their adaptation-translation of *Fidelio*, *Le Nozze di Figaro*, and, above all, *Così fan tutte*. According to Lasalle the name Fonteille is a pseudonym of Carré.

CASPERS, Emile. Seemingly wrote only one stage work, *Le Cousin Babylas* for which his brother Henri composed the music.

CASTIL-BLAZE, François-Henri-Joseph (b. Cavaillon 1 December 1784; d. Paris 11 December 1857). Son of Henri-Sebastien Blaze, a lawyer who was also a good musician and friend of Grétry and Méhul. Francis Hueffer considered Castil-Blaze 'one of the most prolific writers on music and the drama whom France has produced'. Rossini used to refer to him as Castil-Blague! Came to Paris in 1799 to study law, and took lessons at the Conservatoire at the same time. Became sous-préfet of the departement of Vaucluse but in 1820 returned to Paris and published *De l'Opéra en France*, his most important work. Composed a few operas, some sacred music and songs and was music critic of the *Journal des Débats* besides writing numerous articles for other Paris newspapers. His most successful talent, at least commercially, lay in translating and arranging the scores of Mozart, Weber and Rossini.

CHAIGNEAU, Théop... Five works by this dramatist are listed in *The Parisian Stage*. Pt IV, 1851–1875.

CHALLAMEL, Jean-Baptiste-Marie-Augustin (b. Paris 18 March 1819; d. Paris 19 October 1894). First entered business, next became a barrister, finally turned to letters. In 1844 he became a librarian, and so, discovering all forms of literature began to write in all forms (occasionally as Jules Robert), short stories and novels, light articles and serious studies, biographies, histories, accounts of voyages—and libretti.

CHAZOT, Paul de (d. August 1879). Besides helping to translate *Oberon* he wrote at least one libretto with Carré for the Opéra-Comique. Also a great number of songs which were set to music and sung by the baritone, Faure.

CHIVOT, Henri-Charles (b. Paris 13 November 1830; d. Le Vésinet (Seine-et-Oise) 1897). Was first a solicitor's clerk, then joined the railway company P.L.M. as a forwarding agent, ending his career as secretary to the board. He had had his first play produced at the Palais Royal in 1855 and would write about 50 comedies, opérettes and vaudevilles. Collaborated with Alfred Duru for much of his work especially in opérettes for Offenbach, Audran, Lecocq and others.

CHOLER, Adolphe-Joseph (b. Paris 1821; d. Paris 20 January 1889). Dramatist. Was also director of the Palais Royal. Wrote either alone or in collaboration up to 80 stage pieces which included some libretti.

CLAIRVILLE (Louis-François Nicolaïe) (b. Lyon 28 January 1811; d. Paris 7 February 1879). Dramatist. The son of actors. His father had taken the stage name of Clairville. Appeared as a child on the stage of the Théâtre du Luxembourg where his father was directing a very small company. In 1829 presented his first play at the same theatre and so became principal playwright to his father's company. Passed to the Théâtre Ambigu-Comique in 1836 where he inaugurated a series of comic revues which became very popular. With and without collaborators wrote 600 pieces of which 450 were published. His best known libretti are those written (in collaboration) for Lecocq's *La Fille de Madame Angot* and Planquette's *Les Cloches de Corneville*.

COGNIARD, Jean-Hippolyte (b. Paris 29 November 1807; d. Paris 6 February 1882). With his elder brother Charles-Theodore formed the Siamese twins of comedy writing in Paris. Both set out to study medicine but then turned to writing patriotic plays. It was then just after the July revolution. Their very first effort, *La Cocarde tricolore* produced at the Folies-Dramatiques in 1831 ran for 200 performances and gave a French word to the English language—chauvinism, from the role of Nicolas Chauvin, a much wounded yet still idolizing Napoleonic veteran. Hippolyte became director of the Vaudeville in 1845 but resigned after a year. Subsequently directed the Variétés. Both brothers wrote comedies, operettes, vaudevilles and 'féeries'.

CORMON, Eugène (Pierre-Etienne Piestre) (b. Lyon 5 May 1810; d. Paris March 1903). Dramatist. With collaborators wrote dramas, comedies, libretti, of which almost 150 were published. Became stage manager at the Opéra in 1859 and administrator of the Vaudeville in 1874. Maillart's *Les Dragons de Villars*, Bizet's *Les Pêcheurs de Perles* (with Carré away from Barbier), Offenbach's *Robinson Crusoe*, are operas in which he had a hand.

CRÉMIEUX, Hector-Jonathan (b. Paris 10 November 1828; d. Paris 30 September 1892). Dramatist. Studied law and in 1852 was employed as a clerk at the Ministry of State where the Duc de Morny, himself a dramatist, exploited his talents and at the same time gave him plenty of scope to look after his own affairs.

He specialised in parodies. Works by him and in collaboration were performed at the Odéon, Bouffes-Parisiens, Variétés and Théâtre Lyrique. They included Offenbach's *Orphée aux Enfers* and *La Chanson de Fortunio*.

CREUZÉ DE LESSER, Augustin-François (b. Paris 3 October 1771; d. Paris 14 August 1839). Of noble family as the name suggests. First wrote under the name of Auguste. Appointed to the Legation at Parma, later, secretary of the Embassies at Naples and Palermo all of which he recorded in his *Voyage en Italie et en Sicile* published in 1806. Had a highly successful political and diplomatic career, deputy to the Senate for Saône-et-Loire in 1804, created Baron in 1818. Throughout he wrote plays and operas-comiques. Among the latter his *Le Nouveau Seigneur de Village* (with de Favières), composed by

Boieldieu and produced in 1813 is the only one even remotely remembered, undoubtedly because of the composer. Yet when it was first performed at Montpellier where Creuzé de Lesser was then stationed as préfet of Hérault (and, incidentally was having trouble with the students of the famous Montpellier medical school) it was greeted with boos.

DEFORGES, Philippe-Auguste Pitaud (b. Paris 5 April 1805; d. Saint-Gratien (Seine-et-Oise) 28 September 1881). Educated, Collège Bourbon. First, customs officer; in 1830, entered Ministry of War; in 1839 changed again to become head of Record Office. At age 20 he had founded a newspaper, *Le Kaleidoscope* in Bordeaux and later wrote for minor Paris papers. Then turned to the theatre and, in collaboration, wrote a great number of vaudevilles and opérettes, *Le Bijou Perdu* among them.

DELAHAYE, Jules (Living in 1891). Sometime administrator of the Porte-Saint-Martin, later secretary general of the Opéra. Was associated in the writing of 12 stage works.

DELAVIGNE, Jean-François-Casimir (b. Le Havre, 4 April 1793; d. Lyon 11 December 1843). Distinguished poet and dramatist, although his talent was more theatrical than poetic. Championed Bonapartism and liberty but this did not prevent him accepting the post of librarian to the Chancellery from Louis XVIII on the restoration, and later that of librarian to the Palais-Royal from Louis-Philippe. First great success was *Les Vêpres Siciliennes* at the Odéon in 1819 to be followed by *L'École des Vieillards* at the Comédie-Française in 1823. The 1830 revolution inspired the hymn 'La Parisienne' which, with music by Auber became 'La Marseillaise' of the new monarchy. Unusual in that he wrote his plays single-handed except for the libretto of *Charles VI* in which his brother Germain collaborated.

DELAVIGNE, Germain (b. Giverny (Eure) 1 February 1790; d. Montmorency (Seine-et-Oise) 30 November 1868). Elder brother of above. Educated, Collège Sainte-Barbe, Paris, where Eugène Scribe was a schoolmate. They subsequently collaborated in many plays. Unlike Casimir, wrote several libretti. Except for *Charles VI* all were in collaboration with Scribe and included Auber's *La Muette de Portici*, Meyerbeer's *Robert-le-Diable* and Gounod's *La Nonne Sanglante*.

DENIZET, Jules (b. Reims 1827; d. Paris 1878). Educated at local college. At age ten studied the violin and subsequently all the instruments of the orchestra, but apparently none too successfully since in the Philharmonic Society of Reims and in the Garde Nationale he was assigned to the bass drum. Was interested in the sciences and came to Paris in 1855 as a science student, at the same time writing for *Le Gaulois*, *Le Figaro*, *Le Charivari* and other newspapers under his own name besides the pseudonyms of O'Brenn, de Muire, Martial and Louis Ramon. Seems to have written few libretti.

DESARBRES, Nérée (b. Villefranche-sur-Saône 12 February 1820; d. Paris 16 July 1872). Dramatist. Collaborated in a number of opérettes and vaudevilles. In 1856 became secretary to the administration of the Opéra, retiring in 1863, and in 1864 wrote *Sept ans à l'Opéra* to be followed in 1868 by *Deux Siècles à l'Opéra.* Retired to Lyon in 1866 and had some plays produced at the municipal theatre.

DESFORGES, Pierre-Jean-Baptiste Choudard (b. Paris 15 September 1746; d. Paris 13 August 1806). His true father was a distinguished Paris physician, Antoine Petit (1718–1794). Educated, Collège Mazarin and Collège de Beauvais where he began to write verse tragedies. Brief periods studying first medicine, then painting under Vien. In 1765 began to make translations from the Italian and to write for the theatre. Joined the Comédie-Italienne in 1769 and later was a strolling player with an Italian troupe in the provinces. Accompanied by an actress wife set out for St. Petersburg in 1779 where he was well received by Catherine II and earned 5000 roubles in three years. Returning to Paris in 1882, his first marriage was dissolved, he remarried and left the theatre to devote himself to writing. Besides plays and libretti wrote some novels and his memoirs.

DESLANDES, Nicolas-Théodore-Paulin (b. 18..; d. 1866). First was a singer at the Opéra-Comique but lost his voice and then wrote vaudevilles and plays, with success.

DESLYS, (Charles Collinet) (b. Paris 1 March 1821; d. Paris 13 March 1885). A singing actor who performed both in drama and opéra comique in many theatres in the Midi, especially in Toulouse. Returned to Paris in 1846 where the success won by his story 'Les Bottes vernies de Cendrillon', published in *L'Esprit Public* decided him to become a writer. Wrote many novels and stories, plays and libretti as well as political tracts during the 1848 revolution.

DEULIN, Charles (Charlemagne) (b. Condé-sur-l'Escaut (Nord) 4 January 1827; d. Condé-sur-l'Escaut 30 September 1877). Journalist who contributed theatre reviews to various Paris newspapers (in some under the pseudonym Charles de la Mouselle) and later held an appointment at the Arsenal Library. Wrote novels and short stories besides collaborating in many stage works including libretti for opérettes.

DUBREUIL, Ernest (b. 1833; d. near Paris 28 April 1886). Dramatist and journalist writing under his own name and under the pseudonym of Pierre du Croisy. Libretti in collaboration for works performed at the Théâtre Lyrique, Folies-Dramatiques and Athénée.

DUMANOIR, (Philippe-François Pinel) (b. Guadeloupe (Lesser Antilles) 31 July 1806; d. Pau 13 November 1865). Came to Paris in 1816 to the Collège Bourbon. Studied law and at the same time collaborated in writing vaudevilles. From 1836 to 1839 was director of the Variétés. Wrote almost 200 stage works of all genres in collaboration, among them the play *Don César de Bazan.*

DUPIN, Jean-Henri (b. Paris 1 September 1791; d. Paris 5 April 1887). Dramatist. Started out as a bank clerk. Wrote over 200 stage works in collaboration, of which about 50 were with Scribe. Wrote libretti for Théâtre Lyrique, Opéra-Comique and Gymnase but primarily, like Dumanoir, was a writer of vaudevilles.

DUPREZ, Edouard (b. Paris 1804; d. Vaugirard, near Paris 5 June 1879). Younger brother of the famous tenor, Gilbert-Louis Duprez. Began as an actor at the Théâtre de Montmartre, later at the Variétés and Odéon and abroad in Brussels and London. Wrote vaudevilles in which he performed, and it would appear that he also sang as a 'trial', perhaps at the Opéra-Comique. Later wrote libretti and translated the text of several Verdi operas as well as Bellini's *Il Pirata* into French. Also contributed to the press.

DURU, Henri-Alfred (b. Paris 1829; d. 29 December 1889). Was first an engraver. In collaboration wrote many vaudevilles, plays and opérettes including *La Fille du Tambour Major*.

DUVAL, (Alexandre-Vincent Pineu) (b. Rennes 6 April 1767; d. Montmartre, near Paris 9 January 1842). In turn joined navy to fight in the American War of Independence under La Fayette, became architect, draughtsman, volunteer in the National Guard of 1792, actor, theatre director and dramatist. From early 1794 played small roles at the Théâtre-Français, and from 1812 to 1815 was director of the Odéon. He succeeded Legouvé as member of the Académie Française in 1812. After the July revolution of 1830 was appointed administrator of the Arsenal Library. Wrote more than 60 stage works including libretti for the Opéra, Opéra-Comique (Méhul's *Joseph* among them) and a number of books on the theatre. Was an ardent adherent of the old school of dramatists in trying to combat the romanticism of Victor Hugo.

ENNERY, Adolphe Philippe d' (b. Paris 17 June 1811; d. Paris 26 January 1899). Began as a clerk in a drapery store, then turned to journalism and so to the theatre. Collaborated with most dramatists of his time. His first play was produced in 1831, his last in 1885. Was director of the Théâtre Historique for a brief 15 days in 1850. Became administrator of the 'Société Thermale' of the seaside resort of Caboug-Dives and was elected maire of Cabourg. Wrote some 280 works for the theatre, plays, vaudevilles, 'féeries' and libretti which included *Le Muletier de Tolède* (Adam), *Le Premier jour de bonheur* (Auber), *Le Tribut de Zamora* (Gounod), and *Le Cid* (Massenet). Towards the end of his life he wrote novels. He left a fortune of almost 6,000,000 francs and a collection of objets d'art from China and Japan which he bequeathed to the nation.

FAVRE, Adolphe (b. Lille 1808; d. 16 January 1886). Poet and writer of novels, short stories and stage works. Many of his poems were set to music. Also contributed to *La Revue Parisienne*. From 1830 pressed for the return of Napoleon's remains to France.

FOURNIER, Edouard (b. Orléans 15 June 1819; d. Paris 10 May 1880). Historian, theatre chronicler, critic, journalist, dramatist and librettist, he was above all prolific. Editor of *Le Théâtre* from 1853 to 1855.

FURPILLE, Eugène (b. Versailles 1822). Wrote stage pieces, many in collaboration. Was contributor to the *Gazette des Tribunaux*.

GABRIEL, Jules-Joseph-Gabriel de Lurieu (b. Paris 11 February 1792; d. Paris 28 March 1869). Educated Collège Henri IV. Administrator and dramatist.

Known in the theatre by his given name of Gabriel. Held important executive posts in the Ministry of the Interior. Wrote vaudevilles, plays and libretti, almost invariably in collaboration. Wrote administrative tracts as well as stage works under his real name of de Lurieu, and two early pieces under the name of Jules.

GAY, Marie-Françoise-Sophie Nichault de Lavalette (b. Paris 1 July 1776; d. Paris 5 March 1852). Wife of a financier who became 'receveur général' of the Département of the Roer (Rur), under the first Empire. She made her début as a writer in the *Journal de Paris* in 1802. This was followed by many novels and some plays and libretti, among which *Le Maître de Chapelle* (Paër) is the only one now even remotely remembered. In her youth she had had music lessons from Méhul and later wrote words and music of songs which had a socialite vogue in their time. She was a leading salon hostess during the reign of Louis Philippe.

GILLE, Philippe-Emile-François (b. Paris 18 December 1831; d. Paris 1901). Journalist and dramatist. First studied sculpture, then was employed in the Préfecture of the Seine, later became secretary to the Théâtre Lyrique. Contributed to various Paris newspapers including news items to *Le Figaro* under the pseudonym of 'Masque de fer'. Married Massé's elder daughter. Alone and in collaboration wrote plays and libretti, the most notable for Delibes' *Lakmé* and Massenet's *Manon*. Also published collections of poetry and works on art.

GRANDVALLET, Charles. Was associated with Adenis in the libretto of Massenet's first opera, *La Grand'Tante*, performed at the Opéra-Comique in 1867.

GRANGÉ, (Pierre-Eugène Basté) (b. Paris 16 December 1810; d. Paris 1 March 1887). One of the most prolific French dramatists of his time, now completely forgotten. First attempt was a pantomime at the Funambules. Wrote plays, operettes and vaudevilles, almost invariably in collaboration. Also wrote a great number of chansons and topical songs.

GUILLARD, Nicolas-François (b. Chartres 16 January 1752; d. Paris 26 December 1814). At age 14 while still at school in Chartres won a prize for poetry. Then remained unnoticed until he wrote the libretto for Gluck's *Iphigénie en Tauride*. Wrote libretti for operas by Sacchini, including *Oedipe à Colone*, Lemoyne, Salieri, Kalkbrenner, Paisiello and Lesueur. Remarkably for the period, with one exception, all were written unaided.

GUILLIAUME, Jules (b. Brussels 1825; d. Ixelles, near Brussels 19 November 1900). Scholar and writer. A polyglot who translated much from German into French, including (besides *Rienzi*), Wagner's *Judaism in Music*. Secretary-treasurer of the Conservatoire of Brussels.

HOFFMANN, François-Benoît (b. Nancy 11 July 1760; d. Paris 25 April 1828). For a time joined the army but even as a youth had contributed to the *Almanach des Muses*. Settled in Paris in 1784 and in 1785 published a book of verse there. Was literary critic of the *Journal de l'Empire* and in 1807 of the

Journal des Débats. Wrote tragedies, comedies and libretti for the Opéra-Comique and Opéra including *Medée* (Cherubini).

JAIME, (Adolphe Gem) (b. Paris 1824; d. Asnières 4 March 1901). Son of Ernest Jaime (1802–1884) another writer of vaudevilles. Began as an actor in a company of strollers playing in barns, and in 1864 announced that with the help of English capital he was about to build a theatre to seat 3000 in the boulevard de Belleville–an ambition he does not seem to have achieved. Was combined stage manager-administrator of Léon Vasseur's short lived Nouveau-Lyrique in the rue Taitbout in 1879. Alone or in collaboration wrote 73 stage works, plays, opérettes and vaudevilles, and some novels.

KAUFFMANN, A.-Sebastien (b. Lyon, 1800; d. Paris 1868). Combined the positions of journalist, poet, writer of vaudevilles, chansonnier and collector of tolls. Was active in politics as a young man—hostile to Charles X and the Bourbons, favouring Napoleon, the Greek and Polish uprisings and the July revolution—and was involved in the political disturbances in Lyon in 1831. Spent three years in Italy as a journalist while studying the economy of the country and published his findings in the 'Journal des Économistes' and in a book, *Chroniques de Rome.* Wrote voluminously on Freemasonry, one seemingly definitive book going through seven editions, and became editor of the *Revue Maçonnique.* He also wrote novels. Died forgotten, although *La Demoiselle d'Honneur* was still in print in 1931.

LABAT, Eugène (b. Italy; d. October/November 1867). Real name Cavazzi. Dramatist and antiquarian. For many years archivist to the Paris Prefecture of Police. Wrote dramas, comedies and libretti, including one based on the story of Inez de Castro which was submitted to the Opéra, but never set to music.

LANGLÉ, Joseph-Adolphe-Ferdinand (b. Paris 21 November 1798; d. Paris 18 October 1867). The name is occasionally found spelled Langlois. Son of Honoré-François-Marie Langlé, a Monegasque composer descended from a Picardy family which had settled in Monaco in the mid-seventeenth century, and his wife, Angélique-Elisabeth Sue, aunt of the novelist Eugène Sue. Educated at the Lycée Bonaparte, and under the Bourbon restoration appointed 'historiographe' of the Musée Dauphin. Began his literary career as a journalist. For a time it would seem that he also studied medicine (Eugène Sue's father was a well known surgeon), but subsequently became a funeral undertaker! One of his later literary works recounted the return of the remains of Napoleon I from Saint-Helena to Paris in 1840. Wrote stage works alone and in collaboration. His *Maître Pathelin* (Bazin) is still remembered.

LEUVEN, Adolphe de (Comte de Ribbing) (b. 1800; d. Paris 14 April 1884). Son of Count Adolphe-Louis Ribbing, one of the three conspirators involved in the assassination of Gustavus III of Sweden. De Leuven was the name of his maternal grandmother. He very occasionally used the pseudonyms Granval and Adolphe. Alone and in collaboration wrote about 150 stage works of all genres including a great number of libretti. In December 1862 he was appointed director of the Opéra-Comique, a position he held in association successively with Ritt and Du Locle until 1874. He was a close and life-long friend of Alexandre Dumas père.

LOCKROY, (Joseph-Philippe Simon) (b. Turin 17 February 1803; d. Paris 19 January 1891). Was first an actor, making his début at the Odéon in 1827, later playing at the Comédie-Française. As early as 1827 he had also collaborated in some plays with Scribe and from 1840 onwards turned entirely to writing, producing dramas, comedies, vaudevilles and libretti.

LONCHAMPS, Charles de (b. Réunion Island 1768; d. Louviers (Eure) 17 April 1832). Educated at the Collège de Rennes (his family had come from this city). On the death of his father he was left in comfortable circumstances and in 1786 returned to France to claim his inheritance. Two years later, having led an indulgent life meanwhile, he set out for India. While visiting Chandernagore he learned of the French Revolution. The French Governor there, encouraged by the English, was hostile to the new regime, whereupon Lonchamps, at his own expense raised a company of sepoys who attacked and defeated him. Lonchamps returned to France in 1792, where, ironically, he was arrested as a suspect, spending the next seven months in Saint-Lazare prison. On his release he was appointed 'adjoint' to the adjutant-general, Jouy whom he had earlier met in Chandernagore. It was Jouy, later librettist of *La Vestale* and *Guillaume Tell* who encouraged Lonchamps in his literary work. In 1804 Princess Caroline Murat (Napoleon's youngest sister), appointed him her principal secretary, and in the following year, her husband, Jerome Murat, commissioned him an officer in the Austerlitz campaign, where he won the Légion d'honneur. When Murat became king of Naples he appointed him chamberlain and superintendent of the Neapolitan theatres. In 1811, while Lonchamps was on leave in France, Murat decided that all Frenchmen holding official positions must either become naturalised Neapolitans or resign their posts. Lonchamps resigned, not without some bitterness, and retired to Louviers, his wife's home-town, where he spent the remainder of his life. He wrote plays for the Théâtre Français, vaudevilles and libretti, alone and in collaboration and in 1823 published two volumes of verse written mainly while he was in Italy.

MARSOLLIER DES VIVETIÈRES, Bénoît-Joseph (b. Paris 1750; d. Versailles 21 April 1817). Came of an aristocratic family and prior to the Revolution held an official position in the Hôtel de Ville, Paris, but from the beginning was also interested in the theatre. He wrote libretti, particularly for Dalayrac (including *Nina, ou La Folle par Amour*), Méhul and Gaveaux. These operas were performed at the Comédie-Italienne, the Opéra-Comique and the Théâtre Feydeau. He also had some plays produced at the Théâtre Français.

MASSON, Michel (Auguste-Michel-Bénoît Gaudichot) (b. Paris 31 July 1800; d. Paris 23 April 1883). Novelist and dramatist. The child of poor parents, at the age of 10 he was a ballet dancer in the tiny boulevard Théâtre Monthabor. For this theatre he also wrote his first stage piece in which he played a role. There followed a number of artisan jobs during which time, entirely by his own efforts, he managed to educate himself. By 1826 he was producing articles for a number of literary magazines and by 1830 had become a contributor to *Le Figaro*. In the same year he renounced journalism to devote himself entirely to writing novels and stage works. Both categories were written mostly in collaboration and a considerable amount was turned out. His works for the theatre included plays, vaudevilles and libretti.

MEILHAC, Henri (b. Paris 21 February 1831; d. Paris 6 July 1897). Was educated at the Lycée Louis-le-Grand. First worked in a bookshop, at the same time dabbling in journalism under the pseudonym of Thalin. In 1855 he had some plays performed at the Théâtre du Palais-Royal and between this date and 1869 he wrote some 60 stage works mainly in collaboration, and principally with Ludovic Halévy as his partner. The two names, like Barbier and Carré, would become almost inseparable and both would be the authors of many of Offenbach's greatest successes, including *La Belle Hélène*, *La Grande Duchesse de Gérolstein* and *La Périchole*. Their vaudevilles would include *Le Réveillon*, which Johann Strauss in time would make famous as *Die Fledermaus*, and their most important collaboration of all was, of course, *Carmen*. Following this, Meilhac went on to write the libretto of *Manon* with Philippe Gille. He was also renowned as a bibliophile.

MÉRY, François-Joseph-Pierre-Agnès (b. Les Aygalades near Marseille 22 January 1798; d. Paris 17 June 1866). As a young man, in 1815, he took part in the bloody violence in the Midi which led to the return of the Bourbons to the throne, but was nonetheless anticlerical and his satirical attack published against a certain Abbé Eliçagaray landed him in prison for a term of three months, from which he emerged a confirmed liberal and Bonapartist. In 1820 he founded the liberal newspaper, *Le Phocéen* to be followed later by another, *La Mediterranée*. By this time he was also publishing poetry. He was then living both in Marseille and in Paris, and in Paris became editor of the liberal newspaper, *Le Nain jaune*. During the July revolution of 1830 he wrote the words of a patriotic song, 'La Tricolore', which Fromental Halévy set to music and which was sung in the Paris theatres. However, becoming disillusioned with politics he decided to return to Marseille.

From there he travelled widely throughout the Continent, and also to England which he visited in 1838 in the company of the ballet dancer Marie Taglioni. While in Italy he was in close touch with the Bonaparte family, particularly Queen Hortense. On the Bonaparte restoration he returned to Paris where he wrote for *Le Figaro*, but he was journalist, poet, novelist, dramatist and librettist in turn. His plays were produced at the Comédie-Française, the Odéon and the Porte-Saint-Martin, while his libretti reached the Théâtre Lyrique and the Opéra, although here his only memorable effort was his collaboration with Du Locle in *Don Carlos*. By this time he was a very ill man and would not live to see the opera produced.

MESTÉPÈS, Eugène (b. Pau. (Basses-Pyrénées) 1820; d. Paris 15 May 1875). Dramatist and librettist of operas comique and opérettes. Occasionally used the pseudonym, Gaston. For a time was administrator of the Bouffes-Parisiens and in his latter days stage director at the Ambigu-Comique.

MOLINE, Pierre-Louis (b. Montpellier c. 1740; d. Paris 19 February or 12

March 1820). Having graduated Master in Arts at Avignon he set off for Paris where he became a barrister but soon left the bar for literary work. During the Revolution, like most of his artistic colleagues, he eagerly adopted the new principles and became secretary-registrar of the National Convention. Following the dissolution of the Convention he returned to private life. Wrote many works in many forms: poetry, dramas, comedies, libretti. He is best known for his translation of Calzabigi's *Orfeo ed Euridice* for the production at the Opéra in 1774. Also translated Cimarosa's *Il Matrimonio Segreto* for the theatre at Ghent, and Mozart's *Die Entführung aus dem Serail* for the Théâtre Français de l'Opéra Bouffon, Paris.

MONNIER, Etienne (d. 1850). Seemingly a translator whose work was heard at the Hague (*Norma* and *I Puritani*, 1839; *Roberto Devereux*, 1840), Bordeaux (*La Sonnambula*, 1839) and Versailles (*Lucrezia Borgia* performed as *Nizza de Grenade*, 1842).

NAJAC, Emile-Fernand Comte de (b. Lorient (Morbihan) 14 December 1828; d. Paris 11 April 1889). Wrote many comedies, vaudevilles and libretti, mainly alone but some in collaboration. Occasionally signed his works with the pseudonym E. Fernand. In addition to the Théâtre Lyrique, his works were performed at the Opéra-Comique, Bouffes-Parisiens, Folies-Marigny and Variétés.

NUITTER, (Charles-Louis-Étienne Truinet) (b. Paris 24 April 1828; d. Paris 24 February 1899.) Librettist and translator. Was called to the bar in 1849 but soon left it for the theatre. As archivist of the Bibliothèque de l'Opéra he assembled a most important collection of books and documents. Fortunately these had been removed to the present theatre, then unfinished, when the theatre in the rue Le Peletier burned down in 1873. Wrote many vaudevilles, mostly in collaboration, as well as libretti for operas and operettes. Many of his operette libretti were written for Offenbach. Translated *Die Zauberflöte*, *Oberon*, *Rienzi*, *Macbeth*, and *Aida* and many more, almost all in collaboration. He also collaborated in the books of a number of ballets for the Opéra including *Coppélia*, as well as in writing some books on the history of opera which included the story of the new theatre, *Le Nouvel Opéra*. On his death he left bequests of one million francs for Paris artists, and of half a million for the bibliothèque which he had created.

OPPELT, Gustave-Louis (b. Brussels 15 April 1817; d. Brussels 15 November 1888). First entered business but left to study painting under Paul Lauters. He next found employment in the Ministry of Finance, entering as a clerk and advancing to become librarian and associate director. From his early years he wrote verse which was set to music. He also wrote theatre articles for a number of Brussels and Paris newspapers. He would later become professor of commercial sciences at the institute where he was once a student and would write treatises on works which ranged from economics and the history of Belgium (including the Congo) to instructions on the aerial navigation of balloons. He also found time to write vaudevilles and libretti as well as to translate a number of libretti (*Martha*, *I Lombardi* and *Nabucco* among them) into French. Nor did he stop there; he also translated the *Stabat Maters* of Pergolesi, Haydn and Rossini into French!

PICARD, Louis-Bénoît (b. Paris 29 July 1769); d. Paris 31 December 1828). Educated Lycées d'Harcourt and Louis-le-Grand. Intended for legal profession but, like so many writers, abandoned law for the theatre. Established his reputation with *Les Visitandines*. In all he wrote over 100 stage works, some in collaboration with Alexandre Duval. Was also an actor and in time became manager of the Odéon company (the theatre itself had been burned down in March 1799) leading the players in a nomadic existence until 1801 when they again found a theatre in which to settle in Paris. His forte was both as a comic actor and as a writer of comedies and he was much patronised by Napoleon I. Was appointed director of the Opéra in 1807, a post for which he was not particularly suited and did not particularly enjoy—but then patronage usually does entail loss of independence. In 1815 he retired from the Opéra and once again became manager of the Odéon company. In 1821 he retired from all active management, following which he wrote novels and continued to write for the theatre but now almost entirely in collaboration.

PLANARD, François-Antoine-Eugène de (b. Millau (Aveyron) 4 February 1783; d. Paris 13 November 1853). As a member of the aristocracy was imprisoned with his mother during the Revolution. Following the release went to Paris where, in 1806 he joined the Council of State as an archivist, later became executive secretary of the Legislative Section. During his administrative career he also wrote comedies and numerous libretti. The latter, which included *Le Pré aux Clercs* (Hérold) were all produced at the Opéra-Comique. One of his daughters married Adolphe de Leuven.

PLOUVIER, Edouard (b. Paris 2 August 1821; d. Paris 12 November 1876). Began as a leather worker, educated himself and entered literature as a writer of verse. Then wrote dramas, comedies, libretti and many vaudevilles in association with Jules Adenis. He also wrote articles for several newspapers under at least seven different pseudonyms of which Cagliostro seems to have been the most frequently used.

ROYER, Alphonse (b. Paris 10 September 1803; d. Paris 11 April 1875). Best known as director of the Opéra, a post he held from 1856 to 1862. Made his literary début as a novelist and having spent some early years in the East, wrote of his experiences there. He also wrote for the theatre but primarily he was a translator of libretti, usually in collaboration with Gustave Vaëz, and *Lucia di Lammermoor, Don Pasquale*, and a version of *I Lombardi* are among the operas that they arranged for the French stage. His principal original work, again with Vaëz, was the libretto of *La Favorite*. He also wrote a six-volume history of the theatre, and, inevitably, an *Histoire de l'Opéra*. On his retirement from the Opéra was appointed Inspecteur Général des Beaux-Arts.

SAINT-ETIENNE, Joseph-Sylvain (b. Aix-en-Provence 1807; d. Paris 23 October 1880). Librettist and music critic. Also wrote the words of many songs and choruses and translated cantatas and oratorios, including Handel's. Founded a choral group, the Société Sylvain Saint-Etienne in his native Aix.

Also founded the newspaper, *Le Mémorial d'Aix*. Came to Paris in 1844 where he helped to found a second, *La Chanson Française*. Wrote music criticism under his own name and also under the pseudonyms of Sextus Durand and A. de Bovy. Was life long friend of Félicien David who also had lived at Aix from an early age.

SAINT-GEORGES, Jules-Henri Vernoy de (b. Paris 7 November 1799; d. Paris 23 December 1875). After Scribe the most gifted and fertile of all French librettists and a renowned dandy of his day in Paris. His first literary work was a novel, but he then turned to the theatre and wrote vaudevilles, ballets and libretti. In 1829–30 he had a short ruinous episode as associate director with M. Ducis of the Opéra-Comique. Works by him at the Théâtre des Variétés were performed under the pseudonym of Jules. He was six times elected president of the Société des Auteurs Dramatiques and delivered an oration for the society at Rossini's graveside. He collaborated in writing the book of a number of ballets, including *Giselle*, and of over 80 operas of which however only *La Fille du Régiment*, *Martha* and *La Jolie Fille de Perth* tenuously remain in the repertory.

SAINT-LÉON, (Charles-Victor-Arthur Michel) (b. Paris 17 September 1821; d. 2 September 1870). A doubtful name to include in a list of librettists, but in most contemporary notices he is credited (with Alboize du Pujol) as having written *Le Danseur du Roi*. He was a famous ballet dancer and choreographer as well as a violinist whose virtuosity astonished Mayseder and Paganini, both of whom had been his teachers. He and Fanny Cerrito were married in 1845, but they separated five years later.

SAUVAGE, Thomas-Marie-François (b. Paris 5 November 1794; d. Paris 2 May 1877). Wrote vaudevilles, plays and libretti including works for Adolphe Adam and Ambroise Thomas. He was theatre critic of *Le Journal Général de France* and of *Le Moniteur Universel*, and, for the year 1827–28, an unsuccessful director of the Odéon. The catalogue of the Bibliothèque Nationale, Paris lists 75 works by him.

SCRIBE, Augustin-Eugène (b. Paris 24 December 1791; d. Paris 20 February 1861). In his time, the emperor of French dramatists. The complete edition of his 'Oeuvres dramatiques' runs to 76 volumes, of which 26 are taken up by his opera libretti. Ernest Legouvé declares that 'for a score of years he positively held sway over the four principal theatres in Paris; viz., the Opéra, Opéra-Comique, the Gymnase and the Comédie-Française', and indeed as a librettist his work dominated the French lyric stage. Dramatically he can be considered the father of modern opera, for his libretti for the Opéra banished the classical styles of the seventeenth and eighteenth centuries. Allardyce Nicoll points out that he was not just a playwright, but that 'he set up what amounted to a play-factory in which stories were found, invented, or paid for and turned like sausages into comestibles . . . ' Nevertheless, many of his still remembered works were written entirely by himself and included among his libretti, *La Dame Blanche* (Boieldieu), *Fra Diavolo* (Auber), *La Juive* (Halévy), *Les Martyrs* (Donizetti) and *Le Prophète*, *L'Étoile du Nord* and *L'Africaine* (Meyerbeer). *La Muette de Portici* (Auber), *Le Comte Ory*

(Rossini), *Robert-le-Diable* and *Les Huguenots* (Meyerbeer) and *Les Vêpres Siciliennes* (Verdi) were other operas with libretti mainly or partly by him.

SEDAINE, Michel-Jean (b. Paris 4 July 1719; d. Paris 17 May 1797). His father, an architect, wished him to follow that profession, but the father dying he was obliged to become a stonemason. Nevertheless he continued to read and study. He was assisted in his efforts by the architect François Buron (an uncle of the painter David), and in 1756 his first stage work *Le Diable à quatre* with music arranged by Philidor appeared at the Opéra-Comique. More libretti for the Opéra-Comique and the Comédie Italienne followed. By 1765 he was writing for the Comédie-Française. Operatically he is perhaps best known today as the librettist of Grétry's *Richard Cœur-de-Lion* and is considered to be the true founder of opéra comique.

SEVESTE, Jules-Henri (d. Meudon near Paris 30 June 1854). Has already been recorded as director of the Théâtre Lyrique from 1852 until 1854. He collaborated in the libretto of *Les Fiançailles des Roses* (Villeblanche) produced there in February 1852, and the catalogue of the Bibliotèque de Nationale, Paris, lists two vaudevilles dated 1825 and 1827, cross referenced under Edmond and Jules Seveste and two dated 1832 and 1833 by MM Jaime and Jules Seveste. To these titles Bourquelot's *La Litterature Française* adds a 'drame fantastique' dated 1836, in collaboration with Louis-Emile Vanderburch.

THÉAULON DE LAMBERT, Marie-Emmanuel-Guillaume-Marguerite (b. Aigues-Mortes (Gard) 14 August 1787; d. Paris 16 November 1841). Dramatist (yet another who first studied law) with influence in high places. First wrote poetry, then vaudevilles. Held official positions during reign of Napoleon I. Quickly changed his allegiance with the restoration of the Bourbons which caused him some embarrassment when Napoleon returned from Elba. Nevertheless, theatrically he survived the many changes in French politics and in 1821 had the distinction of having works performed at the Opéra, the Opéra-Comique and the Théâtre-Français all at the same time to celebrate the christening of the future Charles X's grandson. Alone or in collaboration he would write more than 250 works in every form and for almost every Paris theatre. His libretti included works for Spontini and Liszt and he was associated with Dumas in writing the play, *Kean.*

THIERRY, Emile. Very difficult to identify. An actor of that name (late of the Bouffes-Parisiens) was engaged by Martinet and Champfleury for the Fantaisies-Parisiennes in 1865, while the *Revue et Gazette Musicale* of 11 March 1855 reports an Emile Thierry, 'a young man, a poet to some slight extent, a very amusing singer of "chansonnettes", and moreover a natural and true actor.'

TRIANON, Henri (b. Paris 11 July 1811; d. Paris 17 October 1896). Commenced as an artistic and literary critic in the Paris press, but then abandoned writing for a time to become a teacher. Later became a librarian and from 1857 to 1859 was associated with Nestor Roqueplan in the administration of the Opéra-Comique. Translated Homer's and Plato's works into French, wrote the story of one ballet, *Orfa*, the libretti for several operas, and, in collaboration, a play in verse for the Comédie-Française.

TURPIN DE SANSAY, Louis-Adolphe (b. Selongey (Côte d'Or) 27 April 1832). Historical novelist and writer of short stories, libretti and over 700 chansons. Some of his books were written under the pseudonym, Philippe de Robville.

ULBACH, Louis (b. Troyes 7 March 1822; d. Paris 16 April 1889). Encouraged in his early work by Victor Hugo whose house he frequented. Became editor of *La Revue de Paris* in 1853, and later contributed to *Le Temps* and *Le Figaro*. In 1868 he founded a radical paper, *La Cloche*, to which Zola contributed and in which Ulbach seems to have attacked impartially both the Empire and later the Commune. Following the overthrow of the Commune he was accused by the Versailles government of having supported it. For this he is said to have received a sentence of three years in prison and a 6000 francs fine, but on appeal this was reduced to three months and 3000 francs. In 1878 he was appointed librarian of the Bibliothèque de l'Arsenal, while at the same time he continued to contribute to several newspapers and magazines. He wrote novels, plays and libretti as well as mémoires and other general works. Occasionally he used the pseudonyms of Ferragus and Jacques Souffrant.

VAËZ, Gustave (Jean-Nicolas-Gustave van Nieuwenhuysen) (b. Brussels 6 December 1812; d. Paris 12 March 1862). Destined for the bar—yet another!—but soon turned to the theatre. Had plays produced in his native Brussels between 1829 and 1834. Later came to Paris where he wrote more plays besides libretti and vaudevilles, mostly in collaboration. During 1849 he was in correspondence with Wagner concerning the translation of libretti into French of works which Wagner was then contemplating, *Wieland der Schmied* and *Jesus von Nazareth*. His libretti included Donizetti's *Rita* and, with Alphonse Royer, *La Favorite*. Among operas translated by him and Royer were *Lucia di Lammermoor*, *Don Pasquale* and *I Lombardi*.

VALOIS, Charles. Little can be discovered about this writer except that he was sometime 'secretaire de l'Isthme de Suez'.

VERNE, Jules (-Gabriel) (b. Nantes 8 February 1828; d. Amiens 24 March 1905). So much is known of this first of the science fiction writers that reference will be confined to his theatre activities. He came to Paris in 1848 and had his first play produced at the Gymnase in 1850. (He qualified as a barrister at the same time, and later would become a stock-broker). He joined the Théâtre Lyrique as secretary during the Seveste regime, remaining there until the arrival of Pellegrin. From the beginning he was deeply interested in opera, an interest encouraged by his friend, Aristide Hignard, also from Nantes, and he was part author of the libretti of most of Hignard's works. These included *Monsieur de Chimpanzé* for the Bouffes-Parisiens, which faintly anticipates Henze's *Der junge Lord*. He also wrote some plays of no particular distinction.

VIAL, Jean-Baptiste-Charles (b. Lyon 1771; d. Paris 1837). Dramatist. Intended for a business career but having had a play successfully performed in Lyon set off for Paris and the theatre. Wrote dramas, comedies, libretti and vaudevilles, usually in collaboration. He was the writer who altered Picard's libretto of *Les Visitandines*, making it more acceptable to the audiences of the pro-clerical France of Charles X and Napoleon III, as *Le Pensionnat de Jeunes Demoiselles.*

WAILLY, Augustin-Jules de (b. Paris 12 September 1806; d. 12 July 1866). Educated at the Collège Henry IV. Came from a literary family. Was first attached to the Ministry of the Interior becoming chef de bureau of the Fine Arts section, but the 1848 revolution led to his retirement to private life. Earlier he had had plays performed at the Gymnase and, under the pseudonym Marie Sénan, at the Théâtre Français. Later he would collaborate in libretti for the Opéra-Comique as well as the Théâtre Lyrique.

WOESTYN, Eugène (b. c. 1813. d. 1876). Journalist and editor of *Le Figaro-Programme.* He also wrote some poetry and, in collaboration, some plays and libretti.

ZACCONE, Pierre (b. Douai 2 April 1817; d. Morlaix (Finistère) 12 April 1895). Popular novelist. First employed as a postal official. Began by writing serials for the Brittany newspapers and had a vaudeville performed at the theatre in Brest. Came to Paris in 1843 where he continued to write novels as well as general historical and sociological works, mostly in collaboration. He also wrote many vaudevilles and libretti.

Nothing can be discovered of the librettist ANDREL.

Appendix E

Adolphe Adam's programme of operas performed at the former Cirque Olympique between November 1847 and March 1848, and names of members of his company.

Dates of first performances of operas at the Opéra National[1]

1847

Nov. 15
LES PREMIERS PAS OU LES DEUX GÉNIES* Prologue 1 a. (Royer and Vaëz)
Halévy, Carafa, Auber and Adam
GASTIBELZA* op. 3 a. (d'Ennery and Cormon) Maillart
Nov. 16
ALINE, REINE DE GOLCONDE op-c. 3 a. (Vial and Favières) Berton
(Re-orchestrated by Adam)
Nov. 23
UNE BONNE FORTUNE op-c. 1 a. (Féréol and Édouard [Mennechet])
Adam
Dec. 22
FÉLIX OU L'ENFANT TROUVÉ op-c. 3 a. (Sedaine) Monsigny
(Re-orchestrated by Adam)

1848

Jan. 22
LE BRASSEUR DE PRESTON op-c. 3 a. (de Leuven and Brunswick) Adam
Jan. 30
LA TÊTE DE MÉDUSE op-c. 1 a. (Vanderburch and Deforges) Scard
March 6
LES BARRICADES DE 1848* op. 1 a. (Brisebarre and Saint-Yves)
Pilati and Eugène Gautier
DON QUICHOTTE ET SANCHO PANÇA op-c. 1 a. (Hervé) Hervé.

[1] Lasalle. *Mémorial du Théâtre Lyrique*, pp. 7–11.

*

First productions of these operas.
Lasalle mentions a number of other ephemeral pieces performed during this period, of no importance musically or dramatically.

Licensed Director: '*Directeur privilégié*', Mirecour; *Co-Director,* Adam; *Stage Director,* Leroy; *Stage Manager,* Thiéblemont; *Assistants,* Fosse and Lecour; *Administrator,* Annet; *Secretary,* Lormier; *Treasurer,* Ouin; *First Conductor,* Bousquet; *Second Conductor,* Gautier; *Ballet Master,* Lerouge; *Chorus Master,* Cornette; *Accompanists,* Cohen and Croharé; '*Contrôleur en chef*', Barthe; '*Machiniste en chef*', Saexe; *Scene painters,* Martin and Wagner.

Artists: '*Premières Chanteuses*', Mmes Chérie-Couraud, Petit-Brière, Decroix, Prety, Potier, Rosset; '*Dugazons*', Mmes Bourdet, Cara, Gautier, Hetzel, Amélie Briere, Feigle, Doulcet, Octave; '*Duègnes*', Mmes Mancini, Derly; *First and Second Tenors,* Raguenot, Huner, Chenet, Lapierre, Fosse, Legrand, Béraud, Lecour, Paublan, Dutillay, Delsarte jeune; '*Tenors comiques*', Joseph Kelm, Hervé; *Baritones,* Pauly, Cabel, Beaugrand, Vallod; *Basses,* Junca, Hure, Pedorlini, Delsalle, Marnin, Fritz; *Dancers,* M. Lerouge and Mlles Richard and Auriol; *Orchestra,* 70 players; *Chorus,* 54; *Ballet,* 28.[2]

² Pougin, p. 192.

Appendix F

The unresolved enigma of 'Prends pitié de sa jeunesse'

Recently music by Verdi to which the words 'Prends pitié de sa jeunesse' had been set was discovered by the musicologist Patric Schmid. The music was later identified as the song 'Il poveretto' composed by Verdi in 1857 to words by Manfredo Maggioni. It is a plaintive ballad type air of the 'When all was young' school (which Gounod introduced into Faust for Mme Nantier-Didiée) but having more style.* The identification prompted further questions. How did 'Prends pitié' enter the French translation of *Rigoletto* in the first place, and when, if ever, was it performed? Seemingly not in Brussels, for following the first performance there, *L'Indépendance Belge* of 28 November 1858 reported, somewhat equivocally perhaps, 'After the quartet . . . there is no other piece, the remainder passes in recitatives and in detached phrases.' Neither is there anything to suggest that it was sung at the Théâtre Lyrique. Both d'Ortigue in *Le Journal des Débats* and the critic of *Le Moniteur Universel* merely comment that Mlle Dubois as Madeleine was the weakest member of the cast.

The first performance of *Rigoletto* in the French language in France took place at Marseille on 13 May 1860. The role of Madeleine was taken by Mlle Elmire who had already sung it in the Brussels première 18 months previously. (The season was organised by Théodore Letellier, who had been director of the Monnaie theatre, Brussels, from 1852 to 1858 and would soon be reappointed.) The *Semaphore de Marseille*, 29 May 1860 fails to record any air sung by Madeleine. On the contrary it complains that both the Duke's air ('Parmi veder le lagrime') and the final duet ('Lassù in cielo') were cut, which makes it extremely unlikely that an air outside the original score should have been included.

There is a further intriguing point. Léon Escudier, the music publisher advertised the Duprez translation of *Rigoletto* in vocal score and other forms in his *L'Art Musical* of 31 December 1863. Advertised too was sheet music of the principal items from the opera, but strangely the last three pieces are listed as follows:

*

I am indebted to Anthony Quigley for calling my attention to a recording of 'Il Poveretto' by the British tenor Donald Pilley issued in 1968 on Saga FDY 2014.

10 Quatuor. 'Un jour, bel ange.'

12 Trio. 'Je ne balance plus'

13 Duo. 'Je sens un corps humain'

It will be noted that number 11 is missing. The same pieces were again advertised in *L'Art Musical* on 31 October 1872, but number 11 is now included between 10 and 12 where it is described as, 'Mélodie, mezzo-soprano. "Prends pitié de sa jeunesse".' In the same advertisement, separate items with the original Italian text are also announced, but there is no version of 'Prends pitié' among them. Finally in the Escudier music catalogue of 1872 (British Library. Hirsch 593 (1–4), 'Verdi—"Le Pauvre" is included under 'Romances and Melodies.'

One could surmise much about this puzzling affair without reaching any definite conclusion. Perhaps these details will help a little towards finding an answer to the enigma, some day.

Appendix G

Annual Receipts 1851–1870

1851	*From the opening on 27 September*	*Fr.*	*134 869*	*c. 50*
1852			*329 335*	*15*
1853			*542 973*	*25*
1854			*457 754*	*95*
1855			*637 589*	*25*
1856			*680 962*	*75*
1857			*831 211*	*95*
1858			*849 214*	*60*
1859			*682 933*	*70*
1860			*588 645*	*90*
1861			*469 410*	*85*
1862			*478 980*	*20*
1863			*862 450*	*00*
1864			*960 798*	*50*
1865			*903 308*	*25*
1866			*1 000 448*	*60*
1867			*1 396 834*	*35*
1868			*387 968*	*40*
1869			*407 807*	*70*
1870	*Up to the closure on 31 May*		*175 146*	*50*

Interpretation of these figures is difficult because they are calculated over calendar years whereas the theatrical year ran from early autumn to early summer, usually 1 September to 31 May. The success of *Les Amours du Diable* and *Le Bijou Perdu* in 1853, *La Fanchonnette* in 1856, *Oberon* in 1857, *Les Noces de Figaro* in 1858, *Rigoletto* (produced 24 December 1863) in 1864 and *La Flûte enchantée* in 1865 may explain the excellent receipts for these years. More difficult to understand are the equally good returns in 1863. Surprisingly the success of *Faust*, *L'Enlèvement au Sérail* and *Orphée* (produced late in the year) is not fully reflected in the 1859 figures. The war against Austria combined with the exceptionally warm summer may have been the reason. Neither did the 1855 Exhibition produce exceptional results but there can be no doubt about the prosperity created by the 1867 Exhibition, which would seem to have been gathering momentum even from the previous year.

BIBLIOGRAPHY

Bibliography I

Books and Printed Articles

Abbiati, Franco. *Giuseppe Verdi*, 4v., Milan 1959.

Arditi, Luigi. *My Reminiscences*, London 1896.

Arnoldson, Louise Parkinson, *Sedaine et les Musiciens de son Temps*, Paris 1934.

Aubin, Léon. *Le Drame Lyrique*, Tours 1908.

Bac, Ferdinand. *Intimités du Second Empire*, 3v., Paris 1932.

Barzun, Jacques. *Berlioz and his Century*, New York 1956.

Beaumont, Cyril W. *Complete Book of Ballets*, London 1951.

Bennett, Joseph. *Forty Years of Music, 1865–1905*, London 1903.

Berlioz, Hector. *Mémoires* (Trans. and Ed. David Cairns) London 1969.

Bidou, Henry. *Paris*, Paris 1938.

Boschot, Adolphe, *Une Vie Romantique: Hector Berlioz*, Paris 1919.

Brand, Erna. *Aglaja Orgeni: Das Leben einer grossen Sängerin*, Munich 1931.

Brockhaus Enzyklopädie, Wiesbaden 1968–74.

Budden, Julian. *The Operas of Verdi*, Vol 1. London 1973.

Carel, Alfred. *Histoire Anecdotique des Contemporains*, Paris 1885.

Carse, Adam. *The Orchestra from Beethoven to Berlioz*, Cambridge 1948.

Castillon du Perron, Marguerite. *Princess Mathilde*, (Trans. Mary McLean) London 1956.

Chorley, Henry F. *Thirty Years' Musical Recollections*, 2v., New York 1926.

Cochin, Charles Nicolas. *Projet d'une salle de spectacle pour un Théâtre de comédie*, Paris 1765.

Combarnous, Victor. *L'Histoire du Grand Théâtre de Marseille: 1765–1919*, Marseille 1927.

Curtiss, Mina. *Bizet and his World*, London 1959.

Davison, J.W. *From Mendelssohn to Wagner*, Memoirs compiled by his son, Henry Davison, London 1912.

Dean, Winton. *Georges Bizet, His Life and Work*, London 1965.

Devrient, Hans. (Ed.) *Briefwechsel zwischen Eduard und Therese Devrient*, Stuttgart 1909.

Du Camp, Maxime. *Souvenirs d'un demi-siècle*, 2v., Paris 1949.

Duprez, Gilbert. *Souvenirs d'un Chanteur*, Paris 1880.

Easton, Malcolm. *Artists and Writers in Paris. The Bohemian Idea. 1803–1867*. London 1964.

Engel, Louis. *From Mozart to Mario*. 2v., London 1886.

Fétis, F.J. *Biographie Universelle des Musiciens*. Paris 1878–84.

Fitzlyon, April. *The Price of Genius.* London 1964.

Fleury, Comte Maurice, and Louis Sonolet. *La Société du Second Empire.* 4v., Paris 1924.

Fouque, Octave. *Histoire du Théâtre-Ventadour.* Paris 1881.

Galabert, Edmond. *Georges Bizet. Souvenirs et correspondance.* Paris 1877.

Glinka, Mikhail I. *Memoirs* (Trans. R.B. Mudge). Oklahoma 1963.

Goncourt, Edmond and Jules de. *Journal* (Ed. Robert Ricatte). 4v., Paris 1956.

Goncourt, Edmond and Jules de and Cornelius Holff. *Mystères des Théâtres,* 1852. Paris 1853.

Gounod, Charles. *Autobiographical Reminiscences.* (Trans. W. Hely Hutchinson). New York 1970.

Green, F.C. *A Comparative View of French and British Civilization, 1850–1870.* London 1965.

Grove's Dictionary of Music and Musicians. (3rd and 5th eds.) London 1928 and 1955.

Guedalla, Philip. *The Second Empire.* London 1922.

Guest, Ivor. *The Ballet of the Second Empire, 1885–1870.* London 1953.

Hahn, Reynaldo. *Thèmes variés.* Paris 1946.

Harding, James. *Gounod* London 1973.

Hegermann-Lindencrone, Lillie de. *In the Courts of Memory, 1858–75.* New York 1912.

Heylli, Georges d'. *Dictionnaire des Pseudonymes.* Paris 1887.

Horne, Alistair. *The Fall of Paris. The Siege and the Commune, 1870–1.* London 1965.

Hostein, Hippolyte. *La Liberté des Théâtres.* Paris 1867.

Humblot, Émile. *Un Musicien Join-villois de l'époque de la Révolution: François Devienne, 1759–1803.* St. Dizier 1909.

Jahn, Otto. *W.A. Mozart.* 4v., Leipzig 1856–9.

Jollivet, Gaston. *Souvenirs de la Vie de Plaisir sous le Second Empire.* Paris 1927.

Lasalle, Albert de. *Mémorial du Théâtre Lyrique.* Paris 1877.

Lasalle, Albert de. *Les Treize Salles de l'Opéra.* Paris 1875.

Lecomte, Louis Henry. *Histoire des Théâtres de Paris: Le Théâtre Historique.* Paris 1906.

Lecomte, Louis Henry. *Histoire des Théâtres de Paris: Les Fantaisies-Parisiennes, etc.* Paris 1912.

Legouvé, Ernest. *Sixty Years of Recollections* (Trans. Albert D. Vandam). 2v., London 1893.

Leroy, Alfred. *The Empress Eugénie* (Trans. Anne Cope). Geneva 1969.

Leroy, Maxime. *Les Premiers Amis Français de Wagner.* Paris 1925.

Loewenberg, Alfred. *Annals of Opera, 1597–1940.* 2v., Geneva 1955.

Lough, John. *Paris Theatre Audiences in the 17th and 18th centuries.* London 1972.

Maréchal, Henri. *Paris. Souvenirs d'un Musicien, 185-.–1870.* Paris 1907.

Massenet, Jules. *Mes Souvenirs, 1848–1912.* Paris 1912.

Osborne, Charles. *The Complete Operas of Verdi.* London 1969.

Pagnerre, Louis. *Charles Gounod, sa vie et ses œuvres.* Paris 1890.

Planché, James Robinson. *Recollections and Reflections.* 2v., London 1872.

Pontmartin, Armand de. *Souvenirs d'un vieux critique.* 10 séries. Paris 1882.

Prod'homme, J.G. and A. Dandelot.

Gounod 1818–1893. 2v., Paris 1911.

Servières, Georges. *Episodes d'Histoire Musicale.* Paris 1914.

Servières, Georges. *Richard Wagner jugé en France.* Paris 1886.

Soubies, Albert. *Soixante-sept ans à l'Opéra en un page (1826–1893).* Paris 1893.

Soubies, Albert. *Soixante-neuf ans à l'Opéra-Comique en deux pages (1825–1894).* Paris 1894.

Soubies, Albert. Histoire du Théâtre Lyrique, 1851–1870. Paris 1899.

Soubies, Albert and Henri de Curzon. *Documents inédits sur le Faust de Gounod.* Paris 1912.

Soubies, Albert and Charles Malherbe. *Histoire de l'Opéra Comique.* 2v., Paris 1892.

Vandam, Albert D. *An Englishman in Paris.* London 1900.

Wagner, Richard. *Briefe* (selected and annotated by Wilhelm Altmann) 2v., Leipzig 1925.

Wagner, Richard. *Lettres Françaises de Richard Wagner.* (Ed. by Julien Tiersot) Paris 1935.

Wagner, Richard. *Mein Leben.* Munich 1915.

Wagner, Richard. *Wagner writes from Paris...* (Ed. and transl. by R.L. Jacobs and G. Skelton). London 1973.

Wolff, Stéphane. *Un Demi-Siècle d'Opéra-Comique 1900–1950.* Paris 1953.

Wolff, Stéphane. *L'Opéra au Palais Garnier 1875–1962.* Paris 1962.

Bibliography II

Newspapers and Periodicals

PARIS			
Almanach de la Musique.		La Presse.	P
L'Artiste.	A	Paris-Magazine.	PM
L'Art Musical.	AM	Revue des Deux Mondes.	RDM
Le Constitutionnel.	C	Revue et Gazette Musicale.	RGM
Le Figaro.	F	Le Temps.	T
La France Musicale.	FM	L'Union.	U
Gazette de France.	GF	L'Universel	UL
Galignani's Messenger.	GM	LONDON	
L'Illustration.	I	The Builder.	B
Le Journal des Débats.	JD	Building News.	BN
Le Journal Illustré.	JI	Illustrated London News.	ILN
Le Journal de Musique.	JM	Music and Letters.	ML
Le Ménestrel.	M	The Musical Standard.	MS
Le Monde Illustré.	MI	The Musical World.	MW
Le Moniteur Universel.	MU	The Orchestra.	O

The letters after the titles are the abbreviations used throughout the reference notes in this book.

INDEX

Index